# VIOTTI AND THE CHINNERYS

*Dedicated to the memory of my mother*

Thelma Morony 1924–1996

# Viotti and the Chinnerys

## A Relationship Charted Through Letters

DENISE YIM

ASHGATE

Published by
Ashgate Publishing Limited
Gower House
Croft Road
Aldershot
Hants GU11 3HR
England

Ashgate Publishing Company
Suite 420
101 Cherry Street
Burlington, VT 05401-4405
USA

Ashgate website: http://www.ashgate.com

**British Library Cataloguing in Publication Data**
Yim, Denise
Viotti and the Chinnerys : a relationship charted through letters. – (Music in nineteenth-century Britain)
1.Viotti, Giovanni Battista, 1755–1824 2.Chinnery, William 3.Chinnery, Margaret 4.Viotti, Giovanni Battista, 1755–1824 – Correspondence 5.Chinnery, William – Correspondence 6.Chinnery, Margaret – Correspondence 7.Violinists – Italy – Biography 8.Composers – Italy – Biography 9.Music patrons – England – Biography 10.Women music patrons – England – Biography
I.Title
787.2'092

**Library of Congress Cataloging-in-Publication Data**
Yim, Denise, 1947–
Viotti and the Chinnerys : a relationship charted through letters / Denise Yim.
p. cm. – (Music in nineteenth-century Britain)
Includes bibliographical references and index.
ISBN 0-7546-3161-3 (alk. paper)
1. Viotti, Giovanni Battista, 1755–1824. 2. Viotti, Giovanni Battista, 1755–1824–Correspondence. 3. Chinnery family–Correspondence. 4. Composers–Italy–Biography. 5. Composers–Italy–Correspondence. I. Title. II. Series.

ML410.V79Y56 2003
787.2'092–dc21
[B]

2003056045

ISBN 0 7546 3161 3

Printed and bound in Great Britain by MPG Books Ltd, Bodmin, Cornwall

# Contents

# List of Figures

# General Editor's Series Preface

Music in nineteenth-century Britain has been studied as a topic of musicology for over two hundred years. It was explored widely in the nineteenth century itself, and in the twentieth century grew into research with strong methodological and theoretical import. Today, the topic has burgeoned into a broad, yet incisive, cultural study with critical potential for scholars in a wide range of disciplines. Indeed, it is largely because of its interdisciplinary qualities that music in nineteenth-century Britain has become such a prominent part of the modern musicological landscape.

This series aims to explore the wealth of music and musical culture of Britain in the long nineteenth century (*c.*1780s–1920s). It does this by covering an extensive array of musicological topics, and situating them within the most up-to-date interpretative frameworks. All books provide relevant contextual background and detailed source investigations, as well as considerable bibliographical material of use for further study. Areas included in the series reflect its widely interdisciplinary aims, and although principally designed for musicologists, the series is also intended to be accessible to scholars working outside of music. Topics include criticism and aesthetics; musical genres; music and the church; music education; composers and performers; analysis; concert venues, promoters and organizations; the reception of foreign music in Britain; instrumental repertoire, manufacture and pedagogy; gender studies; and music in literature, poetry and letters.

Although the nineteenth century has often been viewed as a fallow period in British musical culture, it is clear from the vast extent of current scholarship that this view is entirely erroneous. Far from being a 'land without music', nineteenth-century Britain abounded with musical activity. All society was affected by it, and everyone in that society recognized its importance in some way or other. It remains for us today to trace the significance of music and musical culture in that period, and to bring it alive for scholars to study and interpret. This is the principle aim of the Music in Nineteenth-Century Britain series – to advance scholarship in the area and expand our understanding of its importance in the wider cultural context of the time.

Bennett Zon
*University of Durham*

# Acknowledgements

It is thanks to my doctoral supervisor Emeritus Professor Angus Martin, of the University of Sydney, that this book has come into being. It was he who spoke of my work to Emeritus Professor David Tunley, of the University of Western Australia, who was kind enough to read my dissertation, and to offer encouragement regarding publication. I thank the many editors who replied to my emails and referred me on, most importantly Dr Katharine Ellis (*Music and Letters*), who explained the labyrinthine world of publishing to me, and suggested Ashgate.

I would like to thank Ashgate for giving me the opportunity to publish this part of my dissertation in what is, I hope, an improved form, and I especially thank Rachel Lynch and Dr Bennett Zon, who patiently dealt with the many flaws in my book submission and were kind enough to find a second reader, to whom I am also immensely grateful for his/her detailed pages of comments on my typescript. I would also like to thank Rachel for dealing so patiently with my many queries.

I am very grateful to Ms Helen Yoxall, Archivist of the Powerhouse Museum, Sydney, who has helped with my numerous requests for access to the Chinnery papers since 1992, and her assistant archivists Ms Susan Davidson and Ms Jill Chapman. The music curator at the Powerhouse Museum, Mr Michael Lea, has also been most obliging in answering queries and digging out items from difficult places. I would also like to thank the Museum for permission to transcribe or quote from letters in their Chinnery Family Papers collection and in their E.A. and V.I. Crome collection, and for allowing me to reproduce two of the items as illustrations. I was granted very favourable terms.

I would also like to thank the Music Division of the New York Public Library for the Performing Arts, Astor, Lenox and Tilden Foundations, for permission to transcribe or quote from letters in their Viotti and Viotti/Chinnery collections and to reproduce two items from their collections. I must also thank Frances Barulich, a reference specialist at the same library, who made available their Viotti/Chinnery collection to me in 2000, drew my attention to some other Viotti letters in the Library's possession, and kindly sent me a copy of her article concerning the Viotti/Chinnery collection. Ms Barulich also very helpfully scanned the image which appears here as Figure 10. I also thank the University of Sydney Librarian Mr John Shipp for permission to transcribe or quote from letters in their Chinnery Family Papers collection. The staff in the Library's Rare Book department, and in the Interlibrary Loans department have been particularly helpful.

I extend special thanks to Mrs Judith Curthoys, Archivist, Christ Church College, Oxford, not only for for permission to quote extensively from their Chinnery correspondence, but also for her helpfulness with this publication in other ways. Her friendship is much appreciated. Dr Peter Horton, reference Librarian of the Royal College of Music, London, kindly gave me permission to transcribe or quote from letters in the Library's Viotti collection, and to reproduce some photographs of miniatures from the collection. I also thank Mr Paul Collen, of the Department of Portraits and Performance History at the College, for permission to reproduce images from the College's collection. Dr Horton and Mr Collen were both extremely obliging in answering my queries and in supplying photographs from in the midst of repairs and redecoration. Also in London, I must thank Dr Peter Beal of Sotheby's Department of Printed Books and Manuscripts for sending photocopies of records of auctions.

I am also grateful to Dr Deborah Priest of the Sydney Conservatorium of Music, who, under difficult conditions, read the first part of my typescript, made corrections, offered suggestions, and helped with some 'musical' translations. I also thank Mrs Sue Khouri and Ms Amy Chautard, violin teachers, for kindly answering some questions relating to the violin. Acknowledgements must also go to Madame Marie-André Corcuff and Madame Claire Béchu of the Archives nationales de France for providing me with copies of documents, and Dr Florence Gétreau, Director of *Musique, images, instruments* for assisting me to find photographs.

I have benefited enormously from the help of another Viotti researcher Mr Warwick Lister. He generously allowed me to read his 2002 article in *Music and Letters* before publication, and after visiting Sydney was kind enough to draw my attention to errors in my dissertation, thereby saving me from some embarrassing blunders in this book. He has continued to share ideas and information with me, and I am deeply appreciative of his generous spirit. The resultant intellectual exchange has been stimulating and rewarding.

At Gilwell House in Essex, now home to the Scout Association, I must thank Mr Paul Moynihan, Archivist, and Mrs Pat Stiles, Assistant Archivist, who received me so hospitably in 2002 on the occasion of the repatriation of the Chinnery ashes from France, and who most kindly put at my disposal a whole range of interesting material relating to the history of the property. A collateral Chinnery family descendant Mr Randolph Vigne, whom I met on the same occasion, has with great kindness given me access to all his own research material on the Chinnery family, including private correspondence with Heron-Allen. He knows how appreciative I am of his help, and I thank him sincerely.

To my indulgent husband Tom, my musical son Alexander, my computer expert son Jerome, who helped me format the book, and my steadfast daughter Sascha I extend my deepest gratitude for their patience, advice and loving support over the duration of the writing.

Denise Yim
March 2004

# Abbreviations

| | |
|---|---|
| AF | Adolphus Frederick, Duke of Cambridge |
| CC | Caroline Chinnery |
| GBV | Giovanni Battista Viotti |
| GRC | George Robert Chinnery |
| MC | Margaret Chinnery |
| WBC | William Bassett Chinnery |
| WGC | Walter Grenfell Chinnery |
| WRS | William Robert Spencer |

| | |
|---|---|
| BL | British Library, London |
| Ch.Ch. | Christ Church Library, Oxford |
| Fisher | Fisher Library, University of Sydney |
| NYPL | New York Public Library for the Performing Arts, Music Division |
| Osborn | Osborn Collection, Beinecke Rare Book and Manuscript Library, Yale University |
| PHM | Powerhouse Museum, Sydney |
| PRO | Public Records Office, Kew |
| RCM | Royal College of Music Library, London |

The Chinnery letters in Christ Church Library are arranged chronologically and will be cited by date only except in cases of ambiguity, when the full shelfmark will be given.

| | |
|---|---|
| *AJFS* | *Australian Journal of French Studies* |
| *AMZ* | *Allgemeine musikalische Zeitung* |
| *Annales de la musique* | C. Gardeton (ed.) (1819–20), *Annales de la musique ou Almanach musical pour l'an 1819 et 1820*, Minkoff Reprint, Geneva, 1978. |
| *Art of the Violin* | P. Baillot (1835), *The Art of the Violin*, ed. and trans. by L. Goldberg, Northwestern University Press, Evanston, Ill., 1991. |
| Bachaumont | L. Petit de Bachaumont (1783), *Mémoires secrets pour servir à l'histoire de la république des lettres en France depuis 1762 jusqu'à nos jours*, 21 vols, vol. 20, John Adamson, London [Paris?]. |

| | |
|---|---|
| Burke | *Burke's Genealogical and Heraldic History of the Peerage, Baronetage and Knightage*, 96th edn, Shaw, London, 1938. |
| CFP | Chinnery Family Papers |
| Edgcumbe | R.M. Edgcumbe (1827), *Musical Reminiscences of an Old Amateur Chiefly Respecting the Italian Opera in England for Fifty Years from 1773–1823*, 2nd edn, W. Clarke, London. |
| *FétisB* | F.-J. Fétis (ed.) (1834–44), *Biographie universelle des musiciens et bibliographie générale de la musique*, 8 vols, Leroux/Méline, Brussels. |
| François-Sappey | B. François-Sappey (1978), 'Pierre-Marie-François de Sales Baillot (1771–1842) par lui-même', *Recherches sur la musique française classique* vol. 18, pp. 127–211. |
| Giazotto | R. Giazotto (1956), *Giovan Battista Viotti*, Edizioni Curci, Milan. |
| Goodkind | H. Goodkind (1972), *Violin Iconography of Antonio Stradivari, 1644–1737*, Larchmont, New York. |
| GRC's Travel Journal | The Travel Journals of George Robert Chinnery, 1819–1820, 3 vols, BL Add MS 64093, Add MS 64094, Add MS 64095. |
| Highfill | P.H. Highfill, K.A. Burnim, and E.A. Langhans, (1973–93), *A Biographical Dictionary of Actors, Actresses, Musicians, Dancers, Managers and other Stage Personnel in London 1660–1800*, 16 vols, Southern Illinois University Press, Carbondale, Ill. |
| La Laurencie (1924) | L. La Laurencie (1924), 'Les Débuts de Viotti comme directeur de l'Opéra', *Revue de musicologie*, vol. 5, pp. 110–22. |
| Landon | H.C. Robbins Landon (1976), *Haydn in England 1791–1795*, Indiana University Press, London. |
| MC's Journal | Margaret Chinnery's Journal, PHM 94/143/1 – 3. |
| MC's will | Margaret Chinnery's will, proven Paris, 12 December 1840, Archives nationales, -ET/LX/761. |
| 'Memoir of Viotti' | F. Fayolle (1824), 'Memoir of Giovanni Battista Viotti', *The Harmonicon*, no. 16, April, pp. 55–7. |
| *Mémoires* | S.-F. de Genlis (1825), *Mémoires inédits de madame la comtesse de Genlis, sur le dix-huitième siècle et la révolution française*, 8 vols, Ladvocat, Paris. |
| *MGG* | F. Blume (ed.) (1949–86), *Die Musik in Geschichte und Gegenwart*, 17 vols, Bärenreiter, Kassel. |

| | |
|---|---|
| Michaud | J.-F. Michaud (ed.) (1843–65), *Biographie universelle ancienne et moderne*, 45 vols, reprinted Akademische Druck und Verlagsanstalt, Graz, 1966–70. |
| *ML* | *Music and Letters* |
| *MM* | W. Parke (1830), *Musical Memoirs*, 2 vols, reprinted Da Capo Press, New York, 1970. |
| MMC's Journal | Matilda Chinnery's Journal, March–April [1814], PHM 94/143/1 – 27. |
| *MQ* | *The Musical Quarterly* |
| *New Grove 1* | S. Sadie (ed.) (1980), *The New Grove Dictionary of Music and Musicians*, 20 vols, Macmillan, London. |
| *New Grove 2* | S. Sadie (ed.) (2001), *The New Grove Dictionary of Music and Musicians*, 2nd edn, 29 vols, Macmillan, London. |
| *Notice* | P. Baillot (1825), *Notice sur J.-B. Viotti*, Hocquet, Paris. |
| *Observations* | *Observations désintéressées sur l'administration du Théâtre Royal Italien, adressées à M. Viotti*, Boucher, Paris, 6 February 1821, transcribed in Giazotto, pp. 276–85. |
| Pincherle (1924) | M. Pincherle (1924), 'Quelques Lettres de Viotti à Baillot', *Revue de Musicologie*, vol. 5, pp. 103–9. |
| Pougin | A. Pougin (1888), *Viotti et l'école moderne de violon*, Maison Schott, Paris. |
| *Précis* | *Précis de la vie de J.B. Viotti depuis son entrée dans le monde jusqu'au 6 mars 1798*, 23 March 1798, Viotti Papers, RCM, MS 4118. |
| *QMMR* | *Quarterly Musical Magazine and Review* |
| van der Straeten (1902) | E. van der Straeten (1902), 'J.B. Viotti, wie er sich selbst geschildert', *Die Musik*, vol. 1, nos 18 and 19, cols 1635–43 and 1736–44. |
| van der Straeten (1911) | E. van der Straeten (1911), 'Viottiana', *The Connoisseur*, November, pp. 152–60. |
| *SVEC* | *Studies on Voltaire and the Eighteenth Century* |
| *Thematic Catalogue* | C. White (1985), *Giovanni Battista Viotti: A Thematic Catalogue of his Works*, Pendragon Press, New York. |
| White, 'Chronology' | C. White (1973), 'Towards a More Accurate Chronology of Viotti's Violin Concertos', *Fontes Artis Musicae*, vol. 20, pp. 111–24. |
| Yim | D. Yim (ed.) (2003), *The Unpublished Correspondence of Mme de Genlis and Margaret Chinnery and related documents in the Chinnery Family Papers*, *SVEC*, vol. 2. |

The above edition of letters contains much correspondence that relates to Viotti. Where these letters and documents have been cited in the present book, the number assigned to the document in the *Unpublished Correspondence* will be given after the citation (e.g. Yim, D14).

Viotti compositions listed in White's *Thematic Catalogue* will be cited in parentheses, preceded by the letter W.

All translations within these pages are by the author unless otherwise stated.

# Introduction

> If the admiration of all could be concentrated on one artist alone, it might be said that the violin has never been greater or more beautiful than under the bow of *Viotti*, in that brilliant career he pursued in triumph, with the noble and touching simplicity of his style, the imposing and magnificent nature of his concerti.
>
> *Art of the Violin*, p. 12

Thus spoke Pierre Baillot of Giovanni Battista Viotti (1755–1824), one of the greatest violinist–composers to have lived. To read Baillot's words one would think that Viotti's career had lasted a lifetime. In fact it lasted only a few years, but the influence he exerted on the future course of violin playing has lasted right up to the present. Conversely the concertos of the composer who was in his day repeatedly described as a genius, have not endured and are rarely performed. His Violin Concerto No. 22 in A minor, which was revived by Joachim and revered by Brahms, is the most popular of the few that get a hearing today.

As a performer Viotti completely dominated the stage, having both presence and grace. Baillot described his supreme self-confidence as being similar to Paganini's.[1] Viotti's playing never failed to affect his listeners. His performances were not only technically brilliant, but they contained such emotion that they commonly moved his audience to tears. He was a superb interpreter of his own concertos into which he poured all the sensibility and passion of his own character. His contemporaries also remarked with wonder on his thoroughly spontaneous improvisational skills, claiming that he rarely performed his works as they were written.

As a contemporary of Mozart and Haydn, Viotti was steeped in the Classical tradition, but at the same time was a forward-looking composer whose genius took him to the borders of Romanticism. It has been demonstrated that he influenced Beethoven.[2] As well as 29 violin concertos and two *symphonies concertantes* Viotti composed string quartets, trios, duos, sonatas and some vocal works. His corpus of violin concertos, according to one modern critic, 'represents arguably the culmination of the genre in the eighteenth century'.[3] These concertos were performed throughout Europe in the early nineteenth century, and this fact, together with reviews of Viotti compositions to be found in the nineteenth-century German music journal the *Allgemeine musikalische Zeitung* and the evidence of

---

[1] *Art of the Violin*, p. xviii.

[2] B. Schwarz (1958), 'Beethoven and the French Violin School', *MQ*, vol. 44, no. 4, pp. 431–49.

[3] R. Stowell, review of White's *From Vivaldi to Viotti* in *ML* (1993), vol. 74, p. 295.

Viotti's contemporaries, shows the esteem in which his works were held in their day.

But it is first and foremost as the head of a new violin school that Viotti earned his place in history. When he arrived in Paris in 1782 with his Stradivari violin it was immediately realised that here was a totally new style of violin playing. Tone and expression, precision, and simplicity were the hallmarks of his style, which, unlike that of many of his contemporaries, was free of any affectation. Viotti's impact on Parisian violinists at the end of the eighteenth century led to the adoption of his technique by his pupils and disciples, most significantly by the triumvirate Pierre Rode (1774–1830), Rodolphe Kreutzer (1766–1831) and Pierre Baillot (1771–1842), who would through their 1803 *Méthode de violon* enshrine it as the official teaching method of the Paris Conservatoire, thereby creating the 'French' violin school.

The French method of violin playing subsequently gained currency in Europe and came to be the acknowledged one throughout the nineteenth century. Early nineteenth-century reports published in the *Allgemeine musikalische Zeitung* consistently acknowledge the supremacy of violinists trained in the French school, or disciples of it, and his fellow musicians even then recognized Viotti as 'le Père createur' (the original father) of the violin.[4] In fact it can be shown, through tracing teacher–pupil relationships over three centuries, that Viotti, through his direct link to Corelli, was the pivot from which all modern schools of violin playing evolved.[5]

The pupil who was most influential in disseminating Viotti's technique was Pierre Rode. It was Rode who, during his extensive European tours, not only performed many Viotti concertos but was also recognized by all who heard him as the principal exponent of the French violin school, or, as the *AMZ* was wont to call it, the 'Viotti'sche Schule'. But while it was the itinerant Rode who most effectively spread the French violin method by his playing, it was the more sedentary Baillot who ensured it endured by his teaching and writing, especially through his later, more comprehensive violin treatise *L'Art du violon* (1835).

One of the violinists who came under the influence of Rode was another Viotti admirer, Louis Spohr (1784–1859). Although Spohr had failed in his quest to become a Viotti pupil himself,[6] he was nevertheless a powerful influence in carrying his idol's method forward into the next violinist generation, living almost 30 years longer than Rode, and gaining widespread esteem as both a virtuoso and as a teacher. Spohr's *Violinschule* (1832) was a respected violin treatise that advocated a style that was closer to Viotti's than to that of his virtuosic contemporaries.

The Viotti/Chinnery letters are a valuable source of information on Viotti's pupils, including the young Spaniard Philippe Libon (1775–1838), who studied

---

[4] Jan Ladislav Dussek to GBV, 26 May 1810, NYPL JOB 97-52, item 16.

[5] See chart of teacher–pupil relationships in M. Campbell (1980), *The Great Violinists*, Granada, Frogmore, St Albans, Herts.

[6] L. Spohr (1865), *Autobiography*, 2 vols, trans. from the German, Longman Green, London, vol. 1, p. 13.

with Viotti from 1792 to 1798, Nicolas Mori (1797–1839), who took his lessons at the Chinnery home Gillwell Park from 1808 to 1812, the Brussels-born André Robberechts (1797–1860), and Rode himself. The Chinnery letters support Fétis's assertion that having met Viotti in Brussels, Robberechts became for a number of years Viotti's pupil in London. Robberechts later gave lessons to Charles de Bériot (1802–70), who would become professor of violin at the Brussels Conservatoire, thereby perpetuating Viotti's influence through the Franco-Belgian school.

One Viotti pupil in England who is mentioned in Chinnery correspondence, but who is unnoticed by any Viotti biographer or in any dictionary of music, was Charles Guynemer.[7] Guynemer was Baillot's brother-in-law and ex-pupil, and after his marriage in France (1809), he departed for England.[8] It is likely that Guynemer went to England with a recommendation to Viotti furnished by Baillot, who similarly passed on his pupil Robberechts. Another of Baillot's pupils to whom Viotti gave advice in London in 1814 was the almost unknown Fémy.[9]

Apart from aspiring professional violinists, Viotti gave informal lessons to, or at least condescended to play with, many *amateurs* from the upper classes of English society. The Viotti/Chinnery letters give much information on the most famous pupil in this category, the seventh son of George III, Adolphus Frederick, Duke of Cambridge. They also mention Albertine de Staël, daughter of the lioness of letters Madame de Staël, who procured short-term lessons from Viotti for her daughter during their 1813–14 sojourn in England.

## Viotti's biographers

Viotti has had many biographers. These can be roughly divided into three groups. Firstly there were his French contemporaries: disciple and soulmate Pierre Baillot; violinist–musicologists François-Joseph Fétis (1784–1871) and François Fayolle (1774–1852); French *député* and diplomat Comte Ange-Marie d'Eymar (*c.*1740–1803); and man of letters and music connoisseur Edme-François Miel (1775–1842), who wrote the Viotti entry in Michaud's *Biographie universelle ancienne et moderne*. All of these men, except perhaps Fétis and Fayolle, knew Viotti well, but as they lived in France they were not well-informed of his activities in England.

As far as Viotti's music and playing style are concerned the most reliable evidence comes from Baillot, who maintained close contact with Viotti from 1802 until his death. But neither Fétis's nor Miel's evidence can be dismissed as inaccurate, as the Chinnery letters show. Moreover Miel was a fellow member of the French *Société académique des enfants d'Apollon* (as was Eymar) and an intimate of the Paris Conservatoire professors.[10] Eymar's strange anecdotal evidence has sometimes been called into question, but his accounts of Viotti's

[7] See MC to WBC, *c.*April 1819, PHM 94/143/1 – 17/57.

[8] François-Sappey, pp. 129, 131.

[9] See GBV to Baillot, 12 July 1814, in Pincherle (1924), Letter 2, pp. 105–6.

[10] See below, pp. 116–17.

playing are valuable and his assessment of Viotti's temperament are corroborated by the latter's own letters to members of the Chinnery family.

Secondly there were the late nineteenth–early twentieth-century biographers, of whom the most important was the French musicologist Arthur Pougin, who wrote the first book-length biography of Viotti. But here again Viotti's years in England are a blank, as acknowledged by the author. The English violin enthusiast Edward Heron-Allen (1861–1943) broke new ground with his discovery of a small collection of autograph Viotti material (nine items), which at his death were bequeathed, along with a handful of Chinnery letters, to the Royal College of Music, London. Heron-Allen wrote the Viotti article for the second edition of *Grove's Dictionary of Music*, and had contact with the German musicologist Edmund van der Straeten, who wrote an article for the music journal *Die Musik* in 1902, and another for the English *Connoisseur* in 1911, based on these papers. This material, which included Viotti's short autobiography, enabled biographers to give a more 'factual' account of Viotti's life than had previously been possible, and alerted them to the importance of the Chinnery family in Viotti's life.

In the third group are the twentieth-century scholars Remo Giazotto, Chappell White and Boris Schwarz. The longest and most ambitious, but not the most accurate biography of Viotti was undertaken by Giazotto. This work, containing the first thematic catalogue of Viotti's works, now corrected and completed by White, is riddled with errors. It also includes some rather fanciful inventions, particularly regarding the Chinnery family. White and Schwarz are the most reliable authorities on Viotti.

Clearly a thoroughly revised biography of Viotti is long overdue. Although this book does not purport to be a complete biography, it will attempt to fill some of the lacunae in the above biographies. But it will not discuss in any detail the entrepreneurial aspects of Viotti's life – his attempt to gain control of the Paris Opéra in 1789, the operations of his Théâtre de Monsieur/Feydeau, his managerial role at the King's Theatre, London, or his wine business. Rather it will focus on his life with the Chinnerys after his arrival in London in 1792, giving particular attention to his musical activities, both public and private. Some information on Viotti's life prior to that period will be included.

Although the above biographers have acknowledged the close ties of Viotti with the Chinnery family, none has identified the exact nature of that relationship. The facts have remained hazy, and confusion surrounding the names of the various members of the Chinnery family has been widespread, mainly because of a dearth of biographical data about this family. Now that that information has become available it is possible not only to reconstruct quite accurately the second half of Viotti's life, but also to gain a much deeper insight into Viotti's character and motives.

## The Chinnery Family Papers

The Chinnery Family Papers are the private papers of a late eighteenth–early nineteenth-century English family. They are the most important, and by far the most voluminous source of Viotti manuscript material to come to light in the last 100 years. The CFP collection consists of over two thousand letters, journals, poetry, education material and other miscellaneous papers, with a date range from 1793 to 1843. There are over 120 Viotti letters to members of the Chinnery family, autograph copies of Viotti letters to others, and letters addressed to Viotti. The branch of the Chinnery family that this material issues from is that of William Bassett Chinnery (1766–1827), who was a chief clerk of the British Treasury. All the family papers, including those of Viotti, were kept together by William Bassett Chinnery's wife Margaret Chinnery (1764–1840) until her death. She was the last surviving member of this branch of the family.

The collection first came to the attention of Heron-Allen in 1885, when he was in contact with a supposed family descendant Algernon Greene (b.1843),[11] whose aunt Miss Mary Whitaker Greene had been Margaret Chinnery's companion in her final years, and who had inherited the Chinnery and Viotti papers that were in her possession at her death.[12] Heron-Allen clearly believed that Algernon Greene was a Chinnery descendant, since at the top of a 1798 Viotti letter[13] obtained from Algernon Greene he wrote: 'Written to Miss Caroline Chinnery and given to me in February 1885 by her grand nephew Algernon Greene.' However Margaret Chinnery's deed of succession specifies that although Miss Mary Whitaker Greene, annuitant, was the executrix of her will, she was not a relative.[14] Algernon Greene has also been stated to be a lineal descendant of Viotti, but the writer gives no supporting evidence.[15] Van der Straeten (1902) stated that Algernon Greene's grandmother (Miss Mary Whitaker Greene's mother) had been Margaret Chinnery's closest friend.[16]

Along with the collection of Chinnery/Viotti letters, Miss Mary Greene gave her nephew some family portraits, including one of Viotti painted by Elisabeth Vigée-Lebrun (1805),[17] another by Trossarelli (see Figure 1), some miniatures of various Chinnery family members also by Trossarelli (see Figure 3) and a portrait of Viotti by William Chinnery's brother the portraitist George Chinnery (see Figure 6).

---

[11] Algernon Greene, wealthy copper smelter, was the son of Nicholas Whitaker Greene and Frances Sophia Greene of Basingstoke, Hampshire. The 1881 census showed that he was then living at Egham, Surrey, near Windsor (Information kindly supplied by David Rymill, Archivist, Hampshire Record Office).

[12] MC's will, dated Paris, 26 January 1837.

[13] GBV to CC, 8 October 1798, Viotti Papers, RCM, MS 4118.

[14] Déclaration de succession, 4 May 1841, Archives départementales de Paris, D.Q[7] 3465.

[15] Highfill, vol. 15, p. 188.

[16] Vol. 1, col. 1636. A search for the identity of this person has not produced any result. It might be conjectured that her maiden name was Whitaker, but no female of this name is mentioned in the Chinnery letters, nor is there any record of a marriage between a Whitaker and a Greene between the years 1776 and 1825 in the marriage records of Lambeth Palace Library.

[17] The portrait was still in the possession of the Greene family in 1911, when it was reproduced in van der Straeten (1911), p. 152.

Sometime between 1893 and 1936 the Chinnery Family Papers were acquired by Richard Bentley II (1854–1936), grandson of the nineteenth-century publisher of the same name. On the back of a letter from Margaret Chinnery to Madame Cherubini there is a pencilled note by a Greene descendant, possibly made while taking stock of the collection in anticipation of a sale: 'All these are read, June 17th 1893, ES[?]G'. It is conceivable that Algernon Greene may have sold the collection to Richard Bentley, since the latter's grandfather was a contemporary of the Chinnerys, and probably knew them. On 19 December 1962 and 19 February 1963 there were two important Sotheby auctions in London of the property of the estate of Richard Bentley II, at which various parts of the CFP collection were disposed of. This resulted in the collection being broken up and scattered across the globe.[18]

The part of the collection that contains the bulk of the Viotti papers was donated to the Powerhouse Museum, Sydney by the Australian music and musical instrument collectors E.A. and V.I. Crome in 1973, but it is known that Crome had acquired the papers some years before that. These papers were not among those auctioned by Sotheby's in 1962 and 1963. They may have been sold later by Sotheby's, perhaps to one of the important American or English music manuscript dealers. It is possible that Crome purchased the papers from one of the latter, from whom he purchased other material donated to the Powerhouse Museum. This part of the CFP collection is by far the richest source of information on Viotti, since as well as his 108 letters to members of the Chinnery family, there are innumerable references to him in other Chinnery correspondence and journals.

The Chinnery Family Papers open up whole new aspects of Viotti's life, some rather surprising. As well as giving valuable insight into his musical activities, especially his 1794 Bath Easter concerts, they help date many of his compositions, identify his closest musician friends, recount his 1793 voyage on the Continent, describe his role of music tutor to the young harpist Casimir Baecker, and that of 'literary agent' to the latter's adoptive mother Madame de Genlis, and reveal him in the guise of educational assistant to Mrs Chinnery. The Chinnery Family Papers are also a valuable source of information on various aspects of musical life in London in the early nineteenth century, such as the teaching of music to children, opera at the beginning of the reign of George IV, and above all, on the conduct and structure of small private and domestic concerts.

---

[18] The parts of the collection sold in 1962 include those now held by the NYPL and by Yale University (Osborn collection), and a 1794 Haydn letter to Viotti, cited in Landon, p. 277. The parts sold in 1963 include those now held by Christ Church and Fisher libraries. The CFP collection in Fisher Library was uncovered by the present author in London in 1996 and acquired by Fisher the following year. All of the parts, except that owned by Yale, contain autograph Viotti letters.

## Members of the Chinnery family[19]

*William Bassett Chinnery (1766–1827)*

Chief clerk at the British Treasury, 1799–1812, WBC was on good terms with members of royal family, Duke of Cambridge, Duke of Cumberland and Prince of Wales. He was a collector of antiquities and an amateur cellist.

Married Margaret Tresilian on 21 October 1790, and settled at 5 Mortimer Street, Cavendish Square, London. After 1798 resided at 3 Duke Street, Adelphi on weekdays, and at Gillwell House, Waltham Abbey, on weekends. A lax Treasury auditing system allowed him to amass great wealth using Treasury funds, which could be kept in private bank accounts pending disbursements. Spent lavishly on entertaining, on his household establishment, on holidays, on improvements to the Gillwell Park property, and gave generous loans to friends, including Sébastien Erard and Viotti.[20] His theft, amounting to over £80,000, discovered in 1812. Dismissed from his Treasury post by prime minister Spencer Perceval, convicted of felony, committed to Newgate, but obtained royal pardon from the Prince Regent.[21] All his property and effects sold at public auction, 1812–13.

Fled to Gothenburg, and entered a trading business, 1812–14. Moved to Calais, rue de la Comédie (1814–16), then to Le Havre, 59 rue d'Edreville (1816–23), where he traded in wine, spirits, sugar, tea and coffee. Business foundered, 1823. From 1824 lived with his wife in Paris, where he died, 3 March 1827. Buried in a vault in the Père-Lachaise cemetery. In August 2002 his remains were removed to the grounds of Gilwell House, Essex [22]

*Margaret Chinnery (1764–1840)*

Eldest daughter of Brompton gentleman Leonard Tresilian. Well-educated, intelligent, and an accomplished pianist and musician. Was a much-courted hostess, who knew French and Italian. Educated her own children and those of relatives, based on the principles of French educator and author, Madame de

---

[19] Sources for the following dates in D. Yim (2000), *The Chinnery Family Papers, 1793–1843*, 2 vols, unpub. Ph.D. diss., University of Sydney, vol. 1, pp. 13–27.

[20] A bill of costs submitted by the Treasury Solicitor in 1815 shows that Viotti had borrowed £1,200 from WBC (T1/3535), and Erard £6,000 (T1/3535/16484), cited in M. Scorgie and D. Wilkinson, 'William Bassett Chinnery: 1787–1812. Australia's Premier Accountant and Embezzler', unpub. paper presented at the Conference of the Accounting Association of Australia and New Zealand (AAANZ), Hobart, Australia (extract in *Conference of the AAANZ*, Melbourne, July 1997, p. 115). The paper was sent to me by the authors, whom I thank sincerely.

[21] *Gentleman's Magazine* (1812), vol. 82, pt 1, p. 286.

[22] On 27 August 2002 WBC's and MC's ashes (and those of a young grand niece) were laid to rest beneath the monument erected to the memory of their son Walter Chinnery in the grounds of Gilwell House, now the property of the Scout Association. The service was conducted by Canon Martin Webster, Rector of Waltham Abbey. (Today Gilwell is spelt with three 'l's.)

Genlis.[23] As well as the children listed below MC educated a certain Maria, (b.*c.*1788, surname unknown), whose father was a singer in the Italian Opera at the King's Theatre in March 1814.

Lived at Gillwell House, the property settled upon her by her father on her marriage, 1796–1812 (from *c.*1799 with Viotti). Rented a house at 10 Charles Street, Manchester Square with Viotti, 1812–17. Purchased a house at 17 Montagu Street, Portman Square, where she lived with Viotti, 1817–19, and intermittently until 1824.

With Viotti visited her husband on the Continent yearly from 1814. Purchased a property outside Paris at Châtillon-sous-Bagneux, 1819. Divided the year between Châtillon and London, 1819–23. Returned to London with Viotti, end 1823. Rented a property at 5 Upper Berkeley Street, where Viotti died. Moved back to Paris to live with her husband. Died in Paris, 5 November 1840. Was buried with her husband in the Père-Lachaise cemetery. In August 2002 her remains were removed with her husband's to the grounds of Gilwell House, Essex.

*George Robert Chinnery (1791–1825)*

Eldest son of WBC and MC, and twin brother of Caroline. After his home education at Gillwell, attended Christ Church College, Oxford, 1808–11. Awarded a Studentship (1809), Newdigate prize for poetry (1810), B.A. with first class honours, mathematics (1811), M.A. (1814). Knew five modern languages, as well as Greek and Latin.

Junior clerk, British Treasury (1812–21), assistant clerk of revenue, 1821–23. Belonged to several London gentlemen's clubs, including the United Universities Club, the Albion and Grillion's. Protégé of statesman George Canning, 1814–25. Private secretary to Canning, 1816. Accompanied Canning to Portugal (1815), and on tours of the Continent, 1819, 1820. Transferred to Foreign Office, 1823. Sent to Madrid as British commissioner of claims (in the British merchants' dispute with the Spanish Government), 1824–25. Died suddenly in Madrid, October 1825. It is not known where he was buried.

*Caroline Chinnery (1791–1812)*

Twin sister of GRC. Educated at Gillwell, like GRC, by her mother and various tutors. Taught piano and singing by her mother, harp by François Dizi, and composition by Francesco Bianchi. Musical studies also supervised by Viotti, who wrote sonatas especially for her. Composed some piano pieces which have not survived. Knew French, Italian, German and Latin.

Was courted by high society, including the Prince Regent, for her musical accomplishments. Contracted whooping cough, 1811. Died of miliary tuberculosis aged 20 on 3 April 1812, ignorant of her father's disgrace, in the home of William

---

[23] See D. Yim, 'Madame de Genlis's *Adèle et Théodore*: Its Influence on an English Family's Education', *AJFS*, vol. 38, no. 1, pp. 141–57.

Spencer at 36 Curzon Street, London. Buried with her brother Walter in a vault in Waltham Abbey Church.

*Walter Grenfell Chinnery (1793–1802)*

Younger brother of GRC and CC. Educated by his mother and by Viotti at Gillwell. Most of his studies conducted in French and Italian by Viotti. Accompanied his family and Viotti to Paris, 1802. Died of typhoid fever[?] on his return to London, 19 November 1802. Buried with his sister in Waltham Abbey Church, where there is a marble memorial to both children.

*Matilda Margretta Chinnery (1797–1877)*

Born Madras, eldest child of WBC's brother John Terry Chinnery (1770–1817). Sent to England, 1800. Educated at Gillwell by MC. Achieved the same level of proficiency in music as CC, and also came under influence of Viotti. Shared role of hostess with MC after Caroline died, and entertained guests on piano and harp. Kept a journal [1814], which documents some of Viotti's Philharmonic Society activities. Remained with MC and Viotti for 20 years, until she left England (1821) to marry Captain Samuel Irton Hodgson in India, 1822.

*Margaret Chinnery Girardot (c.1798–1878)*

Née Margaret Chinnery, and known as 'little Margaret' she was WBC's stepsister. Educated with the other children by Margaret Chinnery at Gillwell, where she lived, *c.*1804–11. Played piano and harp, and benefited from Viotti's tutoring. Sent to school (1811), and lived intermittently with MC and Viotti thereafter. Taught piano and harp to young ladies in London. In *c.*1822 married Captain Charles Andrew Girardot (1794–1864).

* * *

From the moment Viotti met the Chinnery family his life became part of theirs. Their closeness is evident from the affectionate terms of address used in the letters. Viotti called William 'mon cher Chin', or simply 'Chin', and in more playful moments 'Gastaldo' or 'Cinnerino' (the last an affectionate allusion to William's small stature). Margaret he called sometimes 'Amica', or 'la cara Padrona', or 'la belle Margaratina'. To all the Chinnery family members, and to many of their friends as well, Viotti was known simply as 'Amico'. Viotti was a loyal friend and supporter of both Margaret and William, and to their children he was a second father.

The relationship between the three adults can only be described as a truly successful *ménage à trois*. Both men idolized Margaret, but although one was her husband by law and the other her companion by choice, never was there any friction between the two. When Viotti was expelled from England under a cloud of suspicion in 1798, William Chinnery was his staunch defender, and when William

Chinnery was in turn forced to flee England in 1812, Viotti was a pillar of support to his wife and a harsh critic of his detractors. Nor was there any subsequent jealousy on William's part when Viotti remained with Margaret after his departure. Indeed he was grateful that his wife had a protector. The yearly reunions of the three friends on the Continent were happy and harmonious.

Was Viotti Margaret's lover? It seems impossible to believe that he was not. He certainly declared his love for her in many of the early letters, especially the 1793 ones from the Continent, when he felt so tormented and lonely. Expressions addressed to Margaret such as 'I love you tenderly',[24] 'Adieu Amica, amica whom I love and honour more each day'[25] indicates his already deep attachment. Margaret reciprocated his feelings. There is no doubt that these expressions of love were genuine, but in an age of both libertine mores and of unembarrassed sentimentalism (as testified by the unrestrained outpourings of feeling in many of the present letters), it is hard to determine if this love was platonic or not. Besides, Viotti's expressions of affection for William were just as strong: 'tell Mr Chi that he is also the only person whom I love with all my heart in this fine country',[26] 'I send you both a thousand tender wishes from the depth of my heart.'[27] A harmonious threesome such as theirs may well have been tolerated in such an era. On the whole it went unremarked.

One of the few persons to have hinted at scandal was the family friend Lord Glenbervie, who reported in his *Journals* rumours that Caroline might have been Viotti's daughter,[28] and who jotted the following suggestive lines in his *Diaries*:[29]

> The name Mrs Chinnery still calls Fiotti [sic] by, of *L'Amico*, and as the husband also always called him, puts me in mind of a song in one of the Italian comic operas acted at Venice (I think) when I was there, in the years 1767–8.

| | |
|---|---|
| Questo Marcello | This Marcello |
| Non è fratello— | Is no little brother— |
| E'un *amico* | He is an *amico* |
| C'è un intrico, | It is an entanglement |
| Egià sapete come va! | To be sure, you know how it goes! |

But there was never any jealousy on William's side for the place Viotti occupied in his wife's heart, and the two men continued the closest of friends until Viotti's death. For Viotti's part, he devoted his life to both William and Margaret. The

[24] 'je vous aime tendrement' (GBV to MC, 20 September 1793, PHM 94/143/1 – 2/10).

[25] 'Adieu Amica, amica que j'aime et j'honore tous les jours de plus' (GBV to MC, 6 December 1793, PHM 94/143/1 – 2/14).

[26] 'dites à M^r^ Chi qu'il est le seul aussi que j'aime de tout mon cœur dans ce beau pays' (GBV to MC, 22 July 1793, PHM 94/143/1 – 2/6).

[27] 'recevés tous les deux mille choses tendres de la part de toute ma sensibilité' (GBV to MC, 13 October 1793, PHM 94/143/1 – 2/12).

[28] S. Douglas (1910), *The Glenbervie Journals*, ed. W. Sichel, Constable, London, p. 145.

[29] S. Douglas (1928), *The Diaries of Sylvester Douglas (Lord Glenbervie)*, 2 vols, ed. F. Bickley, Constable, London, vol. 2, p. 319.

affection in which he held the Chinnerys and his relationship with them may best be described in his own words:

> I made the acquaintance of Mr and Mrs Chinnery, two beings who possess the most estimable qualities to a superior degree. Kind, compassionate, faithful friends, in whose excellent hearts no quality was lacking. As soon as I met them I loved them, and as soon as they met me, they reciprocated the sentiment. Since this happy moment I have devoted my life to them. Nothing in the world— society or amusements— held any attraction for me without them, and their home where I lived as a family member, as a brother, has become my own, [the place] where I would have liked to always be, and never leave.[30]

Viotti was not exaggerating when he wrote these words. He did devote his life to the Chinnerys. Indeed he spent almost half his life with Margaret. His longest separation from her was for four months in the winter of 1821–22. A prophetic confession of Viotti's constancy to the Chinnerys can also be found in an even earlier letter which he ends with the following words: 'Everything is replaced in life, everything passes on, but nothing will replace the attachment I have for you and all your family, and it will pass only with my life.'[31]

---

[30] 'Je fis connoissance avec M$^{r}$ et Mme Chinnery deux êtres qui possedent au suprème degré les qualités les plus estimables. Bons, compatissants, amis fideles, rien ne manque à leur âme excelente. Sitôt que je les ai connus je les ai aimés, et sitôt qu'ils me connurent ils me cherirent de même. Depuis cet heureux moment je leur ai dévoué ma vie. Le monde, la société, les amusemens, rien de tout cela n'avoit d'attrait sans eux, et leur maison ou je vivois comme un parent, comme un frère, est devenue la mienne propre, celle ou j'aurois voulu être sans cesse, celle d'ou je n'aurois jamais voulu sortir' (*Précis*).

[31] 'Tout se succéde tout passe dans la vie, mais rien ne succedera à l'attachement que j'ai pour vous et toute votre famille, et il ne passera qu'avec ma vie' (GBV to MC, 17 April 1793 [*recte* 1794], PHM 94/143/1 – 2/1).

CHAPTER 1

# Before Paris

Viotti was born into an era and country where music was part of everyday life. All over Europe kings, princes and wealthy aristocrats kept their own bands, and members of the upper classes and the well-to-do bourgeoisie liked to give out that they were either *amateurs* who made music or connoisseurs who understood it. In a country like Italy it was not unusual for even families of modest means to own instruments and play for their own entertainment. It was not a subject of wonder then that a father who was a blacksmith should play the horn, nor that his son should have a violin put in his hands at the age of eight. According to a short biography penned by a family friend[1] Viotti showed early promise of an exceptional talent, which fortuitously was noticed and cultivated. The spark of genius that was recognized by others was also recognized by the child. Innocently confident of his ability to handle his instrument, and to impress others, Viotti seemed to step assuredly onto the path that fortune opened before him, never doubting the success that would come his way.

Our knowledge of Viotti's existence before his bursting into prominence in Paris in 1782 is still very blurry compared to the clear picture that now emerges of his post-1792 life. It was until recently based on Viotti's own sketchy autobiography and the anecdotal evidence of Viotti's contemporaries, which has now been supplemented by a thoroughgoing examination of local Turin and Fontanetto records.[2] The records show that Viotti was born in Piedmont in the small town of Fontanetto Po near Turin in the canton of Crescentino on 12 May 1755. Viotti's father Felice Viotto was indeed a blacksmith, and was the owner of the premises from which he worked, G.B. Viotti's birthplace. The address is today via Viotti no. 23.

Viotti's father married his mother Maddalena Milano on 24 February 1746, and Giovanni Battista was born nine years later. Maddalena Milano died in April 1763, probably in childbirth, the year that Pugnani became principal of the second violins in the chapel orchestra of the king of Sardinia. Viotti's father wed again, this time to a Maria Teresa Musetti. From the two marriages issued a total of 18

---

[1] Dr G.B. Negri, deputy mayor of Fontanetto and member of a respected legal family. Negri's manuscript *Note biografiche* (1810) was in the Fontanetto parish archives, but cannot be found there today.

[2] Since the writing of the present book Viotti's early years have been significantly clarified in a meticulously researched article by Warwick Lister (2003) entitled '"Suonatore del Principe": New light on Viotti's Turin years', *Early Music*, vol. 31, no. 2, pp. 233–45. See also R. Raina (1994), 'Nuovi documenti biografici su Giovan Battista Viotti', *Nuova Rivista Musicale Italiana*, vol. 28, pp. 251–6.

children, most dying in infancy. Fontanetto records also show that Viotti had an older sister Anna Adelaide (b.1748), a brother Giuseppe (b.1763), and from his father's second marriage two young half-brothers, Gian Maria and Gian Andrea (later known as André), both of whom had distinguished careers in the French army and were awarded the Legion of Honour. A third half-brother 'l'ultimo fratto Giorgio', mentioned in an 1803 letter from Gian Andrea to Viotti, also had a career in the French army, and at the time of writing was headed for Bengal.[3] There was also a young half-sister Teresa Margherita to whom Viotti stood godfather in December 1782.[4]

According to Fétis, Felice Viotto played the horn and taught his son the elements of music. Giovanni Battista allegedly acquired his first violin from the Crescentino fair at the age of eight. His first teacher is said to have been a certain Giovannini, a lute-playing adventurer whose instruction lasted only one year. In 1766 the young Viotti was recommended to the prominent Turin aristocrat the Marchesa di Voghera as a music companion for her 18-year-old son Prince Alfonso dal Pozzo della Cisterna. The marchesa was allegedly disappointed to find that her son's new companion was a mere child of 11, but luckily for Viotti she was persuaded to keep him by a distinguished musician from the royal chapel who tested his competence with first an easy, then a difficult piece of music, both of which Viotti executed with ease. Fétis, who says that his information came from the prince himself, relates that having heard Viotti reproduce on his violin correctly some opera music that he had heard only once, Cisterna was so astounded that he decided on the spot to instal him in his villa and give him the illustrious Piedmontese violinist Gaetano Pugnani (1731 98) as a teacher. The prince told Fétis that Viotti's education had cost him more than 20,000 francs, which he did not regret because such a talent could never be paid for too highly.[5] Viotti himself lends weight to the truth of this statement when he says that his younger years in Cisterna's palace were spent in typically idle childish occupations alternating with 'an enormous amount of study'.[6]

This period of concentrated study, was, it goes without saying, not wasted on Viotti. But what is not well known, perhaps, is that it was not only musically that Viotti profited from the education given him by his generous benefactor. The precocious young violinist appears to have been left with a deep appreciation of the value of education, and a lasting interest in education methods, evidence of which crops up sporadically throughout his life. Even at such a young age Viotti must have been conscious of the fact that he had been assigned as teacher the most famous violinist in Turin, and soon been made aware that that city, as the capital of

---

[3] Jean-André Viotti to GBV, 9 April 1803, NYPL JOB 97-52, item 8.

[4] Raina, 'Nuovi documenti', pp. 253–4.

[5] *FétisB*, vol. 8, pp. 468. The first part of Fétis's account corresponds almost exactly to Negri's biography, on which G. Degregori's later *Istoria della vercellese letteratura ed arti* (Turin, 1819–24) was based, and which Fétis had probably read.

[6] 'infinment d'étude' (*Précis*). For a sample of some of the subjects Viotti studied see Lister, "Suonatore del Principe", p. 234.

the duchies of Savoy and Piedmont and of the kingdom of Sardinia, was one of the pre-eminent musical centres in Europe, a region of rich musical heritage.

Pugnani's pedigree went back through Somis to Corelli. From Pugnani Viotti inherited a broad, grandiose manner of playing, a forceful bowing style (Pugnani's 'arco magno' was legendary), and a typically Italian rich *cantabile* that was inspired by Tartini's adage 'Per ben suonare, bisogna ben cantare' ('To play well one must sing well').[7] According to Baillot Viotti owed his beautiful style to Pugnani, but was able to avoid the faults of his mentor.[8] In addition, according to Fayolle, it was from Pugnani, a past-master in ensemble playing, that Viotti learned the art of leading an orchestra.[9] Viotti's gratitude to his mentor is shown by his calling himself 'élève du célèbre Pugnani' on the title page of his first concerto, No. 3 in A. (By 1793 the roles would be reversed, and it would be Pugnani who addressed Viotti as 'Celebre Proffeseur de Musique'.)[10] Viotti's admiration for Pugnani in his alleged exclamation 'C'est un Jupiter', gives an idea of what Pougin calls Pugnani's 'exécution mâle' (manly execution),[11] a term that would be repeatedly used to characterize Viotti's own style.

Pugnani would have been about 38 when he acquired Viotti as a pupil. From the letter Pugnani wrote to Viotti in 1793 it is clear that in Turin Viotti was introduced into Pugnani's family, and that the mutual affection between master and pupil endured long after the two had parted ways. The manner in which Pugnani signs off the letter shows that he loved Viotti as a son: 'Adieu. Love me, do not forget me, and know that no one in the world loves you more than your friend Pugnani'.[12]

By 1766 Pugnani had already distinguished himself in performing tours, and for two seasons (1767–68 and 1768–69) he led the Italian Opera orchestra at the King's Theatre, London. Viotti probably did not become Pugnani's pupil until the latter's return from England, having first studied under a Signor Celoniat. By 1773 Pugnani must have deemed Viotti accomplished enough to accompany him on his next tour to London, as a cryptic advertisement in a London newspaper (*Public Advertiser*, 13 May 1773) refers to a trio played by Pugnani, 'Viot' and the cellist Janson.[13] It may have been this voyage that Miel refers to in his notice on Viotti in the *Biographie universelle*, where he states that at the age of 12, Viotti crossed France en route to London with his master.[14] Viotti had in fact just turned 18.

---

[7] Cited in Baillot's *Notice*, p. 5.

[8] *Ibid.*, p. 4.

[9] F. Fayolle (1810), *Notices sur Corelli, Tartini, Gaviniés, Pugnani et Viotti*, Paris, cited in Daniel Heartz (1984), 'Portrait of a Court Musician: Gaetano Pugnani of Turin', *Imago Musicae*, vol. 1, p. 119.

[10] Pugnani to GBV, 16 October 1793, NYPL JOB 97-52, item 1, transcribed in Appendix.

[11] Pougin, p. 13.

[12] See Appendix.

[13] Simon McVeigh (1989), *The Violinist in London's Concert Life 1750–1784: Felice Giardini and his Contemporaries*, Garland Publishing, New York and London, pp. 70–71.

[14] Michaud, vol. 43, p. 586.

In 1773 Viotti entered the orchestra of Turin's Teatro Regio,[15] and in 1775 the king of Sardinia's chapel orchestra, where he occupied the last desk of the first violins for five years. In 1780–81 Viotti and Pugnani made a tour of the Continent, appearing in many different cities and courts of Europe. Viotti wrote of these years:

> When I reached the point where I believed I had something [talent] I left that villa [Cisterna's], intending to travel and develop my talent. Geneva was the first place where I was heard. That was, I believe, in 1780, and the encouragement I was given there made me resolve to continue my travels.[16]

Viotti's reception in Geneva is described in a letter dated 10 January 1780, written by an English music lover on a tour of the Continent, Reverend Thomas Brand to a fellow clergyman in Durham.[17] The 12-week concert series that took place in Geneva in the winter of 1780 featured Viotti as a soloist one week, and Jean-Jérôme Imbault (1753–1832) the other. Surprisingly, Pugnani appeared as a guest performer only. It is clear from Brand's account that of the three violinists Viotti made the greatest impression, Imbault and Pugnani receiving lesser accolades from the writer, and presumably, from the rest of the audience. Brand's is the earliest known account of Viotti's playing, and his assessment encapsulates in one sentence the sentiments of all Viotti's future reviewers: 'His tone and execution are equally great and he is besides a well made handsome man and plays with wonderful ease and grace.'

Viotti's personal appearance certainly counted in his favour, and as can be seen from the Chinnery letters, he dressed with care. But he did not allow appearances to influence his own assessment of other violinists. In Geneva he befriended Imbault, an experienced violinist, but one whose noticeable shyness before the public probably did not allow justice to be done to his performances. Viotti's subsequent professional closeness to Imbault would suggest that he esteemed this violinist's playing more than did the general public.

Encouraged by what was clearly a very enthusiastic reception in Geneva, Viotti decided to proceed to Berne. His *Précis* takes up: 'Already a small degree of celebrity had preceded me to Berne. I did not delay in following it. I was received there with all the kindness I could have desired, and the taste for travelling grew upon me.'[18] On leaving Switzerland Viotti proceeded with Pugnani to Dresden, and then to Berlin, arriving on 21 April 1780.[19]

---

[15] This fact was discovered by Warwick Lister ("Suonatore del Principe", pp. 238–9).

[16] 'Arrivé à l'époque ou je crus d'avoir quelque chose, je quittai cette Villa dans l'intention de voyager et former de plus en plus mon talent. Genève fut le premier lieu ou je me fis entendre. C'étoit ça me semble en 1780, et l'encouragement que j'y reçus me fit résoudre à poursuivre ma route' (*Précis*).

[17] The letter was uncovered by Warwick Lister, who transcribed part of it in his 2002 article 'New Light on the Early Career of G.B. Viotti', *ML*, vol. 83, no. 3, p. 419. Lister also discusses which pieces of music Viotti might have performed at the Geneva concerts.

[18] 'Déjà une petite célébrité me précédoit à Berne; je ne tardai guere à la suivre. Là je fus

In Berlin Viotti was met and lodged by his compatriot the Sardinian minister to the Prussian court Count Carlo Fontana. Fontana, an *amateur* who knew Pugnani well,[20] presented the visitors to the enlightened Prussian monarch Frederick the Great, who was clearly much taken with the gifted young violinist, as he kept him at his court for some considerable time, and, according to Viotti's understated account, often played with him. Viotti's Six quartets for two violins, viola and cello, Op. 1, dedicated to the Princess of Prussia (wife of the king's nephew and successor Friedrich Wilhelm), and his Six trios for two violins and cello, Op. 2, dedicated to Pugnani, could have been performed in Berlin, having been composed, perhaps, for use on the tour.

The charmingly simple tone of the *Précis* of Viotti, whose modesty is evident in all his writings about himself, continues in a bald description of his travels to Warsaw, where the cultured King Stanislas not only heard him play, but according to Miel, also took him on hunting expeditions and included him in all the courtly entertainments. The next court to receive him was that of St Petersburg, where he arrived with Pugnani in early January 1781. There he was treated with equal consideration and respect by Catherine the Great, who allegedly showered him with expensive gifts in a vain attempt to detain him at her court. He also seems to have made a lucrative tour of several Russian cities, including Moscow.[21]

From St Petersburg Viotti returned in early December 1781 to Berlin, where, according to Miel, he performed a violin concerto which he had just finished. It was here that he allegedly had his first encounter with the eccentric violinist Giovanni Giornovichi (1747–1804), or Jarnowick, as he was then more commonly known. Miel's account sounds plausible when he portrays Viotti's embarrassment at having to perform unprepared his concerto before the Prussian court because he had had no time for rehearsal, having spent the whole day copying out parts.[22] This was clearly not a concerto that had been performed in full before. It may have been his No. 2, 4, or 5 (No. 3 being by then already published), all of which, it is believed, could conceivably have been composed prior to Viotti's arrival in Paris.[23]

From Berlin Viotti made his way down to Paris, intending to stay for a few months, but instead remaining for ten years. He arrived in time for the commencement of the *Concert spirituel* on 17 March 1782.

---

reçu avec toute la bienveillance que j'avois pû desirer, et le goût de voyager s'imprima de plus en plus en moi' (*Précis*).

[19] For Viotti's dates in Berlin see Lister, 'New Light', p. 423.

[20] *Ibid.*

[21] Michaud, vol. 43, p. 586; Lister, 'New Light', p. 423; *FétisB*, vol. 8, p. 468.

[22] Michaud, vol. 43, p. 586.

[23] White, 'Chronology', p. 116; Lister, 'New Light', p. 421.

CHAPTER 2

# Paris, 1782–1792

Viotti arrived in Paris leaving in his train a reputation that spread from one end of Europe to the other, but whether the French musical public, or even the musicians themselves, knew of his recent successes seems unlikely. On the other hand it may be assumed that the aristocratic *amateurs* had heard of it from correspondents, especially foreign ambassadors, at the courts Viotti had visited over the previous two years. Indeed the first concert Viotti gave in Paris was a private one. The Parisian commentator and critic of the arts Petit de Bachaumont wrote of the violinists' surprise in his *Mémoires secrets*:

> M. Viotti, a foreign violinist who has not yet performed here, and who by chance made himself known, with rare modesty, for the first time at a small private concert where he made all our great professors drop their bows in astonishment, is to debut at the Concert spirituel during the next fortnight. There are certain amateurs who rank him above any we have ever heard before.[1]

Where might this first private performance have taken place? Perhaps it was at the home of the Baron de Bagge, a violin devotee who used his immense wealth to foster the musical arts, and who offered generous hospitality and useful introductions to many of the newly arrived violinists in Paris. His *hôtel* on the Place des Victoires was famous for its lavish dinners and musical soirées at which he performed with his professional protégés. Fancying himself to be an accomplished violinist and composer, he even presumed to offer himself as a teacher to these professionals, paying them, according to one report, to accept his tuition. According to the same report Viotti was one of them!

> The first artists of France, Germany and Italy were obliging enough to allow themselves to be instructed in what he called his first principles, and Viotti, to whom he had given rooms in his house, took formal tuition from him. The most amusing thing of all was that the eccentric teacher paid the pupil one louis d'or for each lesson. How difficult must it have been for Viotti to keep a straight face; for never did a baron make more horrible grimaces than this one, the moment he took up his violin and bow. His face, his muscles and his entire body were most painfully contorted, and when his playing

---

[1] 'M. Viotti, violon étranger, qui n'a point encore paru ici, qui s'est fait connoître par hasard pour la premiere fois dans un petit concert particulier avec une modestie rare, & fit tomber l'archet des mains de tous nos grand maîtres, doit débuter au concert spirituel durant la quinzaine: il est des amateurs qui le mettent au-dessus de tout ce que nous avons entendu jusqu'à présent' (Bachaumont, 13 March 1782, vol. 20, p. 122).

became passionate the sounds that emanated from his instrument might be confused with the yowling of a cat.[2]

Bagge was a sort of unorthodox Prussian court representative, holding from 1789 the title *chambellan du Roi de Prusse*, which meant that he was certainly in communication with the Prussian court in Berlin,[3] where Viotti had recently played. The Sardinian minister Fontana, with whom Viotti had lodged, may well have provided Viotti with a letter of introduction to Bagge. According to Bachaumont, who had noted Bagge's all-consuming passion for music in his *Mémoires* just three weeks before the above entry regarding Viotti, even this might not have been necessary, since Bagge apparently actively sought out new talent:

> No virtuoso arrives in Paris without his wanting to see him and hear him, whatever the price may be. It is usually in his home that [musicians] are first heard before appearing at the Concert spirituel.[4]

Viotti could have had no better introduction to Paris's musical society, both professional and amateur, than through this intermediary. Moreover it was probably Bagge who proposed Viotti for membership of the new masonic *Société de la Loge olympique*, which would have immediately propelled him into the right circles. The stated aim of the *Société*, established in May 1782 under the arcades of the Palais Royal, was to cultivate music, to give high quality concerts, and to fill the gap left in the city's concert agenda by the demise of the *Société des Amateurs* in 1781.[5] Membership of this fashionable *Société*, was a distinct honour for Viotti, since only a handful of the 364 fully subscribed members were listed as musicians.

Both Viotti's and Bagge's names, along with other aristocratic *amateurs*, mostly members of the Church and the military nobility, figure on the 1786 list of members, where Viotti is noted as also belonging (since 1783) to another masonic lodge, the *Saint-Jean d'Ecosse du Contrat Social*.[6] The exclusivity of this society

---

[2] 'Die ersten Künstler Frankreichs, Deutschlands und Italiens hatten die Gefälligkeit, sich in dem, was er seine eignen Grundsätze nannte, unterrichten zu lassen und Viotti, dem er eine Wohnung in seinem Haus einräumte, nahm förmlich bey ihm Stunde. Das Spashafteste bey der Sache war, dass der seltsame Lehrer dem Schüler für jede Lektion einen Louis d'or bezahlte. Wie schwer mag es aber bisweilen Viotti'n geworden seyn, ernsthaft dabey zu bleiben; denn nie hat wohl ein Baron schrecklicher grimassirt, als dieser, so bald er dir Geige ansetzte und den Bogen ergriff. Sein Gesicht, seine Muskeln, sein ganzer Körper waren in der peinlichsten Spannung und wenn er beym Spielen feurig wurde, so kamen Töner zum Vorschein, die mit den Klagen eines Katers zu wechseln waren' (*AMZ*, 16 September 1801, cols 840–41).

[3] He dedicated his first concerto to Prince Friedrich Wilhelm of Prussia.

[4] 'Il ne vient point de virtuose à Paris qu'il ne veuille voir & entendre, à quelque prix que ce soit. C'est ordinairement chez lui qu'on débute avant de paroître au concert spirituel' (Bachaumont, 20 February 1782, vol. 20, p. 83).

[5] J.-L. Quoy-Bodin (1984), 'L'Orchestre de la Société Olympique en 1786', *Revue de musicologie*, vol. 70, p. 96.

[6] *Ibid.*, p. 98. Many musicians were freemasons, including Haydn, Mozart, Beethoven,

was underscored by the fact that the queen sometimes attended the concerts, given in the Tuileries Palace, forcing the whole assembly, including the orchestra, into full court dress. It appears that Viotti occasionally led the orchestra at the *Olympique* concerts. According to an article in the *Revue et Gazette musicale* his second *Symphonie concertante* (WI:31) was performed here under his direction by Henri Guérillot (1749–1805) and Jean-Jacques Grasset (*c.*1769–1839).[7]

But in 1782 it was the *Concert spirituel* that Viotti had in his sights. Originally established for the performance of ecclesiastical instrumental and vocal works in Lent and on religious holidays when the other theatres were closed, by the end of the eighteenth century secular music had been accepted into its programmes, and it was the performing platform of choice for any new artist ambitious to make a name for himself. It had attracted musicians from all over Europe, especially Italy, since its inception in 1725. The *Concert spirituel* was the grand arbiter of talent in both composition and performance, and the violin concerto was the most admired genre.

The *Concert spirituel* was a fiercely competitive arena. Different from the London concerts in which Viotti would perform a decade later, the *Concert spirituel* presented a long succession of vocal and instrumental artists in the same programme, including virtuosos of the same instrument. In London two rival violinists would never be pitted one against the other in the same programme. But here it was almost the *Concert*'s raison d'être: 'The great benefit of this institution was the opportunity which it afforded the students of music, and the public in general, of hearing, judging, and comparing the compositions of the great masters of foreign schools, and the spirit of emulation which it naturally inspired', wrote the *Harmonicon* in 1824.[8]

The accolades that Viotti received after his first public performance at the *Concert spirituel* were unprecedented. Many artists had been feted by the fickle Paris public, but none had caused a sensation like this. Every major newspaper, music journal and public commentator reviewed the concert. Viotti's playing was praised for its brilliant execution, its exquisite finish, its admirable tone quality, and for the 'unbelievable facility and the clarity with which he executed the greatest difficulties'.[9] Viotti's *adagio* playing was singled out for praise by every single reviewer, and by itself qualified the newcomer as one of the greatest masters, raising him, according to one, to the level of the quasi sacred Lolli.[10]

Until Viotti's appearance the violinists who had made most impression on the French public had been their own venerated masters (Leclair, Gaviniès, L'Abbé *le fils*, Barthélémon, Guénin, the Chevalier de Saint-Georges, La Houssaye), as well as the Italian Lolli, who had been adopted as their own. More recently the

---

Cherubini, and Baillot.

7 Cited in T. Lassabathie (1860), *Histoire du Conservatoire impérial de musique et de déclamation,* Michel Lévy Frères, Paris, p. 63.

8 'Origin and History of the *Concert Spirituel*', *The Harmonicon* (1824), no. 16, April, p. 57.

9 'la facilité incroyable & la netteté avec laquelle il exécuta les plus grandes difficultés' (*Journal de Paris*, 23 March 1782).

10 Bachaumont, 20 March 1782, vol. 20, p. 133. 'Lulli' is written, but Lolli is probably meant.

quarrelsome Giornovichi, in Paris from 1773 to 1779, had fascinated the public as much by his unpredictable behaviour as by the elegance of his playing.

The violinists appearing on the same stage as Viotti in 1782 were indeed unfortunate, especially the German Johann Friedrich Eck, who was making his debut that year. All were eclipsed. The *Almanach musical* wrote:

> MM. [J.-A.] Fodor, Eck, Viotti and [Isidore] Berthaume performed various violin concertos of their own composition or of other French composers. [...] From the first day of Viotti's appearance all those who heard him were unanimous in placing him above all his rivals.[11]

But the French connoisseurs were notoriously jealous and did not like their favourites being displaced by a foreigner. The German violinist Louis Spohr was to write of French critics in 1821: 'It is always a hazardous undertaking for a foreign violinist to make a public appearance in Paris, as the Parisians are possessed with the notion that they have the finest violinists in the world, and consider it almost in the light of arrogant assumption when a foreigner considers he has talent sufficient to challenge a comparison with them.'[12] Therefore it is not surprising that there should be one dissenting voice in the avalanche of encomia. It came from the *Mercure de France* of 20 April 1782, a month after the first concert:

> M. Viotti's supremacy has not been accepted in such a unanimous manner [as that of Viotti's co-star at the Concert spirituel that season, the Italian soprano Mme Mara]; certain connoisseurs claim that his playing is sometimes brusque and harsh, and that he often sacrifices expression and the spirit of his subject to the desire to draw from his instrument extraordinary sounds; and that finally his style of composition is inferior to that of Jarnowick and other well known virtuosos.[13]

The criticism regarding the sacrifice of expression to technical virtuosity was one that was commonly levelled against those violinists who used every trick of the trade to impress the audience. It was a criticism commonly found in the pages of the German music journal the *Allgemeine musikalische Zeitung*, whose writers repeatedly warned aspiring young violinists against attempting feats of virtuosity before acquiring a solid grounding in the fundaments of music. This charge is certainly unjustified with regard to Viotti. No one, apart from the present connoisseurs, has ever accused Viotti of employing these tactics to win over the

---

[11] 'MM. Fodor, Eck, Viotti & Berthaume, ont exécuté différens concerto[s] de violon de leur composition ou d'autres Compositeurs François [...] Dès le premier jour qu'on a entendu M. Viotti, tout le monde s'est accordé à le placer au-dessus de tous ses Concurrents' (*Almanach musical* (1783), vol. 8, pt 1, p. 175).

[12] Spohr's *Autobiography*, vol. 2, pp. 119–20.

[13] 'La prééminence de M. Viotti n'a pas été reconnue d'une manière aussi unanime; des Connoisseurs prétendent que son jeu est quelquefois brusque & heurté, qu'il sacrifice souvent l'expression & l'esprit de son sujet au desir de tirer de son instrument des sons extraordinaires; qu'enfin, son genre de composition est inférieur à celui de Jarnowick & de quelques autres Virtuoses connus.'

public. Expression was the very hallmark of his playing. The demurring critics were quickly silenced, and in the light of the overwhelmingly favourable consensus, it would seem that they were inspired by simple spite, or at the very least, confusion at hearing such an unfamiliar style.

What was it that so surprised Viotti's listeners? Viotti was a brilliant exponent of the traditional Italian *cantabile* style, but in this he was no different from his Italian predecessors. For example Lolli's tone has been described as being exquisitely similar to a tenor or soprano voice, and of Giornovichi it was written that he 'sings excellently in an adagio'.[14] Yet Viotti's *cantabile* was clearly more pervasive than that of his predecessors, with one newspaper writing of his composition that it 'never allows one to forget the beauty of song in even the most learned and elaborate passages.'[15]

Another striking feature of Viotti's playing, and one which was undoubtedly influenced by Pugnani, was his strong bowing arm, which was equally capable of producing the most delicate and touching sounds. In the words of Baillot his was 'a bow of cotton drawn by the arm of Hercules.'[16] 'Manly' and 'powerful' were epithets so commonly applied to Viotti's bowing that they would become clichés. However the less flattering adjectives of the above criticism ('brusque', 'harsh') would dog Viotti's performing life, and may be attributed to his characteristically decisive and confident manner of striking the strings, which, according to one writer, occasionally led to some (forgivable) false notes.[17]

In addition, Viotti's legato bowing was different from the customary springing bowstroke that had gained currency during the previous decade after the example of its principal exponent, Wilhelm Cramer (*c*.1746–99). This made for more sonority and expansiveness, traits which were constantly remarked upon in Viotti's playing. In 1811 the *AMZ* spelled out precisely those characteristics of the Pugnani school, on which, it said, Viotti had so brilliantly improved:

> It is well known that the excellent characteristics of this school flow from the following principles: first, a large strong full tone; second, a joining of this with a powerful, affecting and beautiful singing legato; third, variety, charm, shade and light, all of which must be brought into play through a most diverse range of different bowings.[18]

It was not without some material assistance that Viotti was able to achieve these effects. If Viotti was not the first in Paris to use a Stradivari violin, he was

---

[14] *AMZ*, 12 June 1799, col. 579; and *New Grove 2*, vol. 9, p. 890, respectively.

[15] 'qui ne laisse jamais oublier la beauté du chant dans les passages même les plus savans & les plus recherchés' (*Mercure de France*, 28 April 1787).

[16] 'un archet de coton dirigé par le bras d'Hercule' (*Notice*, p. 9).

[17] *AMZ*, 13 May 1801, col. 559.

[18] 'Es ist bekannt, dass die vorzüglichsten Eigenheiten dieser Schule aus folgenenden Grundsätzen fliessen: grosser, starker, voller Ton ist das Erste; Verbindung desselben zu kräftigem, eindringlichem, schön verbundenem Gesang das Zweyte; Mannigfaltigkeit, Reiz, Schatten und Licht, als das Dritte, muss durch die verschiedensten *Strich-Arten* ins Spiel gebracht werden' (*AMZ*, 3 July 1811, col. 452).

certainly the first violinist with sufficient genius to convince the Parisians of its merits. The violin he used may have been the 1709 'Viotti' (it was not until 1810 that he acquired the 1712 Stradivarius).[19] The key features of his violin were undoubtedly those cited by *New Grove* as being typical of the 'Classical' violin, namely a substantial soundpost and bass-bar and an elongated neck and fingerboard. The 'perfect' proportions of Stradivari instruments not only gave them a fuller tone, but the flatter shape made them easier to hold for virtuoso playing.[20]

At the same time in Paris innovative experiments were being made on the bow by François Tourte *le jeune*, with whom it is likely that Viotti collaborated. The result was a bow that was straight rather than convex, and the stick was thicker and heavier. The increased length, strength, and elasticity of this new bow, combined with its wide, perfectly flat ribbon of hair that enabled a much more even sound, helped give the 'breadth' to Viotti's playing that so astonished his listeners. Baillot defined breadth as the roundness of tone achieved by making the string vibrate as evenly as possible for the duration of the bowstroke.[21] 'There is an indefinable something about a Tourte that seems to increase the player's dexterity of manipulation to an extraordinary extent', wrote one nineteenth-century aficionado.[22] He was undoubtedly referring to the shift in balance towards the frog, which afforded increased manoeuvrability.

But in Baillot's opinion, at the time of his Paris debut Viotti was far from having the finish in his execution that he later acquired.[23] His playing had not yet acquired the simplicity and maturity that future emotional upheavals would impart to it. His mode of attacking the strings of his Stradivarius was full of youthful exuberance and passion.

As a violinist–composer Viotti typically wrote compositions to suit his own style of playing and to exhibit his technical prowess, and he was undeniably proud of his talent. Even in childhood he was aware of his superiority. Viotti's early patron Cisterna spoke of 'son petit orgueil' ('his child's pride') to Fétis, when describing the ease and confidence with which the 11-year-old boy played from sight a difficult piece of music.[24] It is no surprise then that the first concerto the young Viotti performed before the impressionable Paris public (No. 1 in C major), was one that contained many difficulties that were calculated to amaze. This was in fact the third concerto that Viotti wrote, but it was published by Sieber one week after his Paris debut as No. 1 in order to capitalize on the sensation it caused:

> The violin concerto that M. Viotti played for his debut at the Concert spirituel presented a very great number of difficulties which made him produce some very extraordinary

---

[19] See below, p. 147. Goodkind (p. 762) lists ten Stradivari violins that were owned by Viotti, but most were probably purchased on behalf of others rather than for his own use.

[20] *New Grove 2*, vol. 26, pp. 713–15.

[21] *Art of the violin*, p. 227.

[22] H. Saint-George (1896), *The Bow, its History, Manufacture and Use*, The Strad Library, London, p. 51.

[23] *Notice*, p. 4.

[24] *FétisB*, vol. 8, p. 468.

sounds for this instrument. M. Viotti dealt with them with surprising ease; one would almost have thought that he kept returning to the thorny passages merely for his own pleasure, and that he had no other object than to display his power and superiority.[25]

Nothing would have irked a jealous rival more than this effortless display of virtuosity, and the consequence of such a performance in a city where virtuosos competed fiercely may well be imagined.

Like his playing Viotti's composition was of an unfamiliar style. This is brought home by an appraisal of that same concerto made 30 years later:

> He played a concerto of his own composition, and in this could be found, as in all subsequent ones, a stamp of originality which appeared to have reached the highest point in this genre up to then, a fertile imagination, a happy boldness, the full fire of youth, but tempered by a pure and noble taste, which never allowed him to overstep the boundary of what was beautiful.[26]

Baillot, writing one year after Viotti's death, supports the above opinion: 'His compositions were original, but of a style too elevated to be at first appreciated as they deserved to be'.[27] Fétis's comments, coming from still further into the nineteenth century, confirm the previous two comments:

> The imagination that shone from his concertos was an additional pleasure for his audience, for his compositions for his instrument were as superior to those that had been known before as his execution was [superior] to that of his rivals. As soon as this beautiful music was heard the vogue for Jarnowick's concertos vanished, and the French school of violin playing gained wider scope.[28]

---

[25] 'Le concerto de violon que M. Viotti a exécuté pour son début au Concert spirituel présentoit un très-grand nombre de difficultés qui lui ont fait produire des sons très-extraordinaires pour cet instrument. M. Viotti les a passées avec une facilité surprenante; on auroit presque cru qu'il ne faisoit qu'aller & venir pour son plaisir sur les passages épineux qu'il parcouroit, et qu'il n'avoit d'autre objet que de montrer sa force & sa supériorité' (*Almanach musical* (1782–83), vols 7–8, Minkoff Reprints, Geneva, 1972, vol. 8, pt 1, pp. 175–6).

[26] 'Er spielte ein Concert von seinem Composition, und man fand in diesem, wie in allen nachfolgenden, einen Charakter von Originalität, welche das, bis dahin Höchste in dieser Gattung, erreicht zu haben schien, eine fruchtbare Einbildungskraft, eine glückliche Kühnheit, das ganze Feuer der Jugend, aber gedämpft durch einen reinen und edlen Geschmack, der ihn nie über der Linie des Schönen hinausschreiten liess' (*AMZ*, 1 July 1812, col. 435).

[27] *Notice*, p. 4.

[28] 'L'imagination qui brillait dans ses concertos ajoutait au plaisir qu'il procurait à son auditoire; car ses compositions pour son instrument étaient aussi supérieures à ce qu'on connaissait auparavant, que son exécution était au-dessus de celle de ses rivaux. Dès qu'on connut cette belle musique, la vogue des concertos de Jarnowick disparut, et l'école française du violon s'engagea dans une voie plus large' (*FétisB*, vol. 8, p. 469).

The originality of Viotti's early concertos consisted mainly in his treatment of the first movements and the finales, especially the latter, where, according to White, he 'never accepted the exact repetitions of the refrain nor the predictable key sequence and limited character of the episodes,' but rather gave the rondo finale 'enough variety and structural interest to balance the first movement.' Viotti's passage-work, which featured a singing legato tone, also displayed more musical interest and scope than that of his predecessors, and his solo openings were 'markedly idiomatic in style'.[29]

Viotti's success at the 1782 *Concert spirituel* must have set him to work replenishing his repertoire for the 1783 season, when he was even more in demand than the previous year. In 1783 Viotti performed 16 times: at the *Concert spirituel* during the two weeks of Easter, at the benefit of his compatriot Madame Todi in May, and at subsequent religious feasts during the year. This year the praise was unanimous. One early 1783 review in a Paris newspaper sheds light on the negative comments of the previous year:

> Another object of the public's favour, and who this time appears without any rivals, is M. Viotti. His success has been even greater than last year, and we believe that his talent has increased likewise. It was thought that he attacked his notes with more precision and confidence; [that] his style was even more mellow and better developed, and the composition itself more agreeable. He was received with the most deserved enthusiasm, and it appears that the artists are beginning to forgive him for not having been born in France.[30]

In view of his enthusiastic reception from the public the recalcitrant rivals probably had no choice but to admit Viotti's superiority. Other violinists to appear at the 1783 *Concert spirituel* were Viotti's future adherents Rodolphe Kreutzer, Henri Guérillot, and Paul Alday *le jeune*.

Viotti's performance of 8 September 1783 was to be his last public appearance in Paris. This must have been shortly after his return from his hometown Fontanetto, which he visited in the summer of 1783 in order to purchase a house for his father. If his fellow violinists dropped their bows in astonishment at his first appearance, they must have been fairly dumbfounded at this 28-year-old's extraordinary decision to end his career at its height. Viotti's 18-month rise to the peak of his profession (the best violinist in Europe was the common consensus) had been meteoric, and his departure from the performing platform shocked his supporters and has ever since bewildered scholars. But given what is now known

---

[29] C. White (1992), *From Vivaldi to Viotti: A History of the Early Classical Violin Concerto*, Gordon and Breach, Philadelphia, pp. 337, 339, 340.

[30] 'Un autre objet de l'amour du Public, & qui cette fois paroît sans concurrens, c'est M. Viotti. Son succès a été encore plus grand que celui de l'année passée, & nous croyons que son talent est de même augmenté. On a trouvé que ses sons étoient attaqués avec plus de justesse & de sûreté; sa manière encore plus moëlleuse & mieux fondue, sa composition même plus agréable. Il a été reçu avec les transports les plus mérités, & il semble que les Artistes commencent à lui pardonner de n'être pas né en France' (*Mercure de France*, 19 April 1783).

of Viotti's character, it should come as no surprise. Fétis and Miel offer more or less the same explanation.

It was on the occasion of one of the Holy Week concerts at the *Concert spirituel* that Viotti was upstaged by an inferior violinist who threw the audience into raptures with a concerto in which the final rondo had 'a vulgar theme reminiscent of a vaudeville air'.[31] The contemporary music critic Ginguené complained that such misuse of a rondo in a concerto was only too common at the time, and that the melody of these rondos 'almost always has more of the character of a song than of instrumental music'.[32] Viotti's playing had left the audience cold, whereas the mediocre rondo was called for again on a number of subsequent occasions. This undistinguished violinist had all of Paris agog for a week, and although Viotti made no complaint 'his righteous pride was deeply wounded'.[33]

Such a sudden shift of favour was typical of the eighteenth-century Paris public, whose whim was dictated by transient fashion, whose interest was just as easily aroused by gossip attaching to an artist as by his merit, and whose nature was so disputatious. According to one writer attached to the *Allgemeine musikalische Zeitung* it was always the biased members of the audience who clamoured the loudest, thereby giving rise to contradictory judgements about first-rate artists.[34]

A damning indictment of this capriciousness came from a *Mercure de France* writer, who marvelled sarcastically that the public should be in rare agreement over the two rival vocalists Todi and Mara: 'Could it be possible that the French might have made up their minds to do justice to two subjects in the same genre? That they might love one of these singers without trying to put the other down? [...] This would indeed be an interesting new turn of events.'[35] The public was so insistent that one of these artists should be named an outright victor over her rival that the reviewer felt himself compelled to justify the way he went about his task.[36]

Viotti's disciple Pierre Baillot shared this view of ill-educated audiences. Writing much later to a friend that he had 'risked' playing a Tartini concerto to 'those gentlemen who are lovers of quadrilles', he lamented: 'I had made up my mind to risk it in spite of those servants of bad taste who never want to hear what is beautiful because the idea of beauty is not accredited by fashion'.[37]

---

[31] 'un thème vulgaire analogue aux airs de vaudeville' (*FétisB*, vol. 8, p. 469).

[32] *Encyclopédie méthodique: musique*, vol. 1, Paris, 1791, cited in Pincherle (1964), *The World of the Virtuoso*, trans. L.H. Brockway, Victor Gollancz, London, p. 121.

[33] 'profondément blessé dans son juste orgueil' (*FétisB*, vol. 8, p. 469).

[34] *AMZ*, 3 July 1811, col. 453.

[35] 'Seroit-il possible que les François se déterminassent à rendre à la fois justice à deux sujets du même genre? Qu'ils aimassent l'une de ces deux Cantatrices sans chercher à déprimer l'autre? [...] Ce seroit une nouveauté bien intéressante' (*Mercure de France*, 19 April 1783).

[36] *Mercure de France*, 28 June 1783.

[37] 'j'avais résolu de le risquer malgré les valets du mauvais goût qui ne veulent jamais qu'on produise le beau parce que le beau idéal n'est point accrédité par la mode' (Baillot to Montbeillard, 3 April 1798, cited in François-Sappey, p. 177).

Viotti had been accustomed to playing before audiences that were appreciative and knowledgeable. From the time he entered Cisterna's palace until the time of his arrival in Paris these audiences were composed of musically educated nobility and royalty, among whom were the accomplished performer and composer Frederick II of Prussia and his nephew Friedrich Wilhelm, with whom Viotti had played chamber music in Berlin. Stanislas II of Poland was also a cultured monarch who fostered the arts and sciences, and who was after his death keenly regretted by a writer for the *AMZ* who claimed that the best that music had to offer could be heard in Warsaw during his reign.[38] The Empress Catherine II of Russia patronized opera and the musical arts at St Petersburg, even if she herself was tone deaf.[39] Nor was Viotti reliant on the goodwill of the public for his income as violinists of a lesser stature were. It has been alleged that he arrived in Paris already a wealthy man from his takings in Russia and from the generosity of Catherine II. To lose the 100 francs per session that he earned at the *Concert spirituel* was of no great consequence.

Moreover when he left public performing he went straight into a court appointment at Versailles, where in January 1784 he was made accompanist to the queen. Viotti claimed in his *Précis* that it was because of this appointment that he left the public performing sphere. It is certain that Viotti's physical appearance and refinement served him well at court, and his friend Eymar writes of his making quite a splash 'with his amiable face, his calm and sensitive physiognomy, his slim figure, his dress always elegant, his thick blond hair.'[40] But apparently some members of French royalty were no better educated in music (or manners) than the general public. In the words of Fayolle, who relates the much-repeated anecdote concerning Viotti at Versailles in the British music journal the *Harmonicon*:

> His fame at length attracted the notice of royalty. Marie Antoinette sent for Viotti to Versailles. A day was fixed for a concert, in which his powers were to be called into action. All the persons of the court were assembled, and the performance began. Already the first bars of his favourite solo commanded breathless attention, when an outcry was heard in the saloon: *Place à monseigneur le Comte d'Artois!* In the midst of the tumult, the indignant Viotti coolly placed his violin under his arm and walked out of the room, leaving the whole court in amazement, to the great scandal of a numerous assemblage of spectators. Shortly afterwards this singular man made a resolution never again to play in public, which he scrupulously adhered to, as it is related in France, where, ever after, none but his friends enjoyed the envied privilege of hearing him in their private concerts.[41]

---

[38] *AMZ*, 3 July 1811, col. 451.

[39] A. Goodden (1997), *The Sweetness of Life: A Biography of Elisabeth Louise Vigée Le Brun*, André Deutsch, London, pp. 182–3.

[40] 'avec sa figure aimable, sa physionomie douce et sensible, sa taille svelte, sa parure toujours élégante, ses grands et blonds cheveux' (A.-M. d'Eymar (1799–1800), *Anecdotes sur Viotti*, Luc Sestié, Geneva, p. 19).

[41] 'Memoir of Viotti', p. 55.

Here is a different version of when Viotti took the resolution to cease performing. This account coincides roughly with the date given by Miel (Viotti's third year in Paris, or 1784). Whether the mediocre rondo or the rudeness of the king's brother was the catalyst that caused his departure, the underlying reason remains the same – the wounding of Viotti's artistic pride.

According to the English oboist and diarist William Parke, Viotti lost his court appointment because of 'the violence of his ungovernable temper'.[42] It does seem extraordinary that he could have reappeared there after such an incident. Moreover there was another report of a breach of etiquette at Versailles:

> The late queen of France wished to hear Viotti in her private apartments. The concert was arranged, and was to feature an extraordinarily difficult duo that Viotti had composed but not yet played in public, and which he wished to perform on the violin with the famous English cellist Grosdell [Crosdill]. The queen appeared. Viotti was not there. Embarrassed, the orchestra played a few other pieces. Viotti was still not there. A French cellist asked to be shown the violin part, glanced over it, [and] according to Grosdell [Crosdill], beginning confidently, played at sight Viotti's violin part on the cello so well that those present doubted if Viotti himself would have played it any better on the violin. And who was this one-in-a-thousand artist? "Duport!"[43]

Jean-Louis Duport, brother of Jean-Pierre Duport, whom Viotti had met in Berlin, was one of Viotti's earliest and most intimate friends in Paris. A cellist who greatly admired Viotti's violin technique, he applied the same principles to his own instrument. Duport had enjoyed the patronage of the Baron de Bagge and it was probably in the latter's home that the pair first met. He was also a freemason, belonging like Viotti to the *Loge olympique* and to the lodge of *Saint-Jean d'Ecosse du Contrat Social*. He also shared with Viotti the honour of having conferred on him membership of the prestigious musical fraternity the *Société académique des enfants d'Apollon*.[44] On the eve of Duport's death Viotti dedicated

---

42 *MM*, vol. 1, p. 256.

43 'Die letzte Königin von Frankreich wünschte Viotti in ihren Zimmern zu hören. Das Konzert wird angestellt, und soll vornehmlich durch ein ausserordentlich schwieriges Duo glänzen, das Viotti geschrieben, aber noch nicht herausgegeben hat, und das er auf der Geige, und der berühmte englische Violoncellist Grosdell [Crosdill] auf dem Violoncell ausführen wollten. Die Königin erscheint, Viotti ist nicht da. Man ist verlegen, giebt einige andere Stücke: Viotti ist noch nicht da. Ein französischer Violoncellist lässt sich die Violinstimme zeigen, fliegt die durch, sagt Grosdell [Crosdill], er solle getrost anfangen, und führt Viotti's Violinstimme auf dem Violoncell a prima vista, und so vortrefflich aus, dass alle Anwesende zweifeln, ob sie Viotti selber auf der Geige besser ausgeführt haben würde. Und wer war dieser Tausendkünstler? "Düport!"' (*AMZ*, 21 September 1803, cols 866–7).

44 This multinational society admitted artists of both sexes. Each branch held private monthly meetings, and once a year there was a public meeting consisting of a concert, a speech during intermission, and a concluding dinner. The concerts boasted the best performing artists and the most select company (*AMZ*, 19 August 1824, col. 554).

to him his Three divertimenti for violoncello (WV: 19–21) and also an arrangement of the latter for violin (WVa: 7–9).

Viotti remained in Marie-Antoinette's service for two years. It is believed that he performed with Imbault his two *symphonies concertantes* at the Queen's concerts.[45] Here he become acquainted with France's most elevated nobility, as well as with other court musicians, including Rodolphe Kreutzer who had been accepted into the king's music in 1785; Jean-Baptiste Janson, cellist to Monsieur; and pianists Nicolas-Joseph Hüllmandel and Jan Ladislav Dussek, both of whom were close to Viotti in London and made keyboard arrangements of some of his concertos.

Among the courtiers whom Viotti knew well was Joseph-François de Paule de Rigaud, Comte de Vaudreuil, intimate of Marie Antoinette and patron of the artist Elisabeth Vigée-Lebrun, who was herself then busy at Versailles executing several portraits of the queen. Viotti also met the finance minister Charles-Alexandre Calonne, who was responsible for the payment of his royal pension of 6,000 francs (or £150, as Viotti writes in his *Précis*). Hüllmandel, Dussek, Vigée-Lebrun, Vaudreuil and Calonne were all later received by the Chinnerys either at their London home or at Gillwell House in Essex.

Madame Vigée-Lebrun, a pretty and ebullient young lady with an artistic disregard for convention, turned an annexe in the garden of her home in the rue de Cléry into one of the liveliest and most sought-after salons in Paris. It was here that she brought together an eclectic mix of Parisian identities, including other artists, musicians, writers, and courtiers, as well as all the men and women of fashion who liked to circulate in this stimulating environment. In her *Memoirs* Vigée-Lebrun wrote of the musical soirées she held, and singled out two artists for special mention, Viotti and the pianist Hélène de Montgéroult:

> For instrumental music I had as a violinist Viotti, whose playing, so full of grace, of power and expression, was ravishing. I also had Jarnovick, Maestrino, and Prince Henry of Prussia, an excellent amateur, who brought this first violinist besides. Salentin played the hautboy, Hulmandel and Cramer the piano. Mme de Montgerou came once, soon after her marriage. Although she was very young then, she nevertheless astonished my friends, who were very hard to please, by her admirable execution, and especially by her expression; she really made the instrument speak. Mme de Mongerou has since taken first rank as a pianist, and distinguished herself as a composer.[46]

This may have been Viotti's first meeting with Hélène de Montgéroult, the pianist who was to have a special relationship with him both professionally and emotionally, and with whom he would maintain lifelong contact. Since Vigée-Lebrun specifies that it was shortly after Montgéroult's marriage that she came to her salon, the meeting may be dated 1784 or shortly after. Montgéroult's first Paris

---

[45] See *Thematic Catalogue*, p. 39. However I have been unable to find any reference to it in the source quoted (*Mercure de France*, May 1787).

[46] E. Vigée-Lebrun (1903), *Memoirs of Madame Vigée Lebrun*, trans. L. Strachey, Doubleday, New York, p. 36.

teacher was Viotti's close friend Hüllmandel. Later she studied under Clementi and Dussek.

In 25-year-old Hélène, Marquise de Montgéroult, Viotti found a soulmate with whom he could while away whole days of playing and improvising. It was not only Vigée-Lebrun who remarked on Viotti's and Montgéroult's expressive playing. Their unique spiritual accord is described by Viotti's friend Eymar, who accompanied Viotti to the marquise's country house in the valley of Montmorency just outside Paris, where he observed at close hand Viotti's love of nature. Eymar writes of the understanding between the two as they improvised, of first the piano, then the violin taking the lead, so that the melody passed imperceptibly from one to the other. He marvels not only at their execution, but at their science, their creativity and their infallible taste:

> These two great virtuosos are equally knowledgeable in the science of harmony, equally well versed not only in linking of chords, musical phrases and in the natural succession of passionate *accents*, but still more in the theory and practice of all the accessory means by which one can add to effect and expression; both possess the rare gift of invention and the most astonishing creativity. Heaven has endowed them with the deepest sensibility, the purest taste.[47]

The French violinist and critic Eugène Gautier, writing at the end of the nineteenth century, claimed that the feats that Viotti and Montgéroult performed were unheard of in his day.[48] The truth of this is borne out by a remark Dussek made to Viotti in 1810: 'we are sometimes obliged to listen to some of our new *great men*, and watching their efforts to go beyond perfection, we sometimes laugh and sometimes rage at their caricatures.'[49] In the same letter Dussek wrote of Montgéroult's embarking on a theoretical work, undoubtedly her acclaimed tutor *Cours complet pour l'enseignement du forte-piano*, which would be published in 1822. In this work there are clear indications of Viotti's influence, especially in the preface, where she advocates the imitation of the singer's art in order to achieve a good tone. She also devotes a whole chapter to improvisation.

It was in 1790, according to Eymar, that Viotti agreed to play before an audience once more, at the fifth-floor apartment belonging to a *député* of the first Revolutionary government, the National Constituent Assembly. The concert was

---

[47] 'ces deux grands virtuoses sont également profonds dans la science de l'harmonie, également versés non seulement dans l'enchaînement des accords, des phrases musicales, et dans la succession naturelle des accens passionnés, mais encore dans la connaissance et la pratique de tous les moyens accessoires par lesquels on peut ajouter à l'effet et à l'expression; tous deux sont doués du don si rare de l'invention et de la plus étonnante fécondité. Le ciel leur a départi, avec le sentiment le plus profond, le goût le plus pur' (Eymar, *Anecdotes sur Viotti*, p. 37).

[48] E. Gautier (1873), *Un Musicien en vacances,* Leduc, Paris, p. 47.

[49] 'nous sommes quelque fois obligé[s] d'ecouter quelques-uns de nos nouveau[x] *grands hommes* et voyant leurs efforts d'aller plus loin que la perfection, quelque fois nous rions et quelques fois nous nous mettons en colère de leurs Caricatures' (Dussek to GBV, 26 May 1810, NYPL JOB 97-52, item 16).

magnificent and allegedly attracted the fashionable *haut ton* of Paris, who happily climbed the five flights of stairs to enjoy the treat. Rode, Alday, Hüllmandel, Montgéroult, the singer Pierre Garat, the pianist Daniel Steibelt, and even Marie-Antoinette's piano teacher Johann David Hermann were present as performers, and Viotti played a piece by Boccherini.[50]

Viotti's association with sympathizers of the Revolution during these years was noticed. For example it attracted the attention of one of Paris's most vicious gutter journalists, a certain Gauthier, who in his *Journal général de la cour et de la ville* of 26 November 1791, accused Viotti of anti-royalist sentiments, and at the same time launched a vituperative attack on his friendship with Madame de Montgéroult.[51]

But as most of his contemporary biographers have noted, Viotti's interests were not limited to music. He had a lively curiosity in all that was new. His friendships extended across all political persuasions, from the highest of nobles to the more liberal-minded men and women of letters. Among them were writers and librettists Abbé André Morellet, Jean-François Marmontel, and Jean-Pierre Claris de Florian; parliamentary reporter Hugues-Bernard Maret, whose *Bulletin de l'Assemblée nationale* would later merge with Paris's *Gazette nationale*; and giant *femme de lettres* Madame de Staël, whom he had met at different salons. The last two were special friends of Hélène de Montgéroult. Viotti was not alone in taking an interest in the beginnings of the Revolution. Many thinking aristocrats were in favour of the abolition of the iniquities of the *ancien régime*.

One such aristocrat was the controversial writer, educationalist and harp *amateur* Madame de Genlis, who had been mistress to the Duc d'Orléans and *gouverneur* to his children. Madame de Genlis's sympathy for the Revolution was, like Viotti's, restricted to its early days. Her strong interest in music, and her advocacy of the teaching of musical skills to the young led her into friendships with many of Paris's professional musicians and caused her to author a harp tutor. It is likely that she heard and met Viotti somewhere in Paris, either at the Palais Royal where Viotti is alleged to have enjoyed the patronage of or 'had some personal dealings with the Duc d'Orléans',[52] or at some other private venue – perhaps at the salon of Madame Vigée-Lebrun, who knew her well.[53] Madame de Genlis also knew and esteemed Hélène de Montgéroult, on whom she bestows lavish praise in her *Mémoires*, holding her up as a role model for young women.[54] Madame de Genlis would renew acquaintance with Viotti in 1802, the beginning of a chequered relationship which, through Margaret Chinnery, would last until his death.[55]

---

[50] Eymar, *Anecdotes sur Viotti*, p. 28.

[51] Cited in Pougin, p. 64.

[52] *FétisB*, vol. 8, p. 471; Grove, 1st edn, vol. 4, p. 301.

[53] See Vigée-Lebrun's *Souvenirs*, 2 vols, ed. C. Hermann, Paris, 1984, vol. 2, pp. 259–60, where she gives a written 'portrait' of the famous writer.

[54] *Mémoires*, vol. 6, p. 20.

[55] See Yim (ed.), *The Unpublished Correspondence of Mme de Genlis*.

Although Viotti left the public performing arena in 1783, he did continue to participate in private concerts at the homes of aristocratic friends, and also, perhaps, at some of the *grands hôtels*. During the *ancien régime* many of the wealthy French aristocrats kept private orchestras and employed eminent musicians. The dedicated cultivation of music in these establishments lasted right up to the time of the Revolution, broadening immeasurably the performing platform for musical artists and giving generous scope to composers. According to Miel and Fétis Viotti was director of a private orchestra in the Hôtel de Soubise.[56] Pougin, citing a report of Viotti's fellow freemason Ginguené, says that Viotti also directed the orchestra of the Prince de Rohan-Guéméné (to whom Viotti dedicated his Concerto No. 2). According to Ginguené, it was at a private concert at the Prince de Rohan-Guéméné's that Viotti met the diplomat Count Edward Dillon, a member of the Comte d'Artois's entourage, but it cannot have been in the year cited (1778), as Viotti was not yet in France. Viotti and Dillon would meet again at Gillwell in 1807, when the latter carried across the Channel some of Madame de Genlis's books to Margaret Chinnery, and also in 1814 when Dillon was a frequent caller on Margaret Chinnery and Viotti at their London home.[57]

It was in 1785 that Viotti first met his compatriot Luigi Cherubini, with whom he was to strike up a lifelong friendship. He was then living in rented furnished apartments at the Hôtel de Chartres, 40 rue de Richelieu, not far from the Baron de Bagge's residence. Viotti helped Cherubini begin his illustrious career as one of Paris's foremost composers by introducing him to Marie-Antoinette and to the writers Marmontel and Florian who would become his librettists, and was probably instrumental in having Cherubini's works performed at the *Concert spirituel*. He also undoubtedly nominated his friend for membership of the masonic *Société olympique*, for which Cherubini composed his cantata *Amphion*. From 1786, when Cherubini finally settled in Paris, the two shared lodgings until Viotti's departure for London in 1792.

Their residence at 20 rue Notre-Dame-des-Victoires was listed as Viotti's address in the 1786 register of fully subscribed members of the *Société olympique*.[58] By 1791 they had moved to an elegant dwelling with an inner courtyard and two fine circular staircases with magnificent wrought iron banisters at 8 rue de La Michodière,[59] conveniently close to the Opéra. Their home was a *foyer* of musical activity. Viotti consolidated friendships with Paris's established violinists Jean-Jérôme Imbault, who was a fellow member of the *Société académique des enfants d'Apollon*, and who would later publish some of Viotti's Paris concertos; with Henri Guérillot, first violin in the Opéra orchestra since 1784, and who with Imbault performed Viotti's newest concertos before Rode took over

---

56 Michaud, vol. 43, p. 587; *FétisB*, vol. 8, pp. 469–70.

57 P.-L. Ginguené (1800), *Notice sur Piccini*, Paris, p. 144, cited in Pougin, pp. 33–4; Yim, D38; MMC's Journal, 6 April and 7 April [1814].

58 Quoy-Bodin, 'L'Orchestre de la Société Olympique en 1786', p. 98.

59 Pougin, p. 50n; La Laurencie (1924), p. 114; J. Hillairet (1997), *Dictionnaire historique des rues de Paris*, 10th edn, 2 vols, Editions de Minuit, Paris, vol. 2, p. 18.

this honour; with Pierre La Houssaye (1735–1818), who had been first violin in the *Concert spirituel* orchestra at the time of Viotti's performances there; and with Nicolo Mestrino (1748–89) and Giuseppe Puppo (1749–1827), whom Viotti would later make joint leaders of his Théâtre de Monsieur orchestra.

Presumably many other members of the orchestra of the *Société olympique* came to Viotti's home, among them perhaps a certain Vandyck, first violin of the fourth desk, who dedicated his Concerto No. 5 to Viotti in 1788 during the latter's term as director of the orchestra.[60] These seasoned orchestral members would have been useful to Viotti in trialling new concertos, and his close contact with Cherubini may have helped him with his composing, in which he seems to have had little formal training.

Viotti also interested himself in the city's younger talent, and began taking pupils, among whom were August F. Durand (Duranowski) (*c.*1770–1834); Pierre-Jean Vacher (1772–1819), who would perform a Viotti *symphonie concertante* with Charles-Philippe Lafont (1781–1839) in 1797; Louis-Julien Castels de Labarre (b.1771), whose lessons, according to Fétis, were limited to 'a few words of advice',[61] and most importantly, Rode. The 13-year-old Pierre Rode had arrived in Paris from Bordeaux in 1787, begun lessons with Viotti soon after, and continued them until Viotti's departure for England in 1792. Rode appears to have been the only one of his French pupils to have benefited from such a long period of uninterrupted instruction. By 1790, when he made his Paris debut, he was Viotti's favourite.

However two of Viotti's pupils, Jean-Baptiste Cartier (1765–1841) and Paul Alday *le jeune* (*c.*1763–1835), were only ten years younger than himself, showing that these lessons did not follow the traditional master–pupil pattern, as Viotti's had with Pugnani, but were, according to Fayolle, simply given in a spirit of friendship: 'It is well-known that Viotti never gave lessons from interested motives, but that he made friends with those young men in whom he recognized promising talent, and was pleased to instruct some of them.'[62] None of these so-called pupils came to Viotti as a blank slate. All had had previous teachers, and therefore most could more properly be termed followers than pupils.

Even with all this activity Viotti apparently still did not feel professionally fulfilled, and in 1788, at an ominously ill-fated moment, he embarked on what was to be the first of several disastrous attempts to carve for himself a career as a theatre impresario. In an unlikely partnership with the queen's hairdresser and confidant Léonard Autié, Viotti organized a company of shareholders that funded an ambitious new theatre, of which he was the administrator. Viotti's co-lodger

---

[60] Anne Chastel (1976), 'Etude sur la vie musicale à Paris à travers la presse', *Recherches sur la musique française classique*, vol. 16, p. 61.

[61] 'quelques conseils' (*FétisB*, vol. 6, p. 2).

[62] 'On sait que Viotti ne donnait jamais de soins intéressés, qu'il prenait en amitié les jeunes gens auxquels il reconnaissait de grandes dispositions, et qu'il s'est plu à en former plusieurs' (A.-E. Choron and F.-J. Fayolle (1811), *Dictionnaire historique des musiciens: Artistes et Amateurs, morts ou vivants*, 2 vols, reprinted Georg Olms, Hildesheim, 1971, vol. 2, p. 237).

Cherubini, who had been in Turin from October 1787 to March 1788 working on his opera *Ifigenia in Aulide*, may have provided the spark that ignited Viotti's enthusiasm for the project, as his return to Paris was very close to the date Autié petitioned the king's minister (June 1788) for the *privilège* which was to be granted for 30 years.[63]

Viotti committed all he possessed to the venture. Under the patronage of the Comte de Provence (future Louis XVIII), and housed in the Tuileries Palace in the same room that the *Concert spirituel* used, the new theatre aimed to re-establish in France a high quality Italian comic opera company, and to present French opera. Known originally as the Théâtre de Monsieur, it was forced to change its name and its location when the Revolution trundled the court out of Versailles and back to the Tuileries Palace. After a period of performing under extremely trying conditions, an experience that Viotti was destined to repeat in 1819 when he took over the directorship of the Paris Opéra, new premises were built in the rue Feydeau, from which the theatre, fearing an open connection with royalty, now (July 1791) took its name.

Ever the perfectionist, Viotti wanted the best Italian *buffa* singers that Europe had to offer, but there is no evidence that he travelled to Italy to recruit them himself. A report in the Lyons newspaper the *Petite Chronique lyonnaise* shows that on 11 March 1789 Paul Alday performed a *symphonie concertante* in that city with a certain 'Vauthy', who, it has (wrongly) been assumed, was Viotti. This same Vauthy had also appeared on stage with Alday on 11 May the previous year in Paris. Even in an English or German newspaper a misspelling of Viotti's name at this date would have been highly unlikely. In a Parisian publication such as the *Calendrier musical*, where the other mention of Vauthy occurs, it would have been unthinkable: the editors were far too familiar with 'le célèbre Viotti', as he was then known.[64]

However a report in London's *Morning Post* of 23 September 1789 indicating that Viotti was expected in London some time in the winter of 1789–90 might suggest that Viotti visited that city in order to seek out Italian singers. Among the many excellent Italians recruited for the Théâtre de Monsieur were Brigitta Banti, Luigi Raffanelli, Stefano Mandini, Bernardo Mengozzi, Giuseppe Viganoni, Carlo Rovedino, and Anna Morichelli, some of whom were to appear later at Viotti's Opera concerts at the King's Theatre in London, and – at least those among them who possessed the most refined manners – in the Chinnery drawing room. Viotti had much of the other expertise he needed for the theatre already at his fingertips. His friend Cherubini acted as musical director and provided insertion arias and ensembles for the repertoire of the comic opera composers Pergolesi, Paisiello,

---

[63] Archives nationales O1 1683, item 155. I thank Warwick Lister, who kindly provided this date and its source.

[64] See L. Vallas (1971), *Un Siècle de musique et de théâtre à Lyon (1688–1789)*, Minkoff Reprints, Geneva, p. 448; *New Grove 2*, vol. 1, p. 334; *Calendrier musical universel* (1789), vol. 10, Minkoff Reprints, Geneva, p. 76.

Cimarosa and others. Many of his violinist friends were made members of the theatre's orchestra.

Perhaps encouraged by the initial success of this first venture, Viotti, six months later, took the over-ambitious step of applying to the king for the exclusive *privilège* to administer the Paris *grand opéra*, the *opéra comique* and all vocal and instrumental concerts not only in Paris, but in the whole of France. In return he would deposit three million *livres* in the royal coffers (in half-million instalments over six months) for which he wanted a five per cent per annum interest. As the correspondence with the king's minister dragged on and his backers applied more pressure on him, Viotti's voice took on a more insistent edge, until finally the minister took umbrage and refused him outright.[65]

During this time Viotti's concertos continued to be performed to much acclaim by his confreres at the *Concert spirituel*, including two successful Easter performances in 1787 by Guérillot and Imbault of Viotti's new *symphonies concertantes*. The *Mercure de France*, now long accustomed to Viotti's absence in the public performing arena, but aware of his prominence in private societies, took to calling him an *amateur*:

> The fifth novelty was a *symphonie concertante* for two violins by M. Viotti. Much original passage-work and figures of harmony, which were as charming as they were learned, earned him the most brilliant success. If we have reason to regret the brilliant execution of this *amateur*, who has brought violin talent to its highest point, we are at least comforted by the hope of enjoying more of his compositions, which are no less precious. The grace, the accuracy of intonation, [and] the precision with which M. Guérillot & M. Imbault executed it, leaves nothing to be desired.[66]

The performance of the second *symphonie concertante* was given equally gushing praise by the *Mercure de France* of 28 April 1787. One month later the same newspaper advertised the sale of the first symphony, published by Imbault, with the reminder that it had recently been performed at the *Concert spirituel*. The writer pointedly added that he was sure that the *amateurs* (that is, the prospective purchasers) would concur with the encomia accorded this work when it was reviewed in the two previous issues.[67]

The new Théâtre de Monsieur also became a forum for the performance of Viotti's latest concertos in the interval between opera acts, as was common practice in theatres of the day. In 1790 Rode made his debut there, playing Viotti's

---

[65] See 'Mémoire au roi concernant l'exploitation du privilège de l'Opéra demandé par le sieur Viotti', Paris, 1789, transcribed in Giazotto, pp. 246–58.

[66] 'La cinquième nouveauté, étoit une symphonie concertante à deux violons, par M. Viotti. Beaucoup de traits neufs, des tournures d'harmonie aussi agréables que savantes, lui ont mérité le plus éclatant succès. Si l'on a lieu de regretter l'exécution brilliante de cet amateur, qui a porté au plus haut point le talent du violon, on est consolé dumoins par l'espoir de jouir encore de ses compositions, qui ne sont pas moins précieuses. La grace, la justesse & la précision avec laquelle M. Guérillot & M. Imbault l'ont exécutée, n'ont rien laissé à désirer' (*Mercure de France*, 7 April 1787).

[67] *Mercure de France*, 26 May 1787.

Concerto No. 13. In 1791 and 1792 Viotti instituted a *Concert spirituel* at his theatre (now Feydeau) in Holy Week, after the original series ceased in 1790 as a result of the abolition of royal privileges. According to Fétis Rode performed Viotti's Concerto Nos 3, 13, 14, 17 and 18 at these Holy Week concerts.[68] Baillot specified that at the Théâtre Feydeau *Concert spirituel* of April 1791 Rode performed the Viotti Concerto nos 17 and 18, and that the *tutti* of the latter was applauded as much as one of Haydn's symphonies presented at the same concert.[69] These concertos, like the *symphonies concertantes*, were quickly engraved and advertised in the French press, entering the modern repertoire soon after their initial performance. This was not the case for Viotti's London concertos, which would typically wait ten years to be published, most having been first published as piano concerto arrangements.

Baillot and Rode were both engaged in the Théâtre de Monsieur/Feydeau orchestra (Rode in 1789, Baillot in 1791). Kreutzer had moved to Paris from Versailles in 1789, and Baillot, whose natural bent for letters led him to take a law degree in 1790, came to Paris in 1791 wishing to make a career in music. However the need to support his family forced him to abandon his poorly paid post in the Feydeau orchestra to take a public service position in the Finance Ministry after only five months, and it may be seen from the formal tone of the correspondence between Baillot and Viotti when Baillot informed Viotti of his resignation, that although there was a mutual respect between the two, they were not yet on the intimate footing that would later exist between them.[70]

Meanwhile the Revolution continued its inexorable course. Those musicians who decided to remain in Paris throughout the turmoil had to make adjustments to their repertoire, but despite an enforced patriotism, the musical situation was not all bad. Music might even be said to have flourished at the hands of the Revolution, since the Ecole de musique de la Garde Nationale, headed by Bernard Sarrette, formed the nucleus of the Institut national de musique, which in turn gave birth on 3 August 1795 to the Conservatoire nationale de musique. The Paris Conservatoire was the earliest formalised music-teaching institution in Europe, and was to be the model of all those that followed. Even the Germans, who considered themselves to be the trendsetters in music, had nothing but praise for it:

> The Paris Conservatoire must be, without any national prejudice, considered as one of the finest institutions of its kind in Europe. It cannot be compared with any other, not even the Neapolitan Conservatorium; and this is as much on account of the manifold consideration given to *all* branches of music and their application, as on account of the large number of composers, professors and and illustrious artists that this institution counts among its members.[71]

---

[68] *FétisB*, vol. 7, p. 447.

[69] *Notice*, p. 6.

[70] See François-Sappey, pp. 134–5.

[71] 'Das pariser musikalische Conservatorium lässt sich, ohne alle National-Parteylichkeit, als eine der schönsten Anstalten dieser Art in Europa betrachten. Vergleichen können wir diese Anstalt mit keiner andern, nicht einmal mit dem neapolitanischen Conservatorium;

The Conservatoire, situated on the corner of the rue du Faubourg-Poissonnière (no. 11) and rue Bergère (no. 2) on the site of the old *hôtel des Menus-Plaisirs*, would establish its own library, publish its own music and textbooks, run its own shop, and from 1797 hold the famous yearly concerts at which the prizewinning students would perform. It would employ Paris's top instrumentalists, vocalists and composers as teachers. Cherubini, along with the composers Gossec, Méhul, Grétry and Le Sueur, would be made teaching inspectors, Baillot, Kreutzer and Rode, professors of violin, and Hélène de Montgéroult professor of piano forte.

But Viotti was not in Paris to witness these historic musical developments. Even though he tried to render himself inconspicuous by donning the uniform of the National Guard, he was well aware that his close association with royalty put his life at risk. Narrowly missing the August massacre of the Swiss Guards, Viotti reluctantly abandoned his home, his friends, his theatre and his assets, and fled to England. It was 22 July 1792.

---

und dies sowohl wegen der mannichfaltigen Rücksichten, welche auf *alle* Fächer der Musik und deren Anwendung genommen worden, als wegen der grossen Menge von Komponisten, Professoren und berühmten Künstlern, welche diese Anstalt unter ihre Mitgleider zählt' (*AMZ*, 11 March 1801, col. 411).

CHAPTER 3

# London, 1793

Viotti's first meeting with the Chinnerys took place in a climate propitious to the flowering of a musical friendship: London in the 1790s was immersed in music. On 19 February 1791 the *Morning Chronicle*, which regularly reported on musical activities in its pun-loving daily column the 'Morning Mirror' or 'Glass of Fashion', stated: 'The present is the age of Music. The taste of JOHN BULL, which before was fond only of the *substantial*, seems now to be transferred to *sound*.' The rage for music, that 'espèce de fureur' that had swept Paris in the years leading up to the Revolution, overtook London a decade later. Music was everywhere in public and private life. There was opera, ballet, oratorios, public and private concerts, musical clubs and societies, and a corresponding number of opera houses, concert halls, theatres, inns, taverns, coffee houses, and private drawing rooms to accommodate them. There were so many musical societies (11 in all), that it was possible to go to a concert on every night of the week, including Sunday, when – because of the ban on public entertainments on the Sabbath – special dispensation had to be granted by the Archbishop of Canterbury.

The most frequented venues for musical entertainments in London were the King's Theatre, Haymarket, where Italian opera was performed; Drury Lane and Covent Garden, where English opera and the Lenten Handel oratorios were held; the Vauxhall and Ranelagh Gardens, open-air venues for concerts and variety shows; and, as the fashionable West End concerts gained ascendancy over all other musical entertainments, the Hanover Square Rooms, where the hugely popular concerts of the same name were held.

The Hanover Square concerts were a series of 12 weekly concerts which took place each year, beginning in February 1791, when the German immigrant violinist Johann Peter Salomon (1745–1815) pulled off a coup by bringing Haydn to London. Salomon commissioned Haydn to compose new works, and preside over the performance of them, for the 1791–92 and 1794–95 seasons, thereby goading the English love of music to fever-pitch. In the years that Haydn appeared at them, the Hanover Square concerts were the rage of fashionable London.

The Hanover Square Rooms were fitted out in a manner that allowed 500 of the *élégants* of London society to listen to music in maximum comfort, with carpets, sofas along the side walls, and ample lighting and heating. The orchestra comprised about 40 members seated in amphitheatre formation, and according to a report in the *Berlinische musikalische Zeitung* of 29 June 1793, which from that time began to publish a weekly letter from London, the acoustics were excellent.[1]

[1] Cited in Landon, p. 189.

The number of concert reviews that finished with the comment that 'the Room was very brilliantly attended' attests to the class of clientele the concerts attracted.

When Viotti arrived in London Salomon had been engaging musical artists from the Continent for the past two seasons. Over the next three years, as the Revolution became bloodier, and more artists fled from France, Salomon was responsible for bringing together the most brilliant collection of instrumentalists, vocalists and composers in Europe. 'Nothing less than the demolition of one Monarchy, and the general derangement of all the rest, could have poured into England and settled such a mass of talents as we have now to boast. Music as well as misery has fled for shelter to England', wrote the *Morning Chronicle* on 15 February 1793. The Chinnerys would certainly have been subscribers to Salomon's Hanover Square concerts, being among the 'Gentry', if not 'Nobility', at whom Salomon's advertisements in the newspapers were pitched.

It is not clear from the letters how Viotti first came to meet the Chinnery family. Giazotto, without giving any supporting evidence, claims that he met them in March 1793, through Adolphus Frederick, future Duke of Cambridge, who, he says, was already a frequent visitor to the Chinnery home.[2] The latter may or may not have already been acquainted with the Chinnerys at this time, but it is unlikely that he introduced Viotti to the Chinnerys in 1793, as the young prince was then serving in the Hanoverian army, and did not return to England until September of the same year.

It is more likely that the Chinnerys met Viotti shortly after his arrival in London in the second half of 1792, perhaps at a private dinner in honour of the famous newcomer. The introduction may have been made by Adolphus Frederick, or even by Salomon himself, whom the Chinnerys appear to have known quite well. The young music-loving Chinnery couple were even then leading a gay social life in the city thanks to their connections, and when Viotti arrived in London an ambitious *emigré* of reduced means, they would have been in a position to offer him assistance, if not exactly patronage. By the familiar tone of the earliest letter in the Chinnery collection from Viotti to Margaret Chinnery, which begins 'I left you yesterday in sorrow my dear good Amica. My heart was heavy and filled with my customary sadness', and ends with fond sentiments for 'the three little monkeys'[3] (the young Chinnery children), it would appear that he had known her and her family for longer than the two-month period that would have elapsed since Giazotto's hypothetical date of meeting.

When Viotti arrived in England many of his Paris colleagues were already there. His pianist friends Dussek and Hüllmandel had arrived in 1789 and 1790 respectively, and the Polish violinist Feliks Janiewicz (1762–1848), who had made his debut at the *Concert spirituel* in 1787 and subsequently become a member of the Duc d'Orléans's chapel orchestra, had arrived towards the end of 1791.

---

[2] Giazotto, p. 134.

[3] 'Je vous ai quitté hier avéc chagrin ma chere bonne amica, j'avois le cœur gros, et l'âme s'est remplie de sa tristesse ordinaire' […] 'les trois petits marmots' (GBV to MC, 30 May 1793, PHM 94/143/1 – 2/3).

Announcements in the *Diary, or Woodfall's Register* in 1792 show that Salomon and Janiewicz were the featured violinists at Salomon's Concert, and Giornovichi and Wilhelm Cramer at the rival Professional Concert.

Viotti's name appears for the first time as a featured soloist at Salomon's Hanover Square concerts in the *Morning Post* of 1 January 1793, whose reporter wrote that 'Salomon is resolved to make a bold stand against all opposition. He is to have, in addition to MARA and HAYDN, the celebrated VIOTTI, supposed to be the first Violin in the world.' In order to emphasize the exclusivity of his concerts Salomon advertised that 'VIOTTI the celebrated Violin [...] will perform no where else in public.'[4] As the *Times* advertisements show, Viotti would perform in all 12 of the weekly concerts, drawing the crowds that might otherwise have stayed away owing to Haydn's non appearance. (Haydn had been billed to appear in the 1793 concerts, but had excused himself for health reasons.)

It was not a practice of the newspapers of the era to identify instrumental pieces performed at these concerts, and reviews were only intermittent. The early concerts tended to be given long reviews, which then grew shorter and petered out completely at the end of the season. The space, the editors claimed, was wanted for more important news. Admittedly the news of early 1793 had been sensational. Louis XVI had lost his head (21 January) and France had declared war on England (1 February) by the time Salomon's Hanover Square concerts began on 7 February.

The *Oracle* of 8 February 1793 gave an unusually generous amount of space to its review of the first concert:

> The compositions of VIOTTI are yet, if possible, more exquisite than his Performance. They seem to have been inspired among the artless luxuriance of the VEVAI— The subjects remind us of the simple melodies of Music in her infancy, dwelling on
>
> "The sweetest length of Notes"
>
> Nature has suggested all of it— The subject seems to be caught from the Nightingale, and the modulated varieties of transition from the Lark. His tone is astonishing upon the instrument, particularly upon the first string— the strength of his hand is remarkable, and the flexibility at the same time incredible.— His taste and feeling are the finest we have witnessed.

The reviewer dwells on the artlessness and simplicity of Viotti's composition, qualities that were revered by an age imbued with classical ideals. But he speaks in such general terms that the reader would not even be aware that he was referring to a new violin concerto, were it not that the fact had been announced in the papers two days before.[5]

Typically, new concertos were presented at times when they would make most impact, that is, at the first concert of the season and at the composer's benefit concert. Of course additional new concertos might be given at any other time during the season, but since the performer had limited leisure for composing between concerts, these tended to be the exception rather than the rule. According

---

[4] *Morning Chronicle*, 11 January 1793.

[5] *Morning Chronicle*, 6 February 1793.

to the newspaper announcements Viotti performed only two new concertos this year, one of which may have been the original version of his Concerto No. 20 in D major, with the slow movement from his Concerto No. 8.[6] The concerto was given an enthusiastic review by the *Allgemeine musikalische Zeitung* in 1799, when, as the first of Viotti's London concertos to be published on the Continent, it was released by Pleyel. The writer remarked, significantly, that it was written in a manner designed to show up the skill of the performer. He particularly recommended the beautifully developed final movement, 'which is full of feeling, and which has some brilliant passages very deftly woven into it.'[7]

The other new concerto performed in 1793 can now be identified with certainty as Concerto No. 21 in E major, which, as the October 1793 letter from Pugnani to Viotti shows, was composed for the 1793 season. Pugnani writes: 'I have played one of your latest concertos in E major. It pleased me very much, the style is new, and [it] is well written.'[8] Pugnani was probably given a copy of the manuscript by Salomon, who, the letter reveals, had just passed through Turin. The comment shows that Viotti's compositions had by 1793 undergone a significant evolution from the *galant* style that would have been familiar to Pugnani.

The reviews at the time of Viotti's first appearances before the London public are redolent of the earlier Paris reviews. But now Viotti's playing was more mature, and his taste surer. Taste, according to the experts, was not something that could be learned. It was implicit in any understanding of beauty, to which all human endeavour should tend, wrote one music theorist, whose next remark was particularly applicable to Viotti: 'Everything that sustains animal lust destroys taste, and everything that awakens an understanding of nature fosters it.'[9]

The new concerto that Viotti performed at the first concert appears to have been repeated at the second and third.[10] The audiences of these years tolerated repeat performances of a favourite composition, and even demanded them. After the second concert the *Morning Chronicle*'s praise was effusive. Having remarked on the regrettable circumstances that brought such an array of talent to England, the reporter singled out Viotti as an example:

> This reflection, we own, is misplaced; but the incomparable Viotti, now spared to us by the ruin of the French Court, presented it to our mind. It is impossible to speak of this man's performance in common terms, and therefore we may be pardoned the rhapsody. His execution is not more astonishing by its difficulty, than it is delightful by its

---

[6] See White, 'Chronology', p. 121.

[7] 'gefüllvolle Satz, in welchem brillante Stellen sehr schicklich verwebt sind' (*AMZ*, 17 July 1799, col. 680).

[8] See Appendix.

[9] 'Alles verdirbt den Geschmack, was die thierische Lust unterhält, und alles fördert ihn, was reinen Natursinn erweckt' (*AMZ*, 29 March 1809, col. 406).

[10] See *Morning Chronicle*, 20 February 1793, where 'the New Concerto Violin, Signor Viotti, as performed last Thursday' is announced.

> passion. He not only strikes the senses with wonder, but he touches the heart with emotion.[11]

'Emotion', 'feeling', 'sentiment' and 'soul' were such commonly repeated refrains concerning Viotti's playing that reviewers invariably prefaced their use of them with the apology that they could find no other terms to describe how Viotti's playing affected them. Many were incredulous that such a talent existed:

> Such an assemblage of powers as this performer exhibits, almost exceeds belief. His strength, delicacy, execution, and taste, render his performance indeed the first musical treat ever heard. A general rapture burst forth at every interval.[12]

What seemed to strike most listeners was Viotti's ability to impart fiery passion and yearning tenderness to the same piece. The *Oracle* made a comparison with Giornovichi, who was 'elegant' and 'graceful' but not as 'grand' as Viotti:

> VIOTTI is original and sublime— he reaches at unattempted grandeur— and he never fails. What may be expected of him is impossible to conceive.— He has a soul capable of magnifying Simplicity into the Wonderful.— His music is yet better than his performance.[13]

After the third concert the *Oracle* (22 February) favourably compared Viotti's concerto to 'the divine Works of Haydn.' Of the fourth the *Morning Chronicle* (1 March) wrote that 'the *Amateurs* were again highly gratified by the exquisite performance of *Viotti*, in a charming *Trio* of his own composition', but did not specify if the work was new. For most of the other concerts Viotti was announced as performing simply a 'Concerto Violin'. These were probably Paris-composed works that the London audiences had not yet heard.

Halfway through the 1793 series the demand for tickets from non-subscribers had risen to such a height that Salomon was obliged to place repeated advertisements in the newspapers offering single tickets at a cost of half a guinea, while at the same time politely but firmly pointing out the limitations of the rooms. The twelfth and final performance of the 1793 series was on Thursday 2 May, and a week before that Viotti held his benefit concert (26 April), for which a new concerto and a new duet were announced. (The eleventh concert was on the eve of his benefit, which is probably why his appearance was brief: he played a violin *obbligato* to Mara's aria.)

The 1793 Pugnani letter to Viotti proves that his Concerto No. 21 in E major was performed at the 1793 Salomon concerts. But at which one? In 1803 a German reviewer of this same concerto, although he did not think it one of Viotti's best, remarked, as had Pugnani, on its novelty and originality:

---

[11] *Morning Chronicle*, 15 February 1793.

[12] *Diary, or Woodfall's Register*, 15 February 1793.

[13] *Oracle*, 20 February 1793.

> There are few violin concertos which are distinguished by novelty and originality in the passages, by powerful yet also melodious movements, by meaningful *tuttis* that are suited to the whole, by a fitting accompaniment and solid character, and which at the same time can show to advantage the complete virtuosity of the performer.[14]

He went on to comment on the character of the composition, thereby enabling a comparison to be made with the English reviewer's comments on the Viotti concerto performed at the first concert:

> It has a fiery and at the same time tender character; the accompaniment and harmony is rich and throws into relief the main voice uncommonly well; the *tutti* movements are powerful and the *soli* brilliant; the passages have, apart from a certain uniformity and frequent repetition, much *bravoure*— and on account of this it may be rightly recommended to and welcomed by many violin players.[15]

The epithets 'fiery', and 'much bravoure' are so much at odds with the English reviewer's nightingale–lark evocation of the concerto performed at the first concert, that it is tempting to conclude that these reviews were not describing the same piece of music, and that it was not Viotti's Concerto No. 21 that was performed at the first concert, but rather that it was performed at his benefit.

The advertisement for Viotti's benefit gives his address at the time as 47 Curzon Street, Mayfair. It also gives a list of the performers who assisted Viotti on this evening, thereby identifying the musicians with whom he had the closest rapport. They were Signor Bruni, Mesdames Krumpholtz and Mara, and Salomon, with whom Viotti performed one of his newly-composed duets. Viotti returned the favour for his friend, repeating the same duet, by popular demand, with Salomon at the latter's benefit on 9 May. It was probably the same duet, billed as 'Double Concerto, for two principal Violins', that was also performed at the twelfth concert.[16] The finale of Viotti's benefit was a symphony by Haydn, but even this did not overshadow Viotti's own popularity.

By the end of the 1793 season Viotti's reputation was established, his London debut having been accomplished with as much *éclat* as his introduction to Paris a decade earlier. His second career in the public arena was now successfully launched.

---

[14] 'Der Violinkonzerte, die sich durch Neuheit und Originalität der Passagen, durch kräftige und auch melodiöse Sätze, durch bedeutende, dem Ganzen angemessene Tuttis, durch zweckmässige Begleitung und festgehaltenen Charakter auszeichnen, und womit sich zugleich der Spieler in seiner ganzen Virtuosität zeigen kann, giebt es wenige' (*AMZ*, 7 September 1803, col. 828).

[15] 'Es hat einen feurigen und zugleich zarten Charakter; die Begleitung und Harmonie ist reich und hebt die Hauptstimme ungemein; die Tuttisätze sind kräftig und die Soli glänzend; die Passagen haben, ohngeacht einer gewissen Einförmigkeit und öftern Wiederholung, viel Bravour— und deshalb wird es mehrern Violinspielern mit Recht empfohlen werden können und willkommen seyn' (*Ibid.*, cols 828–9).

[16] *Times*, 1 May 1793.

CHAPTER 4

# Letters from the Continent, 1793

The earliest series of letters in the CFP collection are twelve letters from Viotti to Margaret Chinnery and three to William Chinnery, dated May–December 1793. They are some of the most interesting from a historical point of view, throwing light on a period of Viotti's personal life unmentioned by any of his biographers. The letters describe his voyage to Italy across the war-torn Continent in 1793, highlighting his second close encounter with the French Revolution. They were written before Viotti moved into the Chinnery home, but betray an intimacy of feeling which leaves us in no doubt that he was already on very close terms with the family. Unfortunately no letters from the Chinnery side of the correspondence survive.

The Revolution was approaching its bloodiest phase, and the instability of government in France was beginning to worry even the English supporters of revolutionary principles. From the time of the first meeting of the Estates General in May 1789, to July 1793, when Viotti's Continental journey began, the French Revolution had been through four successive upheavals leading to as many changes of government. The original National Constituent Assembly, among whose members Viotti counted several friends, was succeeded in 1791 by the much more left-wing Legislative Assembly. This in turn was replaced in 1792 by the Convention, which was dominated by the Girondin section of the Jacobin club. In June 1793 the Montagnard section of the Jacobin club gained control of the Convention and instigated the draconian Committee of Public Safety, marking the beginning of the Terror.

In his *Précis* Viotti says that he made friends with certain members of the first Assembly, because in those uncertain times everybody sought protectors: 'In that terrible turmoil everyone tried to have a protector in the [Constituent] Assembly. I did likewise: my fortune and life depended upon it, and I must confess that I knew some members who seemed to me to be good and honest men.'[1] The identity of the men cannot be cited with certainty, but according to later evidence in the *Reminiscences* of Michael Kelly, who was manager of the King's Theatre in London from 1793 for 30 years, two of them might have been Alexandre de Lameth and Adrien Duport (whom Kelly calls 'Dupont'). Kelly reported that he had been invited by Viotti to dine at the Crown and Anchor Inn with 'three of the greatest revolutionists', including these men, who had both been members of the

---

[1] 'Chacun tachoit dans cette affreuse confusion d'avoir un appui dans quelque membre de l'Assemblée; je l'ai taché de même, ma fortune et ma vie en dépendoient, et je dois avouer, qu'il m'a parû en avoir connû d'honnetes et de bons' (*Précis*).

Constituent Assembly, and the Duc d'Aiguillon. It is easy to see why Viotti cultivated their friendship, as they were cultured men and not only shared Viotti's passion for music, but according to Kelly, the duke had even been his pupil:

> The Duke D'Aiguillon, one of the twelve Peers of France, who, in former days, had an immense fortune, was a great patron of the arts, and so theatrical, that he had a box in every theatre in Paris. He was particularly fond of music, and had been a scholar of Viotti. I passed a pleasant day with these émigrés, who were all men of high endowments, and truly polished manners; nor did they seem at all depressed by change of circumstances; all was vivacity and good humour.[2]

The Duc d'Aiguillon may have been one of the many aristocratic *amateurs* with whom Viotti consented to play duets, presumably giving some instruction on the side. Reduced to his last shilling in London, the duke subsequently begged Kelly to employ him as a music copyist, as none of the other French *émigrés* would come to his aid.[3] Although Kelly describes the men as 'three of the greatest revolutionists', they were certainly more moderate than the members of the ministries which were to come, and all three had been obliged to flee France because of their views. Viotti claims not to have known personally a single member of 'that second [Legislative] Assembly':

> In 1792, as my affairs were taking an ever more serious turn and I could foresee more trouble, and more horrors from that second Assembly which had just replaced the first, and in which I fortunately did not know a single member, I made the decision to sell what I possessed, liquidate the debts of my unfortunate theatre and abandon a country where an honest man could no longer live in peace, where I had suffered so many persecutions, and where I had lost almost everything. Indeed I left before the distressing arrest of the royal couple and I went to England on 21 or 22 July of the same year.[4]

What he fails to mention, however, is that although he may not have known any member of the Legislative Assembly, he did have a very good friend who was a representative of the body that succeeded it, the Convention. This was the respected journalist-turned-diplomat Hugues-Bernard Maret, a lover of music who had frequented the same Paris salons as Viotti. Maret was the son of the highly esteemed and learned Dijon doctor Hugues Maret, who had himself written a book on music. The trusted Maret had been sent to England twice by the French foreign

---

[2] M. Kelly (1826), *Reminiscences*, ed. R. Fiske, OUP, London, 1975, p. 222.

[3] *Ibid.*, p. 223.

[4] 'En 1792 mes affaires prenant de plus en plus une mauvaise tournure prévoyant de nouveaux malheurs, de nouvelles horreurs de cette seconde assemblée qui venoit remplacer la première, et dont j'ai eu le bonheur de n'en pas connoître un seul membre; je me décidai à vendre ce que je possédai, liquider les dettes de mon malheureux théâtre et abandonner un pays dans lequel un homme honnête ne pouvoit plus vivre en paix, ou j'avois essuyé tant de persécutions et ou j'avois presque tout perdû. Je le quittai en effet avant la douloureuse arrestation de ses Souverains, et me rendis en Angleterre le 21 ou le 22 de juillet de la même année' (*Précis*).

minister Lebrun at the end of 1792 and at the beginning of 1793 in a secret last-ditch attempt to prevent war between the two countries. In June he would be named French ambassador to Naples, with the delicate mission of persuading the king, Marie-Antoinette's brother, to remain neutral in the war between France and Austria.

The earliest Viotti letter in the CFP collection is dated 30 May 1793,[5] and sets the mood for the deep melancholy which pervades all his letters of the 1793–94 period. Written from a rural retreat, it is one of three letters dating from the two-week period from the end of May to mid-June. All the letters are hand delivered by a Mr Smith, almost certainly Charles Smith, the Chinnery friend with whom Viotti was later to go into a wine partnership. The letter speaks of his heavy heart in spite of the beauty of nature that surrounds him, and attests to the truth of all the accounts of Viotti's contemporaries who describe his brooding nature, his sensitive temperament and his profound love of nature. According to Eymar: 'Never did a man place so much store on the simplest gifts of nature; never did a child enjoy them more.'[6] The letter was penned at five in the morning, another detail that supports the truth of Eymar's observation that Viotti was a morning person, for whom the evening was a time of sadness: 'Viotti awakes, like the birds, at the crack of dawn [...] then his face lights up and comes alive with nature [...] But correspondingly, when the sun sets he sinks into a melancholic torpor.'[7] This statement is confirmed by Viotti's own description of dusk as 'l'heure triste' (the melancholy hour).

The only clue to the location of the house from which Viotti is writing is a cryptic reference to 'Castel Beare' in his second letter. Castle Beare was the name of a handsome country seat on Castlebar Hill, Ealing, then a small hamlet lying about six miles to the west of London. In 1793 the property probably belonged to the Whig politician Henry Beaufoy, and the previous owner had been a Mr Graham.[8] Viotti has been invited to dinner at Mrs Graham's house in London, and asks Margaret to make sure this lady receives his letter declining the invitation. It is apparent that Viotti is one of a number of house guests, and that he feels sufficiently at ease to keep himself apart from the rest of the company and to wander in the countryside according to his whim.[9]

---

[5] GBV to MC, 30 May 1793, PHM 94/143/1 – 2/3.

[6] 'Jamais homme n'attacha tant de prix aux plus simples dons de la nature; jamais enfant ne sut mieux en jouir' (Eymar, *Anecdotes sur Viotti*, p. 31).

[7] 'Viotti s'éveille, comme les oiseaux, au moment où le soleil commence à poindre à l'horizon [...] alors sa physionomie se dévoile et se ranime avec la nature [...] Mais aussi, quand le soleil se couche, il devient triste et languissant' (*Ibid.*, p. 34).

[8] Henry Beaufoy (d.1795) was M.P. for Great Yarmouth. The rate books show that he took over the property in 1791 after Graham's death (*c*.1790). I would like to thank Dr Jonathon Oates, Archivist of Ealing Library, for this information. I am also indebted to David Hawgood, whose website Genuki first alerted me to the name of the property, and who subsequently sent me detailed information from Peter Hounsell's local history book, *Ealing and Hanwell Past* (1991), Historical Publications, London.

[9] GBV to MC, 12 June [1793], PHM, 94/143/1 – 2/5.

It is probable that the Hüllmandels, who were Viotti's first musician friends in England, were also among the house guests at Castle Beare. Madame Hüllmandel, referred to familiarly as 'l'Amica Hull—', is mentioned in the third letter as having accepted the same dinner invitation that Viotti declined.[10] Salomon's Hanover Square concerts having finished on 2 May, Viotti had clearly been invited to spend a couple of weeks in the country before his departure for the Continent in July.

Viotti's second letter, dated 8 June 1793, throws some light on the length of his acquaintance with the Chinnerys. In accepting a dinner invitation from Margaret he says eagerly that he will come any day she cares to nominate, asks if his suit is ready, and requests it to be sent to him by Smith so that he will be able to make himself handsome for the occasion. The suit he has with him is still his old French one and it is now too tight, making him look like a trussed piece of roast beef.[11] Most certainly these are not the words of a friend of short acquaintance. Nor are his words of thanks for the suit in the third letter, written four days later, in which he says he will wear it with all the more pleasure knowing that it was Margaret who chose it for him.[12]

It is in the last of these three letters that Viotti mentions his first visit to the Chinnery property Gillwell Park, which until 1796 was used by them as a summer residence. Viotti says that he will go with the Chinnerys to their 'farm' on 22 June, and remain there until his departure, regretting that he will be unable to stay for the entire summer. He reassures Margaret that he will like the farm in terms that make his attachment to her abundantly clear. Sentiments of affection and loyalty take up a large part of all Viotti's letters to Margaret. Wherever she is, he is happy to be. Whenever he is absent from the Chinnerys he is miserable. Although he is looking forward to his approaching visit to Gillwell, he worries that his melancholy disposition will clash with Margaret's natural gaiety.[13]

What occasioned this severe melancholy? The thought of his forthcoming journey to Italy to settle his family's affairs after the death of his stepmother definitely contributed to it. But it was not only this. Viotti had apparently received bad news from France, almost certainly regarding his soulmate Hélène de Montgéroult. According to Gautier, who bases his account on Eymar's, Hélène de Montgéroult was arrested and incarcerated in the Conciergerie for several days in February 1793.[14] Allegedly her musical colleague Bernard Sarrette, then in charge of the music of the National Guard, was able to plead for her release on the grounds that France could not afford to lose such an important pianist. According to Gautier, Sarrette hit on an ingenious way of softening her captors by showing off her improvisational skills in a stirring rendition of *La Marseillaise.* This imaginative display of her talents supposedly resulted in a standing ovation and her subsequent release. She then set about planning her flight from France with her

---

[10] *Ibid.*

[11] GBV to MC, 8 June 1793, PHM 94/143/1 – 2/4.

[12] GBV to MC, 12 June [1793], PHM 94/143/1 – 2/5.

[13] *Ibid.*

[14] Gautier, *Un Musicien en vacances*, pp. 50–52.

elderly husband. This flight, in which Viotti took a close interest, forms the substance of the 1793 letters written by Viotti to the Chinnerys from the Continent.

The only public explanation that Viotti gives for this journey is in his *Précis*, where he states that he was obliged to return to Italy to put the family affairs in order after the death of his (step)mother. Viotti's *Précis* reads:

> However I was obliged by the death of my mother to leave once again. Therefore I set off on 21 July 1793, crossed Germany, the Tyrol, and proceeded via Venice to my homeland. I settled my affairs, and those of my brothers, then still children, and set out again for Switzerland, Germany, Flanders, which then belonged to the Emperor, returning towards the end of December to London, resolved to settle there and never leave again.[15]

This is a perfectly truthful account, corroborated by Viotti's own letters from the Continent. What he omits, however, is that there was a second reason for making the voyage, and that was to keep a rendez-vous, probably to be in Venice, with Madame de Montgéroult and her travelling party. As the *Précis* was written in 1798 to convince the British Government of his innocence of any Jacobin activities, this omission is understandable. The brief mention of this journey made by Miel is therefore also accurate when he says that Viotti made it to help friends in distress. As for his assertion that Viotti travelled incognito, this was certainly true, as Viotti took care that none but his closest friends in England (the Hüllmandels and the Chinnerys) knew of the journey. Miel writes: 'Viotti saw Italy [again] only much later, going via Switzerland. Devotion to friendship played a large part in this decision: he thought he could be of use to friends in distress, and he set out, incognito.'[16]

About one month before Viotti's departure for the Continent Hélène de Montgéroult and her husband had left Paris, having arranged for the latter to be given a fictitious diplomatic post in Naples. As a sea passage to this port was out of the question, owing to the siege of Toulon by the British navy and her Allies, and as the route through the Austrian-ruled northern provinces of Italy was closed, the only possible way was the circuitous route through Switzerland. This took them through the Swiss Confederate State of the Grisons, and south through the small adjoining region of Valtellina, a long narrow valley which was the main route linking the Tyrol to the Duchy of Milan. Situated as it was, Valtellina was a region over which both the French and the Austrian governments wanted influence. At

---

[15] 'Je fus cependant obligé de m'en absenter encore. La mort de ma mère m'y força. J'en partis donc le 21 juillet 1793, je traversai l'Allemagne, le Tirol, et me rendis par Venise dans ma Patrie. Je mis ordre à mes affaires, à celles de mes frères encore enfants, et me remis en route par la Suisse, l'Allemagne, la Flandre alors appartenant à l'Empereur, et me retrouvai vers la fin de décembre à Londre résolû de m'y établir de manière de n'en plus sortir.'

[16] 'Viotti ne vit que fort tard l'Italie, où il se rendit par la Suisse. Le dévouement de l'amitié entra pour beaucoup dans cette détermination; il crut pouvoir servir des amis dans la peine, et il se mit en route; mais il garda l'incognito' (Michaud, vol. 43, p. 588).

some point while the Montgéroult party was proceeding through Valtellina, they were arrested by Austrian soldiers and taken to Mantua, where they were thrown into the dungeons of the former ducal palace. This much emerges from the ensuing Viotti letters.

By an apparently strange coincidence, the real French ambassador to Naples Hugues-Bernard Maret is known to have also been arrested, along with his party of 12, on about 14 July 1793, in this same valley, at the same time, and were taken, ten days later, to apparently the same prison in Mantua. The ambush took place in the village of Novate by a group of men dressed as bandits, but who were really, according to Maret's own later evidence, Austrian soldiers acting on orders from Vienna. Their imprisonment lasted 30 months. Could it be that Hélène de Montgéroult and her husband were part of the French diplomatic party that was arrested? As has been seen, Hélène de Montgéroult knew the urbane music-loving Maret, who had almost certainly attended her salon in Paris. Viotti certainly knew him, as the present correspondence proves. According to Rufer, the German historian who documented the whole Novate adventure in 1941, not only did Hélène de Montgéroult know Maret, but she was his 'beloved'! According to Rufer it was she who had persuaded her husband to join Maret's diplomatic party in order to flee France, a fact confirmed by Viotti's letter to Margaret Chinnery of 4 September 1793, and by Maret's own evidence.[17]

After spending a month with the Chinnerys at Gillwell, Viotti departed for Dover on 21 July 1793, the date given by him in his *Précis*, and confirmed by the Chinnery correspondence. In Dover he was met by a friend of the Chinnerys who helped him obtain good horses and a carriage, a berth on the packet and an inn to rest at until his departure. Still in a despondent mood, he sat down to write to the Chinnerys saying that he felt that he was headed for 'a jeremiad of troubles'.[18] On 22 July at 9 pm he set sail from Dover on a packet bound for Ostend, where he arrived at 8 am the following morning.

The opening words of his next letter are interesting: 'It has been a long time since I had such a fast and pleasant crossing.'[19] How many times had Viotti crossed the Channel before? Clearly not a reference to his recent 1792 crossing, this statement implies that Viotti had made at least two previous crossings. His first visit to London had apparently been with Pugnani in 1773,[20] and it has been suggested by Fétis that Viotti made another voyage to London with Pugnani just prior to settling in Paris in 1782. Fétis asserted that Viotti's appearances in London were so successful, both for his fame and fortune, that certain lords tried to

---

[17] A. Rufer (1941), *Novate: Eine Episode aus dem Revolutionsjahr 1793*, Büchergilde Gutenberg, Zurich, p. 29; PHM 94/143/1 – 2/9; Maret's account is cited in Michaud, vol. 26, p. 530, where Novate has been wrongly transcribed as 'Novale'.

[18] 'une Jeremiade de peinnes' (GBV to MC, 22 July 1793, PHM 94/143/1 – 2/6).

[19] 'depuis longtems on n'avoit fait une traversée aussi prompte, et aussi agréable' (GBV to MC, 25 July 1793, PHM 94/143/1 – 2/7).

[20] See above, p. 14. There remains the possibility that Viotti accompanied Pugnani to England in 1767 for a short stay only, but there are no newspaper reports to prove it.

persuade him to stay.[21] But no evidence of a 1782 visit to England exists, and given Viotti's own contradictory account of the route he took to Paris in 1782, it seems very dubious. However there was mention of an intended visit in the winter of 1789–90 in the *Morning Post* of 23 September 1789, under the heading 'MUSIC':

> London will abound with instrumental performances this winter. GIARDINI, VIOTTI, and young WEICHSEL, brother of Mrs. BILLINGTON, will certainly be here. [...] VIOTTI, who, according to MARA's account, is the first performer in the world on the violin, will only play in select parties, as he is a man of good fortune.

The next letter, written from Ghent, informs Margaret that he has been given a warm welcome by a merchant friend and his family, with whom he has been staying for a few days: 'I arrived at Ghent, where I was received most tenderly by a fine man, a worthy merchant of this town, who loves me as a son, a son whom he had the misfortune of losing at the age of 18, and to whom I had given lessons out of friendship.'[22] Clearly Viotti had been to Ghent before. Moreover it seems that he stayed in this town long enough to make an impression on the inhabitants, who, on hearing of his arrival, flocked to stare at him. He gives an amusing account of the way they made him feel – like a freakish animal on display at the village fair. Viotti does not mention visiting Ghent in his *Précis*, when he speaks of his 1780–81 performing tour through Europe, and it was a long way west of the route he describes. Unlike the other cities that Viotti visited on this tour, Ghent did not have a royal court, but it did have many wealthy merchants, who emulated the life of royalty with their patrician residences and cultivation of the arts. The city also possessed several theatres, including an opera house. It may have been that Viotti came to Ghent in the winter of 1789–90 seeking singers for his new Paris theatre, and was persuaded to give a concert there. Perhaps he visited Ghent en route to England, taking the packet at Ostend instead of Calais.

At the home of his friends, named Smed, Viotti plays his violin for the first and last time during his five-month absence from England. On this occasion, as on so many others, Viotti's playing produced tears in his listeners. The family was already grieving for a dead son, perhaps killed in one of the many battles for Flanders between France and Austria over the previous three years. Viotti's own sensitive nature contributed to the effect he was able to produce on his instrument, and sympathetic identification with his friends' grief made him weep with them:

> After dinner I entertained this good papa, his wife and two daughters— one of whom was married— with a good piece of music. I was barely halfway through the first part, when, whether from the revival of some sad memory, or from being moved by the music, tears began to roll down the cheeks of the married daughter. A moment later the

---

[21] *FétisB*, vol. 8, p. 469.

[22] 'Je suis arrivé à Gand, ou j'ai été reçû avéc toute la tendresse possible par un brave et digne homme Négociant dans cette ville, qui m'aime comme son fils, un fils qu'il a eû le malheur de perdre à l'âge de 18. ans, et à qui j'avois par amitié donné des leçons' (GBV to MC, 25 July 1793, PHM 94/143/1 – 2/7).

youngest daughter also began to weep, then the mother, then the father and I. We could not help ourselves. I could not see through my tears, and stopped playing to join in the very moving concerto of tears.[23]

The second letter from the Continent comes from Frankfurt, and is dated 3 August. Viotti had left Ghent, accompanied by the Smed family, for Brussels on 26 July. He did not spend long in Brussels, setting out almost immediately for Frankfurt, and arriving a fortnight after leaving England. The going was slow because of the poor condition of the roads, and undoubtedly also because they were clogged with regiments of soldiers. Most of this letter is taken up with expressions of friendship, feelings of regret at being obliged to travel in a direction which takes him away from his friends, rather than towards them, and assurances that Margaret is his only 'amica' in England. He ends his letter, as always, with fond wishes for the Chinnery children (twins George and Caroline, who are not quite two years old, and baby Walter, just three months old), and a recommendation to Margaret not to let them forget how to pronounce his name – 'Amico'. He also sends greetings to the Chinnery friend 'Monsieur Grenfile [Grenfell]'.[24]

The third letter to Margaret, from Baden [im Aargau] in Switzerland, dated 4 September 1793, is not sent through the post as the previous two were, which means that Viotti found a friend to carry it for him. A whole month has elapsed since the last letter. Perhaps any intervening letters went astray, or perhaps Viotti did not write any, not liking to entrust their sensitive contents to the post. Viotti does mention a letter he has written Margaret from Venice on 13 August (now lost), and it is not clear if Margaret ever received it. There is no other letter from anywhere in Italy. It is a pity that Viotti's letter from Venice is missing, because it may have contained details of his plans to meet up with the French ambassadorial party. The opening words of his letter from Baden make it clear that he was by then aware of his friends' plight, and had tried to visit the men in prison, but being unsuccessful, had pursued Madame de Montgéroult until he finally caught up with her in Baden.[25]

But how did Viotti know what the Montgéroults' plans were? From a letter from Hélène de Montgéroult herself perhaps? Although it was extremely risky to send letters between France and England at this time, it seems that Viotti took the risk (and paid the price, if these letters were the cause of his expulsion from Britain in 1798). It is possible that one of his letters to France that he mentions in his *Précis* – the fourth, which he emphasized was of a personal nature – was an answer

---

[23] 'Aprés dinné j'ai regalé ce bon Papa sa femme, et ses deux filles, dont une mariée, d'un bon morceau de musique; appeine étois-je à la moitié de la premiere partie que, soit par un douloreux souvenir, soit par sensation musicale, de grosses larmes tombent des yeux de la fille mariée, un moment aprés la Cadette l'imite, la mere fait de même, et le pere et moi sans pouvoir nous en empecher nous faisions comme elles; je ne voyois plus clair je quitte le violon pour faire un concert de larmes trés attendrissant' (*Ibid.*).

[24] Pascoe Grenfell (1761–1838), wealthy copper merchant of Taplow House near Windsor.

[25] GBV to WBC and MC, 4 September 1793, PHM 94/143/1 – 2/9.

to one of Hélène de Montgéroult's. A remark in his letter to Margaret of 30 May 1793, in which he asks her to forward a letter addressed to 'my poor French friends',[26] fearing that it may not reach them, points to this being the case. If Viotti did have plans to meet his friends, it was most likely to have been in the neutral Republic of Venice, as there seems no other reason for his going there. However at the time of his departure from England on 22 July, it seems unlikely that he would have known of their arrest.

After his two unsuccessful peace-brokering missions to Britain to meet British prime minister Pitt, Maret had returned to a dangerous situation in France. By the end of May 1793 the Girondins had been deposed, to be replaced by the Jacobin extremists who constituted the majority of the notorious Committee of Public Safety. Maret's friend Lebrun, the moderate Girondin minister for foreign affairs, was under house arrest, later to be executed, but was able to save Maret from the same fate by sending him on the diplomatic mission to Naples. Maret's brief was to travel via Venice and Florence to ascertain the sentiments of these republics towards France.

Maret's biographers Ernouf and Rufer both state that the Montgéroult couple was in this diplomatic party, Ernouf describing the Marquis de Montgéroult as 'an ex [royal] office-holder, charged with a special mission for Naples.'[27] In fact, according to Rufer and Viotti, Montgéroult had a fictitious diplomatic post created for him by Maret.[28] Rufer asserts that in 1795, when the French Directory paid Sémonville 192,000 and Maret 134,000 francs in compensation for their loss of income as a result of their imprisonment, Madame de Montgéroult received 3,000 francs for the personal effects purloined from her husband, but nothing by way of compensation for income, as her husband had held no appointment.[29]

The journey from Paris via Lyons in revolt, and on through Switzerland, had not been easy for this group. Maret was to meet up in Geneva with Sémonville, whose destination was Constantinople. Sémonville came laden with extravagant gifts from the French Republic with which to impress the Sultan. The lumbering line of carriages had difficulty negotiating the narrow alpine tracks. According to Rufer, their caravan consisted of two bulky English berliners and two enormous *diligences*, the berliners being drawn by six and the *diligences* by four horses. There was also a cabriolet drawn by two horses. Their progress was both conspicuous and slow.[30]

After Geneva the French party's route took them through Berne, then on to the small Swiss town of Baden about 20 kilometres from Zurich, where the French ambassador to the Swiss Confederate States François Barthélemy warned them of the presence of Austrian spies in Switzerland. He advised them not to travel on the

---

[26] 'mes pauvres amis de France' (GBV to MC, 30 May 1793, PHM 94/143/1 – 2/3).

[27] 'Montgeroult, ex-officier général, chargé d'une mission particulière pour Naples' (A.-A. Ernouf (1884), *Maret, duc de Bassano*, 2nd edn, Perrin, Paris, p. 167).

[28] Rufer, *Novate*, p. 29; GBV to WBC and MC, 4 September 1793, PHM 94/143/1 – 2/9.

[29] Rufer, *Novate*, p. 210.

[30] *Ibid.*, p. 23.

Austrian side of the Alps, but to go via Chur. He also told them that they were travelling far too conspicuously and that they should split up into smaller groups and abandon their coaches, which advice they ignored.[31]

Thus it was that the French diplomatic party walked right into the trap set for them by the Austrians and their Swiss collaborators in the small village of Novate on the northern-most shores of Lake Como in the neutral territory of Valtellina. Having called a halt, the accompanying guards left the French travellers to go ahead to arrange the escort for the next stretch of the journey. While waiting for them to return, the travellers all repaired to the local *osteria*, with the exception of Madame de Montgéroult, who entered the village church, where she sat down at the organ and began to improvise. This attracted the attention of the curate and a few locals, who approached her wanting to know if she were a member of the French party who had just arrived. Upon her answer in the affirmative, the curate supposedly warned her to flee. His warning came too late. Hélène de Montgéroult had no sooner informed her group of the danger, than they were surrounded by a large number of men dressed as bandits, who had appeared from the direction of the lake. All the men, with the exception of the very young Montholon, were arrested and thrown shackled into a sloop, which carried them across the lake to Gravedona. Their baggage was seized and all their effects confiscated. The women, their female servants, and the children were left destitute on the shore. They were allowed to return to Chiavenna, where they were to await orders from the Milan authorities.[32]

According to Rufer, Madame de Montgéroult reacted hysterically ('Citizen Montgéroult seemed to lose her head'),[33] rushing from the scene of the ambush in indecent haste, leaving Madame de Sémonville and her children to catch up later. Rufer gives far more information about Madame de Montgéroult than does Ernouf. Although only vague sources are cited to back his assertions, it does seem that he has read Hélène de Montgéroult's correspondence,[34] as many of his claims tally with Viotti's account. Viotti also testifies to Hélène's hysterical state, describing the piteous condition in which he found her in Baden in his letter of 4 September.[35] Viotti's account is sympathetic whereas Rufer's is not. Clearly Viotti shared his friend's emotional upheaval. Rufer also reports that the Archduke Ferdinand of Milan sent the two ladies 100 *louis d'or* each, by way of a small compensation. He says that Madame de Sémonville proudly refused the enemy's money, but that he cannot be sure of being able to say the same for Madame de Montgéroult.[36] Viotti reports that she also indignantly refused any help from the Archduke.[37]

---

[31] Michaud, vol. 26, p. 530; Rufer, *Novate*, pp. 30–31.

[32] Rufer, *Novate*, pp. 100–118.

[33] 'Die Bürgerin Montgeroult schien den Kopf verloren zu haben' (Rufer, *Novate*, p. 118).

[34] This appears to be among the French papers in the Vienna State Archives.

[35] GBV to WBC and MC, 4 September 1793, PHM 94/143/1 – 2/9.

[36] Rufer, *Novate*, p. 120.

[37] GBV to WBC and MC, 4 September 1793, PHM 94/143/1 – 2/9.

Rufer even hints that Madame de Montgéroult was a lady of easy virtue, claiming that she shared rooms with 'some private person' in Baden. This 'private person' was none other than Viotti! He kept her company and consoled her after her arduous 20-league ride on horseback from Novate to Baden. '[Hélène] is ill and in a piteous state', he wrote to Margaret. 'They still have not returned any of her belongings, nor any of her papers which constitute all the titles to her fortune. She does not know what is to become of her, what to do, or where to turn. What a dreadful position to be in!'[38]

It is possible that Viotti heard of the ambush of the French diplomatic party as he passed through the Tyrol in August en route to Italy. News of their capture had spread fast through the Swiss Confederate States, where sentiments were reportedly sympathetic to the French. However he would have definitely learned of his friends' arrest from the French ambassador in the Republic of Venice, François Noël, whom he may have met in London in 1792. From Venice Viotti seems to have gone straight to Mantua, as described at the beginning of his letter of 4 September. This sequence of events would seem plausible in view of the fact that it was from Venice (on 13 August) that he asked the Chinnerys to send a bank draft for £200 which was intended for his friends in distress.[39] But if this is the case, it is difficult to imagine when he had time to fit in a visit to his hometown of Fontanetto in Piedmont on the other side of Italy. According to Maret the prisoners were transferred to Mantua on 24 July, having first been detained for ten days in Gravedona. Presumably then, Viotti would have reached Mantua about three weeks after his friends.

In Mantua the French were held in the dungeons of the decaying old castle. It was the height of summer and burning hot days were succeeded by cold nights. The air was thick and humid and conditions insalubrious. Malaria was a risk. Viotti's testimony of the unhealthy climate as 'pestilencieux', the separation of the prisoners from each other, and the lack of reading and writing material, is borne out by Maret's own account.[40] Conditions were so harsh that all the prisoners except Maret came down with swamp fever, most dying within six months of their imprisonment. Among the dead was the Marquis de Montgéroult.

Viotti's arrival in Baden is noted by Rufer. The latter claims that Viotti had just arrived from Venice, and that he testified publicly, along with Madame de Sémonville and another Swiss dignitary, that he had seen the whole of Valtellina ready to rise up in revolt at the crime which had been perpetrated against the French diplomats.[41] Viotti does not mention making this public attestation in his letters, but it is in keeping with his character and his ready indignation at injustice.

---

[38] '[Hélène] est malade et dans un état à faire pitié. On ne lui a encore rendu aucun de ses effets, ni de ses papiers qui sont tous les titres de sa fortune. Elle ne sait que devenir, que faire, ni ou donner de la tête; quelle affreuse position!' (GBV to MC, 20 September 1793, PHM 94/143/1 – 2/10).

[39] GBV to WBC and MC, 4 September 1793, PHM 94/143/1 – 2/9.

[40] Michaud, vol. 26, p. 530.

[41] Rufer, *Novate*, p. 123.

Although he calls him by name, Rufer does not seem to recognize the famous violinist, referring to him simply as Madame de Sémonville's compatriot.

Viotti's letter of 4 September contained an enclosure from Hélène to the British prime minister Pitt (missing), informing him of the outrage that had been committed. Viotti asked William Chinnery to pass it on, knowing that William, as a chief clerk of the Treasury, knew Pitt well enough to deliver the note in person. He undoubtedly also knew of the two private meetings which had taken place in London between Maret and Pitt, and of the regard in which Pitt held Maret. Madame de Montgéroult's appeal to Pitt must have been on the basis that Pitt might have been able to influence the Austrians in their favour, but with the Terror gaining momentum and Marie-Antoinette's head about to fall, it was a vain one. However Viotti was confident that Pitt would act on the letter, and in a subsequent letter to William advised him to keep safe any reply that Pitt might make, and to wait for an opportunity to have it carried by a friend, as any letter entrusted to the post would certainly compromise their friend.[42]

By 20 September Hélène had learned of the death of her 60-year-old husband, which is described by an outraged Viotti in his letter to Margaret from Baden of the same date. Ernouf notes that the Parisian newspaper *Le Moniteur* reported the death on 8 October 1793, intimating that Montgéroult had committed suicide. Viotti's account is different. He reports that conditions in the prison and the old man's distress combined to bring on a fatal asthma attack which killed him on 2 September. According to Viotti Madame de Montgéroult had been pressing the Austrian authorities for the previous five weeks for permission to join her husband in prison, without receiving a reply. On this detail Rufer gives an identical account, adding, however, that once her husband was dead Hélène transferred all her attentions to Maret, to whom she began writing hysterical love letters, which, Rufer says, he fortunately never received, as they were intercepted by the Austrian guards.[43] Viotti gives no hint of any such letters, simply expressing his indignation at the treatment of Hélène's elderly, gout-stricken husband, whose only reason for leaving France was, he says, his health and peace of mind.[44]

Hélène de Montgéroult's predicament made a strong impression on Viotti. His sensitive nature and his horror of injustice combined to plunge him into black pessimism: 'Oh my friends, how unhappy is man's lot on earth! For my part I am more than ever convinced that happiness is a chimera.'[45] Montgéroult's death caused him to fear that the same fate would overtake Maret: 'This event should spur all honest men into taking action to preserve poor Maret's health, and even his life. We have had no news since that fatal moment.'[46] Viotti's own health was

[42] GBV to WBC, 24 September 1793, PHM 94/143/1 – 14/1.

[43] Rufer, *Novate*, p. 205.

[44] GBV to MC, 20 September 1793, PHM 94/143/1 – 2/10.

[45] 'Oh! mes amis qu'on est mal à son aise dans ce monde! Pour moi je suis plusque jamais convaincû que le bonheur est un chimere!' (*Ibid.*).

[46] 'Cet evenement doit redoubler la zele de tous les honnetes gens pour sauver la santé, et même la vie de ce pauvre maret; nous n'avons pas de ses nouvelles depuis ce fatal

severely affected. In the same letter he says he has been suffering for the past fortnight from a double tertian fever ('une fièvre double-tiérce').[47] The next letter, addressed to William Chinnery, is entirely taken up with discussion of the bank draft. Viotti was impatient for it to arrive:

> As soon as I have received it, not being of any further use to my poor friends, I shall set off on my return journey to England, to return to you and to your kind-hearted other half, to pour into your bosom the sadness that overwhelms me. [I shall also] nurse my health that has for so long suffered from so many severe shocks. I am so thin and pale that you would not recognize me.[48]

The draft, which Viotti had wanted addressed to either the French ambassador Barthélémy in Baden, or poste restante, Zurich, did not arrive. He asked William, who had organized the draft through Viotti's banker Hammersley,[49] to take all the necessary precautions to avoid the loss of the money, and in a clear reference to his losses during the French Revolution, wrote: 'It is not that I need the money at this very moment, but I have been so persecuted by Fortune in my life that I must economize as much as possible, so that if I have any more setbacks they will not leave me without a bare minimum.'[50]

Viotti's letter of 8 October from Zurich testifies to his frayed nerves. He chastises Margaret bitterly for not writing, saying that by this omission she is adding to his woes. Finally, giving the draft up for lost, he asks William to cancel it, and writes that he will be making his way back to England in two weeks. In this and the following letter from Zurich he stresses how dire his need is for comfort: 'In truth I have great need of your consolation, for ever since leaving you I have experienced nothing but pain and bitterness.'[51] Having at last received a letter from Margaret, the first since Frankfurt, he is relieved but still mournful. On 21 October Hélène de Montgéroult departed Zurich to return to the land she had tried to flee.

---

moment' (*Ibid.*).

47 *Ibid.*

48 'Si tôt que je l'aurai reçüe, ne pouvant être plus utile à mes pauvres amis je me remetterai en route pour revenir en Angleterre, revenir auprés de vous, de votre aimable moitié, verser dans votre sein la tristesse dont je suis accablé, et remettre un peu une santé qui depuis long tems à [sic] souffert de si rudes atteintes. je suis si maigre, si pâle que vous ne me reconnoitriés plus' (GBV to WBC, 24 September 1793, PHM 94/143/1 – 14/1).

49 William Hammersley was also the banker for the Opera. Messrs Ransom, Morland and Hammersley of Pall Mall were listed in the *Times*, 2 February 1795, as one of the outlets where subscriptions to the 1795 Opera concerts could be purchased.

50 'Ce n'est pas que j'aye besoin d'argent dans ce moment cy, mais j'ai tant été persecuté par la Fortune dans ma vie, que je dois ménager le plus possible affin que si les coups me frappent encore, ils ne portent pas du moins sur l'absolû nécéssaire' (GBV to MC, 13 October 1793, PHM 94/143/1 – 2/12).

51 'En vérité j'ai bien besoin de cette consolation, car depuis que je vous ai quittée je ne me suis nourri que de douleur et d'amertume' (GBV to MC, 8 October 1793, PHM 94/143/1 – 2/11).

'Never before have I felt so keenly how unbearable life can be at times', wrote Viotti.[52]

In two of his letters to the Chinnerys Viotti asks to be remembered to Hüllmandel.[53] In the second he asks them to warn Hüllmandel not to write to Hélène. These words would suggest that Hüllmandel also had been following the fortunes of his former piano pupil, and was privy to the details of Viotti's journey. This was not the case for Salomon, for although Viotti tells Margaret that he has written to Salomon, presumably to reassure him about the date of his return, he says that he did not tell him either where he was or what he was doing on the Continent.[54]

The Chinnerys shared Viotti's concern for Hélène, and had written to her in Baden, prompting her promise of everlasting loyalty: 'She charges me to tell you and Mrs Chinnery that she has an undying affection for you. She is deeply grateful for the concern that both of you have shown for her troubles. She reiterates that she will never forget it.'[55] Hélène de Montgéroult did keep her friendship for the Chinnerys alive. She received them in Paris in 1802, and in 1819 would pay Margaret a visit in London. Viotti finishes his letter of 13 October by saying that Hélène would write herself, and it would be her last letter for a long time, as any future correspondence with England would spell her death sentence.[56]

One letter written by Viotti from Switzerland at this time is not part of the CFP collection.[57] Dated Baden, 2 November 1793, it is addressed in a correct Republican manner to 'Citizen Maret, Wife of the District President' of the *département* of the Côte d'Or – Maret's sister-in-law in Dijon. Hugues-Bernard Maret had an older brother in whose house Hélène de Montgéroult intended to seek refuge on her return to France. Viotti wrote to have news of his friends, opening his letter with the words: 'Today is the day the posts arrive from France and Mantua. I hope that the latter [post] will bring me news of your brother, my friend [Maret], but I also hope that the former will bring me news of yourselves and of our unhappy friend [Hélène de Montgéroult].'[58] 'Mantoue' has been wrongly transcribed by Giazotto as 'Mentone'. With Viotti's handwriting, this is an

---

52 'jamais je n'ai si bien senti combien la vie est insuportable dans certains momens' (*Ibid.*).

53 GBV to MC, 20 September 1793, PHM 94/143/1 – 2/10; GBV to WBC, 24 September 1793, PHM 94/143/1 – 14/1.

54 GBV to WBC and MC, 4 September 1793, PHM 94/143/1 – 2/9.

55 'Elle me charge de vous temoigner ainsi qu'à M[dame] Chinnery un attachement innalterable, votre Sensibilité à vous deux pour ses peines l'a penetrée de reconnoissance; elle me repete souvent qu'elle ne l'oubliera jamais' (GBV to WBC, 24 September 1793, PHM 94/143/1 – 14/1).

56 GBV to MC, 13 October 1793, PHM 94/143/1 – 2/12.

57 It is transcribed in Giazotto, p. 266. No source is given.

58 'C'est aujourd'hui jour des courriers de France et de Mentone [*recte* Mantoue]. J'espere que l'un m'apportera des lettres de votre frère et mon ami, mais j'espère aussi que l'autre m'apportera de vos nouvelles et celles de notre malheureuse amie' (GBV to Mme Maret, 2 November 1793, cited in Giazotto, p. 266).

understandable error, but the wrong transcription causes the reader to miss the whole point of the letter.

It is clear from the tone of the letter that Viotti does not know Maret's brother's wife personally. He makes the pointed remark that all good Republicans must be comrades. This was obviously intended as a 'politically correct' way of addressing a fellow Republican in one of the bloodiest years of the Revolution, in the event that the letter was intercepted by French authorities. But if they were politically correct in revolutionary France, these terms were quite the opposite in Britain, and it was ironic that this letter, if known to the British Government, may have been used in evidence against Viotti at the time of his expulsion from Britain five years later.

From Zurich on 8 November 1793 Viotti addresses a second letter to William Chinnery. He expresses relief that he has at last received a letter from his friend: 'Oh! How it did me good to hear from you! An angel from heaven would not have been better received by me than the messenger bearing the letter that I had been awaiting so impatiently.'[59] He is soothed by the knowledge that the Chinnerys are well, and love him still and think of him. In spite of his recent traumatic experiences his health is surprisingly good, 'for in the face of so many cruel storms even a colossus would have succumbed.'[60] He reiterates that it is three weeks since Hélène left Zurich and he still has had no news of her.

Viotti goes on to compliment William on his French, which he (Viotti) had been teaching him. The fact that William Chinnery does not know French well would explain the preponderance of letters to Margaret Chinnery in 1793. William's French subsequently improved, and within a few years he was able to read and write French and Italian with sufficient accuracy to correspond with his friend. Viotti informs William that he will return to London via Ghent, where he will again stay at the home of Smed. He had already begged Margaret to write to him there at 'place d'arme'.[61] He also reassures William – who must have reproached Viotti for not having played at all during his journey – regarding his ability to take up his instrument again after such a long estrangement from it:

> Since leaving you I have not touched my violin. Do not scold me. In my present situation the high notes of the instrument are incompatible with my pain. I will take it up again when my reason begins to return to me. You know that thanks to the gift that nature has given me, it will not take me long to pick it up again and that a week will suffice to bring me up to the same performing standard as last year. Therefore do not hold it against me and rest assured that I will succeed.[62]

---

[59] 'Oh! que votre Souvenir m'a fait du bien! On m'auroit annoncé un ange descendû du Ciel que je ne l'aurois pas mieux reçû que le messager qui me l'a remise cette lettre que j'attendois avéc tant d'impatience' (GBV to WBC, 8 November 1793, PHM 94/143/1 – 14/2).

[60] 'car au millieu de tant de crueles bourasques, un Colosse y succombroit' (*Ibid.*).

[61] GBV to MC, 8 October 1793, PHM 94/143/1 – 2/11.

[62] 'Depuis que je vous ai quitté je n'ai pas touché mon Violon. Ne me grondés pas, ma situation est telle que les sons égus de cet instrument sont incompatibles avéc mes

This special gift that Viotti possessed of being able to regain quickly his superlative playing skills after a long period away from his instrument has been remarked upon with admiration by his contemporaries. The implication in the above passage that William heard him play a year previously lends support to the hypothesis that Viotti already knew the Chinnerys at the end of 1792.

Viotti arrived in Ghent on or about 6 December 1793, on which date he wrote to Margaret of his delight on finding three of her letters waiting for him. Again he says that the Chinnery letters are like balm to his woes:

> On my arrival here I found three of your letters. My first care before reading them was to thank Heaven that He did not entirely abandon me, and that my friends, my dear friends who have ever remained close to my heart, still love me. After these thanks I opened the letters. Oh my good Amica, how they comforted this poor unfortunate who has suffered for so long!… thank you, thank you.[63]

Viotti's reply to a remark of Margaret's regarding his mental equilibrium shows that his religious faith was strong:

> I would have lost it [my reason] even more if the confidence that I have always had in Divine Providence had not supported me. But my dear Amica I am no less at odds for that with this infernal world into which I have been born merely to suffer trials a thousand times worse than death.[64]

Viotti rested in Ghent for ten or twelve days before embarking for Dover. The Smeds again offered him hospitality and comfort, but it was on the Chinnerys that his hopes devolved to relieve his present misery. He begged them to find him an apartment and a servant in their own neighbourhood: 'An insignificant individual like me does not need much. My only wish is that it be close to your little house. I do not care about anything else'.[65] He also enclosed a letter to Hüllmandel, asking

---

sensations douloureuses. Je m'y remetterai lorsque la raison aura pri[s] plus d'empire sûr moi. Vous savés que grace aux dons que la nature m'a fait, il ne me faut pas longtems pour me remettre en train et que huit jours suffiront pour que je sois tout aussi digne d'être entendu que l'année passée; ainsi ne m'en voulés pas et soyés tranquille sur mes Succès' (GBV to WBC, 8 November 1793, PHM 94/143/1 – 14/2).

63 'J'ai trouvé en arrivant ici trois de vos lettres; mon premier soin avant de les lire a été de remercier le Ciel de ce qu'il ne m'avoit pas entierement abandonné; et que mes amis mes bons amis que j'ai sans cesse gardés dans mon cœur m'aiment toujours. Aprés ce remerciement je les ai ouvertes ces lettres. oh ma bonne amica qu'elles ont fait du bien à ce malheureux qui souffre depuis si long tems!... merci merci' (GBV to MC, 6 December 1793, PHM 94/143/1 – 2/14).

64 'Je l'aurois perdue bien plus encore si la confiance que j'ai toujours conservée dans une Providence Divine ne m'eut soutenu mais ma chere amica je n'en suis pas moins brouillé avéc cet infernal monde ou je ne suis placé que pour éssuyer des déchirements d'ame mille fois pire que la mort' (*Ibid.*).

65 'Il ne faut pas grand chose pour mon chetif individû, je veux seulement qu'il soit prés de votre petite maison. Le reste m'est égal' (*Ibid.*).

if his friend could accommodate him for two or three days until he moved into his own apartment: 'I am embarrassed to owe him this small favour because of his wife, but I would be in a fix otherwise, and anyway he is a good man and loves me sincerely.'[66] He added that he was counting on Margaret to revive his interest in music:

> You will make me take up music again when I return to you, won't you Amica? In the five months that I have totally abandoned it everyone, wherever I went, has tried to stop me on my journey. They did everything possible and impossible to make me play, and built golden bridges to attain their ends, but I ignored them all, and my [violin] case has remained constantly closed. Harmony has irritated me ever since the events in my life obliterated the harmony of my being. If this antipathy continues I shall probably continue to act in London as I have during my voyage.[67]

From the above letters it is possible to form an idea of the route that Viotti followed on his journey to Italy and back again. As stated in his *Précis* he reached his homeland via Germany, the Tyrol and Venice. Understandably wishing to give the Revolution a wide berth, he did not choose to cross into France at any point. Therefore the route he took after leaving Frankfurt was undoubtedly the most direct one for reaching Venice – through Stuttgart, Munich and Innsbruck in the Tyrol. His movements after Venice remain hazy. When did he fit in the visit to Fontanetto to attend to his family affairs? There is no indication in his letters that he went to Piedmont at all, although there was conceivably time for him to have done so between leaving Venice and arriving in Baden. He could just as easily have retraced Madame de Montgéroult's steps by entering Switzerland from the northwest of Italy, and indeed this accords with the route he gives in his *Précis*. Since the main reason for the journey was to settle his family affairs, we must assume that he did go to his birthplace. But the letter dated October 1793 and addressed to Viotti at Ghent from a disappointed Pugnani (see Appendix) shows that he did not visit his old teacher in Turin.

The following is a hypothetical outline of Viotti's itinerary, based on the evidence in his *Précis* and the present letters. The dates in brackets are either the dates of letters written from the place in question or dates which are adduced from information given in other letters: Dover (22 July), Ostend (23 July), Ghent (25 July), Brussels (26 July), Frankfurt (3 August), Innsbruck in the Tyrol [n.d.], Venice (13 August), Mantua [n.d.], Fontanetto [n.d.], Valtellina [n.d.], Baden (4,

---

66 'Cela me fache de lui devoir ce petit plaisir à cause de sa femme, mais je me trouverois dans l'embar[r]as sans cela, et d'ailleur il est bon lui il m'aime sincerement' (*Ibid.*).

67 'N'est-ce pas amica que vous me ferés reprendre la musique quand je serai auprés de vous? Depuis cinq mois je l'ai totalement abandonné, partout ou j'ai passé on a voulu m'arreter on a fait l'impossible pour m'entendre on m'a fait des ponts d'or pour en venir à bout, j'ai fermé l'oreille à tout, et mon étui a été constemment fermé. L'harmonie me contrarie depuis que les evenemens de ma vie ont effacé celle qui éxistoit dans mon etre. Si cette antipathie continue je continuerai probablement de faire à Londre ce que j'ai fait dans mon voyage' (*Ibid.*).

20, 24 September), Zurich (8, 13, 20 October, 4, 18 November), Ghent (6, 17 December). As can be seen, it was a five-month journey, not a one-and-a-half-month one, as claimed by Giazotto.[68] Nor did Viotti go to Vienna or Leipzig.

Viotti's last letter from the Continent is addressed to William. He again compliments him on his astounding progress in French:

> Why am I not in a position for you to pay me the same compliment about my English? Alas, I have forgotten the little I knew, but what have I not forgotten in the cruel situations in which I have found myself. It is saying a lot that I am even alive. Providence has intended that I be preserved for my friends, or perhaps for even greater misfortunes.[69]

He has finally received news of Hélène, whose health is poor. He bemoans the fact that, for reasons which he will explain on his return, she was forced to return to 'cet Enfer' (that Hell). In one last misanthropic outburst he wails that with his temperament he will probably be doomed to find peace only in the grave: 'when one is born as I was, my dear friend, with an extremely sensitive nature, one must accept one's lot and submit to incessant suffering, expecting peace only when a good clod of earth covers us, separating us from the rest of humanity.'[70]

That Viotti tested the Chinnerys' friendship to the limit during these months of unalleviated despair is certain. But his own loyalty to his friends was tested and found unshakeable when, 19 years later, the Chinnerys' own problems began.

---

[68] Giazotto, p. 134.

[69] 'Que ne sui-je dans le cas que vous me fassiés le même compliment dans la langue Anglaise? helas j'ai oublié le peu que je savois, mais que n'ai-je point oublié dans les crueles situations ou je me suis trouvé. C'est encore beaucoup que j'existe. La Providence a voulu me conserver pour mes amis, peut être pour des malheurs encore plus grands' (GBV to WBC, 17 December 1793, PHM 94/143/1 – 14/3).

[70] 'Lorsqu'on est né comme moi mon cher ami avéc une sensibilité extreme il faut prendre son parti et se vouer à des souffrances qui se renouvellent sans cesse, et n'attendre le repos que lorsqu'un bon morceau de terre nous aura couvert et separé du reste des humains' (*Ibid.*).

CHAPTER 5

# The Hanover Square concerts, 1794

Viotti returned from the Continent just two months before the start of Salomon's 1794 concerts in the Hanover Square Rooms. These were awaited in the capital with high expectation because of Haydn's much publicized participation in them, and since Viotti was Salomon's second crowd-puller, it was not surprising that the organizer was anxious to know the date of the violinist's return. Haydn, too, was to keep Salomon in suspense. When the great composer did not arrive in time for the first concert that had been announced for 3 February 1794, Salomon was obliged to postpone by a week the commencement of the concerts.

On his return to London Viotti moved into the house that William Chinnery had taken for him at no. 34 Wells Street, Oxford Street, the address given by Doane's *Musical Directory* for 1794. It was just across the road from the Chinnerys' own home at 5 Mortimer Street.[1] William had also hired a manservant for him, Henry. Viotti was almost certainly in daily contact with the Chinnerys, which would explain the lack of letters during this period. However there is a small bundle of five hand-delivered notes to the Chinnerys which seem to be of this period, although only one is dated. On the outside of the letter dated '13. f. 94' is written, in Viotti's hand, 'Several letters from Amico to Amica in our early days.'[2]

The first letter is a short half-page note to Margaret enquiring after her cold. Viotti himself is resting in bed with a painful foot ailment, probably gout, a recurrent malady often mentioned in his correspondence with the Chinnerys. He asks Margaret to make some domestic purchases for him – two music portfolios and a 'moffiniere' (muffin maker?), and announces that he will call on the Chinnerys 'before the Spaniard arrives' at five o'clock.[3] 'L'Espagnol' was almost certainly Viotti's Spanish pupil Philippe Libon. The letter ends with assurances of Viotti's everlasting faithfulness: 'Adieu my good Amica. Never forget that all my life I shall be the best of all [your] friends.'[4]

The next letter contains further enquiries after Margaret's cold, and the news that his foot is now better. He wishes uncharitably that Margaret's hoarseness had

---

[1] The address given by the *Morning Chronicle* of 7 May 1794 in its advertisement for Viotti's benefit concert, 16 Charles Street, corner of Wells Street, near Middlesex Hospital, is the property next door (R. Horwood (1813), *The A to Z of Regency London*, ed. P. Laxton and J. Wisdom, Harry Margary, Lympne Castle, Kent, 1985, p. 24).

[2] 'Plusieurs lettres de l'Amico à l'Amica dans nos premiers temps' (GBV to MC, 13 F[ebruary] 1794, PHM 94/143/1 – 2/16).

[3] 'avant que l'Espagnol arrive' (GBV to MC, *c.*February 1794, PHM 94/143/1 – 2/22).

[4] 'Adieu ma bonne Amica n'oubliés jamais que toute ma vie je serai le meilleur de tous les Amici' (*Ibid.*).

rather been inflicted on her sister Marianne, whose singing voice is not as sweet as Margaret's. Although the letter is undated, it can be shown to have been written in late January or on one of the first three days of February 1794, as Viotti says he was caught out by a false report of Haydn's arrival in London.[5] (Haydn arrived on 4 February.) In the same letter Viotti mentions an invitation to an evening party from Madame Hüllmandel, and in another he passes on her offer to lend her house at Brompton to the Chinnerys, perhaps for a summer holiday. Hüllmandel had married into a large fortune in Paris,[6] and was apparently still living in comfort.

On 13 February Viotti writes, in rather ambiguously suggestive language, that he is sending Margaret a new concerto he has just finished:

> I am sending you, Amica, another of my new children. I desire that you receive it with friendly indulgence and that you never lose patience with it. You understand of course that I mean a concerto, for what else could I be referring to, I who am but a poor solitary soul, with such an ardent unrequited heart!...[7]

This was clearly a violin concerto composed for the 1794 season, written out fair for Margaret, perhaps as a token of his gratitude for her support and forbearance during his darkest hours of gloom.[8] Since Margaret was an accomplished pianist, Viotti intended that she should perform it as a piano concerto, a conversion that she was quite capable of making herself. It was common in the late eighteenth century for violin concertos to be first performed by *amateurs* as piano concertos. All that was required for the concerto to be played without orchestra was for the player to begin at the first solo entrance, omitting the opening *tutti*, and proceed through to the end, including later *tuttis*.[9]

Speculation about Viotti's new compositions for the coming season was rife, with the *Oracle* of 25 January 1794 writing: 'Viotti has been selecting some fine thoughts for *Concerto playing*, which for sublimity and simplicity is unequalled'. Viotti's mention to Margaret of 'another' new concerto implies that he had already written more than one. Under the terms of his contract with Salomon for the 1794 Hanover Square concert series, Viotti, like Haydn, was required to produce new compositions, and, as was the custom, he would start the season with a new work.

---

5 GBV to MC, *c.*3 February 1794, PHM 94/143/1 – 2/15.

6 GBV to MC, *c.*1794, PHM 94/143/1 – 2/23; *AMZ*, 15 December 1802, col. 198n.

7 'Je vous envoye amica un autre de mes nouveaux Enfans je desire que vous le receviés avéc l'indulgence de l'amitié et que jamais vous ne vous fachiés contre lui. Vous sentés bien que c'est d'un concerto dont je veux parler, car comment pourrai-je parler d'autre chose moi pauvre etre isolé de tout, l'ame si ardente et si vide de ce qui pourroit la rendre sattisfaitte!' (GBV to MC, 13 F[ebruary] 1794, PHM 94/143/1 – 2/16).

8 In White's 'Chronology' (p. 122) he notes that the autograph of the slow movement of Viotti's Concerto No. 24 is written out with unusual care on small pocket-sized sheets, and surmises that it was intended as a gift to an admirer. It is tempting to imagine that the recipient was Margaret, and if so, reinforces the argument that this concerto was written for the 1794 season.

9 T.B. Milligan (1983), *The Concerto and London's Musical Culture in the Late Eighteenth Century*, UMI Research Press, Ann Arbor, Mich., p. 34.

Which work might Viotti have presented first? A review of the second concert in the *Morning Chronicle* of 19 February, in which Viotti repeated his new concerto of the first concert, did say that it was in a minor key. On the basis of instrumentation, it has been suggested that it might have been his Concerto No. 24 in B minor.[10] The second movement of this concerto, the *andante sostenuto*, might well have produced in Viotti's hands the 'exquisite' tones of the second movement described below:

> VIOTTI produced a new Concerto, in which his own execution was most delicate and touching; nothing could be more exquisite than his tones in the second movement. We have no doubt but both these pieces will be called for again; for they are to be ranked among the finest productions of which music has to boast.[11]

In view of Viotti's frame of mind on his return from the Continent it is not surprising that the concerto was in a minor key. Baillot wrote of the use of the minor key that it was 'the natural expression of trouble and loss' and conveyed 'the most profound melancholy [...] which acts more strongly than joy on suffering hearts and tender souls,' all the better to soothe them.[12] Certainly the second movement of the Concerto No. 24 is full of poignant melancholy. The testimony of the *Oracle* that the concerto was '*simple* and *affecting*, like his genius',[13] shows that it touched the audience deeply. The first movement, too, is full of passion and underlying tension.

All the reviewers were impressed with Salomon's organization of the concerts. The *Sun* joined in the general praise:

> The Concerts under the management of HAYDN and SALOMON commenced for the season last night, and we were glad to see the taste of the Public manifested in a large and elegant Audience. Indeed, it would be wonderful if a Concert, which can boast the united powers of HAYDN, VIOTTI, SALOMON, and MARA, with an ample and a[d]mirable Band, did not excite a very liberal patronage. The grand instrumental trial of last night was a New Overture by HAYDN, a composition of the most exquisite kind, rich, fanciful, bold, and impressive. VIOTTI displayed all his fine taste and astonishing execution in a Violin Concerto, which, though deeply scientific, was no less pleasing.[14]

The last comment was undoubtedly a tilt at those erudite composers who were apt to display their knowledge of music so ostentatiously that they descended into pedantry. Viotti, on the other hand, was able to display all his 'science' without detracting in any way from the strong emotion present in his music. In the 1794 concerts Viotti was joined by his friend Dussek, who had come over to Salomon's concerts from the now defunct Professional Concert. Madame Mara was again the

---

[10] *Ibid.*, p. 136.
[11] *Morning Chronicle*, 11 February 1794.
[12] *Art of the violin*, pp. 276–7.
[13] *Oracle*, 11 February 1794.
[14] *Sun*, 11 February 1794.

featured female soloist but she took ill before the second concert, affording the 'unfortunate emigrant' Madame Ducrest (Madame de Genlis's sister-in-law) an opportunity of making herself known in London.

The *Morning Chronicle*'s review of the second concert was comprehensive. It began with a tribute to Salomon, went on to review the performances of the newcomers, and finished by extolling 'the genius of Haydn, astonishing inexhaustible, and sublime'. Viotti's playing was accorded nearly as much space as Haydn's. But the reviewer could not quite put his finger on Viotti's style. At the beginning of 1794 Haydn's influence had not yet been fully felt, but so affected was Viotti by his recent experiences, that it would be strange if the brooding disenchantment that he felt with the world were not transferred to his compositions, giving them the lyrical, pre-Romantic cachet that has been noticed in his works of this period. At the same time the concerto retained elements of the old *galant* style, causing the reviewer's uncertainty:

> Viotti played a concerto in a minor key, the composition and performance of which were alike masterly. In style it was neither perfectly ancient nor modern, though it partook of the beauties of both. His power on the fourth string is indeed great; but, like power in general, it is liable to abuse. To speak proverbially, "He harps a little too much on one string." He played however with uncommon sweetness, feeling, and effect.[15]

Power on the G string was a fundamental characteristic of Viotti's bowing style. The adherents of the Viotti school believed, like Viotti, that no other string had as much authority. It was this string that 'establishe[d] the empire of the violin'; it was 'the tenor voice in all its beauty', and 'the deeper this voice is, the more it enables expression to reach the sublime.'[16]

The reviewer for the *Sun* had no reservations about Viotti's playing, writing:

> The wonderful new Overture of HAYDN, performed on the first night, was repeated last night, amidst the wondering plaudits of the Audience. The first movement was *encored*. VIOTTI also repeated his fine Concerto of the former night, which was, if possible, more charming than before.[17]

Of the 12 concerts of Salomon's 1794 series Viotti played in all but the third, sixth, eighth and tenth. In no other concert announcement is there mention of a new concerto, except for his benefit, where two are announced. The Viotti reviews continued to call him a 'masterly performer' and emphasised his ability to affect his audience. After the fourth concert the *Morning Chronicle* of 5 March wrote: 'Viotti we have never heard with greater pleasure; the sweetness and perfections of his tones were enchanting, as were the feelings they inspired.'

---

[15] *Morning Chronicle*, 19 February 1794. Milligan (*The Concerto*, p. 147) cites Concerto No. 24 as a good example of Viotti's mixture of 'ancient and 'modern' tendencies.

[16] *Art of the violin*, p. 250.

[17] *Sun*, 18 February 1794.

Again in the fifth and seventh concerts Viotti was praised for giving soul to his music. The concerto he performed in the fifth concert can be identified as his No. 5 in C major by the review in the *Oracle* of 13 March 1794, which clearly identifies the Swiss melody *Ranz des Vaches* that is introduced into the second movement:

> Viotti performed a most beautiful Concerto, in which he introduced the movement, whose effects arouse that *Amor Patriae* in the SWISS, which makes them sicken after the blessings of a distant home. In truth, there is such a divine simplicity in the strain, it corresponds so well with our impressions from that country, and its most happy inhabitants, that to hear it without emotion is impossible.

It is significant that Viotti chose to perform this concerto, having been so recently in Switzerland, where his experiences were so very different from those when he had first heard this beautiful alphorn melody used to call the cows to milking. Perhaps he was trying to lose himself in the music, as he did when he first heard it, describing his sensations in a lyrical piece of writing that he copied out for Margaret Chinnery:

> My thoughts wandered at random, and my footsteps were equally undirected. My imagination was not occupied with any particular object, and my heart lay open to every impression of pensive delight. [...] I fell into that kind of profound reverie which so totally absorbed all my faculties, that I forgot whether I was on earth.[18]

The *Morning Chronicle* praised Viotti's restraint in not trying to impress his listeners, but rather to arouse an emotive response in them:

> The masterly performance of VIOTTI exceeded all former example; his power over the instrument seems unlimited. The grand mistake of Musicians has been a continued effort to excite amazement. VIOTTI, it is true, without making that his object, astonishes the hearer; but he does something infinitely better— he awakens emotion, gives a soul to sound, and leads the passions captive.[19]

It was commonly agreed among musicians of taste that exciting amazement should be the last of the true artist's aims. It was also a commonly evinced view in the German newspaper the *Allgemeine musikalische Zeitung* that music played without feeling was worthless. In a long article regarding all aspects of performance the writer makes it clear that a virtuoso who does not touch the heart of his listeners is not worthy of the name.[20]After the seventh concert the reviewer gives a little advice to aspiring musicians. Holding up Viotti as an example, he says:

---

[18] *Ranz des Vaches*, Viotti Papers, RCM. Translation by G. Hogarth (1848), *Musical History, Biography and Criticism*, Da Capo Reprint, New York, 1969, p. 59.

[19] *Morning Chronicle*, 12 March, 1794.

[20] *AMZ*, 11 August 1802, cols 759–60.

> But musicians who aspire after excellence should never forget that if they want [i.e. lack] passion, the defect cannot be compensated by any other excellence, however great. VIOTTI again produced the most rapturous sensations; he indeed possesses not only sweetness, vigour, and every variety that the bow and the finger seem capable of affording, but he adds the grand ingredient, soul, without which music is either insipidity, trick, or noise.[21]

Viotti's compositions are again under scrutiny after the ninth concert:

> Some of the connoisseurs profess to like the playing of Viotti better than his Music.—Judgements differ: we will not pretend to affirm they are mistaken; we can only say, though his Compositions partake of the Old French School, there is yet a richness, unity, and grandeur in them, that in our opinion place them far beyond the jigs, quirks, and quackery, in which modern music is so apt to indulge. Not that we are the enemies of modern music: it has many essential improvements, but it has no few radical vices.[22]

It is clear from the above that Viotti had performed one of his French concertos, and that certain connoisseurs had found it old fashioned. This was not surprising, given Haydn's influence on contemporary music, and the evolution that even Viotti's London-composed concertos had undergone.

The reviewer of the eleventh concert, like many of Viotti's contemporaries, described him as performing 'in a grand and impressive style'.[23] This grand performance style was unique to Viotti, and was something not even his pupils were able to emulate. In 1821 George Chinnery was to write of Nicolas Mori's performance of a Viotti concerto: '[he] possesses none of the grandioso which Amico's works require to do them justice.'[24]

Violin duets performed by Viotti and Salomon had been a popular attraction in the 1793 Hanover Square concerts, and were continued in 1794. In the twelfth and final concert the audience was delighted by a Viotti–Salomon duet played 'in a very bold and finished style'.[25] Viotti also played at Haydn's benefit on 2 May, and led the band for Salomon's benefit on 28 May. His own benefit was given on 23 May. No mention of Viotti was made in the *Morning Chronicle*'s review of the Haydn benefit, nor was there a review of his own.

The *Morning Chronicle* announced that for the Viotti benefit there were to be two new concertos, one of which was for viola.[26] One of these appears to be what was to become his most popular concerto, No. 23 in G major, known as the *John Bull*, which, as a piano transcription by Dussek, was advertised by the latter's publishing firm Dussek, Corri and Company in the *Times* of 16 December 1794 as 'VIOTTI'S celebrated New GRAND CONCERTO IN G as Performed at his

---

[21] *Morning Chronicle*, 26 March, 1794.

[22] *Morning Chronicle*, 9 April 1794

[23] *Morning Chronicle*, 7 May 1794.

[24] GRC to MC, 21 March 1821, Fisher 2000 – 7/10.

[25] *Morning Chronicle*, 15 May 1794.

[26] *Morning Chronicle*, 20 May 1794. No viola concerto is listed in White's *Thematic Catalogue*.

Concert, Hanover Square' (see Figure 4). Although the Viotti benefit concert referred to in this advertisement could theoretically be that of 1793, it is more likely to have been that of 1794, since the closer the date of the advertisement to the date of the concert, the greater the saleability of the music. Moreover with Dussek performing alongside his admired friend in Viotti's 1794 benefit, what could be more natural than his mentioning the concert on the title page of his publication? Dussek would later dedicate to Viotti his Piano Concerto in E-flat major, Op. 70. From a friendly remark he made about the Chinnery family in the letter informing Viotti of this dedication,[27] it is evident that the pianist was one of the musicians who visited the Chinnerys with Viotti during these years. He may even have made the transcription of the *John Bull* concerto with Margaret Chinnery in mind, and have listened to her perform it.

Therefore not only did Viotti not lose his musical skills during the five months of 1793 that he did not touch the violin, but his playing clearly gained in passion and soul, which were, according to all the reviewers, the very hallmarks of his musical genius. The power and emotion detectable in his playing and his music on his return from the Continent gives credence to his friend Eymar's statement that for a musician to be able to put life into his playing and his compositions he must possess 'a heart that is wracked alternately by the tenderest affections and the most ardent passions, never knowing any rest.'[28] This description fits Viotti to a tee.

Viotti was a consummate performer, polished and confident. But the glamorous persona portrayed by the above newspaper reviews is very much at odds with the private one revealed in his letters to the Chinnerys. Viotti's misanthropic humour continued for months after his return from the Continent. In February 1794, wishing to send gifts to his friends in Ghent, he wrote to William, who was to frank the packages at the Treasury, 'I imagine that the small gifts that I wish to send to Ghent have not yet been delivered to you. Let us wait for them with all the patience that is needed in this miserable universe. I am only too aware of how much one needs resignation!'[29]

---

[27] Dussek to GBV, 26 May 1810, NYPL JOB 97-52, item 16.

[28] 'un cœur qui, tantôt tourmenté par les affections les plus tendres, et tantôt dévoré par les plus fougueuses passions, ne connaisse jamais de repos' (Eymar, *Anecdotes sur Viotti*, p. 5).

[29] 'j'imagine qu'on ne vous a pas encore porté les petits cadeaux que je veux envoyer à Gant. Attendons les avéc patience, il en faut dans ce miserable univers et je sens bien combien il faut de la resignation!' (GBV to MC, 13 February 1794, PHM 94/143/1 – 2/16).

CHAPTER 6

# Letters from Bath, 1794

The absence of Viotti in Salomon's tenth concert of 1794 was probably due to the fact that he had only three days earlier returned from Bath, where he had performed at Rauzzini's famous Passion Week concerts. An account of these is given in a series of seven letters dated 16–25 April 1794 from Viotti to Margaret Chinnery in the Powerhouse Museum CFP collection. Noted by Kenneth James in his *Concert Life in Eighteenth Century Bath*,[1] these Viotti concerts have gone unnoticed by all Viotti's biographers.

Two letters in the series bear the date 1793, but it is clear that Viotti has wrongly dated them. The letter from Bath which seems to be the earliest is dated 'Bath ce 17. avril jeudi Santo 1793'. Several anomalies become immediately obvious. Firstly, the 17 April was not a Thursday in 1793. It was not even Easter, since the newspapers of that year report that Easter fell between 21 March and 4 April. Secondly, Viotti was at this time performing in Salomon's Hanover Square concerts, which began on 7 February and continued weekly until 2 May 1793, with the exception of Passion and Easter weeks. As final proof that Viotti was not in Bath for the Easter concerts of 1793 there are the Bath newspaper announcements for the Passion and Easter week concerts of that year, which make no mention of Viotti. The *Bath Herald and General Advertiser* of 23 March 1793 announces Viotti's colleague Janiewicz as the featured violinist.

The substitution of 1794 for 1793 makes the day of the week correspond to the date, and proves that the 17 April was indeed 'jeudi Santo'. Moreover, when the two '1793' letters are slotted in chronological sequence into the 1794 letters from Bath, immediate sense is made of Viotti's first remark in the opening sentence of the 17 April letter regarding some tickets that Margaret has sent him. These are mentioned in Viotti's letter of 16 April 1794, and appear to be tickets to Salomon's benefit concert in London, which was to take place on Wednesday 28 May. Salomon must have wanted Viotti to try to sell them in Bath, but Viotti is not optimistic about his chances of success:

> I think it is useless for Salomon to send me the tickets. From what I can tell, no one will ask me for any, and it would be impossible for me to offer a quarter of one to anyone. However if he intends to send them to me let him do so. I shall have enough space to bring them back.[2]

---

[1] Unpub. Ph.D. diss., University of London, 1987.

[2] 'Je pense qu'il est inutile que Salomon m'envoye les billets. A vüe de Pays, il me semble que personne ne m'en demandera, et il me seroit de toute impossibilité d'en offrir le quart d'un à qui que ce soit; laissé le faire cependant si son intention est de me les expedier,

The letter dated '17 April 1793' begins with a tender acknowledgement of Margaret's letter, indicating the depth of his affection for his protectress. It is clear that he eagerly awaits the arrival of her letters:

> I have just this minute received the tickets and your letter, my dear good Amica. It is always between eleven and twelve midday that I receive what you are kind enough to send me. Therefore that is my favourite time of day. All the other pleasant happenings in my life are insipid.[3]

As Viotti was one of the featured soloists in the Hanover Square concerts in 1794, his visit to Bath had to be fitted in between the ninth concert (7 April) and the eleventh (5 May), in which he was due to perform. Easter and Passion Weeks fell in this period, which was long enough to give Viotti time to travel to Bath and spend nearly two weeks in that city. Viotti's first letter from Bath, dated 16 April, shows that he arrived on the 12th:

> I cannot believe that only four days have passed since I saw you, Amica. It feels as though it has been at least a month, but it is true that the fourth day is not yet over! Ah how time drags, and how carefully it conceals its wings when truly good friends are separated![4]

Once the letters are in correct sequence, they give a colourful vignette of the 1794 Bath Passion Week concerts and their attendant social activities. It is thanks to Margaret Chinnery's insistence that Viotti give a full account of his concerts and activities in Bath that we owe the informative detail of these letters. Once again it is unfortunate that no letters from Margaret's side of this correspondence have been preserved.

Viotti was in Bath at the invitation of Venanzio Rauzzini, the Italian *castrato* who had come to London in 1774 to perform in the Italian opera at the King's Theatre. Three years later he had retired to Bath where he instigated the highly successful Bath concerts at the New Assembly Rooms. There were three concert series throughout the year – in winter, at Easter, and the most popular of all in autumn. The music presented at these concerts was of a consistently high standard, and Rauzzini was able to attract world class musicians. Viotti's own music had first been heard in Bath in December 1789 when young George Bridgetower

---

j'aurai assés de place pour les rapporter' (GBV to MC, 16 April 1794, PHM 94/143/1 – 2/17).

3 'Je reçois à l'instant ma chere, ma bonne amica les billets et votre lettre, c'est toujours entre onze heures et midi que je reçois ce que vous avés la bonté de m'envoyer, aussi c'est ma plus belle heure de la journée, toutes les autres belles choses qui m'arrive[nt] sont toutes insipides' (GBV to MC, 17 April 1793 [*recte* 1794], PHM 94/143/1 – 2/1).

4 'Je ne peux pas me persuader amica qu'il n'y ait que quatre jours que je ne vous ai vüe, il me semble qu'il y a un mois au moins; cependant il est bien vrai que le quatrieme n'est pas même passé encore! Oh que le tems est décrépit, et qu'il cache soigneusement ses ailes quand de veritables et bons amis se separent!' (GBV to MC, 16 April 1794, PHM 94/143/1 – 2/17).

performed one of his concertos. It continued to be heard regularly at Rauzzini's concerts throughout the 1790s, performed by both professional musicians and by *amateurs*, and his concertos were also performed between acts in Bath theatre productions.[5]

The fashionable spa that Bath was in the eighteenth century made it a favourite resort for London's high society. A perusal of the *Bath Herald and General Advertiser*'s column listing the visitors who came to Bath in those years in search of health and pleasure reveals names of some of the leading lights in fashion, not only of Britain, but also of Europe. In 1791 Madame de Genlis had brought the daughter of the Duc d'Orléans here, along with her other female charges. It was the favourite haunt of politicians, military officers, clerics, actors and musical artists alike, and in the last decade of the eighteenth century it was largely music that made it so.

Rauzzini had enjoyed success as a performer on the Continent and in London, and was a highly respected teacher, counting among his pupils the English singers Michael Kelly, Nancy Storace and John Braham. According to the testimony of more than one of his contemporaries, Rauzzini was 'proverbially handsome' and extremely personable. Michael Kelly, who in his *Reminiscences* makes much of his good looks and good humour, says that Rauzzini was 'beloved and respected' by the inhabitants of Bath, and that he was so well liked by his musical colleagues, that they willingly gave their services to him *gratis*:

> I have known Mrs Billington [the most popular female singer on the London stage at that time] renounce many profitable engagements in London, when Rauzzini has required the aid of her talents, and at her own expense, travel to Bath, and back to London, as fast as four horses could carry her, without accepting the most trifling remuneration. The singers engaged at the King's Theatre were always allowed by the proprietors to give him their gratuitous assistance.[6]

This is not to say that Rauzzini took advantage of his colleagues. The takings from the Bath concerts were meagre, the subscription tickets being very moderately priced, and he supplemented his income by giving singing lessons. The hospitality Rauzzini provided to visiting musicians was legendary. To counter criticism levelled at him for his over-fondness of company, causing him severe financial difficulties, the oboist William Parke wrote in his defence:

> Rauzzini was compelled by circumstances to entertain a number of popular singers and musicians, who came to Bath to serve him, and for which they received little, or perhaps no other remuneration. Indeed no man less respected than Rauzzini was, could have carried on these concerts, and have produced them as he did, a succession of singers of the first eminence, at a subscription amounting to no more than about two shillings and ninepence per night! being less than a third of those at the concerts in London.[7]

---

[5] See James, *Concert Life in Eighteenth Century Bath*, p. 1016.

[6] Kelly, *Reminiscences*, p. 234.

[7] *MM*, vol. 2, p. 54.

One of the eminent musicians who was entertained by Rauzzini in Bath was Haydn, who went there four months after Viotti in August 1794, accompanied by the Irish flautist Andrew Ashe and the Italian violinist, singer and composer Giambattista Cimador. Haydn recorded in his Notebook that Rauzzini was 'a very nice and hospitable man. His summer house, where I stayed, is situated on a rise in the middle of a most beautiful neighbourhood, from which you can see the whole city.'[8] Viotti also was shown hospitality by Rauzzini, and like countless musicians before him was affected by his charm, agreeing to go beyond his stipulated contract and give four concerts instead of two. In his letter of 17 April he tells Margaret: 'As far as Rauzzini is concerned, I found him to be such a good honest man that I promised to play four times instead of twice, as we had agreed.'[9]

Because of his busy schedule of rehearsals and recitals it was not until Viotti had been in Bath almost a week that he was free to explore the countryside:

> I cannot yet tell you about the country around Bath, as I have not yet been outside the city. But I have had a look around the city and can pronounce myself very happy with it. It is built in the shape of an amphitheatre, all in stone, with many crescent shaped areas that give it a very pretty air. I spend my time rehearsing in the mornings and performing in the evenings. On Friday I shall be at liberty. I shall take a horse and roam all over the countryside and report what I have seen. What joy this excursion would give me if a certain lady of my acquaintance, who rides very well, who even knows dressage, and always likes to gallop, were to accompany me! How beautiful I would find everything! Instead of which, I already know that my outing will be marred by desires and regrets. That is almost always how life is. Happy are those who are able to employ their time in a way that gives least cause for regret.[10]

In the event Viotti was received by Rauzzini on Good Friday at Perrymead,[11] at the same country house where Haydn was to stay. Viotti's description of the elevation of the location matches Haydn's, although it is expressed in rather more lyrical terms:

---

[8] Cited in Landon, p. 266.

[9] 'Pour ce qui regarde Rauzzini je l'ai trouvé si bon homme si honnête que je lui ai promis de jouer quatre fois au lieu de deux comme nous en etions convenus' (GBV to MC, 17 April 1793 [*recte* 1794], PHM 94/143/1 – 2/1).

[10] 'Je ne puis pas encore vous parler des environs de Bath, je ne suis point sorti de la ville, j'ai parcourû celle ci cependant et j'en suis fort content. elle est bâtie en espece d'Amphitheatre, toute en pierre avéc beaucoup de Places en Croissants qui font un trés joli effet. Je passe ma vie à repeter le matin et à jouer le soir. Vendredi je n'aurai rien à faire. Je mont[e]rai à cheval je courrerai par tout et vous rendrai compte de ce que j'aurai vû. Comme cette promenade me feroit plaisir, si une certaine Dame de ma Connoissance, qui monte trés bien à Cheval, qui sçait les dresser même, et qui aime à toujours gallopper, étoit avéc moi! Comme je serois disposé à trouver tout bien! Au lieu de cela ma promenade se passera j'en suis sûr d'avance à desirer, et à regreter. C'est presque toujours ainsi que la vie s'écoule, heureux ceux qui savent l'employer de maniere à avoir le moins d'occasion possible de regreter le tems perdû' (GBV to MC, 16 April 1794, PHM 94/143/1 – 2/17).

[11] Woodbine Cottage, Perrymead, just outside the city boundary at Widcombe.

> Yesterday I spent all my time in a cottage in the country, or rather in the garden adjoining it, that belongs to Mr Rauzzini. I left the town all alone at one o'clock. I took a country path lined with all kinds of trees laden with flowers. This path rises gently and leads to a sort of forest that crowns a hill looking down on the entire city. It was there that I stopped to contemplate beautiful Mother nature and her inconceivable creator.[12]

The dates of Rauzzini's Easter concerts, at all of which Viotti performed, were 15, 16, 17 and 19 April, as shown by his letters and by the *Bath Herald and Register* announcement of 5 April 1794. This announcement also listed the principal vocal performers and the principal instrumental performers, with a reminder at the end that 'The Performers of the Band and Chorus are requested to attend the Rehearsals every day at twelve o'clock precisely.' Viotti was advertised as: 'The much celebrated Mr. VIOTTI, who will play a CONCERTO on the VIOLIN every evening.' Rauzzini was taken to task by the *Bath Chronicle* of 20 November 1794 for referring to Viotti by the over-used epithet of 'much celebrated', saying that his description was 'rather more suited to a fair-ground artist or a Punch and Judy performer', and asserting that Viotti's merits were too great for such 'trite encomiums'.[13]

No reviews of the concerts exist in any of the Bath newspapers, but Viotti's own impressions are given in his letters to Margaret. On the day after the first concert he wrote in typical understatement: 'Last night I played a concerto. I carried it off moderately well, and I received the impression that the audience, which was very large, was satisfied.'[14] But by the end of the third concert he was disenchanted with the English lack of emotion and gave Margaret the following account of the frigid response to a supposedly successful concert:

> Yesterday I performed for the third time. I was moderately pleased with myself. People said that I had great success, but I assure you, Amica, that I was completely unaware of it. They have a strange way of showing it, you must agree! I confess to you my dear Margaritina that I cannot accustom myself to this cursed coldness. In truth I am more inclined to believe that your dear compatriots are ignorant logs than to allow them, as they will have, any deep sensibility. It is very fortunate that I have a decided passion for music, and that I love it for its own sake and for mine, otherwise I think I would very soon lose my taste for it.[15]

---

[12] 'J'ai passé hier tout mon tems à la campagne dans une maisonette, ou plutot dans le jardin qui en depend appartenant à M$^{r}$ Rauzzini. Je suis sorti de la ville à une heure tout seul, j'ai passé par un chemin champêtre bordé d'arbres de toutes especes et chargés de fleurs. Ce chemin va en montant et conduit à une espece de forée qui couronne une montagne de la quelle on domine sur toute la ville. C'est la ou je me suis arreté pour contempler cette belle nature et son inconcevable auteur' (GBV to MC, 19 April 1794, PHM 94/143/1 – 2/19).

[13] Cited in James, *Concert Life in Eighteenth Century Bath*, p. 1015.

[14] 'J'ai joué hier au soir un concerto, je m'en suis tiré passablement, et il m'a parû que la compagnie qui étoit très nombreuse, a été sattisfaite' (GBV to MC, 16 April 1794, PHM 94/143/1 – 2/17).

[15] 'J'ai joué hier pour la 3$^{me}$ fois, j'ai été passablement content de moi: on dit que j'ai

This was another aspect of public performing that frustrated Viotti and added to his aversion to the public in general. It was quite a different experience from the one he had had in Paris. In France things were as they seemed. In England they were not. A lack of enthusiasm in England did not necessarily equate with a lack of appreciation, but it was no less frustrating for that. Being a self-confessed warm-blooded Italian, whose feelings were in his own words 'brullante'[16] (ardent), it took Viotti a long while to become accustomed to the phlegmatic English temperament, and to come to appreciate the other virtues of the stolid John Bull.

Viotti does his best to provide the details of Bath life that Margaret wants, but he misses the company of the Chinnerys, and not yet having shaken off his melancholy from his voyage on the Continent, is in no mood to enjoy himself:

> You desire to know what I am doing. Alas I am leading a very gloomy existence, in spite of having everything at my disposal to make it pleasant. I made many acquaintances after the first concert. It is the custom here to gather together in a large room after the music to chat and to take tea. That is very agreeable for someone who is able to enjoy it, but I, who am something of a bear, am always in a hurry to leave.[17]

But he does meet one lady who earns his approval:

> However when I have finished my letter I shall call on a lady by the name of Miss Browne, a great patron of Janiewicz, and one of the elegant ladies of these parts. She and her mother have been overwhelmingly kind to me. As early as the first rehearsal they begged that I would send them four dozen tickets to my benefit concert. Such kind enthusiasm is worth the effort of delivering them myself, is it not?[18]

---

beaucoup de succés, je vous assure Amica que je ne m'en apperçois pas du tout. Ils ont une singulière maniere de le témoigner il faut en convenir! Je vous avoue ma chere Margaritina que je ne saurois m'accoutumer à cette maudite froideur, en verité je suis plus porté à croire vos chers compatriotes des buches, des ignorans, que de leur accorder comme ils le pretendent une sensibilité concentrée. Il est bien heureux que j'aye une passion décidée pour la musique, que je l'aime pour elle même et pour moi, sans cela je sens que le gout m'en passeroit bien vite' (GBV to MC, 18 April 1794, PHM 94/143/1 – 2/18).

[16] GBV to MC, 21 April 1793 [*recte* 1794], PHM 94/143/1 – 2/2.

[17] 'Vous desirés savoir ce que je fais. Helas je mêne une vie fort maussade tout ayant de quoi la passer fort agréablement. J'ai fait beaucoup de connoissances après le premier concert. L'usage est ici de se rassembler après la musique dans une grande salle pour causer et prendre du Tea. cela est fort agréable pour quelqu'un qui sait en jouir, mais moi qui suis un peu ours je suis toujours pressé de m'en aller' (GBV to MC, 17 April 1793 [*recte* 1794], PHM 94/143/1 – 2/1).

[18] 'J'irai cependant quand j'aurai fini ma lettre chés une nommée Miss Browne grande protectrice de Yanniewiz et une des élégantes de ce pays ci. Elle et sa mere m'on[t] comblé d'honnetetés; elles m'ont prié dès la première repetition de leur envoyer quatre douzaines de billets de mon benefice. Cet Empressement aimable vaut bien la peine que je les leur apporte moi même n'est-ce pas' (*Ibid.*).

The Miss Browne mentioned in the above letter was the daughter of the Hon. Mrs Browne, of no. 3 Burlington Street, Bath. Her father was probably Abraham Browne, an eminent violinist in the 1750s, who had been leader of the king's band and later music director of Ranelagh Gardens. She and her mother were great patrons of visiting musicians, and Miss Browne herself was an accomplished *amateur*, who sang in one of Rauzzini's 1793–94 winter concerts. Haydn also met Miss Browne on his visit to Bath, and describes her in his Notebook as 'a charming person of the best *conduit*; a good pianoforte player, her mother a most beautiful woman.'[19]

In his following letter, dated 18 April, Viotti gives an account of his visit to Miss Browne's. He is agreeably surprised to find that she is not like a typical Englishwoman, but is warmer and more forthcoming. It was fortunate, he claimed, that there were some charitable, sensible members of society, otherwise one would be tempted to 'aller se pendre' (go and hang oneself). However he persists in his damning judgement of the majority of the Bath set, and compares them unfavourably with his friends who live in Mortimer Street, saying that they are all foolish and insipid compared to the Chinnerys. In his typically self-deprecating style Viotti refers to himself as 'le racleur' (the fiddler). Viotti's modesty, both on stage and off, would have appealed to the English, who, according to Parke, did not like pretension in their performing artists. In Parke's opinion, 'For artists to feel proud of their successful exertions is natural; but [...] they should wear their "blushing honours" with grace, and receive them with due humility.'[20] A decade earlier Viotti had impressed his first Paris audience with this same trait. Fétis, too, claimed that Viotti never sought 'l'éclat de la vogue' (to be the height of fashion).[21]

By the end of his stay Viotti was obliged to revise his initial harsh opinion of the Bath women, and in his last letter he wrote:

> I have already made the acquaintance of many people, and people much more likeable than I had at first believed. Of course I am referring to the female sex, for as for men, I do not know what their habits are. But why don't these cursed women show themselves immediately for what they are, instead of presenting faces of marble on first meeting?[22]

Viotti dismisses the men out of hand. It is only the women who interest him, but he would prefer them to be warm from the start like his favourite, Margaret Chinnery, and thinks they would do well to take lessons from her in order to acquire some of her charming and engaging manners.[23]

---

[19] Landon, p. 267; *Bath Chronicle*, 27 February 1794.

[20] *MM*, vol. 1, p. 301.

[21] *FétisB*, vol. 8, p. 470.

[22] 'J'ai déja connû beaucoup de monde, et du monde beaucoup plus aimable que je n'avois crü d'abord, bien entendu du monde femme, car hommes, oh ceux la je ne scais pas ce qu'ils font. Mais pourquoi ces maudites femmes ne se montrent-elles pas tout de suitte ce qu'elles sont, au lieu de se présenter avéc un visage de marbre au premier abord?' (GBV to MC, 23 April 1794, PHM 94/143/1 – 2/20).

[23] *Ibid.*

Viotti's benefit concert was announced in the *Bath Herald and Register* on Saturday, 19 April 1794:

NEW ASSEMBLY-ROOMS
Mr. VIOTTI most respectfully informs the
Public, that his BENEFIT CONCERT will
be on *Wednesday next*, April 23, 1794.

Tickets 5s. each, to be had at his lodgings, No. 1,
Princes-street, Queen-square, Libraries, Pump-room,
Lintern's Music shop, and New Rooms.
To begin at half past seven o'clock.

On 23 April Viotti writes to Margaret that the day of his benefit has finally arrived and he has much to do, but he is extremely happy because he will soon be back in London. He counts on receiving another two letters from Margaret, which he calls riches that will do his heart good. Although he thinks his benefit will be well attended, he does not expect to take big profits:

> Everyone is coming to the concert this evening, but in spite of that I do not think I will make my fortune. The season is too advanced for Bath. There is not one tenth of the number of visitors that there are in autumn. That does not matter, as long as it is soon over.[24]

Nor were the tickets priced to yield handsome profits, judging from the above notice. Viotti's observation tallies with Haydn's, who writes in his Notebook in August of the same year:

> The city is not thickly populated, and in Summer one sees very few people; for the people taking the baths don't come till the beginning of October, and stay through half of February. But then a great many people come, so that in the year 1791, 25,000 persons were there.[25]

In his letter of 23 April Viotti mentions a very grand supper that he attended at the home of a Mr Alexander and his two daughters, whom he had met in Paris. There were 100 guests invited, and after the French fashion, card games were played. Viotti enjoyed this evening, as it reminded him of France and French customs.

In an earlier letter Viotti had asked Margaret to thank Libon for what was probably an offer to come to Bath to assist at his master's benefit, perhaps to lead the orchestra while Viotti performed his concerto. It says much for the standard of the Bath orchestra that Viotti was able to decline the offer of his famous pupil. As can be seen from the number of rehearsal reminders inserted in the Bath

---

[24] 'Tout ce monde vient au concert ce soir, malgré cela je ne crois pas que je m'enrichirai beaucoup. La saison est trop avancée pour Bath, il n'y a pas la 10^me^ partie du monde qu'il y a en Automne. Ce ne fait rien pourvû que cela passe vite' (*Ibid.*).

[25] Cited in Landon, p. 266.

newspapers, the 150 members of the orchestra put in a lot of practice for these concerts, and under the directorship of Rauzzini it came to be known as the leading provincial orchestra outside London.[26] Viotti writes to Margaret: 'If you see Libon thank him for his thoughtfulness and his offers. If the orchestra had been very bad I would have accepted, but not only is it not bad, it is almost good.'[27] Libon would appear the following year in London concerts with his master and with Haydn.

It was considered a mark of friendship among the musical fraternity to perform at each other's benefit concerts. The favour was understood to be mutual, which is why there was indignation when Madame Mara allegedly did not return the favour for Viotti in Paris in 1782.[28] It was an occasion to put personal jealousies aside to enable the concert-giver to gain maximum financial profit. Salomon performed at Viotti's benefit in 1793, and Viotti returned the favour for his friend the same year. Viotti also led the band at Salomon's benefit in 1794, and performed at Haydn's benefit concerts in both 1794 and 1795.

Among the other invitations that Viotti received in Bath, was one from a 'Mr Tâte', perhaps William Tate the portrait painter, who exhibited at the Royal Academy in London, but who lived in Bath during the last years of his life, about this time. Viotti says in his letter of 17 April that he has accepted an invitation from that gentleman and his daughter to go to dinner and supper at their home whenever it pleased him, and it pleased him to go the following evening (Good Friday). On Easter Sunday he has accepted an invitation from a lady whose name he cannot remember.[29]

In his letter to Margaret of 18 April Viotti makes a cryptic remark about Haydn, who had by then been in London for two months:

> You did well to demand the sonatas from Papa Haydn. The way in which he went about handing out manuscripts to all and sundry when he should have offered them to you first is something that has always been on my chest. I have always meant to complain to him about it.[30]

Why should Haydn have given his manuscripts to Margaret before any other? Did he owe her any favours? Was Haydn one of the eminent musicians who played at the Chinnery concerts? In this case it is especially regrettable that Margaret's letters to Viotti are lost, as they might have thrown some light on the subject.

---

[26] *Bath Chronicle*, 20 November 1794.

[27] 'Si vous voyés Libon remerciés le de son attention et de ses offres, si l'Orchestre avoit été bien mauvais, je les aurois acceptées, mais non seulement il est passable mais il est presque bon' (GBV to MC, 17 April 1794, PHM 94/143/1 – 2/1).

[28] See Bachaumont, 29 April 1782, vol. 20, p. 211. Bachaumont's claim that Mara was jealous of Viotti seems dubious in view of the fact that in London they were clearly on the best of terms.

[29] GBV to MC, 17 April 1793 [*recte* 1794], PHM 94/143/1 – 2/1.

[30] 'Vous avés bien fait d'exiger des Sonates de ce Papa Haydn, c'est une chose que j'ai toujours eû sur le cœur, de le voir donner au tiers et au quart des manuscrits qu'il auroit dû offrir à vous la premiere. C'est un reproche que je comptois bien lui faire' (GBV to MC, 18 April 1794, PHM 94/143/1 – 2/18).

Margaret Chinnery must certainly have been on good terms with Haydn to have been in a position to demand manuscript music from him. Viotti attributes his unthinking behaviour not to any malice, but to the fact that he is German(!): 'Although this kindly old gentleman is a very great genius he seems to have very little tact or judgement. What do you expect? He lurches along in the German way, and whoever happens to be in his path gets it [the music].'[31] However he bears Haydn no real ill will, as at the end of the same letter he sends his regards to 'Papino', using his own affectionate version of the popular sobriquet 'papa Haydn'. In the same letter Viotti speaks of Salomon. As with his comments on Haydn, his remarks are in answer to something Margaret has said in her letter, and are rather flippant. It appears that Salomon has been discussing Viotti with Margaret. Viotti suspects him of jealousy:

> Why does Salomon talk about me so much? Is he in love with me?... how foolish I am to even ask you why. As if I do not already know the answer! If his anguish were real he would indeed be pitiable. If I were him, instead of giving way to jealousy I would work until I had just as much skill as the next fellow.[32]

These six letters from Bath, and one from London, open a window on musical life in Bath in 1794, and corroborate Viotti's contemporaries' assertions about his sensitive nature, his distrust of the public, his love of nature and his faithfulness in friendship. But more than anything else, it is the last characteristic that emerges as the most striking feature of the letters. Viotti's devotion to the Chinnerys dominates all other topics. In every letter he desires to be told of the activities of his friends, of their health, whether the children speak of him, and unfailingly extends these enquiries to Margaret's two sisters, who are frequently with them. His affection for George, now aged three, is particularly strong, and it is evident that it is in these early years that the quasi-paternal bond that was to last for life was forged. In his letter of 16 April he regrets that in two (missing) earlier letters from Bath he disappointed George by not mentioning him at greater length, but says by way of reparation: 'Give the good little fellow a thousand hugs from me. I am extremely impatient to see him again, and to show him that I shall always be his best friend.'[33]

Viotti's last week at Bath was spent in eager anticipation of being reunited with the Chinnerys. That he was far happier performing in the intimacy of the

---

[31] 'Il me semble qu'avéc un trés grand Genie ce bon Vieillard a trés peu de tacte et de discernement; que voulés vous il agit à l'almande, par bond et par saut, celui qui se rencontre sur son chemin attrappe' (*Ibid.*).

[32] 'Pourquoi Salomon vous parle-t-il tant de moi? Est-ce qu'il est amoureux de moi?... que je suis bête de vous en demander la raison, est-ce que je ne la sçais pas? Si son tourment étoit réel il seroit bien à plaidre. Moi à sa place, au lieu de me livrer à la jalousie je travaillerois tant jusqu'à ce que j'eusse autant de merite qu'un autre' (*Ibid.*).

[33] 'embrassés le mille fois ce bon petit Enfant, j'ai une impatience extreme de le voir bientôt en etat de sentir que je serai toujours son meilleur ami' (GBV to MC, 16 April 1794, PHM 94/143/1 – 2/17).

Chinnery hearth among friends than in the public arena is evident from all his letters, and especially from his playful blasphemy in a letter appropriately dated 'Vendredi Le S$^{t}$' (Good Friday) in which he writes:

> It seems to me that the days have far more than twenty-four hours, and that the hours are filled with minutes that drag interminably. Surely my exile must finally come to an end! I am looking forward to that moment more impatiently than the Jews await the Messiah. This will not have been a Holy Week for me but a Satanic Week. May the Great Being pardon my sacrilege. But after all, what has He to pardon me for? He knows He has given me a sensitive heart which can only be nourished by friendship, and which is ill at ease away from his friends.[34]

Early on the morning of Friday 25 April Viotti was back in London writing Margaret a hurried note announcing his return. Bath was a 12-hour coach journey from London. The Bath newspapers advertised two post coach services to London daily, one departing each morning at six o'clock, and one in the afternoon at five o'clock, both 'with Four Horses all the Way', and both departing from the White Hart Inn and Tavern, and arriving at the Golden Cross, Charing Cross. Viotti took the Thursday overnight coach, hoping he would not have to share the coach with a 'cracheur' (spitter) as he had done on his recent journey from Dover.[35] In his letter of the previous day he had written eagerly to Margaret: 'Tomorrow it will be I who shall accompany all the world's letters on the road', and hoped for a letter from her before the coach left at five.[36] The brief letter of the 25$^{th}$ betrays his burning impatience to see Margaret again. In fact he is so eager to see her that he is bathed, coiffed and dressed, ready to fly to the Chinnery home long before she has even woken:

> It is no longer from Bath, but from London that I am writing, my dear good Amica, to tell you that thanks to Heaven, to a good coach and good horses, I am no longer far away from you. I am coiffed, dressed and ready to fly to my friends' house. I am only waiting for you to be awake, for I am sure you are still asleep. Tell me when that fortunate hour may be, but above all let me not come before you are quite ready and in your little drawing room. If I came before that I would get too impatient waiting for you. My God, what happiness![37]

---

[34] 'il me semble que les jours ont beaucoup plus de vingt quatre heures, et que les heures sont remplies de minutes qui s'ecoulent d'une lenteur insupportables. Il faudra bien que mon exile finisse à la fin! J'attens ce moment avéc bien plus d'impatience que les juifs attendent le Messia. Ce ne sera pas une semaine sainte que j'aurai passé mais une semaine diabolique. Le Grand Etre me pardonnera bien mon impiété, mais plutôt qu'a-t-il à me pardonner lui qui sait qu'il m'a donné un cœur sensible qui ne se nourrit que d'Amitié, qui est mal à l'aise loin de ses Amis?' (GBV to MC, 18 April 1794, PHM 94/143/1 – 2/18.)

[35] GBV to MC, 21 April 1793 [*recte* 1794], PHM 143/1 – 2/2.

[36] 'Demain ce sera moi qui accompagnerai sûr la route les lettres de tout le monde' (GBV to MC, 23 April 1794, PHM 94/143/1 – 2/20).

[37] 'Ce n'est plus de Bath c'est de Londre que je vous écris ma chere bonne Amica, pour vous dire que grace au Ciel, une bonne voiture et de bons cheveaux je ne suis plus loin de

According to Bath newspaper announcements Viotti was also the featured violinist for Rauzzini's 1794 autumn concerts, but surprisingly there are no letters of this period to be found in the CFP collection. The *Bath Herald and Register* of 8 November 1794 bears an advertisement placed by Rauzzini on 29 October 1794 announcing eight (weekly) subscription concerts to begin Wednesday 12 November in which 'the much-celebrated Mr. VIOTTI is engaged for the greatest number of the Concerts.' However Viotti's name does not appear on a program until the third concert, when it was announced that he would play a concerto.[38] His name is also on the programs of the fourth and sixth concerts.[39]

Janiewicz, who was also in Bath that autumn, had, the *Bath Journal* of 8 December announced, 'with the most friendly good nature' forborne to perform, 'not being the Violin for the season.' With the exception of Miss Parke's benefit, for which Janiewicz led the orchestra (which Viotti had magnanimously not objected to), this was indeed the case. The *Journal* also commented that 'Viotti and Janiewicz are the only two violins of great merit now in England who are on terms of Friendship – their stiles are so very different that neither jealousy nor comparison can exist or be made between them.'[40] Be that as it may, it is clear from these letters that there was no doubt in Viotti's mind as to who possessed the superior talent.

The *Bath Chronicle* of 18 December 1794 announced that Viotti would not play again until Wednesday 24 December, the date of Rauzzini's benefit concert at which was to be performed a 'Grand Selection of Sacred Music'. Viotti was billed to play a concerto in the second act.[41] A review of 'Mr Rauzzini's Sacred Concert on Christmas Eve' was inserted in the *Bath Herald and Register* on 27 December 1794. Each of the vocalists was named and appraised, but not the instrumentalists, who were included in the general encomium at the end of the article as having 'met the approbation of those critical *Amateurs* who abound in this city.'

In October 1794 Viotti had been appointed acting manager of the King's Theatre in London. It would be difficult to believe that he could fulfil his obligations in both places were it not for an announcement that appeared in the *Bath Chronicle* of 18 December 1794 stating that 'when VIOTTI signed his articles as Manager of the London Italian Opera, he had a clause inserted which enables him to fulfil his engagements at Rauzzini's Concerts.' As the violin for the autumn season at Bath, Viotti would have been expected to lead at all the concerts where he was not the soloist, entailing a weekly commitment. It is probable that he travelled to Bath for an overnight stay only, which would explain the lack of

---

vous; Je suis coiffé habillé et pret à voler chés mes amis, je n'attens pour cela que votre reveil, car surement vous dormés encore; faites moi dire cette heure fortunée, mais surtout ne me faites pas aller chés vous sans que vous soyés prête tout à fait dans ce petit salon. Si j'y venois avant je m'impatienterois trop à vous attendre; mon Dieu quel bonheur!' (GBV to MC, 25 April 1794, PHM 94/143/1 – 2/21).

38 *Bath Herald and Register*, 22 November 1794.

39 *Bath Journal*, 1 December 1794 and 29 December 1794.

40 *Bath Journal*, 8 December 1794.

41 *Bath Herald and Register*, 20 December 1794.

correspondence with Margaret Chinnery. Viotti fulfilled his commitment up to the time of Rauzzini's benefit, then departed. Janiewicz took his place for the remaining two concerts.

CHAPTER 7

# The Opera Concert and Chinnery concerts, 1795

1795 would be the busiest year in Viotti's musical career in England. Not only was he acting manager of the King's Theatre for the 1794–95 season, he was also musical director of the newly formed Opera concerts, so called because they took place in the Great Room at the Opera House (King's Theatre). This 'New Room', inaugurated at the beginning of 1794, had been promoted as the largest concert room in England,[1] narrowly defeating the Upper Room at Bath for this honour. A correspondingly large orchestra of at least 60 members would fill it, although this number came nowhere near the size of the Bath orchestra. The Opera Concert took over from the Hanover Square concerts as London's premier concert series following Salomon's temporary retirement as a theatre entrepreneur owing to alleged financial difficulties. Salomon placed an explanatory advertisement in the *Morning Chronicle* stating that the situation on the Continent made it impossible for him to continue to bring talented vocalists to England. He took the opportunity of thanking those who had made his 1794 concerts so successful, especially Haydn, Viotti and 'all the other Professors, who honoured him with their assistance'.[2]

Like Salomon's concerts previously, the Opera Concert featured a mixture of vocal and instrumental music. The *Morning Chronicle* carried the same advertisement for the new concerts right through January, giving the names of the famous artists, with Haydn at the head, (Wilhelm) Cramer as leader of the band, and 'the whole to be under the direction of Mr VIOTTI, who will also occasionally furnish new Pieces of Music.' As director, Viotti was responsible for the selection of performers and music. He also sometimes led the orchestra.

There were to be nine concerts, held fortnightly. Because of the popularity of the series an additional two concerts would be scheduled at the end of the season, making a total of eleven. Viotti featured in only five of the eleven. He was announced in the first additional concert of 21 May, but his place was taken by Salomon on the night.[3] He also performed a concerto at Haydn's benefit (4 May), at Dragonetti's (8 May) and at Ashe's (8 June). The aim of the theatre proprietor, it was stated, was 'to combine the most eminent talents, Vocal and Instrumental, now in England.' Haydn would remain in England until June.

---

[1] *Morning Chronicle*, 25 February 1794.
[2] *Morning Chronicle*, 14 January 1795.
[3] *Morning Chronicle*, 25 May 1795.

Among the new solo performers who joined the concerts this year was the famous Italian soprano Brigida Banti, who had made her London debut in the title role of Francesco Bianchi's *Semiramide* at the King's Theatre in April 1794, in which she sang a Guglielmi air accompanied by a violin *obbligato*, originally played by Cramer and afterwards by Viotti (in 1795 and 1798). There were also her fellow singers from Paris Anna Morichelli and Carlo Rovedino; cellist Christopher Schram; and double bass player Domenico Dragonetti, who had arrived in England in late 1794 accompanied by amateur violinist Gaetano Bartolozzi and by Bianchi himself.

The advertised composers included Muzio Clementi, Martin y Soler, and Banti's composer of choice Francesco Bianchi, who all bravely consented to have their new compositions aired alongside Haydn's. Most of these artists would have a close association with Viotti and with the Chinnerys. According to Salomon the musical talent that the Opera Concert united was: 'such an assemblage as no Country in the World can now exhibit'.[4] Viotti was equal to the task of directing all this talent, and performed his duties to the satisfaction of all, according to intermittent comments in the *Morning Chronicle*, one of which stated: 'The selection for last Monday evening, was made with that happy discrimination which the director, Viotti, has shewn through the whole course of these Concerts.'[5]

Nevertheless it cannot have been easy for Viotti to juggle his administrative and musical duties. If Viotti's experience in 1814 and 1815 as a director of the Philharmonic concerts is any indicator, in his administrative role he must have been swamped with applications for free tickets from both the public and from fellow musicians. For example when Haydn wanted a free ticket to Banti's benefit in December 1794 it was to Viotti that he turned.[6] A *c.*January 1795 letter from Margaret to William Chinnery shows the pressure that Viotti was under: 'Amico is forever at the Opera House, & I am convinced from the specimen I had on Saturday night that he has a great deal to do – he desires however to add a word or two for you —'. Viotti takes up, in the impatient tone noticeable in his voice whenever he speaks of the theatres in which he has worked in the capacity of impresario: 'I have just this minute arrived from my great devil of a House. I am very pleased to have arrived in time to remind you not to forget Amico.'[7] From this, and from evidence in the other 1795 letters, it would appear that although Viotti was not yet living with the Chinnerys, he spent all his free time at their Mortimer Street home. The 'specimen' which still needed a great deal of work was clearly one of Viotti's new concertos for the 1795 Opera concerts.

Three new Viotti concertos were announced for the 1795 season, one at the first concert (2 February), one at the seventh (27 April), and one at Ashe's benefit

---

[4] *Morning Chronicle*, 3 February 1795.

[5] *Morning Chronicle*, 15 April 1795.

[6] Haydn to GBV, 19 December 1794, cited in Landon, p. 277.

[7] 'j'arrive dans la minute sortant de ma grande Diable de maison, je suis bien aise d'être arrivé à tems pour vous dire qu'il ne faut pas oublier l'Amico' (MC to WBC, *c.*January 1795, Fisher 2000 – 18/1).

(8 June). The 'specimen' mentioned by Margaret Chinnery was apparently intended for performance at the first concert. Viotti must have found time to complete it successfully, as the day after the first concert, the *Morning Chronicle* of 3 February wrote: 'The new Concerto of Viotti both in composition, execution, and taste, was a capital performance: each movement gave great pleasure, but especially the *adagio*, which, for sweetness of harmony, we have scarcely heard surpassed.'

The *adagio* was, according to a contemporary commentator, 'the grand object of regard with the Composer – equally so with the Performer; it is the *ultimatum* in study and in practice; it is, in either, the summit of perfection, and therefore attained by few'.[8] Viotti was one of the few who attained it, and indeed it was his music and playing that sparked the fashionable preference in London for this slow movement above all others. The *adagio* was the most remarked upon facet of his composition and performance. Fayolle wrote just after his death: 'Nothing could exceed his brilliancy in the *allegro*, but it was in the more difficult *adagio*, in that movement which tries and displays the master, that his powers were unrivalled.'[9]

Viotti's second new concerto was performed at the seventh concert, when the *Morning Chronicle* wrote of 'a new Violin Concerto by Viotti, who played with a degree of power and energy, unexpected even from him (in his hands this little instrument is itself an Orchestra)'.[10] This year Viotti did not give his own benefit, the traditional occasion for presenting a new composition, as a benefit was not written into his contract with the theatre management. But he did perform a new concerto at Ashe's benefit, a fitting occasion, since as it was Haydn's last appearance in England, it attracted intense public interest.

Concerning the concerto Viotti performed at Haydn's benefit, one member of the audience deemed that its musical content was only slight.[11] This may have been his Concerto No. 20, which, it has been proved, was performed (but not necessarily composed) sometime during the 1795 Opera concerts.[12] In arguing for an earlier date of compostion for this concerto, White notes 'the simplicity of the orchestra and of the texture'.[13] The contrast between an earlier Viotti concerto and one composed in close proximity to Haydn, and with an enlarged Opera orchestra, would have been noticeable to a connoisseur. An idea of which of his concertos were popular with his contemporaries is given by Fayolle in 1824: 'Of the compositions of Viotti, those we would principally recommend to the attention of the amateurs of instrumental music, are his concertos in G, in A minor, in D and in E minor.'[14] It is not possible to identify which concertos are meant – except for the

---

[8] *Harmonicon*, vol. 2, no. 16, p. 270, cited in Milligan, *The Concerto*, p. 29.
[9] 'Memoir of Viotti', p. 55.
[10] *Morning Chronicle*, 29 April 1795.
[11] Manuscript notes appended to a hand-bill for Haydn's benefit, cited in Landon, p. 307.
[12] See White's *Thematic Catalogue*, pp. 24, 43.
[13] White, 'Chronology', p. 121.
[14] 'Memoir of Viotti', p. 56.

popular No. 23 in G major – but it is likely, especially since Fayolle was by then living in England, that all are of London origin.

The title pages of certain editions of keyboard arrangements of Viotti violin concertos help identify the concertos Viotti performed in 1795. Viotti's pianist friends Dussek and Hüllmandel both published arrangements of his violin concertos in 1795. Dussek's arrangement of Viotti's Violin Concerto No. 25, announced as having been performed at the Opera Concert in his February 1796 publisher's catalogue, would seem to indicate that it was composed for the 1795 Opera concerts.[15] Similarly, the epithet 'new', which appears on the title page of Hüllmandel's arrangement of Viotti's Violin Concerto No. 20, 'A new grand concerto with accompaniments as performed at the Opera Concert',[16] could be interpreted as indicating that this concerto was also composed in 1795. However this reasoning does have pitfalls. The *British Union-Catalogue* lists an edition of 'Viotti's new grand concerto (in A) as performed at the opera concerts, arranged for the piano forte' by T. Latour, published by Bland and Weller's, London, *c.*1798.[17] This turns out to be an arrangement of Viotti's Violin Concerto No. 9 in A major, certainly not new at the time of the Opera concerts. Here the 'new' clearly refers to the arrangement rather than to the original violin concerto.

Viotti also joined Haydn this year in playing for royalty. The official *St James's Chronicle* of 3 February 1795 reported 'a grand Concert and Supper, at Carlton House' given by the Prince of Wales for his family as well as for 'a select party of the Noblesse of both sexes.' The concert was led by Salomon, and the music consisted chiefly of Haydn's symphonies and a concerto played by Viotti.[18] Having made the acquaintance of the Duke of Cambridge soon after his arrival in England, it is possible Viotti received other invitations to perform before members of the royal family. English society was well aware of his status as a 'gentleman musician', which placed him above the rank and file of London's musical artists. As such he was included rather than excluded from the royal dining table, as can be seen from the large number of such invitations mentioned in the Chinnery letters.

In the second concert (16 February) Viotti played a duet with Salomon, and in the fourth (2 March) Viotti and his pupil Philippe Libon performed a concertante for two violins, both composed by Viotti. In the ninth (18 May) Viotti was again a featured soloist but owing to the lack of a published programme it is not known if he performed a new concerto. The review stated simply that 'VIOTTI, in particular, was never heard to greater advantage.'[19] The reviews of the Viotti–Libon performance were favourable, the *Sun* calling it 'one of the most charming treats of the evening' and praising Libon for cutting a very respectable figure 'even

---

[15] See Milligan, *The Concerto*, p. 136.
[16] *British Union-Catalogue*, ed. E. Schnapper (1957), Butterworths, London, p. 1044.
[17] *Ibid.*
[18] Cited in Landon, p. 283.
[19] *Morning Chronicle*, 21 May 1795.

on so near a comparison with his master.'[20] The *Morning Chronicle* of 3 March 1795 predicted a promising future for Libon:

> Viotti and his scholar, Mr. Libon played a Concertante for the two Violins, which gave great satisfaction. The talents of Viotti are well known; and the youth, his scholar, discovers an ear uncommonly chaste and delicate. His body of tone is not yet sufficient; but it will become more powerful when he gains greater confidence; it scarcely can be more sweet. The Concertante, as a composition, has great merit, and does honour to its author, Viotti.

It was at this fourth concert that Haydn conducted the first performance of his 'Drum Roll' Symphony (No. 103 in E flat), the extended violin solo of which, it has been claimed, was written for Viotti, but which was actually played on the night by Wilhelm Cramer, who led the orchestra that evening.[21]

Viotti's concertos were known in London before his arrival there, and had been performed at the Hanover Square concerts during Haydn's first visit to England in 1791–92, as well as previously at other venues. Significantly, the performers were mostly women or children who had a connection with France.[22] At the 1795 Opera concerts the Swedish violinist Madame Gillberg performed a concerto by Viotti at her benefit on 23 April. Female violinists were not given much credence by the male reviewers, who usually had more praise to offer for their beauty than their playing:

> A Lady of the name of Guilberg […] played a Concerto on the Violin. Her youth and beauty, added to a delicate, though rather feeble tone, a brilliant shake, and great neatness of execution, interested her hearers, who expressed their approbation with repeated plaudits. The Adagio in particular (composed by Viotti, much to his honour) she played in a chaste and charming style.[23]

After the sixth concert, at which Gillberg again performed a violin concerto, the reviewer wrote that in spite of her youth, beauty and delicate playing, 'we should prefer the masculine and matured powers of VIOTTI, or SALOMON.'[24] Nor did male performers think the violin an appropriate instrument for a woman. Louis Spohr made his disapproval quite plain to his new wife, who could play the violin well enough to execute some of Viotti's duos with her husband. He nevertheless dissuaded her from continuing on this instrument, urging her to concentrate on the harp instead.[25]

---

[20] *Sun*, 3 March 1795.

[21] See W. Lister (2001), 'Wilhelm Cramer and the Opera Concert Orchestra: "Damnatio Memoriae"', *ML*, vol. 82, no. 1, p. 78.

[22] For example Mme Gautherot, the *amateur* Mme de Sisley, 12-year-old George Bridgetower, 5-year-old Julian Baux, and Mr Wilson Junior.

[23] *Morning Chronicle*, 24 February 1795.

[24] *Morning Chronicle*, 15 April 1795.

[25] Spohr's *Autobiography*, vol. 1, p. 91.

The English oboist William Parke also demonstrated his bias by remarking that although the Parisian violinist Madame Gautherot displayed great ability, 'the ear, however, was more gratified than the eye by this lady's masculine effort.'[26] Nor was Viotti without prejudice on this subject. While admitting that his compatriot Madame Gerbini was an excellent violinist, the reason he gave for her being so was not flattering: she had a 'masculine strength', and moreover he found her 'as ugly as sin'.[27] It is ironic then that Viotti's concertos found such favour with female performers. Viotti's remark concerning masculine strength is a telling one. Viotti had admired Pugnani's 'exécution mâle' and this was one aspect of his own playing that connoisseurs and colleagues most appreciated. Indeed a 'manly' execution came to be expected of any violinist who undertook to perform a Viotti concerto.[28]

It was during 1794 that the Chinnerys appear to have commenced their regular musical parties in London. Their home at Cavendish Square in the fashionable West End, where they lived for the first six years of their marriage before moving to Waltham Abbey in Essex, was attractive to professional musicians and to London society alike. Margaret's Uncle Henry's [Holland] opposition to their move to the country – Waltham Abbey was 12 miles and a two-and-a-half-hour carriage ride from London – on the grounds that his niece's position in society would be jeopardized[29] indicates just how popular the Chinnerys were in London. There is no doubt that Viotti was the magnet that drew the fashionable world to their doorstep, but the Chinnerys nevertheless had sufficient wealth and *bon ton* to provide the lavish suppers in the form that was expected. Margaret Chinnery played the piano on these occasions and William Chinnery also made his contribution on the cello. His teacher was another gentleman musician, the wealthy John Crosdill.

Margaret was a practised hostess of some considerable finesse, whose skill consisted in assorting like personalities at her parties, and her fluency in French and Italian put all her foreign guests at their ease. The eagerness with which famous musicians, both from England and from the Continent, sought invitations to her parties is remarked on by James Cochrane in his biography of William Spencer at the beginning of the 1835 edition of the latter's *Poems*:

> At the house of his friend Mrs C______y, whom he frequently visited in London, and at Gilwell, Mr. Spencer's taste for music was amply gratified. This lady's repute as a first-rate performer on the piano-forte was very high; and her house was the resort of all those most distinguished for their skill in music. Her daughter, in whom she cultivated this and every other talent, seems to have united in a singular degree, beauty, learning, and accomplishments [...] Every foreigner of eminence in the musical profession was

---

[26] *MM*, vol. 1, p. 120.

[27] 'laide comme le peché' (GBV to WBC, 14 August 1812, PHM 94/143/1 – 14/9).

[28] *AMZ*, 9 March 1808, col. 377.

[29] MC to GRC, 14 [*recte* 15] January 1808, Ch.Ch., MS xlviii, a. 42a, fo 4. Henry Holland (1745–1806) was the fashionable London architect who carried out the first extensions on the Prince of Wales's Carlton House.

> anxious, on his arrival in London, to be introduced to Mrs C______y; so that those who were really fond of music were sure to find it in perfection in her house. There Mr Spencer met Viotti, the first violin player of his day, a very fine composer, and a man of abilities independently of his particular art.[30]

The writer goes on to list the bass Giuseppe Naldi, the contralto Josephina Grassini and the harpist Casimir Baecker as eminent musical artists who were to be met at the home of Mrs Chinnery. There were in fact many more, as the Chinnery letters of these years will show.

There is evidence in the Viotti letters that these concerts took place weekly, on a Wednesday. One of Viotti's letters from Bath, dated [Wednesday] 16 April 1794, makes it clear that it was he who helped Margaret organize them and he who was the star performer. It seems that Margaret was wondering whether to continue the concerts while Viotti was in Bath. Viotti thought his own absence would enable his rivals to enjoy some unaccustomed limelight. Serenely certain of his own superiority, Viotti wrote:

> You do well my good Amica, to hold your musical party a week from today. Too long an interruption might disrupt the regularity of our small parties, and anyway it is not a bad thing to have one without Amico. Salomon's and Janiewicz's light will shine the more brightly for it.[31]

Although Janiewicz and Viotti did not indulge in rivalry, and Salomon also was on good terms with Viotti, it must have been a rare opportunity for these excellent violinists to be heard at a distance from their popular friend. As a testimony to Salomon's ability, the *Morning Chronicle* had written after the second Opera concert: 'The Duo, by VIOTTI and SALOMON, we may safely affirm, could not have been better performed by any other two men existing – perhaps not so well. Masterly as VIOTTI truly is, SALOMON was no less sweet, various, and impressive.'[32] It is obvious from the letter that Janiewicz and Salomon were regular performers at the Chinnery concerts.

The desire to be seen and heard at Margaret Chinnery's musical parties apparently induced would-be guests to abandon other engagements in favour of hers, as shown by Viotti's confession of an indiscretion in one of his early 1795 letters to Margaret:

> I am afraid my dear friends that I have committed an indiscretion. Yesterday I met Bartolozzi and Cimador and told them that you intended inviting them on *Wednesday*. They told me that they were already engaged, but that if they received this invitation

---

[30] 'Biographical Memoir of the Hon. William Robert Spencer', in W.R. Spencer (1835), *Poems*, 2nd edn, Cochrane, London, pp. 59–60.

[31] 'Vous faites bien bonne Amica d'avoir votre musique d'aujourd'hui en huit, une trop longue interruption pourroit peut-être deranger l'ensemble de nos petites parties, et d'ailleurs il n'est pas mal qu'il y ait une sans l'Amico. Le soleil Salomon, et le soleil Yanieviez brilleront mieux' (GBV to MC, 16 April 1794, PHM, 94/143/1 – 2/17).

[32] *Morning Chronicle*, 17 February 1795.

> from you they would throw over their first engagement. Both live at no. 207 Piccadilly. Do as you think best. In any case you might invite them for the evening only.[33]

By the last statement Viotti meant that the pair could, without embarrassment, since it was an established society convention, be invited just for the music after dinner. Giambattista Cimador was an Italian singer and violinist of noble birth who had moved to London in 1791. He was a particular friend of Haydn in England, having accompanied him to Bath the previous year. Gaetano Bartolozzi, son of Francesco Bartolozzi who engraved many of the musicians' benefit concert tickets, was also a friend of Haydn. He married the English pianist and pupil of Clementi, Therese Jansen, in May 1795, and Haydn was a witness at the wedding. Although Viotti's letter is undated, it was certainly written before May 1795, since Bartolozzi was still unmarried and sharing lodgings with Cimador.

It was from among Viotti's musical colleagues at the Opera House that Margaret drew most of the musical talent for her parties. Two of the Opera Concert composers who assisted at the Chinnery concerts were Francesco Bianchi, who had come to London to direct his popular opera *La Vendetta di Nino*, and Muzio Clementi, who along with Haydn pledged new pieces of music for the Opera concerts. Clementi showed his appreciation of the Chinnery hospitality by dedicating three sonatas to Mrs Chinnery, which he published in *c.*1800. In the review of the André (Offenbach) edition of these sonatas in the *Allgemeine musikalischen Zeitung* (advertised in February 1801 as Op. 20, but reviewed as Op. 29) the critic expresses astonishment that such an excellent composer as Clementi should condescend to arrange such mediocre ('mittelmässig') things as Viotti's cello duos(!) But he does concede that the sonatas might furnish entertainment for three players seeking to amuse themselves with something easy, which, unknown to him, seems to be the very purpose for which they were written.[34]

Another who enjoyed the Chinnerys' society was Viotti's Paris friend Dussek, who dedicated a sonata (in B flat, Op. 24) to Mrs Chinnery. This sonata, known as the 'Mrs Chinnery', was a favourite teaching piece of nineteenth-century piano professors until the 1860s, when Dussek compositions started to go out of fashion, according to one English music journal.[35] Dussek, like Clementi, was now involved

---

[33] 'J'ai peur mes chers amis d'avoir commis une indiscretion. J'ai rencontré hier Bartolozzi et Cimadoro, et leur ai dit que vous comptiés les inviter pour *mercredi*. Ils m'ont dit qu'ils étoient engagés mais que s'ils recevoient cette invitation par vous ils enver[r]oient au Diable leur premier engagement. tous les deux demeurent N.° 207 Piccadilly. faites ce que vous voudrés la dessus, en tout cas vous pourriés ne les inviter que pour le soir' (GBV to MC, [early 1795], PHM 94/143/1 – 2/24).

[34] Clementi adapted for pianoforte, violin and violoncello the first book of Viotti's Six duets concertanti for two violoncellos, Op. 6, dedicated to John Crosdill (WIV: 37–42). I thank Michael Kassler for drawing the Chinnery dedication to my attention. See also *AMZ*, 10 June 1801, cols 621–2.

[35] 'Impromptus', *The Musical Standard*, 2 June 1888, p. 343. I thank Frances Barulich of the NYPL (Music Division) for kindly sending me the article.

in a music publishing business in London. His arrangement of Viotti's Concerto No. 25 in A minor was also dedicated to Mrs Chinnery.

Other performers at the Chinnery concerts were Christopher Schram, a cello soloist in the 1795 Opera concerts who earned plaudits for having a good tone, a firm hand, and great musical science;[36] former Théâtre Feydeau vocalists Madame Morichelli and Carlo Rovedino, who were also well reviewed throughout the 1795 season; Domenico Dragonetti, who made such an impact on the British public with his double bass virtuosity, especially his effortless performance of Viotti duets; and Salomon, who, having abandoned his role of impresario, continued to perform as a soloist. With Viotti on such a close footing with Haydn, and in the light of Viotti's comments to Margaret in his letter from Bath 18 April 1794, it is highly probable that he too joined his colleagues in the Chinnery drawing room.

By mid-1795 the Chinnery musical parties had been moved to a Sunday. A letter from Margaret Chinnery to her husband in Bristol, which can be dated *c.*13 July 1795 from the postmark, informs him that:

> Friday & Saturday passed as usual, yesterday we had the Sunday Party, the Morichelli's came, Cimador & Bianchi were absent on account of Colds & Sir Peter Burrel & Mr Bigge were the only People who came in the Evening, Clementi played three or four Sonata's, & certainly I never heard him play so well— they performed the Overture to the Frascatana, twice, & Morichelli sung the two best Airs in the Opera— I do not much think you will see these Morichelli's again, as they propose leaving London on Saturday or very early on Sunday.[37]

As well as being a soloist at the Opera Concert, Madame Morichelli had been engaged by Viotti to perform in the 1794–95 season of the Italian opera at the King's Theatre, where she had received favourable reviews. The season ended on 11 July 1795, and according to the above letter, she and her husband left England shortly afterwards. She had also performed with Viotti in Haydn's benefit concert on 4 May. Clementi, Cimador and Bianchi were all popular composers in London, and in the 1795 Opera concerts Bianchi presided at the harpsichord for the performances of his new works. Muzio Clementi also shared the honour of presiding at the keyboard during this season, but his place at the forefront of London composers was now usurped by Haydn. After this he turned increasingly to teaching and later to music publishing, and would become Viotti's most important London publisher.

Like the professional musicians, members of London's fashionable society were eager to be invited to Margaret's home. Viotti, whom they were always certain of finding there, was just as accomplished a host as he was musician. On this occasion, with William Chinnery away in Bristol, Viotti not only entertained the guests with his playing, but helped with the domestic arrangements for the evening and kept the guests provided with conversation:

---

[36] *Morning Chronicle*, 17 March 1795.

[37] MC to WBC, *c.*13 July 1795, Fisher 2000 – 18/2.

> Amico was all Attention the whole Day, that he took every possible care that I should not have the least Trouble or Difficulty, & was so obliging as to find Conversation at Supper for Sir Peter Burrell until 2 oClock in the Morning when Sir Peter & Mr Bigge took their leave. The Dutchess of Hamilton & Miss Muir sent me their cards last Friday, of course I imagine they mean to be invited for next Sunday, which I shall not fail to do this Evening.[38]

The format of Margaret Chinnery's musical parties was similar to that of the Nobility Concerts, but on a much smaller scale, that is, dinner for a select few, followed by music beginning at about nine, followed by a substantial supper at midnight. The cost of hosting such concerts cannot have been cheap, and William Chinnery was conspicuous in his spending. Indeed when his erstwhile benefactor George Rose was questioned in the House of Commons at the time of William's defalcation in 1812, he testified that after his marriage Chinnery had 'launched into considerable expense, by having a large establishment, giving concerts, which were attended by performers of the first celebrity, and several noblemen.'[39] There is no mention of any payment to musicians in the Chinnery letters, nor does one get the impression of money changing hands from Cochrane's account. It may well have been a case of 'bread-and-butter concerts', as they were termed by the profession.

Bread-and-butter parties are described by William Parke in his *Musical Memoirs* as 'those to which professors of talent are invited to dinner, or to a supper, where a little music is given in a friendly way in the evening. These parties gave birth to benefit concerts; for as the professors so invited could not satisfy their own butchers and bakers by such engagements, they hit on the expedient of taking annual benefits, to afford their exalted friends an opportunity of returning the favour by taking tickets.'[40] In other words, prominent professional musicians were prepared to perform free or for very little at these concerts in order to secure the patronage of what Parke calls the '*haut ton*' at their paying concerts. Unless they were a Haydn or a Catalani[41] these professors were generally not very highly paid. Their benefit concert was the one opportunity of the season they had of taking clear profits, so that it was in their interest to establish a network of wealthy patrons.

Parke makes the comment that Salomon's connections were extensive and that he devoted a great portion of his time to bread-and-butter concerts. The latter must have thought that the Chinnery society was worth cultivating, but Parke did not, as shown by the following anecdote recounted in his *Musical Memoirs*:

> When I played the principal oboe and concertos at Salomon's popular concerts at Hanover Square, in the year 1796, Salomon, on one of the nights said to me, "Mr Chinnery has requested me to say, that he will be glad if you will perform at his concert

---

[38] *Ibid.*

[39] *Gentleman's Magazine* (1812), vol. 82, pt 1, p. 469.

[40] *MM*, vol. 2, pp. 16–17.

[41] Haydn allegedly made 24,000 gulden from his two visits to England, and the popular Italian soprano Angelica Catalani earned over £5,000 in her first season in London.

> on Sunday evening next. You will meet your old friend Crosdill there, Viotti, and myself; and he begged me to add that as it will be on a Sunday night, when there is nothing to do, he will pay you one guinea". Feeling indignant at the proposition, I replied,— "What would you think of me if I were to play for a person so situated in life as Mr. Chinnery is, for one guinea, when you, a brother professor, pay me three?"[42]

It was well known in London that William Chinnery was a wealthy man, and Parke naturally felt he had every right to feel insulted by such parsimony. That he was offered money at all is interesting, probably indicating that he was only a slight acquaintance of the Chinnerys. The above comments were put forward by Parke to refute the commonly held belief that William's deficit in his Treasury accounts was due to 'his extravagant custom of giving concerts'. Parke opined that 'a more absurd reason for his delinquency could not be adduced, because several of the most eminent musicians, Crosdill, Viotti, Salomon, &c, who visited him, received no remuneration whatever.'[43] Parke clearly had no idea of the intimacy of the Viotti/Chinnery friendship.

There certainly were some members of the *haut ton* who took advantage of the professors by inviting them home to supper merely to show them off before their friends. Parke relates the story of the oboist Fischer, who, nettled at being invited to supper and told to bring his oboe, retorted 'My Lord, my oboe never sups!'[44] Perhaps that is the category in which Parke placed the Chinnerys, but there were certainly many others who did not.

---

[42] *MM*, vol. 1, pp. 303–4.

[43] *Ibid.*, p. 303.

[44] *MM*, vol. 2, p. 17.

CHAPTER 8

# Last solo performances and exile, 1796–1798

In the autumn of 1796 the Chinnerys moved out of London to Gillwell House in Essex, for the sake of the education of their children. Because it was impossible for William Chinnery to live so far from Whitehall he retained for a short while a house at 39 Mortimer Street, Cavendish Square where he stayed on week days, coming down to Gillwell on the weekends. Viotti lived close by, and from that date until March 1798 divided his time between London on week days and Gillwell on weekends, as William did. The Chinnerys must have spent some of the first eight months of 1796 converting the former summer residence into a home, and it is hard to imagine Viotti not being on hand to help. This, and the fact that he was already making plans to go into a wine business, would explain his mysterious absence from the performing stage in 1796. The establishment of Viotti's wine business was probably the principal reason for this hiatus in his musical career. Always financially ambitious, Viotti may have tired of his meagre instrumentalist's earnings (£300 as orchestral leader, compared to Banti's £1,400 as principal vocalist),[1] and decided to try to earn back some of his former wealth.

It was apparently at the end of 1796 that Viotti entertained his 'Revolutionary' French friends at the Crown and Anchor Inn, which raised Michael Kelly's eyebrows.[2] The Crown and Anchor at the Strand had a long concert room attached to it, and was home to the Academy of Ancient Music and to the Anacreontic Society, of which Viotti was undoubtedly a member, since he dedicated his Three duets for two violins, Op. 18, to its president Joseph Chaplin Hankey. With aristocratic and wealthy *amateurs* for members, the Anacreontic Society was used as a trial ground for new music, especially Mozart's, whose music remained unheard at the public concerts of this time. Having no public performances scheduled for 1796, Viotti may have spent more time participating in the activities of this semi-private club, and also, perhaps, in composing. Intriguingly, Viotti has been identified as the composer of the music to a new ballet, *Apollon Berger*, premiered at the King's Theatre on 27 September 1796 (revived 1803), and choreographed by the ballet-master Gallet.[3]

---

1 W.C. Smith (1955), *The Italian Opera and Contemporary Ballet in London, 1789–1820*, Headley Bros, London, p. 36.

2 Kelly, *Reminiscences*, p. 222.

3 Smith, *The Italian Opera*, pp. 45, 69. The composition is not listed in White's *Thematic Catalogue*. Gallet is ambiguously identified in the *Morning Chronicle* of 27 September

It was also in 1796 that Viotti signed an agreement with Ignaz Pleyel, the French composer, violinist and pianist who had recently turned music publisher, to sell four of his compositions. One of these was his revised Concerto No. 20 with the new *adagio* movement, which he may have composed in the first half of 1796. The other works sold to Pleyel were his Three trios for two violins and cello, second book (WIII:7–9), and the same trios arranged for pianoforte. Pleyel came to London to conclude the contract, signed on 19 August 1796 at Viotti's residence, which was stated to be at no. 27 Edward Street, Cavendish Square.[4] Returning in early September to Paris, Pleyel met Baillot and made available Viotti's manuscripts to him. On 6 October Baillot wrote to his friend François de Montbeillard: 'We have [...] played some new trios by Viotti, in manuscript, at Pleyel's house, as well as some quartets by the latter. He has promised us other new works, which have whetted our appetite.'[5]

A letter from Margaret at Gillwell to William at 39 Mortimer Street, which appears to date from early 1797, shows that she expected both her 'beaux' to travel down to Gillwell on weekends together: 'As I was sitting here in the little Music Room last night expecting you, I was much surprised to see Amico come in alone, he gave me your Pacquet & told me *his* coming had been very doubtful, I am glad he did come, for as I fully expected you I should have thought something extraordinary indeed must have occurred to have prevented either of you from coming down'. A comment in the same letter would suggest that Margaret was planning a special dinner on Sunday evening, probably with music. William had been sequestered at the Treasury office working on the Budget when Margaret wrote: 'Amico is complaining bitterly of your confinement, & I doubt whether we should not both, at this moment, vote against Mr. P[itt] if we were in the House of Commons. – You will see Amico tomorrow probably & can then make any arrangement you like respecting Sunday's Dinner.'[6]

Another letter of the same period, from Margaret at Gillwell to William at the Treasury Chambers, may be dated from the postmark 1 March 1797. It concerns her removal to town with the children, probably for the concert season. In it Margaret asks him to ensure that 'the children's apartments, except the room where Amico slept' are well aired before their projected arrival. She also gives instructions for the unpacking of some music books that she is sending ahead: 'I should like to have the Books taken out and the Basket returned, but I can only trust *you* or *Amico* to do this for me, & as you will not be at Home you had better call & ask him to take them out for me.'[7]

---

1796 as the ballet's 'composer'.

[4] F. Lesure (1984), 'Deux contrats d'édition de Viotti (1796–1802)', in R. Elvers (ed.), *Festschrift Albi Rosenthal*, Schneider, Tutzing, p. 221.

[5] 'Nous avons [...] fait de nouveaux trios de Viotti, manuscrits, chez Pleyel, ainsi que des quatuors de ce dernier. Il nous a promis d'autres ouvrages nouveaux qui excitent notre appétit' (Baillot to Montbeillard, 6 October 1796, cited in François-Sappey, p. 181).

[6] MC to WBC, [early 1797], Fisher 2000 – 18/3.

[7] MC to WBC, *c.*1 March 1797, Fisher 2000 – 18/4.

The 1797 Opera concerts had commenced on 6 February, and Viotti had been appointed orchestral leader and musical director, replacing his friend Wilhelm Cramer, who had held the position for the previous two seasons. Probably owing to an overall drop in music subscribers the concerts were this year joined to the opera subscription. Salomon had abandoned his short-lived Hanover Square concerts and had come back over to the Opera Concert as a featured soloist with Viotti. Viotti's colleagues Janiewicz and Giornovichi had decided to absent themselves from the competition, and had gone to Ireland with the flautist Ashe to participate in Dublin's fashionable and lucrative concert series, where, it was reported, a Viotti piano concerto (arrangement) was performed by a Dr Clarke at Giornovichi's benefit. There were but few London reviews this year, and the only mention of Viotti was in his capacity as a forceful leader, who gave the orchestra character, and 'rendered it most truly interesting.'[8]

Only five performances by Viotti at the 1797 Opera concerts can be confirmed, owing to the lack of advertised programmes for the sixth and the eighth concerts. He performed a concerto in the first (6 February), the fifth (20 March) and the twelfth (5 June); and a new concerto in the ninth (8 May), which was repeated by popular desire in the tenth (15 May). He also performed a duet with Salomon at the latter's benefit (1 May), and a concerto and another duet at Dragonetti's benefit (29 May). The last was a duet with a difference. It created a stir in the musical world, as it was a violin duet performed with violin and double bass. An account of Viotti's surprise the first time he heard Dragonetti play the violin part on his double bass is given by the Dragonetti biographer Francesco Caffi.[9] Initially believing Dragonetti's offer to take the second violin's part to be a joke, Viotti was in the end overcome with awe at his partner's skill. The public concert for which they were rehearsing was a brilliant success, with the players even changing parts.

Another contemporary who commented on Viotti's admiration for Dragonetti's virtuosity was the celebrated nineteenth-century *salonnière* the Comtesse de Boigne, whose friendship with Viotti and the Chinnerys dated from the early 1800s when she was living in England, and endured until Viotti's final years. She was present at a 'great concert' given by the Portuguese ambassador in London in *c.*1804, at which Viotti and Dragonetti accompanied the guests in a dance of the tarantella. At the end of the dance the two players engaged in a friendly contest, which consisted of Viotti's improvising successively more elaborate variations on the air, which Dragonetti immediately replicated on his instrument. The contest supposedly ended with Viotti throwing down his violin in frustration and exclaiming: 'What can one do? He has the Devil in his body or in his double bass!'[10]

---

[8] *Morning Chronicle*, 7 February 1797. See also *Freeman's Journal*, 2 March 1797.

[9] Cited in F. Palmer (1997), *Domenico Dragonetti in England (1794–1846): The Career of a Double Bass Virtuoso*, Clarendon, Oxford, p. 190.

[10] A. de Boigne (1907–13), *Memoirs of the Comtesse de Boigne*, 4 vols, ed. C. Nicoullaud, Heinemann, London, vol. 1, pp. 138–9. Adèle de Boigne's parents, the Marquis and Marquise d'Osmond were also friends of Viotti and the Chinnerys. The marquise was

A Chinnery letter of the winter of 1796–97 makes it clear that there was no animosity between Viotti and Cramer over the latter's replacement as leader of the orchestra, since in writing to William about plans to receive company at Gillwell, Margaret names Cramer as one of the guests. Margaret looks forward to William's arrival the following day (Saturday) and mentions the severe winter weather, saying 'we do not however mind all this, our various Occupations of a Morning, & our Music & Conversation of an Evening makes the time pass with incredible Swiftness'. Viotti and Dragonetti, who by then were firm friends, were already at Gillwell: 'Amico & Drago send you a great many good wishes & are, they say, impatient for tomorrow Even$^{g}$ that you may be here again'.[11]

Another letter that was penned during the 1797 concert season was from Viotti in London to the Chinnerys at Gillwell. Dated 'Samedi 7, 97' and addressed in playful Italian to 'Mr & M$^{rs}$ Chinnery all famoso Gillwello', Viotti, who has been detained in London by rehearsals, announces that he will be joining his friends at Gillwell on the morrow: 'Adieu dear Padrona, adieu dear Gastaldo. Tomorrow, thanks be to God who created Sunday, I also shall be enjoying the country air.'[12] Earlier in this letter is a clue that would seem to indicate that Viotti has moved, and is now occupying much larger premises – so large that he complains that when William is not with him the house is turned into a vast deserted palace: 'Since my Gastaldo has not been here the house seems twice as large. It's a sad empty palace. Yesterday evening seemed interminable. I spent it idly alone by the fire from six o'clock onwards – that is what comes of being too accustomed [to company].'[13]

These words leave no doubt that the Chinnerys' company was indispensable to Viotti's well-being. His sparse leisure moments were spent either dining with William or awaiting the moment when he could flee London for Gillwell. Margaret continued to contribute to Viotti's sartorial elegance ('A thousand thanks, Amica, for the velvet. I chose a green suit and now I do not know if the black collar will go with it')[14] and William continued to tease him about his libertine life in London. In exasperated tones Viotti chides William for his insinuations: 'How the devil has Gastaldo got it into his head that I have been dining and partying here there and everywhere? Except for the day at Mrs Kingsman's with whom I wanted to discuss

---

born Eleanor Dillon, and was the sister of Count Edward Dillon (see above, p. 31).

11 MC to WBC, winter 1796–97, Fisher 2000 – 18/5.

12 'Addio Cara Padrona, addio Caro Gastaldo. Demain grace à Dieu qui a établi le Dimanche, je jouirai aussi de l'air de la Campagne' (GBV to MC, Saturday 7, 1797, Fisher 2000 – 2/1).

13 'Depuis que mon Gastaldo n'est plus à la maison elle me paroit deux fois plus grande, c'est un palais désert et triste. La soirée de hier m'a parû longue à ne plus finir, je l'ai passée seul depuis 6. heures près du feu à ne rien faire de bon— voila ce que c'est d'avoir été trop bien accoutumé!' (*Ibid.*).

14 'Je vous remercie Amica mille fois pour le velour, j'ai choisi un habit verd et je ne sçais si le colet noir ira maintenant' (*Ibid.*).

my wines, the rest of the time was spent in taverns as dark as chimneys where I ate my soup after very tiring rehearsals.'[15]

The last remark suggests that at the same time that he was toiling at the Opera house, he was also conducting a wine business. In his *Précis*, written about one year later, Viotti stated that he sank all that he possessed into a partnership with Mr Charles Smith with whom he lived for a 14-month period: 'It was also to this rarest of friends, this good Mr Chinnery, that I was obliged for having recommended me to one of the finest men in the world, an excellent character, Mr Charles Smith, with whom I shared all I possess and with whom I lived happily for 14 months which passed like a day.'[16] The address of Smith's premises where Viotti joined him in business was 3 Duke Street in the Adelphi. The 14 months corresponds to the period between January 1797 and March 1798, when Viotti was forced to leave England. The above 1797 Viotti letter would appear, then, to have been written from Smith's. When Viotti was exiled in March 1798 William moved in with Smith and continued to live there during the working week until the time he fled England in disgrace in 1812.

According to an apocryphal report circulated by the journalist brothers Escudier, this residence had a wine shop on the ground level and spacious and elegant living apartments above. The tenor Pierre Garat had supposedly paid Viotti a visit in London in January 1810, and was astounded to find him in the guise of a merchant, busy directing operations amidst a confusion of bottles, casks and pitchers. Viotti, he said, managed quite successfully to combine the life of a merchant by day with the life of a gentleman musician by night. The city merchant was still a great artist, Garat had allegedly pronounced in great amazement, after attending a dinner at Duke Street in company with leading British politicians and literary figures, at which Viotti had played one of his own concertos.[17]

A Viotti letter to an unidentified Italian lady appears to date from the early period of Viotti's residence at Duke Street, and concerns the publication of one of his songs by the singer–publisher Felippo Trisobio. The song in question is

---

[15] 'Ou Diable le Gastaldo a-t-il pri [sic] que je m'amuse tant en dinnant parci par la en fête? éxcépté le jour chés Mrs Kingsmann à qui je voulois parler de mes bouteilles, le reste a été dans des Cabarets noirs comme la cheminée que j'ai mangé ma soupe après des repetitions très fatiguantes' (*Ibid.*). Mrs Kingsman was probably the widow of Thomas Kingsman (d.*c.*1791), who had been a colleague of William at the Treasury.

[16] 'C'est encore à cet ami rare, à ce bon Mr. Chinnery que je dois de m'être appuyé à un des plus parfaits honnêtes hommes qu'il y ait au monde, à un caractère éxcellent, à Mr. Charles Smith enfin avec qui j'ai confondu tout ce que je possède et avec qui j'ai vécu paisiblement quatorze mois qui sont écoulés comme un jour' (*Précis*).

[17] M. and L. Escudier (1856), *Vie et aventures des cantatrices célèbres, précédées des musiciens de l'Empire et suivies de la vie anecdotique de Paganini*, Dentu, Paris, pp. 65–7. The date of the story is erroneous, for Lord Byron, one of the supposed guests, was at that time on a tour of Turkey and Greece. A more probable date would be 1797 or early 1798, when Viotti was still residing at these premises, and did give dinners for musicians and others at which he probably played, but Byron was then still a child. I thank Warwick Lister for prompting me to re-examine the story.

probably the favourite Viotti polacca the 'Amanti che nel core', arranged from the finale of his Concerto No. 13 for Paisiello's opera *La serva padrona*, and first performed in Paris at Viotti's Théâtre de Monsieur in 1789.[18] The opera was performed at the King's Theatre on 29 May 1794, when the aria was sung by Banti. The present letter is in reply to a female patron who seems to have offered to help boost the sales (by subscription) of Trisobio's book of music[19] by purchasing several copies. In the letter Viotti is highly critical of Trisobio, whose manners, he says, are as bad as his singing. Trisobio had been to Viotti's house on a number of occasions, but once he had brought a friend, and both had behaved so badly that Viotti had given orders for them to be evicted. In spite of this Trisobio had been shameless enough to send Viotti his publication, asking a guinea for it. Viotti paid the guinea only because he thought Trisobio must have been in need of the money, and returned the book. Viotti assured his would-be patron that she was under a misapprehension if she thought that he endorsed the book. The misunderstanding probably arose, he suggests, from her seeing Banti's name in the dedication.[20]

The weekly Opera concerts opened on 5 February 1798 with Viotti again leader of the orchestra. The year promised to be a busy one for Viotti, who was already rehearsing hard in January, as a letter to Margaret Chinnery at Gillwell attests. Viotti was preparing to come to Gillwell the following day (a Wednesday), and regretted not having been part of the Chinnery musical party the previous day, as his favourite pupil Rode was with them:

> What did you do yesterday? Did our good friend [WBC] play some music? I hope that if he did fiddle he did not not derive much pleasure from it, as I do not like him enjoying himself in that way when I am not with him. I would have given anything to have gone and joined you all! Instead of which I was lumbered with three long hours of rehearsal, and what is even worse, I had a detestable dinner afterwards at our place, which lasted until three in the morning, and which bored Smith and me to tears. [...] Did Rode remain with you?[21]

---

[18] See White, *Thematic Catalogue*, p. 171.

[19] Viotti's polacca may have been part of a collection of songs. Such publications were popular with the *amateurs*.

[20] GBV to unknown Italian lady, *c.*1797, Fisher 2000 – 38/1.

[21] 'Qu'avés vous fait hier, notre bon Ami a-t-il bien musiqué? j'espere que s'il a raclé, il ne l'a pas fait avéc beaucoup de plaisir, je n'aime pas qu'il en aye dans ce genre quand je ne suis pas avéc lui, j'aurois donné quelque chose de bon pour aller vous rejoindre tous! Au lieu de cela j'ai eu sür les épaules trois grandes heures de repetition et pis que tout cela encore, j'ai eu après un dinner détestable chés nous qui a duré jusqu'à 3. heures du matin et ou Smith et moi nous nous sommes ennuyés autant que possible [...] Rode est il resté avéc vous?' (GBV to MC, Tuesday 23 J[anuary 1798], NYPL JOB 97-52, item 2.) The letter can be precisely dated by taking into consideration firstly the month. The letter J could only refer to January, given the discussion about concert rehearsals (there were no concerts in late June or July). The year must have been between September 1796 (when the Chinnerys moved to Gillwell) and March 1798 (when Viotti went into exile). The 23 January falls on a Tuesday in 1798.

The guests at the above dinner were Viotti's fellow performers at the King's Theatre: the singing pair Michael Kelly and Mrs Crouch, along with latter's four-year-old niece; Giuseppe Viganoni, member of the opera company since the 1795–96 season; 'une autre Dame bien laide' (another very ugly lady), whom Viotti did not know; and his friend Dragonetti. The reason for Rode's untimely visit is not stated. His arrival in England coincided with a period of intense Government scrutiny of every French citizen in the kingdom, and is puzzling, unless it can be explained by Fétis's assertion that he was shipwrecked on the English coast when returning from Hamburg to his hometown Bordeaux, and could not resist paying a visit to his old teacher in London.[22] Perhaps to sway public opinion in Rode's favour Viotti arranged for his gifted pupil to give a performance at the New Musical Fund concert at the King's Theatre on 22 February. The advertised programme in the *Morning Herald* reads:

> Act II. […] Concerto Violin, Mr. Rode, (a Pupil of Signor Viotti) being his first public performance in England, and who has very obligingly postponed his departure to the Continent to aid this laudable Institution.[23]

Viotti had performed concertos in the first two Opera concerts of the season (5 and 12 February). The concerts were still the height of fashion, attracting a 'brilliant audience', including as usual the Prince of Wales, who attended the first concert. Viotti's 'great spirit and ability' in leading the orchestra was praised, and his concertos were still very much appreciated by London audiences: '[Viotti] played a *Concerto* of his own composition, which received a double portion of applause due to a piece so ably written, and brilliantly executed.'[24]

The review of the second concert was short, and simply stated that Viotti's performance was much applauded.[25] In the third concert of 19 February Viotti played another violin–double bass duet with his friend 'Drago', which the public now looked forward to as eagerly as it had the earlier Salomon–Viotti duets: 'The CONCERT at the King's Theatre, last night, afforded an admirable treat to the Musical Amateurs. The performance was in the first style of exellence, and the delight which it imparted was universal.'[26] This performance was to be Viotti's last as a soloist.

At the beginning of March Viotti was ordered by the British Government to leave the country, under suspicion of harbouring Jacobin sympathies. Rode, who was still in England, was banished with him. According to a report in the *Morning Herald* Viotti had been engaged to perform that year at Mrs Second's concerts in

---

[22] *FétisB*, vol. 7, p. 447. Fétis claims that Rode's shipwreck took place before his teaching appointment at the Paris Conservatoire, but he may have been referring to the date Rode commenced teaching (1799), rather than the date of his actual appointment (1795).

[23] *Morning Herald*, 19 February 1798.

[24] *Morning Herald*, 6 February 1798.

[25] *Morning Herald*, 13 February 1798.

[26] *Morning Herald*, 20 February 1798.

Dublin at 100 guineas per night.[27] It is not unlikely that Janiewicz had told him of the lucrative earnings to be had in Ireland, but as far as the Government was concerned even an announced intention to visit Ireland might have seemed suspicious in 1798, the year of the Irish rebellion.

Viotti was reported as having used 'heinous and sanguinary expressions'[28] – an allegation that was patently ludicrous – and protested his innocence vehemently, publishing an affidavit in several London newspapers. The *Morning Herald* printed his declaration in the original French accompanied by an English translation, and preceded it by the remark that in spite of the testimonies of support from numerous respectable members of the community, the [prime minister] Duke of Portland persisted in his determination to proceed with the order of banishment.

> Declaration of J.B. Viotti
>
> I have received an order from Government to quit a country which is dear to me, and which I consider as my own. I obey; but in declaring to the whole world, to all those who are acquainted with my name, that I go without having to reproach myself with any thought, word, or deed; that I have never interfered in any political affair whatever; that, during the six years I have passed in England, I have never written a syllable that either directly or indirectly related to its political concerns, or to those of any other country; that I have never held any conversation to which the smallest degree of blame could attach; and, in short, that I have never frequented any Coffee-house, any Tavern, any Club, or any suspected Society.
>
> I have testified the above assertion on oath, and I call the Supreme Being to witness the truth of my declaration. I hope the many respectable persons to whom I am well known, will answer at any time for the purity of my conduct; and my peaceful conscience assures me, that I shall in the end be fully justified.
>
> J.B. Viotti.
>
> Duke-street, Adelphi, March 4, 1798.[29]

There can be little doubt that the Chinnerys encouraged Viotti to take this course of action and that they were active in pressing their influential friends to support his cause, as testified by the *Times*'s report of 5 March that 'much interest was made to keep him [Viotti] here'. It is also clear from the above that Margaret Chinnery put her able pen to work to render the translation both succinct and appealing. The attestation also appeared in Paris newspapers, where his banishment was attributed to a cabal of jealous musicians. The machinations of fellow musicians was also the reason given by William Parke, who believed the resentment may have been caused by the manner in which Banti, who had featured in all the Opera concerts since 1795, allegedly manoeuvred to have Viotti replace Wilhelm Cramer as leader of the orchestra for the 1797 season.[30] But this seems an unlikely explanation given that Cramer himself apparently bore Viotti no grudge.

---

[27] *Morning Herald*, 29 March 1798.

[28] Cited in Pougin, p. 77; see also *MM*, vol. 1, p. 256.

[29] *Morning Herald*, 5 March 1798.

[30] *MM*, vol. 1, p. 254.

It is impossible to know who was responsible for sowing the seeds of doubt in the Government's mind. At a time when the Irish plot for a French invasion of Britain had just been foiled, and every public meeting in a coffee house or tavern was regarded with suspicion, when it was imagined that London was crawling with Revolutionaries, it cannot have been hard for a grudge-bearer who knew of Viotti's sympathy for the original principles of the French Revolution to initiate malicious gossip. Viotti had supposedly had an association with the Duc d'Orléans, and had certainly befriended former members of the Constituent Assembly as well as a Jacobin Government representative (Maret).

The extent of Government nervousness is evident from the proceedings of the House of Commons published in the *Times* of 23 February 1798, under the heading 'French Emigrants', in which it is reported that the secretary of war Dundas had said 'that a motion had been made last session concerning Emigrants, founded on an idea that there were more of them in the country than was consistent with its security'. Although it was conceded that 'it was a subject on which it was impossible for Ministers to obtain more than a general knowledge', any Minister who 'was acquainted with with any facts upon which an investigation could be set on foot' had a 'duty to communicate them to the Executive Government.'

Somebody did communicate his doubts about Viotti, and although it may be impossible to ascertain who the initiator of the rumour was, it was stated by William Chinnery in a letter to Margaret in 1812 that one person who was antagonistic towards Viotti was George Rose, former senior secretary of the British Treasury. In the letter William intimates that Rose had raised doubts about Viotti's allegiances in the House of Commons. In contrast, William praises the conduct of the Government paymaster-general Charles Long for supporting his own objection to the accusations against Viotti:

> He never failed shewing me the sincerest kindness, & on a particular Moment in the Affair of Amico, when old Rose did everything in his power to exasperate Mr Pitt & Government against me for the part which I "presumed to take against the 'Order of the Day'". M. Long— without my being aware of it, did in the most generous Manner take my part on the occasion with Mr Pitt, which thwarted my Enemy completely & he never once afterwards said another word about Amico.[31]

The specific fact that was responsible for confirming Viotti's guilt in the Government's eyes may have been the one suggested in a King's Theatre announcement published in the *Times* of 5 March 1798: '*Salomon* led the Band for the first time these two years, in the place of *Viotti*, who has been sent out of the country, under the authority of the *Alien Bill*. He left town yesterday [...] Viotti is said to have been in the Republican armies.' Viotti was certainly never in the

---

[31] WBC to MC, 16 May 1812, PM 94/143/1 – 7/12. It was Rose who had drawn prime minister Perceval's attention to the fact that Chinnery appeared to be living beyond his means, thereby initiating the enquiry which eventually brought William undone in March 1812.

French Republican armies, but the mistake may have arisen because of the precaution he took, when the Revolution began to gain momentum, of donning the uniform of the National Guard. The *Morning Herald* of 6 March contradicts the *Times*'s report, saying that Viotti 'had not left town yesterday', that it was Rode who had served in the French army, and that 'the inoffensive and gentlemanly VIOTTI has never had the smallest concern either with the present French Rulers, or any of their partizans.' Indeed this newspaper makes Rode the villain of the piece, asserting that Viotti's case was 'entirely separate and distinct from his', and that Viotti did not accompany Rode when the latter departed on Friday [2 March].

It is known that Viotti chose Hamburg as an asylum. Indeed he did not have much choice in the matter. Because of the war with France there were only two European ports open to him, Lisbon and Hamburg. When the packet service between Dover and Calais closed in 1793, English packets continued to ply between Falmouth and Lisbon, and between Harwich and Helvoetsluis in Holland until 1795, when Holland went over to France, closing this port also to British shipping. Hamburg then became the only point through which the British ships could conveniently reach the Continent,[32] and they left from Yarmouth. The *Morning Herald* of 10 March 1798 carried, under the heading 'The Naval Register', the following announcement, dated Yarmouth, 8 March: 'Sailed the KING GEORGE packet, Captain DEAN, [for Hamburg], with mails and passengers, among whom was Mr. VIOTTI, who was ordered out of the kingdom.' (The *Times* carried an identical announcement, but with the erroneous departure date of 3 March.) As the voyage took at least 36 hours, Viotti would have arrived in Hamburg on 10 or 11 March.

At the time Hamburg was a flourishing commercial centre. Its wealthy inhabitants, including a community of English merchants and a large diplomatic corps, supported a vigorous musical culture with music academies (concerts), several orchestras, and even its own Vauxhall Gardens for *amateurs*. It was therefore a popular stopover for travelling musicians, especially those en route to or from England,[33] offering aspiring artists ample opportunity to showcase their talents. Louis Spohr records a visit to this port in the spring of 1802, when his teacher Franz Eck was to give a concert in the *Logensaal* on the Drehbahn.[34] Hamburg was a free port, accessible to all Europeans regardless of nationality. There were no passport embargoes, as there were in other ports. It was a city full of French royalists, but ironically, also full of French Revolutionaries and spies. Coincidentally, Madame de Genlis happened to be there at the same time as Viotti. But this was before the time that Viotti and Madame de Genlis were well acquainted, and their paths almost certainly did not cross during the two weeks that their visits overlapped.

---

[32] A.H. Norway (1895), *History of the Post-Office packet service between the years 1793–1815*, Macmillan, London and New York, pp. 109–10. Pougin's (p. 78) assertion that Viotti travelled to Hamburg via Holland is therefore erroneous.

[33] See *AMZ*, 2 October 1799, col. 31.

[34] Spohr's *Autobiography*, vol. 1, pp. 18–19.

The few surviving details of Viotti's exile are found in the *Morning Herald* report of 29 March 1798, in the *Allgemeine musikalische Zeitung* of 14 August 1799 and in accounts of his contemporary biographers, notably Miel's. According to Miel an Englishman living near Hamburg heard of Viotti's arrival and offered him a cottage on his estate in a secluded location, where he promised to leave him in peace except for a weekly dinner invitation.[35] The *Morning Herald* report, based supposedly on letters from Hamburg from Viotti himself, confirms this: 'he [Viotti] laments his banishment in affecting terms, and states, that he has retired to a thatched cottage, a few miles from that city, aloof from all intercourse with mankind, confirming the well-founded opinion of the inoffensiveness of his manners and his attachment to the country, from which he has been exiled!'

The 1799 report in the *Allgemeine musikalische Zeitung* specifies that Viotti lived on the estate of a certain George Smith of Altona, whose house was situated at Schönfeld, one mile from Hamburg. The *AMZ*'s Hamburg correspondent named four violinists who had visited Hamburg the previous winter, but who were not heard in public there. These were Viotti, Jarnowick, Bingel and Spitz. The correspondent regretted not having met Viotti before his recent (*c.* August 1799) departure for England. He had been assured by his friends that Viotti, 'apart from his somewhat strong *tremolando*, was a truly excellent player and moreover was by all accounts a very courteous and pleasing man', adding that the same could not be said of Jarnowick.[36]

Viotti's friend Smith in Schönfeld cannot be identified with certainty, as no letters from Viotti in exile to Margaret or William Chinnery have been found (only two 1798 letters to their children Walter and Caroline). He may have been a British merchant. The Chinnery correspondence makes it clear that the London friend Charles Smith was not the same person who lived in Schönfeld, but the two Smiths may have been relatives. Regarding Viotti's alleged August 1799 departure from Hamburg, the date cannot be verified owing to a lack of published passenger lists, but it is likely that he travelled to Cuxhaven to take a mail packet back to England, since at this time the only British ships leaving from Hamburg were trading vessels that sailed under armed convoy. A perusal of the shipping news in the London newspapers of August and early September 1799 reveals that there were indeed intermittent arrivals in Yarmouth of large numbers of passengers on packets from Cuxhaven during these months.

A letter Viotti wrote to William in 1812 at the time of the latter's own search for a safe asylum provides the intriguing detail that George Smith had a young daughter to whom Viotti was very attached, attached enough to refer to her as his daughter: 'We advise you to stay in Stockholm or go and live in Jutland with the father of my daughter, with my good friend Mr Smith, until you are able to return. You will lead a simple, quiet life there; he [Smith] will be enchanted with your

---

[35] Michaud, vol. 43, p. 588.

[36] 'sein etwas starkes *tremulando* abgerechnet, wirklich vortreflich spielen, und dabey en sehr artiger and gefälliger Mann seyn soll' (*AMZ*, 14 August 1799, col. 762).

company and you will not be too unhappy.'[37] The words 'father of my daughter' are ambiguous. Does Viotti mean that this girl is his own daughter who has been placed in Smith's custody (in which case Smith's protection of Viotti during his exile would be explained), or does he mean that she was in fact Smith's daughter who became as close to him as a daughter? Familial relationships were assigned fairly indiscriminately to dear friends, as can be seen elsewhere in Chinnery and Viotti correspondence.

This daughter reappears, married to a Mr Büsch, at Oxford in 1811, and pays a visit to George Chinnery. George states in a letter to his mother that Mr and Mrs Büsch had visited Viotti and the Chinnerys at Gillwell in 1806. The couple had been living at Cheltenham, not far from Oxford, for the previous four years. Mrs Büsch was full of solicitous enquiries after the inhabitants of Gillwell, especially after Viotti, to whom she had written only ten days previously. George was struck by the fact that she continually referred to Viotti as her father.[38] The object of her affection was at the time laid low by a severe tooth-ache, but was touched by his 'daughter's' solicitude: 'Poor Amico has got a pan on his face, and a swelled cheek, and is in a suffering state, but is pleased with Mrs Büsch's kindness', wrote Margaret.[39]

Although Viotti did not appear in public at all while in Hamburg, it is likely that the weekly dinner invitation issued by Smith afforded him the opportunity of meeting certain friends of Smith in private gatherings, including, perhaps, some of the travelling musicians such as the three above-mentioned violinists and the Romberg cousins – frequently mislabelled brothers – violinist Andreas (1767–1821) and cellist Bernhard (1767–1841), who were there at the same time. The *AMZ*'s correspondent from Hamburg also noted the presence of ten-year-old violinist Julian Baux, who had performed a Viotti concerto in London in 1794. It is not impossible that Viotti may have listened to the boy play, and have given him, if not formal instruction, then at least some informal advice. (Perhaps for this reason the *AMZ* calls him a Viotti pupil.)[40] Another person Viotti might have met while in Hamburg was the Danish inventor and man of parts Hans Henrik Ploetz, described by Madame de Genlis in her *Mémoires* as having invented a new way of notating music with Viotti.[41]

If the upsetting events of March 1798 had the same effect on his nerves that those of Paris had in 1793, Viotti would have been plunged into a deep melancholy and a craving for solitude. It was an ideal time for composing, and indeed it was in Schönfeld that he composed his Six duets for two violins, Op. 5, published in

---

[37] 'Nous vous conseillons de rester à Stockholme ou d'aller en Juteland vivre avéc le pere de ma fille, avéc mon bon Ami M[r] Smith jusqu'à ce que vous puissiez revenir. Vous menerez là une vie simple [et] douce; il sera enchanté de votre compagnie et vous ne serez pas trop malheureux' (GBV to WBC, 30 March 1812, PHM 94/143/1 – 14/4).

[38] GRC to MC, 30 September 1811, Ch.Ch. Mrs Büsch's letter is missing.

[39] MC to GRC, 3 October 1811, Ch.Ch.

[40] *AMZ*, 24 April 1805, col. 490.

[41] Vol. 5, p. 51. See also Lister, 'New Light', pp. 424–5.

Hamburg in two books by Jean August Böhme. They were dedicated to 'M^r^ & M^me^ Chinnery', whose efforts to prevent his deportation and hasten his return were keenly appreciated. The Viotti portrait appearing on the title page is a reproduction of the portrait by George Chinnery, brother of William Chinnery (see Figure 5).[42] The annotation on the title page that the work was 'le fruit du loisir, que le malheur me procure' (the fruit of leisure afforded me by misfortune), and that some pieces had been 'dicté par la peine, d'autres par l'espoir' (dictated by sorrow, others by hope) reflected Viotti's frame of mind at the time of composition, as did the music itself.

According to an *AMZ* music reporter who reviewed the duets in two separate issues, this change of mood was evident in the first two duets, especially in the last movement of No. 2 in E minor. The reviewer preferred the second book containing the last three duets, Nos. 4, 5 and 6, which he felt were 'even more perfect [...] more fluently developed, and [which] contained more new ideas' than the first two, and were entirely worthy of their illustrious composer:[43]

> They require, as do all Viotti's things, a very dexterous and steady hand and extraordinary skill with the bow in order to be able to express without difficulty and without any obvious effort the frequent casually-tossed-in but difficult-to-execute staccatos, and the tied notes that have been packed in, all the while keeping the correct time. As well, there are little idiosyncracies that presuppose one's own treatment, which nevertheless are indicated by all sorts of signs, little suspended notes, crescendo and diminuendo signs etc, in such a way that one gets a fairly clear idea of the Viotti manner of execution, although this is self-evident from the structure and character of his things.—
>
> The spirit or the soul of the playing can in no place in the world— not even in Paris— be rendered in the engraving, and so will always remain a matter of feeling and individual interpretation that the player himself must acquire.[44]

---

[42] According to Heron-Allen the original portrait had belonged to Julian Marshall, and was exhibited at the Music [International Inventions] Exhibition in [London], 1885 (Heron-Allen to Randolph Vigne, 12 February 1927, private correspondence of Randolph Vigne).

[43] 'ist noch vorzüglicher [...] mit noch mehr Fleiss ausgearbeiteten, und mit mehr neuen Gedanken' (*AMZ*, 11 December 1799, col. 203). See also *AMZ*, 24 July 1799, cols 717–18.

[44] 'Sie fordern, wie überhaupt die Viottischen Sachen, eine sehr fertige and sichere Hand, und eine ausserordentliche Gewandtheit des Bogens, um die häufigen leicht hingeworfenen aber schwer zu executirenden stakkirten Figuren, und gegen die Taktbewegung angedrückten und gebundenen Sachen ohne Schwerfälligkeit und studirt scheinende Mühe auszudrücken. Sie haben mitunter Cappriciositäten, die ein eigenes Manöver voraussetzen, welches indess durch allerley Signaturen, kleine Vorhalte, Verstärkungs- und Schwächungszeichen etc. angedeutet ist, so, dass man eine ziemlich deutliche Idee von der Viottischen Vortragsmanier erhält, ob sie zwar an sich schon aus dem Bau und Charakter seiner Sachen selbst hervorgeht.— Der Geist, die Seele des Spiels lässt sich an keinem Orte in der Welt, also auch in Paris nicht in Kupfer stechen, und also wird das wohl immer Sache des Gefühls und der individuellen Abstraktion bleiben, die der Spieler sich selbst erwerben muss' (*AMZ*, 11 December 1799, col. 203).

It was while he was in Schönfeld that Viotti gave lessons to the promising young Friedrich Wilhelm Pixis (1785–1842), then just 13 years old. Viotti is said to have been so impressed with his young pupil's playing that he wrote duets for him.[45] Although he had only two months in which to work with the boy, the master's inimitable style must have made a lasting impression on him, as he adopted it as his own, and from this time on his name was associated with Viotti's wherever he travelled in Europe. In a eulogy dedicated to the Pixis brothers by a music enthusiast at the time of their visit to Hanover in September 1799 the poet claimed to perceive strains of Viotti emanating from Friedrich's instrument.[46] Friedrich Pixis became himself a famous professor at the Prague Conservatoire, where he founded the Prague violin school.

The only surviving Chinnery letter from this time is dated *c.*December 1798, and in it Margaret congratulates William on his promotion to chief clerk at the British Treasury. On the approach of the first Christmas since 1793 spent without Viotti Margaret writes: 'We shall be merrier than I thought this Christmas'.[47] There is no adequate account of Viotti's activities between the time he left Schönfeld in *c.*August 1799 and April 1801, the date of an entry in Margaret Chinnery's education journal proving that Viotti was back in England and living at Gillwell: 'Walter will read with Amico and learn his lesson.'[48] However a report in the *Oracle* of 21 February 1800 that Viotti was already living in England incognito, 'the worst of all states for a Musician, who ought at least to be heard, if not seen', was probably true, since there was no other place where he could, or would wish to go in the intervening period. In his *Précis*, which contains many of the same protesting expressions of innocence that are to be found in his public declaration, Viotti makes it clear that he is impatient to be back in England:

> Now I conclude this Précis, and fully confident of your good will, fully certain of my irreproachable conduct, I shall await the end of my misfortunes, nourished by hope. May it happen soon, may I soon see that happy Island where I left my heart and all my possessions. Then I shall give eternal blessings to Heaven and to my liberators, and shall forever live as I have always lived, as a loyal and faithful subject of His Britannic Majesty.[49]

There is a note accompanying the *Précis* stating that Viotti gave it to Mr Coleman Macgregor in Hamburg. Macgregor was described as the British consul

---

[45] *New Grove 2*, vol. 19, p. 816.

[46] *AMZ*, 16 October 1799, col. 55.

[47] MC to WBC, [December 1798], Fisher 2000 – 18/6.

[48] 'Walter [...] lira avec l'Amico & apprendra sa leçon' (MC's Journal, 4 April 1801, p. 127).

[49] 'Je finis ici ce Précis et plein de confiance en vos bontés, bien certain de ma conduite irreprochable, j'attendrai me nourissant d'espoir la fin de mes malheurs. Puisse-t-elle arriver bientôt, puisse-je bientôt revoir cette Isle heureuse où j'ai laissé toutes mes affections, où j'ai laissé tout mon bien. Alors je benirai sans cesse le Ciel et mes liberateurs, et sans cesse je vivrai comme j'ai toujours vecu en loyal et fidèle sujet de S.M. Britannique' (*Précis*).

in Tenerife, and was presumably then en route to England. He was in all likelihood a friend of the Chinnerys, who were well acquainted with highly placed members of society, including many foreign and British envoys, and who, like the rest of London society, were not averse to using the influence of these friends when the need arose.

As a letter from Viotti at Gillwell to Margaret, temporarily in London, dated May 1801, shows, Viotti was living at Gillwell as contentedly as the cows that were being steadily introduced there to stock the farm, and indeed probably had been since his unpublicized return from exile in *c.*autumn 1799. Relieved to be back in England, exonerated of the unjust charges that had banished him to Hamburg, and liberated from the constant rehearsals and the deadlines that had dogged his performing life in London, Viotti took pleasure in the simple delights of the country. He described an exhilarating eight-mile horseback ride without wind, which he hated (Viotti had his own horse 'Sweep'), and announced the arrival on the farm of the new cow, surrounded 'by our two heifers, the little foal and the entire sheep family.'[50]. This idyllic farmyard scene, he says, is far more to his liking than the mud and smog of London. He begs Margaret not to stay away too long, but to return soon 'dans nos champs' (to our fields).

[50] 'de nos deux genisses, du petit poul[a]in et de toute la famille des moutons' (GBV to MC, 20 May 1801, PHM 94/143/1 – 2/25).

CHAPTER 9

# Paris, 1802

In August 1802, during the Peace of Amiens, Viotti accompanied the entire Chinnery family for a two-and-a-half-month visit to Paris. The visit is documented in the Chinnery/Genlis correspondence that is part of the CFP collection. It is also mentioned in Margaret Chinnery's education journal and in a letter from Baillot to his friend Montbeillard.[1] The twins George and Caroline were almost 11 years old, and Walter nine. The *Allgemeine musikalische Zeitung* carried an announcement of Viotti's arrival, along with Banti's, dated 20 August, in which it was regretted that neither artist would appear in public.[2] The primary aim of Margaret's visit was to meet her mentor in education methods, Madame de Genlis. Viotti's was to revisit the city which many of his contemporaries thought was his favourite, in spite of his mixed fortunes there, and revive old musical friendships. He did not come with a view to resettling there, nor did he seek employment.

Another British musician who arrived in Paris about a month before Viotti, and kept a journal of his experiences there, was the nineteenth-century English conductor and composer George Smart. His descriptions of the custom houses at Dover and Calais, the crowd of a thousand onlookers on the Calais pier, the lumbering Paris diligence and the uncomfortable three-day voyage to Paris must have mirrored the Chinnery party's experience.[3] The *amateur* Lord Edgcumbe was also among the British tourists. He wrote in his *Musical Reminiscences*: 'Of French music the less said the better', and his scathing dismissal of the *grand opéra* ('that human ears can bear it is marvellous')[4] would be a comment that was still being voiced 20 years later.

In Paris Viotti and the Chinnery family lodged at the Hotel de l'Empire, rue Cerutti (now the rue d'Artois), just behind the Chaussée d'Antin, and it was here that they received visits and held the small musical parties, 'ces réunions intimes', that Baillot refers to in his *Notice*. It was exactly ten years since Viotti had left behind his close friend Cherubini in that strife-torn city, and it may be imagined that this now illustrious Paris composer was one of the first he went in search of on his arrival. Since Viotti's departure Cherubini had wed (1794) a French woman, Anne-Cécile Tourette. Viotti introduced the Cherubinis to the Chinnerys in 1802

---

[1] Yim, *The Unpublished Correspondence of Mme de Genlis*; MC's Journal, 3 September 1802, pp. 146, 149; and Baillot to Montbeillard, 29 October 1802, cited in François-Sappey, p. 182.

[2] *AMZ*, 8 September 1802, col. 815.

[3] G. Smart (1907), *Leaves from the Journals of Sir George Smart*, ed. H.B. Cox and C.L.E. Cox, Longman, Green and Co., London, pp. 11–16.

[4] Edgcumbe, p. 91.

and Cécile Cherubini and Margaret Chinnery became lifelong friends, reunited at each successive Viotti/Chinnery visit to Paris. George Chinnery would lodge with the Cherubinis during his 1814 sojourn in Paris, and Cherubini would stay at the Chinnery home in London during his 1815 visit to England.

In the same month that Viotti arrived in Paris Cherubini founded his publishing house, a co-operative venture with his colleagues Rode, Isouard, Méhul, Boieldieu and Kreutzer. The firm, which would last only until 1811, aimed to help prevent composers being exploited by publishers.[5] The timing may not have been coincidental, since Viotti was one of the first to sign a contract with this house and must have arrived in Paris with a portfolio of manuscripts under his arm. Dated 25 September, the Viotti contract stipulated that six of his concertos (Nos 21, 22, 23, 24, 25 and 26, to be known henceforth as Concertos A, B, C, D, E and F, that is, his first six London concertos except for No. 20, which had already been sold to Pleyel), and three sets of string trios (Op. 17, Op. 18, Op. 19) were to be sold immediately, and that the publishers would have exclusive rights to all future compositions. Concerto No. 22 was dedicated to Cherubini. The price for these works was generous: 1,080 *livres* (francs) for concertos and trios alike, compared to the 300 *livres* paid by Sieber, Viotti's former Paris publisher, for a trio by the flautist François Devienne. And the payment instalments were swift, putting ready cash in Viotti's hands which could be poured straight into his wine business.[6]

Needless to say the other friends whom Viotti was most eager to see were his pupil Rode and his disciple Rodolphe Kreutzer. The former had returned to his hometown Bordeaux after his expulsion from England in 1798, and resumed his Conservatoire post in Paris in 1799. Rode was then Paris's favourite violinist, having made a reputation for himself throughout Europe. As his travels had taken him to many German cities, his concerts were closely followed by the *Allgemeine musikalische Zeitung*, which was fond of comparing him with his master, and with other French violinists. One of the newspaper's reporters opined that Kreutzer's talent seemed to be the result of much hard work, whereas Rode's seemed natural to him.[7] Another thought that 'next to the concertos of a Viotti, those of Rode were surely in every respect the best and had the most intrinsic merit.'[8] Yet another elaborated on the different performance styles of Rode and Viotti:

> The style of one is quite different from that of the other. Viotti does more; what Rode does is more elegant and cleaner. The former has more power, the latter more grace. Viotti allows himself to be carried away by his passion, he dares, loses himself, and then his boldness does not always have a happy outcome; Rode always remains in control of himself, is always pleasant, always pure, but at times he becomes a little cold; he never sinks, but nor does he elevate himself enough; Viotti, carried away by his fire sometimes strikes some false notes, and those critics who are more sensitive to

[5] *Petites Affiches*, 7 December 1802, cited in Pougin, p. 175n2.

[6] See Lesure, 'Deux contrats d'édition de Viotti', pp. 222–6.

[7] *AMZ*, 9 July 1800, col. 714.

[8] 'Nächst den Konzerten eines Viotti, dürften die von Rode wohl allerdings die besten und gehaltvollsten seyn' (*AMZ*, 11 February 1801, col. 352).

mistakes than to beauties, have made much of this small failing; Rode always remains correct, he never offends the ear, but he seldom stirs the soul to the point where [one] happily forgives such mistakes. Genius eclipses mistakes; but the art of eschewing mistakes does not substitute for genius.[9]

Kreutzer's career had also flourished, and as well as being a respected professor at the Conservatoire, where he taught some famous violinists, including Lafont and Massart, he had made successful concert appearances in Paris, sometimes with Rode. In addition, he had turned to composing for the theatre, a risky undertaking, as shown by a letter he addressed to the administrator of the Paris Théâtre des Arts in 1801.[10] The career of Baillot, the third member of the famous Paris violin triumvirate, had remained largely in the shadows owing to circumstances beyond his control. However he had competently and assiduously filled Rode's post at the Conservatoire during his absence, and in March 1799 received his official appointment as professor of violin of the second class.

In 1801 the Conservatoire had been the target of criticism in the Paris press for its excessive operational costs and inefficient teaching methods. In February 1802 its head Bernard Sarrette replied to the attacks in his speech 'Observations on the state of music in France.' Reforms were instituted, and one outcome was the decision to prepare some official teaching manuals. Thus was born the *Méthode de violon*, jointly created by Baillot, Kreutzer and Rode, but in reality largely the work of Baillot. It was officially adopted by the Conservatoire on 23 February 1802, published in 1803, and put on sale at its music shop at 152 rue du Faubourg-Poissonnière for 24 francs. It was this short treatise that was the forerunner of Baillot's later and much more fully developed *Art du violon*. Here was the first violin treatise to explore all the ramifications of the new Tourte bow. Here three main principles of violin teaching were established: first, instruction in the basic elements of music (solfège); second, instruction in technique; third, practice, using as models the works of both ancient and modern composers. Of the latter Viotti's figured the most prominently. The *Allgemeine musikalische Zeitung* carried a ringing endorsement of this method in its issue of 24 August 1803 (col. 794).

---

[9] 'die Manier des Einen von der Manier des Andern durchaus verschieden ist. Viotti macht mehr; was Rode macht, ist eleganter und netter. Jener hat mehr Kraft, dieser mehr Grazie. Viotti lässt sich durch sein Feuer hinreissen, er wagt, er verliert sich, und dann ist seine Kühnheit nicht immer glücklich; Rode bleibt immer Herr seiner selbst, immer angenehm, immer rein, aber zuweilen wird er etwas kalt; er sinkt nie, aber erhebt sich auch nicht genug; Viotti'n entschwischen in seiner Heftigkeit zuweilen einige falsche Töne, und die Kritiker, die empfindlicher für Verirrungen als für Schönheiten sind, haben viel Aufhebens von diesem kleinen Unglück gemacht; Rode bleibt immer richtig, er beleidigt das Ohr nie, aber er erhebt das Gemüth auch selten zu der Begeisterung, die dergleichen Verirrungen gern verzeihet. Das Genie überstrahlt Fehler; aber die Kunst, Fehler zu vermeiden, ersezt das Genie nicht' (*AMZ*, 13 May 1801, cols 558–9).

[10] R. Kreutzer and N. Isouard to Citoyen Bonnet, 21 ventôse [11 March 1801], PHM E.A. and V.I. Crome collection, A8213, petitioning for compensation for a failed production of their opera *Flaminius à Corinthe*.

The stamp of Baillot's philosophy, which emphasized the formation of the whole human being rather than just the musician, and which came to the fore in his 1835 *Art du violon*, was already in evidence in this first brief *Méthode*. This concept was a novel one for the time, and was remarked on by the English music journal *Quarterly Musical Magazine and Review*, which lauded 'the liberal ideas which the professors of the conservatory endeavour to inspire':

> It should seem strange, that after so many ages, and after so many treatises on the art of playing such an instrument as the violin, it should have been thought necessary to compose a new instruction book. [...] why multiply them unnecessarily? It forms a part of the plan of the French conservatory, to inculcate the philosophy of art, together with the practice, and though the maxims introduced into their books are few, brief, and sketchy, yet they can hardly fail to impel the student to use his understanding as well as his fingers, and at the same time that these observations set him a thinking, they will teach him to form high and honourable notions.[11]

The Conservatoire professors believed that it was not enough to produce a mere technician. They aimed to produce a true artist, who spent his life 'in search of the *beau idéal*, which according to his judgement will consist in whatever touches and exalts his soul.'[12] This quotation from the *Méthode* resounds with echoes of Viotti, who had left Paris just before the *Méthode* was published. Since it was Viotti's playing that had inspired all three of the authors of this treatise, and since all three acknowledged him as their master, it may be imagined that it was not only Viotti's technique that formed the foundation of their instruction method, but also his philosophy that governed it.

Viotti's compositions were used not only as models for violin practice: they were also used exclusively as examination pieces in the Conservatoire's end of year *concours* (competitive examinations), and were performed at the yearly prizegiving concerts. First instituted in 1797, the original object of these concerts was to give the pupils practice in performing both ancient and modern music, to train orchestra leaders, and, in the case of those pupils studying composition, to perform the works of the prizewinners. By 1802 the concerts had become the well respected but modestly named *exercices publics*, some of the most popular public concerts in Paris. From the paying public's point of view these '*exercices*' constituted a yearly musical treat of the highest standard, and were looked forward to by Paris's true music connoisseurs.

At some time during his stay in Paris Viotti was persuaded by his disciples to give a private concert in a small room of the Conservatoire, so that the pupils could hear their venerated master. According to Fétis, some believed Viotti was too old to be a force to be reckoned with, but they were to be surprised:

---

[11] 'Rode, Baillot, and Kreutzer's Method of Instruction for the Violin', *QMMR* (1824), vol. 6, no. 24, p. 528.

[12] *Ibid.*, p. 529.

> It was still the same fire, the same brilliance, the same good taste, the same grandiose manner that had been admired before; the style of his compositions had broadened and been perfected. It was during this visit that he introduced to Paris his delicious concertos designated by the letters A, B, C, etc, his trios, and several other works.[13]

Baillot, the musician with a poetic bent, wrote lucidly and evocatively of the impression Viotti's playing made on his listeners. He added to Fétis's list of Viotti's compositions that were heard during this visit the duets dedicated to Mr Cary (WIV: 28–30) and those dedicated to Mr and Mrs Chinnery (Op. 5), which Viotti had composed in Hamburg. Touched by the wording of the last dedication, Baillot recognized an unmistakably affectionate character, or *accent*, in Viotti's playing, calling it 'a most amiable conversation between two noble-spirited people united in the tenderest friendship.'[14] He considered that Viotti's performance was that of a far more mature violinist than the one who had left Paris ten years earlier. Viotti was no longer possessed by a youthful desire to impress, but played with a naturalness and simplicity that Baillot believed to be the hallmarks of a true artist:

> Here is a rare and remarkable thing! The more expert he became in his art, the more natural he sounded. The naivete that is the dominant feature of a number of his works is a virtue that cannot be praised highly enough: it proves both the release of his soul and the purity of his taste. Not once did a vain desire to shine tarnish these happy gifts of nature; each day he became more expressive, and in his compositions he followed his heart, and it was to the heart that he addressed himself always. He did not aim for accolades, but for another kind of success, success precious in a very different way for [the performer] who cherishes above all the happiness of acquiring a friend in every one of his listeners.[15]

The above remarks were penned by Baillot at the end of Viotti's life. In August 1802 Baillot was still only a casual acquaintance of Viotti, a former member of his Feydeau orchestra who had been obliged by financial constraints to leave after playing in it for only six months. He did not participate in the Chinnerys' private music concerts at the Hotel de l'Empire until six weeks after their arrival. The reason he gives for his long-awaited admission is the same one

---

[13] 'C'était encore le même feu, le même brillant, le même goût, le même grandiose qu'on avait admiré autrefois; le style de ses compositions s'était agrandi et perfectionné. Ce fut dans ce voyage qu'il fit connaître à Paris ses délicieux concertos désignés par les lettres A, B, C, etc., ses trios, et plusieurs autres ouvrages' (*FétisB*, vol. 8, p. 472).

[14] 'c'est la conversation la plus aimable de deux personnes d'un esprit élevé, unies par l'amitié la plus tendre' (*Notice*, p. 9).

[15] 'Chose rare et bien digne de remarque! plus il avança dans son art, plus il conserva de naturel. La naïveté qui règne dans un grand nombre de ses morceaux, est un mérite qu'on ne saurait trop louer: elle prouve à la fois l'abandon de son âme et la pureté de son goût. Jamais un vain desir de briller n'altéra ces heureux dons de la nature; il devint chaque jour plus expressif, n'écrivit que d'après son cœur, et c'est au cœur qu'il s'adressa toujours. Aspirant peu aux applaudissemens, il ambitionna un autre genre de succès, succès bien autrement précieux pour qui met au-dessus de tout le bonheur d'acquérir un ami dans chacun de ceux qui l'écoutent' (*Notice*, pp. 9–10).

mentioned by Rode in his letter to Margaret Chinnery a few days later – Rode's recurrent arm ailment. Baillot stepped in to replace his friend when Rode was no longer able to play. In his letter to Montbeillard of 29 October 1802 Baillot described the ailment as an erysipelas, a type of acute streptococcal dermititis with a clearly defined area of redness and swelling, also known as St Anthony's fire:

> I shall begin with some quite melancholy news which is very distressing to me [...], Rode's arm ailment, a very stubborn erysipelas which manifested itself strongly and then went to his head. These recurrent attacks make me very worried for him [...] Viotti stayed here for two and a half months. He departed nine days ago and is to return this winter. It was six weeks before I could gain admittance to his hotel, but since Rode's arm ailment it is I who have always accompanied our dear master, who is, from the accounts of those who heard him in the old days, more beautiful, more expressive, more expansive, more sublime than ever. He has retained all his passion, all his fire. [Our] admiration is spread equally between his playing and his composition. I have finally heard him properly. I listened with every fibre of my soul, with my ears, I would even say with my eyes at the stretch [...] I accompanied him playing the beautiful duo in F minor seven or eight times. He seemed pleased with me [...] I could not shake off one regret however, and that was that my poor friend was not at my side to hear this kind Viotti who has nourished us for so long, and to whom we are indebted for having forged a path which no one will be able to follow after him. He came here with Mrs Chinnery and her children, a charming family with whom he lives contentedly.[16]

Rode and Baillot had remained close during the Revolutionary years – or as close as Rode's itinerant lifestyle would allow – and both had formed a strong friendship with Hélène de Montgéroult on her return to France. She had had no further brushes with the Committee for Public Safety after 1793, having remained out of Paris until the establishment of the Directory (October 1795), when her

---

[16] 'Je commencerai par quelques nouvelles assez tristes, par des choses qui m'ont bien affligé [...], un mal au bras survenu à Rode, une hérésypèle [sic] très opiniâtre qui est d'abord sortie avec force et qui s'est jetée à la tête. Ces accidents répétés m'inquiètent beaucoup pour lui [...] Viotti est resté ici pendant deux mois et demi. Il est reparti il y a neuf jours et doit revenir cet hyver. J'ai été plus de six semaines sans pouvoir être admis chez lui, mais depuis le mal de bras de Rode, j'ai toujours accompagné notre cher maître, qui est, à ce que m'ont assuré ceux qui l'ont entendu autrefois, qui est, dis-je, plus beau, plus expressif, plus grand, plus sublime que jamais. Il a conservé toute sa vivacité, toute sa fougue. L'admiration est partagé entre son jeu et sa composition. je l'ai enfin bien entendu. Je l'écoutais de toutes les facultés de mon âme, de toutes mes oreilles, je dirais de tous mes yeux [...] Je lui ai accompagné sept à huit fois le beau duo en *fa* mineur. Il a paru content de moi [...] Un regret ne me quittait pas, c'est que mon pauvre ami ne fût pas à mes côtés pour entendre ce bon Viotti qui nous a nourri depuis si longtemps et auquel on doit d'avoir frayé une route que personne ne pourra suivre après lui. Il est venu ici avec Madame Chinnery et ses enfants, famille charmante au milieu de laquelle il vit heureux' (Baillot to Montbeillard, 29 October 1802, cited in François-Sappey, pp.182–3). The duo in F minor mentioned here is one of those from the second book of Op. 5. The *AMZ* (11 December 1799, cols 203–4) singles it out for special mention on account of its feeling and taste, and gives advice on how it should be played.

name was erased from the list of *émigrés*. In November 1795 she had been appointed professor of pianoforte of the first class at the Conservatoire, a post she was to keep until 1798. From Baillot's 4 July 1796 report[17] that she had left Paris for her country house near Dreux (for the summer), and that Rode had written to her there from Hamburg, it is clear that she had resumed a normal routine and was no longer fearful for her life. Madame de Montgéroult was naturally another whom Viotti and the Chinnerys saw much of during this visit.

Under the Directory Viotti's old Feydeau Theatre had been home to some vibrant concerts featuring Rode, Baillot, Kreutzer and other professors from the Conservatoire. In 1800 after a brief visit to Spain, Rode had been named solo violinist to Napoleon, and in summer 1802, Rode, Kreutzer and Baillot were made members of Napoleon's private orchestra. One German writer thought that Paris was in dire need of such an institution, since in the whole of the previous winter there had only been three or four concerts,[18] the only regular concert series being the Concert de la rue Cléry. But Baillot was disenchanted with the bad organization of the First Consul's concerts, complaining that the musicians were treated worse than servants.[19] Napoleon also carried on the Revolutionary tradition of celebrating national festivals with rousing outdoor orchestral performances. George Smart heard Rode lead Napoleon's orchestra at the 14 July concert in the illuminated Tuileries gardens just before Viotti's arrival, but was disappointed with the programme, which consisted only of 'overtures and choruses' and 'some very noisy pieces'.[20]

Without having had any further contact with his admired mentor since their cordial separation in 1791, Baillot had retained his profound admiration for Viotti's compositions, playing them often at private and public concerts. Like Viotti, Baillot lived for the high artistic ideal, and regretted the fact that the drudgery of his professional posts denigrated the true art of music, writing 'when one practises the trade one must renounce art'.[21] The lofty view of music that Baillot shared with Viotti undoubtedly led to the two becoming soulmates, as attested by their future correspondence.

It is clear from Baillot's 1802 letter to Montbeillard that Baillot came to know the Chinnerys well during their sojourn in Paris, as did all of Viotti's musical friends who were invited to the Hotel de l'Empire for private concerts. On 16 October Margaret Chinnery celebrated her birthday at the hotel with a small *fête domestique*. These domestic celebrations, of which the cornerstone was music, were held to commemorate any important family occasion, and were popular among the bourgeoisie and upper classes. They demanded the involvement of each family member in some capacity, especially the children. Dedicatory verses set to

---

17 Baillot to Montbeillard, 4 July 1796, cited in François-Sappey, p. 181.

18 *AMZ*, 23 August 1802, col. 781.

19 Baillot to Montbeillard, 6 December 1802, cited in François-Sappey, p. 178.

20 Smart, *Leaves from the Journals*, p. 31.

21 'quand on fait le métier il faut renoncer à l'art' (Baillot to Montbeillard, 19 August 1805, cited in François-Sappey, p. 145).

music (*romances*), and sometimes even small *comédies* were performed by friends and family members in honour of the occasion. The three *romances* that were sung on this occasion have been preserved in the Powerhouse Museum, although none of the music survives. From the handwriting at the top of each it is clear that Viotti was the organizer of the fête.

The first *romance* was by Madame de Genlis,[22] with whom Viotti and Margaret had by now made contact and become close friends, although the grand lady herself was unable to be present. It was to Viotti that she made her excuses, pleading work pressures, and saying that such occasions made her weep uncontrollably.[23] Cherubini set the poem to music and all three children participated in its rendition. It was a typical maternal eulogy filled with all the appropriate sentiments of filial piety. The second was a poem composed by the Chinnery children's French tutor Maître Bataillard for Caroline to sing to the popular French tune of 'Lise chantoit dans la prairie'.[24] The third consisted of two eight-line stanzas of rhyming couplets written by Baillot to be sung by Madame Cherubini to her new friend 'Mrs La Padrona Cara'. The importance of music in their friendship is spelt out in Baillot's lines: 'To celebrate my friend […] I invoke harmony, which animates everything.'[25]

Other musicians who were almost certainly present at the party were Rodolphe Kreutzer, Hélène de Montgéroult, and Francesco Bianchi, who was also then in Paris. That the Paris musicians were very fond of the Chinnerys, and had been told much about the charms of Gillwell, where they had all been invited, is shown by a letter written by Rode to Margaret at the end of the family's visit. Addressed to 'Madame Chinnery, Gillwell', Rode, who is still afflicted with his arm ailment, preventing him from playing, writes somewhat glumly:

> Paris le 17 brumaire an 11 [8 November 1802]
>
> It has already been more than three weeks since good, amiable Madame Chinnery departed. I would have missed the life I led at rue Cerutti even more were it not for the arrival of my family who have been in Paris for twelve days. My poor young sister has been so ill that my anxiety knew no bounds. Finally, thanks to the care of Dr Süe, she is now much better. My arms are still in a pitiful state. In truth, one must have the patience of a saint to cling to the sad and monotonous life that I am obliged to lead, not being able to use my arms for anything at all. Pardon me, Madame, for mentioning such unpleasant details, but I am really downcast whenever I think of my tedious situation.— I learned from Cherubini that you had arrived safely at Calais and I hope the same was true of the rest of your journey.—
>
> There you are *reinstated* at Gillwell as though nothing had changed. Everyone has taken up the thread of his life, and I am sure no one gives any more thought to us poor Parisians than one would to the grand Turk. That is not the case for us here. All those

[22] *Romance faite pour le jour de naissance de Mme Chinnery* (PHM 94/143/1 – 1/3; Yim, D14).

[23] Mme de Genlis to GBV, [16 October 1802], Fisher 2000 – 38/2 (Yim, D12).

[24] PHM 94/143/1 – 25/1.

[25] 'Pour fêter mon amie / […] / J'invoque l'harmonie / Qui fait tout animé' (*Couplets chantés par M$^{de}$ Cherubini à Madame Chinnery*, PHM 94/143/1 – 1/4).

who were fortunate enough to be admitted to the hotel de l'Empire when you were living there, Madame, retain very fond memories of the dear Padrona, speak about her incessantly, and have formed a very delightful image of the Englishwomen of Gillwell. Speaking of Gillwell, I should like to know if you are making preparations to enlarge it in order to be able to receive all those you have invited to visit you there. The favour that you intend to bestow on so many makes me almost jealous. Fortunately I shall get in early, and I shall shortly be reserving my room. But first I wish to make a little tour, and all that prevents me is my health.

Adieu Madame, be assured of my boundless devotion and my constant affection,

P. Rode
rue St George
n° 35 behind the
rue de Provence

All my best wishes to good Mr Chinnery, to dear Amico, and to the sweet children. Please be kind enough to accept also the respectful greetings of Mama and my sister. Mr Bianchi, whom I saw the day before yesterday, is slightly ill. I believe he has a tendency to indifferent health, and his anxiety for his wife from whom he has had no news, only exacerbates it. Unfortunately I am unable to see him as soon as I would wish, being obliged to look after my own health and stay at home, but I shall send to know how he does.[26]

---

[26] 'Voila déja plus de trois semaines que l'aimable & bonne Madame Chinnery est partie. cette privation de la vie que je menais rue cérutti m'auroit encore parue plus sensible sans l'arrivée de ma famille qui est à paris depuis quinze jours. ma pauvre petite sœur a été malade au point que mon inquiétude était sans bornes. enfin graces aux soins de M. Süe, elle est maintenant beaucoup mieux. mes bras sont toujours dans un état pitoyable. en verité il faut avoir la patience d'un saint pour tenir à la vie triste & monotone que je suis obligé de mener, ne pouvant me servir de mes bras pour quoi-que ce soit. pardon, Madame, de vous entretenir de détails aussi peu aimables, mais je suis vraiment de mauvaise humeur toutes les fois que je songe à l'ennui de ma position.— j'ai appris par Cherubini que vous étiéz arrivée à Calais sans accident & j'espere qu'il en aura été de même pendant le reste du voyage.— vous voilà maintenant *reinstallée* à Gillwell comme si rien n'était. Chacun a repris le cours de ses occupations, & je suis sur qu'il n'en est pas plus question de ces pauvres habitants de paris, que du grand turc auquel on ne songe guère. nous ne sommes pas de même ici, & tous ceux qui ont été assez heureux pour être introduits à l'hotel de l'empire lorsque vous l'habitiez, Madame, conservent un souvenir bien affectueux pour la chère pa[d]rona; en parlent sans cesse, & ont depuis, conçu une idée bien avantageuse des anglaises de Gillwell. à propos de Gillwell, je voudrais bien savoir si vous vous préparez à le faire agrandir pour recevoir tous ceux que vous avez invités à vous y venir voir? cette faveur que vous comptez accorder à tant de monde, me rend presque jaloux. heureusement que je m'y prendrai à l'avance & que j'irai retenir ma chambre dans quelque tems, mais je veux auparavant faire une petite tournée & je n'attends pour celà que le rétablissement de ma santé.— adieu Madame, agréez l'assurance de mon devouement sans bornes & de l'affection inaltérable de mes sentiments pour vous / P. Rode / rue S.$^{t}$ george / n° 35 derrière la / rue de provence. / Mille & mille choses au bon Monsieur Chinnery, au caro amico, & aux aimables enfants. Veuillez bien recevoir aussi Madame, avec quelque intéret les salutations repectueuses de Maman & de ma sœur. Mr. Bianchi que j'ai vu avant-hier est un peu malade. il a je crois naturellement une mauvaise santé, que l'inquiétude où il étoit relativement à sa femme dont il ne recevoit aucune nouvelles [sic], n'a fait qu'accoitre. je [ne] peux

The doctor mentioned in this letter was Pierre Sue, Paris surgeon and president of the school of medicine. He was the Chinnery doctor in Paris, and attended Margaret when an illness prevented her from returning to England earlier with her husband. Viotti and the children stayed on with her. In visiting Margaret at the Hôtel de l'Empire Dr Sue would certainly have met Viotti, who, according to Miel, co-operated with him in some anatomical observations: 'We have heard from Dr Sue that Viotti had on several occasions played pieces of music of every kind for him, expressly to enable him to observe the movements of the wrist. He would stop on and off in each position at the request of the anatomist.'[27]

The respectful tone of the above Rode letter is in direct contrast to the playful punning one sent to 'Monsieu Bayot membre / du Concervatouar de / meusiq au concervatouar/ rü bergaire / a paris' exactly nine months later from Hanover.[28] Rode, in company with his colleague the cellist Jacques-Michel Hurel de Lamare (who co-authored the letter, and was the principal punster), had embarked on the first stretch of his above-mentioned tour, and was still suffering from the same arm complaint. Lamare wrote:

> Rode who is half responsible for the style of this letter will give up his concert on the First Consul's birthday— first arm would be a little more fitting— and is making preparations to leave for Russia where he should have been already had it not been for this cursed handicap. He is obliged to take the waters half a league from here and that is what has forced him to remain a few days longer with us. He hopes that his *friends* will not bear him a grudge for not having written, but he says that you all know him well enough [to understand] that his laziness in no way changes his sentiments towards you.[29]
>
> [There follows a paragraph from Rode in which he admires Lamare's play on words, announces the latter's intention of following him to St Petersburg at the end of autumn, adds a few jokes of his own, and finishes with an illuminating list of friends, including the Viotti biographer Miel,[30] whom he charges Baillot to embrace.] We charge, nay

---

malheureusesment [pas] le voir aussi [tôt] que je desirerais étant moi-même obligé de me soigner & de rester chèz moi, mais j'enverrai savoir de ses nouvelles' (Pierre Rode to MC, 8 November 1802, Fisher 2000 – 4/3).

27 'Nous avons entendu dire par le docteur Sue que plusieurs fois Viotti avait joué devant lui des morceaux de tous genres, exprès pour lui permettre d'observer les mouvements du poignet, s'arrêtant à chaque instant et dans toutes les positions, à la demande de l'anatomiste' (Michaud, vol. 43, p. 589).

28 Rode and Lamare to Baillot, 8 August 1803, PHM E.A. and V.I. Crome collection, A8213.

29 'Rode qui est de moitié dans le style de cette lettre va lâcher son concert le jour de naissance du 1[er] Consul, 1[er] bras vaut un peu mieux et il se prépare à partir pour la Russie où il devoit être sans cette futule incommodité. il est obligé de prendre les eaux a une demie lieue d'ici et c'est ce qui le force à rester encore quelques jours parmi nous. il espere que *les amis* ne lui en voudront pas de ne pas avoir écrit, mail il dit que vous le connoissez tous et que sa paresse ne change pas ses sentimens pour vous' (*Ibid.*).

30 The presence of the name Miel in this list of luminaries of the Paris Conservatoire would indicate that he was on an intimate footing with them, and therefore lends much greater credence to his anecdotes on Viotti in Michaud (vol. 43).

command you to embrace our mothers, our sisters, friends Tariot, Baudiot the Latinist, the purist, the Jansenist; Grassouillet [Grasset, who must have been corpulent], Kreutzer, Bernard, Miel, Montbeillard, Auber, his wife, his daughter, Félix, Auguste, Pradher, Dominique, Salentin, Rey, Frédérick Duvernoy, d'Alvimar, Janson the elder and the younger, Ernest the whistler, and Plantade the jokester; and finally poor Le Sueur.[31] Deus sit nomen benedictus. This last is à la Baudiot. So!... Give us news of Auber and Vienney. We should like to know if they are still in London.

Adieu, dear and trusty friend. We are thinking of you and would dearly love to hear from you. Write immediately and address your letter Hamburg, poste restante.

Rode and Hurel de Lamare[32]

A month earlier Rode had played at Brunswick at the court of Louis Spohr's patron Carl Wilhelm Ferdinand, Duke of Saxe-Gotha. Spohr was enchanted with his playing, writing in his autobiography 'I had no hesitation in placing *Rode*'s style of play (then still reflecting all the brilliancy of that of his great master *Viotti*), above that of my instructor *Eck*, and to apply myself sedulously to acquire it as much as possible by a careful practice of *Rode*'s compositions.'[33] Spohr's 'still' is significant in light of the last two letters. Given Rode's arm complaint it seems extraordinary that he could play as well as he did at Brunswick, and it is very probable that the later deterioration in his playing, noticed in Paris (1808) and in Vienna (1812) was a result of this same cruel blight. There is no evidence that Rode ever fulfilled his promise to Margaret Chinnery to visit Gillwell after his tour, although he did visit her in France many years later. The prolonged state of war between France and England was undoubtedly the reason for the French musicians', as well as Madame de Genlis's, plans to visit Gillwell being thwarted.

It was not only with musicians that Viotti renewed contact in Paris in 1802. It is to be expected that he went in search of many of the aristocratic *amateurs*, and men and women of letters and of the other arts whom he had frequented in the salons of pre-Revolutionary Paris. A letter from the artist Hubert Robert to William Chinnery speaks of the Duc de Rohan, who wants Viotti to sell a Vigée-Lebrun painting for him in London. Hubert, apparently an *habitué* of the Hôtel de l'Empire, wrote of his gratitude to the Chinnerys 'as well as to my dear old friend Viotti, who promised to give me news of himself and also to see what he could do

---

[31] The composer Jean-François Le Sueur had been dismissed from the staff of the Conservatoire in September 1802.

[32] 'Nous te chargeons, te sommons, d'embrasser nos meres, nos sœurs, les amis Tariot, Baudiot le latiniste le puriste, le janséniste; Grassouillet, Kreutzer, bernard, miel, Montbeillard, auber, son épouse, sa fille, félix, auguste, pradere, dominique, salentin, Rey, frédérick duvernoy, d'alvimar, Janson ainé et cadet, ernest le siffleur, & plantade le farceur; enfin le pauvre le Sueur. deus sit nomen benedictus. ceci est à la Baudiot. bon!... donne nous des nouvelles d'auber & de Vienney. Nous voudrions savoir s'ils sont encore à Londres. adieu notre chèr & féal. nous pensons à toi & desirons vivement de tes nouvelles. écris nous de suite & adressez la lettre à hambourg poste restante. / Rode et Hurel de Lamare' (Rode and Lamare to Baillot, 8 August 1803, PHM E.A. and V.I. Crome collection, A8213).

[33] Spohr's *Autobiography*, vol. 1, p. 61.

in London about Mme Lebrun's beautiful portrait of Mme Dubarry. If this favour could be done for the Duc de Rohan, to whom it belongs, he would be very grateful. He paid 6,000 francs for it, and would like to sell it for 3,000.'[34]

One of the most renowned teaching institutions in Europe was operational in Paris at this time. It was the Abbé Sicard's School for Deaf Mutes in the rue St Jacques, administered by the wealthy French philanthropist Laffon de Ladébat, whom, judging by the mention of his name in several letters, Viotti and the Chinnerys knew quite well. The school gave monthly public demonstrations of its pedagogic methods, a favourite attraction for the many foreigners then visiting Paris. There is evidence that the Chinnerys, and almost certainly Viotti, who, like Margaret Chinnery, took a keen interest in the practical application of different education methods, attended at least one of these sessions during their stay.[35]

Viotti also sought out his old friend Hugues-Bernard Maret, who had returned to Paris after his prison ordeal of 1793–95, and who was to rise to great heights as Napoleon's most trusted henchman. In an 1812 letter William wrote of the family's 1802 visit that 'we saw & lived a great deal with *Maret* at Paris'.[36] There was also the Comte de Vaudreuil, the writer and librettist Charles Brifaut, and a certain Mademoiselle Esmangard, all mentioned in a later letter from Madame Vigée-Lebrun, who was herself then also in Paris.[37]

The other significant Viotti friendship dating from Paris, 1802, was the one he formed with France's most notorious and prolific lady of letters, Madame de Genlis. The six letters addressed to Viotti from Madame de Genlis have been transcribed in *The Unpublished Correspondence of Mme de Genlis*.[38] The letters show that Viotti and the Chinnerys had frequent social intercourse with the famous educationalist, writer and harpist, and met some of her friends and family members. The author took a keen interest in Viotti's music, and claimed that his promise of a rondo, which she received from him before his return to England, was the catalyst for her return to harp playing after a lapse of two years.[39] Madame de Genlis knew many of the *ancien régime* musicians, including Monsigny, Kreutzer and Cherubini, and came to hear Viotti play at the Hôtel de l'Empire, bringing her 12-year-old adopted son and pupil Casimir Baecker, to whom she dedicated her harp tutor. He later achieved some small fame as a harpist.[40]

---

[34] 'ainsy qu'a mon bon et ancien ami viotti qui m'avoit promis de me donner de ses nouvelles et de ce qu'il auroit pu faire a Londres pour le beau portrait de m[de] dubary par m[de] Le brun. Si on pouvoit rendre ce service au duc de Rohan a qui il appartient il en seroit bien reconnoissant. il a eté payé 6 000[ff] et il desiroit en avoir 3 000[ff]' (Hubert Robert to WBC, 13 November 1802, Fisher 2000 – 19/3).

[35] See Miscellaneous Verse, PHM 94/143/1 – 32/5, which contains some examples of the question–response drills that were a feature of the school's teaching method.

[36] WBC to MC, 16 May 1812, PHM 94/143/1 – 7/12.

[37] Elisabeth Vigée-Lebrun to MC, 7 July 1816, Fisher 2000 – 8/2.

[38] D. Yim (ed.) (2003), *SVEC*, vol. 2.

[39] Mme de Genlis to MC, [October 1802], Fisher 2000 – 6/10, 6/13 (Yim, D10 and D15).

[40] In 1811 the *AMZ* would describe Casimir as a successful young composer and virtuoso who was capable of performing very difficult piano pieces on the harp, but dismissed

It was to Viotti that Madame de Genlis addressed her letters of condolence on the death of young Walter Chinnery shortly after the family's return to London, having heard the news from Cécile Cherubini.[41] She also asked Viotti for help in having her latest novel *La Duchesse de La Vallière* published in England.[42] The novel quickly became a bestseller in France, and was published in England in 1804 by the French *émigré* Jean-Gabriel Peltier. It is not known if it was Viotti who facilitated the novel's publication in England, but it is known that he knew Peltier, who kept a bookshop at Golden Square in London, where the Chinnerys and Viotti purchased their French books.[43] Madame de Genlis thanked Viotti profusely for his 'arrangements' in her letter of 5 April 1803, calling him 'très dear amico', and confiding to him details of her recent unhappy exile.[44]

There is also an intriguing reference to a visit to Italy planned by Viotti at the end of 1802 in an October letter from Madame de Genlis.[45] It is clear that Viotti had been intending to travel on to Italy after accompanying Margaret to Calais at the end of their stay in Paris, but when Margaret did not find her husband waiting at Calais Viotti chaperoned her across the Channel.[46] Baillot's mention of Viotti's impending return to Paris that winter[47] shows that his musician friends were also expecting to see him en route from Italy to London later in the season. But the voyage must have been cancelled owing to the sudden death of Walter Chinnery on 19 November. Viotti would certainly not have deserted his friends at such a painful moment, and the fact that Madame de Genlis was still addressing letters to him at Gillwell between November 1802 and April 1803 is proof that he did not go.

At the end of 1802 relations with Madame de Genlis were still smooth and happy, and both Viotti and Margaret Chinnery returned to London charmed by their new friend. Margaret was more than ever inspired to continue to implement her friend's methods in her children's education, and Viotti was a willing collaborator.

---

Mme de Genlis's harp tutor as mediocre (*AMZ*, 23 January 1811, cols 67–8). See also *Annales de la musique pour l'an 1820*, p. 177.

41 Mme de Genlis to GBV, 18 November 1802, 30 November 1802, 3 December 1802, NYPL JOB 97-52, items 4, 5, 6 (Yim, D20, D21, D24).

42 Mme de Genlis to GBV, 25 February 1803, NYPL JOB 97-52, item 7 (Yim, D25).

43 See MC to GRC, 27 March 1810, Ch.Ch.

44 Mme de Genlis to GBV, *c.*5 April 1803, NYPL JOB 97-52, item 9 (Yim, D26).

45 Mme de Genlis to MC, [October 1802], Fisher 2000 – 6/8 (Yim, D8).

46 Mme de Genlis to MC, 7 November 1802, Fisher 2000 – 6/17 (Yim, D19).

47 Baillot to Montbeillard, 29 October 1802, cited in François-Sappey, p. 182.

CHAPTER 10

# Music at Gillwell, 1801–1807

Margaret Chinnery's education journal (1801–1807),[1] based on the one that Madame de Genlis kept to document the education of the Duke of Orléans's children and described in her novel *Adèle et Théodore*, shows just how large an influence Viotti had on the Chinnery children's education. It is also a source of much information on the family's activities during these years, and provides a systematic account of the Chinnery children's home education undertaken by Margaret with the help of various tutors. There are also intermittent references to company received at Gillwell and weekend parties and concerts, descriptions of all these being continued in Margaret's correspondence with her son at Oxford between 1808 and 1811. These writings show Viotti's closeness to the Chinnery children, and to their young relatives also educated at Gillwell: Matilda Chinnery, 'little Margaret' Chinnery, and a certain unrelated Maria to whom Margaret was also very attached, who was the daughter of an unnamed musician, and who may have been introduced into the Chinnery household by Viotti.

At the beginning of the nineteenth century music was an integral part of the lives of the educated members of society. It had a place in every lady's drawing room, and mothers had long been reminded by the many prominent newspaper advertisements placed by music instructors that they had a duty to provide their children, especially daughters, with at least some elementary music skills as part of their education. One such advertisement opened: 'Music being considered as one of the most polite of all the liberal sciences, and one of the chief ornaments of a finished education, it ought to claim the attention of all those who have it in their power to acquire a knowledge therein'.[2]

Viotti's influence on the Chinnery children's musical education was of course enormous. But equally important, surprisingly, was his contribution to their general education. Margaret's dependence on his help in this domain was so great that he might fairly be termed her assistant. His influence is detectable from the time of the children's earliest childhood to their adolescent years. Viotti's qualifications for the role of educator were not inconsiderable. His own education had been taken care of by Prince Alfonso dal Pozzo della Cisterna, who presumably not only taught him how to live in the company of kings and princes, but also gave him the thorough eighteenth-century liberal education of a gentleman, including the then mandatory grounding in classical studies, as attested by the frequent allusions to classical mythology in Viotti's letters. Viotti's biographer Miel confirms that his

[1] MC's Journal, 2 vols in one exercise book. In both French and English.

[2] *Morning Chronicle and London Advertiser*, 19 January 1782.

education had been 'soigné' (meticulous), and writes glowingly of Viotti's natural curiosity and intelligence, his interest in literature, physics, botany and anatomy, his aptitude for physical activities, and his urbane manners and animated, witty conversation.[3] Fayolle also speaks of Viotti's quick intellect, his judgement, and of the strength and refinement of his mind.[4] All this is confirmed by the Chinnery letters and journals.

Viotti's predilection for and patience with these pedagogic activities demonstrate what all his violin pupils have proven, that he was a gifted and dedicated teacher. Two often quoted 1798 letters written by Viotti to seven-year-old Caroline and five-year-old Walter Chinnery from his exile at Schönfeld are much better understood if one understands something of Madame de Genlis's method of education, which emphasized the need to keep children fully occupied. Accordingly, days were strictly regimented at Gillwell and the children's occupations were divided among intellectual and physical activities, and the acquisition of all the elegant accomplishments: the practice of a musical instrument, singing, drawing, dancing, and later, versification. Reference to some of the elements of the Genlis education method are to be found in these two Viotti letters, the first dated 18 June 1798, and addressed to Walter:

> I assume, my dear Walter, that you are behaving like a big boy, and that you are reading big books, that you are doing your arithmetic well, and skipping well,[5] and that you are doing all your activities well with mama and mamselle.[6]
>
> As I believe that you are doing all that, it is only fair that I give you proof of my approval, and that is why I am writing you this letter. I hope you will like it, and when mama writes and tells me that you are continuing to be a good boy I shall write you another one. Dear Walter, you must take good care of your garden and plant some flowers so that when I return you will be able to give me a pretty bouquet.[7]
>
> Are you looking after your violin? You must take good care of it, and your brother George also, so that your *amico* can show you how to play it. Tell mamselle that I have not forgotten her, embrace papa and mama for me, and keep loving me with all your heart.
>
> Your amico Viotti[8]

---

[3] Michaud, vol. 43, p. 589.

[4] 'Memoir of Viotti', p. 56.

[5] One of the physical fitness exercises recommended by Mme de Genlis in her education novel *Adèle et Théodore.*

[6] Mlle Virginie St Evay, the French governess who lived with the Chinnerys at Gillwell.

[7] Like the eponymous protaganists of *Adèle et Théodore*, the Chinnery children had a gardener to help them tend their own garden beds and give them simple instruction in botany.

[8] 'Je suppose, mon cher Walter, que vous vous conduisés comme un grand garçon, que vous lisés maintenant dans de grands livres, que vous comptés bien, vous sautés bien et que vous faites bien toutes vos affaires avec maman et mamselle. Comme je crois tout cela, il est juste que je vous donne aussi une preuve de mon estime, et c'est pourquoi je vous écrits cette lettre. J'espère qu'elle vous fera plaisir, et quand maman m'écrira que vous continués à être bien bon, je vous en écrirai une autre. Il faut mon cher Walter que vous ayés bien soin de votre jardin, que vous y plantiés des fleurs pour avoir de quoi me donner

It is clear from the letter that Walter and George were taking violin lessons from Viotti. But they did not continue for very long, and there is no mention of them in Margaret Chinnery's education journal. The only other reference to these lessons is in the January 1798 letter from Viotti to Margaret:

> Are you looking after George? Does he remember a few notes? Do take care of this [aspect of his music studies], I beg you, as I think that that is the only thing that I would not be capable of teaching him. For the rest, I am perfectly confident.'[9]

This extraordinary confession may perhaps be explained by the fact that all Viotti's previous pupils except Rode had been adult violinists. All, including the young future pupil Pixis, had been schooled in the basics of music before Viotti took over their tuition. In Viotti's own violin method he states that a young pupil should not take up a violin before he has 'a clear idea of the notes, their position and their length'.[10] Viotti's case was unusual in that era, when professors began training their pupils very young, and often had them on the performing stage by the age of eight or nine. The Chinnery boys were the youngest of all his pupils, and the only ones to have begun their violin studies with no prior knowledge of music.

The letter to Caroline Chinnery, dated 8 October 1798, also focussed on education, in particular her musical education. The sonatas mentioned by Viotti in the first sentence were probably the Three sonatas for piano with accompaniment for violin (WVIa: 10–12), arranged from his own Duets for two violins, Book 1.[11] Most of Viotti's keyboard solos listed in White's *Thematic Catalogue* would have been intended for Margaret Chinnery or her daughter Caroline, accompanied by himself on the violin and William Chinnery or another musician on the cello:

> I was just busy composing some pretty little piano sonatas for you, with violin accompaniment, when a letter from your dear Mama informed me that you were much neglecting your music. This news was all the more distressing since Mama added that it was your bad humour that was preventing you from making progress!
> As I am sure that all this will not last very long and that you will soon again be your normal sweet amiable self, I shall continue to compose for you, and I shall finish the sonatas so that on my return you may play them for me very nicely and I may have the

---

un joli bouquet à mon retour. Avés vous soin de votre violon? Il faut le bien conserver, votre frère George aussi, afin que votre *amico* puisse vous montrer. Dites à mamselle que je me rappelle bien d'elle, embrassés papa et maman pour moi, et aimés moi toujours de tout votre cœur. / Votre amico Viotti' (GBV to WGC, 18 June 1798, privately owned letter cited in Pougin, p. 79).

9 'Avés vous soin de George? Se rappelle-t-il de quelques notes? Ayés en soin je vous prie, car il me semble que c'est cela seul que je ne serois pas en état de lui apprendre, pour du reste [sic] j'en suis sur' (GBV to MC, 23 J[anvier 1798], NYPL JOB 97-52, item 2).

10 'une idée claire des notes de leur position et de leur durée' (Viotti's *Méthode* (fragment), in M. Pincherle, 'La Méthode de violon de J.B. Viotti', *Feuillets d'histoire du violon*, Paris, 1927, p. 175).

11 See White's *Thematic Catalogue*, p. 135. They cannot have been the sonatas suggested by van der Straeten (1902), col. 1739, since these were already published by *c.*1785.

pleasure of accompanying you. I shall send them to you as soon as I learn from your dear good Mama that you have rediscovered your taste for music, for that beautiful and agreeable art that gives so much pleasure to everyone.
Adieu my dear Caroline, embrace young Walter for me, remember me to Mamselle, and talk about me often with your excellent Mama and your good Papa. I hope I will soon hear that you still deserve all Amico's esteem and friendship.
J. B. Viotti
Your letter gave me great pleasure, and I thank you for it.[12]

It is evident that the rigorous methods that Margaret Chinnery applied to her daughter's later musical education were also applied from the age of seven, and that Viotti even then was helping Margaret to enforce discipline by applying Madame de Genlis's rule of giving rewards for good behaviour.

Another two letters, both dated 20 May 1801, from Viotti to Margaret show that Viotti had been left at Gillwell to supervise the children's educational programme while Margaret was in London consulting a physician. In what appears to be the first of the two letters Viotti states that the day's education journal, kept by the governess in Margaret's absence as a record of the children's behaviour and activities, and read aloud each morning at breakfast, was satisfactory. He also reports, with charming candour, that Caroline's piano lesson had been compromised by the effects of some medicine that Margaret had issued orders for her to be given.[13] In the second letter he gives details of another music lesson:

> So far they have all behaved wonderfully. This morning Caroline worked on her *Canti Kermi* like a little angel. She even took much pleasure in it, even though before beginning she would have preferred to practise her sonata. But as the tuner arrived at half past one, I took the opportunity to set her to work in my room scribbling out some musical notes. George was at the other end of the table writing to you.[14]

---

[12] 'J'étois justement occupé à composer de trés jolies petites sonates de Pianoforte pour vous, avec un accompagnement de Violon, lorsqu'une lettre de votre chère Maman m'a appris que vous négligés beaucoup la Musique. Cette nouvelle m'a d'autant plus mis au désésjoir, que Maman ajoute que c'est votre humeur qui vous empêche de faire des progrès! Comme je suis sur que tout cela ne peut durer que quelques moments, que vous redeviendrés promptement aussi douce, aussi aimable que vous l'avés été, je continuerai à composer pour vous, et je finirai les sonates afin qu'à mon retour vous me les jouiés *très bien* et que je puisse avoir le plaisir de vous les accompagner. je vous les enverrai aussitôt que j'apprendrai de votre chère et si bonne Maman, que vous avés repris votre gout pour la Musique, pour ce bel art si agréable, et qui fait tant de plaisir à tout le monde. Adieu ma chère Caroline, embrassés votre petit Walter de ma part, rappellés moi au souvenir de Mamselle, et parlés de moi souvent avec votre excellente Maman et votre bon Papa. J'espère que bientôt j'apprendrai que vous merités toujours toute l'estime et toute l'amitié de l'Amico. / J. B. Viotti / Votre lettre me fait bien plaisir, et je vous en remercie' (GBV to CC, 8 October 1798, Viotti Papers, RCM).

[13] GBV to MC, 20 May 1801, PHM 94/143/1 – 2/25.

[14] 'Jusqu'ici tous se sont comportés à merveille; Caroline a travaillé ce matin comme un petit ange au *Canti Kermi*, elle a même fait cet ouvrage avéc beaucoup de plaisir, quoiqu'avant de commencer elle eût preféré travailler à sa sonate… Mais l'accordeur

Between February and April 1802 when Margaret was again ill Viotti once more took over educational duties: 'our good Amico began to attend to the children's studies occasionally as time permitted; and during the last three or four weeks he presided regularly, and they pursued in some sort, their usual plan of studies.'[15] Throughout the whole of Walter's short life it was Viotti who read with him and corrected his writing, so that at the age of eight Walter spoke and wrote both French and Italian better than his native English.

Margaret's education journal, like Madame de Genlis's, included daily timetables ('plans de journées'), yearly progress reports ('connaissances acquises'), and lists of texts and pieces of music studied. The Journal shows that at the age of nine Caroline's musical studies began in earnest. On wet days, when she was not outside tending her garden before breakfast, she played scales for half an hour, and after breakfast practised for another hour and a half. She had daily piano lessons from her mother, or sometimes from Viotti, and three days a week she spent an hour in the early afternoon preluding with Viotti or studying composition. The method that Margaret used to teach her daughter piano was largely based on Madame de Genlis's, and is described by her in an 1806 letter to her cousin.[16]

From 1801 Viotti's King's Theatre colleague Francesco Bianchi came to Gillwell every Sunday to give Caroline instruction in thorough bass and composition. Bianchi and his wife of one year, soprano Jane Jackson, were among the several musicians introduced to the Chinnerys by Viotti, who, like the harpist Dizi, and members of the King's Theatre ballet corps Joubert and Boisgérard, were subsequently employed as the Chinnery children's tutors. From September to October 1801 the Bianchis spent a seven-week period at Gillwell as resident music tutors. Bianchi gave Caroline an hour's lesson in counterpoint in the morning and an hour in accompaniment in the afternoon, and by the end of October she was beginning to be able to accompany from the score. Madame Bianchi gave George some rudimentary instruction in time and notes and in singing, and also gave Maria singing instruction.[17]

At the same time Bianchi devoted two hours a day to teaching George the first principles of geometry, and left an extract from his unpublished manuscript *Dell'attrazione armonica* at Gillwell for George to continue to read after his departure. Extracts of Bianchi's theoretical work were translated into English after his death by his wife and published periodically in the English *Quarterly Musical Magazine and Review* in 1820 and 1821.[18] There is evidence that Viotti studied the

---

étant venû à une heure et demie, j'ai jugé à propos de la faire travailler à barbouiller des notes dans ma chambre; George étoit à l'autre bout de la table à vous écrire' (GBV to MC, 20 May 1801, NYPL JOB 97-52, item 3).

[15] MC's Journal, 4 May 1802, p. 143.

[16] MC to B. Crawfurd (copy), 6 February 1806, in MC's Journal, pp. 122–5, and transcribed in Yim, *The Chinnery Family Papers*, pp. 318–21. See also Mme de Genlis's *Adèle et Théodore, ou Lettres sur l'éducation*, 3 vols, Libraires associés, Paris, vol. 1, pp. 67–9.

[17] MC's Journal, 14 October 1801, p. 142.

[18] The one that George read was probably 'On geometrical proportions [in music]', *QMMR* (1820), vol. 2, no. 8, pp. 434–47.

work carefully. The 1885 letter from Algernon Greene to Heron-Allen in the Viotti Papers in the Royal College of Music refers to a two-volume manuscript of the 'Treatise on the theory and practice of counterpoint of Signor Maestro Bianchi', copied by Viotti with the author's permission.

Although George did not continue with his violin lessons, Viotti had an input into his education in other ways. For example in 1804 when the Chinnerys were seeking a tutor qualified to teach classics and mathematics to prepare George for Oxford, it was Viotti who contacted a German friend in Altona, who in turn procured for them a young graduate from the University of Göttingen, C.L. Trumpf.[19] Trumpf was required to give lessons to the other children also, and to keep an education journal in French, and report weekly to Viotti or Margaret on his pupils' progress. Viotti oversaw Trumpf's programme, and smoothed any disagreements with Margaret, giving him the wise advice to submit to Margaret's will.[20]

Margaret's 1801 progress report is full of praise for her ten-year-old daughter's rapid progress in composition, which, even allowing for the exaggeration of maternal pride, seems barely credible:

> The progress of Caroline in music continues to be astonishing for her age, and if M. Bianchi were able to give her continuous instruction she would have already learned all there is to know of the rules of composition and of accompaniment &c. When she puts her mind to it she can quite correctly write parts for four, three or two instruments. She is ten years old today, and it seems impossible to have mastered such a difficult science at that age, but several witnesses will attest to the fact [that she has]. She also knows how to compose sonatas. But ideas have not come to her yet, so that her first three pieces I regard as proof of her learning, rather than of her *genius*, which has not yet developed. Madame Bianchi had begun to teach her singing, but after 3 or 4 lessons I saw that it would not be in a good style; so I found an excuse to place her in Mr Bianchi's hands for singing also. Her voice promises very well; but up to now I have allowed her to sing only very little, for fear of harming her health. Now that she has reached ten years of age she may sing more.[21]

---

[19] See G. Schmeissen to GBV, 10 May 1804, NYPL JOB 97-52, item 10; and MC's Journal, 14 November 1804, p. 74.

[20] Herr Trumpf's Journal, 3 and 4 February [1805], Fisher 2000 – 48.

[21] 'Les progrès de Caroline dans la musique continuent à être étonnantes pour son âge, & si M. Bianchi pouvait lui donner des soins constants, elle aurait deja appris tout ce qu'on pourra apprendre des règles de la composition, de l'accompagnement &c. Quand elle s'y applique elle sait mettre très correctement les parties, en ecrivant à quatre instruments, à trois, & à deux. Elle a aujourd'hui 10 ans, et il parait impossible à cet age de posseder une science aussi difficile, mail il y a plusieurs temoins de ce fait. Elle sait aussi comment il faut s'y prendre pour composer des sonates. Mais les idées ne lui viennent pas encore de manière que quoiqu'elle en ait composé trois premières morceaux [sic] je les regarde plutôt comme des preuves de sa science, que du *génie*, qui n'est pas encore developpé. Mad[me] Bianchi avait commencé à lui apprendre à chanter mais apres 3 ou 4 leçons j'ai vu que ce ne serait pas d'un bon stile; ainsi j'ai trouvé un prétexte pour la remettre entre les mains de M. Bianchi pour le chant aussi. Elle annonce une très belle voix; mais jusqu'ici je l'ai laissé chanter fort peu; crainte de nuire à sa santé. Maintenant qu'elle a 10 ans

In a letter written after his return from Paris at the end of 1802 to his old masonic friend Pierre-Louis Ginguené, now director general of public education in Paris, Viotti cites Caroline's progress in composition as proof of the efficacity of Bianchi's theoretical treatise as a teaching tool:

> I think I would insult your intelligence if I were to endeavour to tell you about the originality, the profundity, and the merit of his system. However, since I have been witness to the way he puts it into practice, and since I have closely followed the way he proceeds in his lessons to a ten-year-old child, I feel it is my duty to inform you that this child knows as much about composition, about the source and use of harmony as any great composer.[22]

That is not to say that Caroline was not a normal ten-year-old in every other respect. Her misdemeanours such as impertinence, stubbornness, and reluctance to do piano practice are typical of a child of that age. In Margaret's Journal there is also evidence of the inevitable mother–daughter friction during music lessons. On one occasion Margaret entered the room to find 12-year-old Caroline displaying bad temper during her lesson with Viotti. But Viotti, like a parent to the children, was not above reprimanding them himself when the need arose. He scolded them for rudeness, taxed them with coldness when they did not show enough feeling for a sibling's troubles, called them to attention when, absorbed in their occupations, they were disinclined to reply to a guest's polite enquiry, and even had a hand in forming their table manners.

In Margaret's Journal the progress reports list the piano pieces learned by Caroline and show that the music studied was without exception by modern composers, most of whom were Viotti's friends. In 1801 Caroline learned pieces by Clementi ('*5 sonates*…Op. 4 & 37'), Steibelt ('3 sonates Op. 35'), [J.C.] Bach ('un Duo de Pianoforte'), Dussek ('2 sonates…Op. 14'), Schobert ('presque deux sonates' – almost two sonatas).[23] In 1802 she studied pieces by Viotti (one concerto in A minor – undoubtedly No. 25, of which Dussek's piano transcription was dedicated to Mrs Chinnery); by Dussek (one concerto in B flat); by [J.B.] Cramer (one sonata in A major), and also played through a lot more music in order to practise sight-reading. Margaret reported: 'She plays the piano with precision and taste, and *her touch* is charming for her age. She has a charming evenness, and she always plays her *pedal points*, *variations* and ornaments straight from her head like the good professors.'[24]

---

accomplis, elle pourra chanter davantage' (MC's Journal, [3 September] 1801, p. 138).

22 'Je croirais faire tort à vos connaissances si j'entreprenais de vous parler de l'originalité, de la profondeur et du mérite de son système. Cependant, comme j'ai été témoin de sa manière de le mettre en pratique, que j'ai suivi constamment sa marche et ses leçons vis-à-vis d'un enfant de dix ans, je me fais un devoir de vous assurer que cet enfant est aussi instruit dans la composition, dans la source et l'emploi de toute l'harmonie, qu'un grand compositeur peut l'être' (GBV to Ginguené, *c.*1802, privately owned letter cited in Pougin, p. 83).

23 MC's Journal, [3 September] 1801, pp. 138–9.

24 'Elle joue du Piano avec precision, et gout, et *son toucher* est charmant pour son age; elle

In 1803 Caroline studied pieces by Mozart (six sonatas), by Dussek (one sonata), by Cramer (two sonatas and '1 grand quartetto'),[25] and by Clementi (one sonata). She also studied eight books of scores by Bianchi and others, and scores and fugues by the Italian composer Fedele Fenaroli. Margaret's Journal entry of 4 February [1804] quotes Viotti as saying that Caroline had 'never played Dussek's sonata so well' (probably Dussek's Op. 24, dedicated to Margaret Chinnery). Caroline continued to advance in her musical studies in 1804:

> She reads scores prettily, and after going over them a little in the morning, is able to execute them quite well in the evening. I can truthfully say, *better* than most professors. She has forgotten none of the theory— and I perceive more facility in her preluding. M. Bianchi says that her knowledge of music is profound.[26]

Just after her thirteenth birthday Caroline began harp lessons. Her harp teacher was the acclaimed Dutchman François Joseph Dizi, who helped make the harp the popular instrument it was in London at the beginning of the nineteenth century. Viotti clearly had a hand in arranging these lessons also, as an 1806 letter written from Gillwell to Dizi attests. The letter was written to apologize for the confusion surrounding the payment of an account owing to the absence of the Chinnery governess, who normally kept a record of the number of visits. Viotti explained that Caroline had been temporarily forbidden to play or sing by her doctor, but that she and her mother, and he himself, would be pleased if Dizi paid them a visit, both for the pleasure of seeing him, and to settle the account in question.[27]

In a family whose lives were so completely dominated by the study and enjoyment of music, it is not surprising that Viotti should have composed pieces especially for them, as he did for other favourite pupils. This would explain the comment of a reviewer that some of Viotti's string trios were not true examples of their genre, but rather accompanied sonatas, and that, moreover, they were suited to less experienced violinists.[28] It is clear that Viotti preferred this form because it allowed him to take the dominant part in playing with pupils or amateur musicians.

Viotti also wrote many short vocal pieces to be performed at Gillwell with guests or on special occasions such as birthdays. His cantata 'Au fond d'une sombre vallée' for soprano (probably sung by Caroline) and piano (probably played by Margaret), of which the autograph copy carries the annotation 'Per il

---

a une egalité charmante, et elle fait toujours ses *points d'orgue*, *variations* et agrements de tête comme les bons professeurs' (MC's Journal, 3 September 1802, p. 148).

[25] In 1803 J.B. Cramer published a piano quartet in E flat, Op. 28.

[26] 'Elle lit joliment les partitions, et après les avoir parcouru un peu le matin, elle les execute assez bien le soir; je puis dire avec vérité, *mieux* que la plupart des professeurs. Elle n'a rien oublié de la Théorie et en preludant je m'apperçois de plus de facilité. M. Bianchi dit qu'elle est profonde dans la science de la musique' (MC's Journal, 3 September 1804, p. 155).

[27] GBV to Dizi, 5 October 1806, transcribed in Giazotto, p. 268.

[28] Review of two sets of Three trios for two violins and cello, Op. 16 and Op. 17 (*AMZ*, 2 November 1803, col. 76–7). However a later writer for the same journal thought that these trios were among his best (*AMZ*, 1 July 1812, col. 439).

giorno natalizio del caro Padre Chinnery' (WVII:1), was composed for William Chinnery's birthday (3 March), perhaps as part of the *fête domestique* for the year 1805, when there is an entry in Margaret's Journal for a proverb and a dance performed by the children for their father's birthday. Viotti himself was the recipient of fond birthday verses in French penned by Caroline on 12 May in 1807, 1808, 1809 and 1810 (the last in English). All pay tribute to his music, and the 1809 verses were set to music by Caroline.[29]

Among Caroline Chinnery's papers in the Powerhouse Museum collection is a page of undated writing in Viotti's hand entitled 'Palais de l'Esperance' (Palace of Hope),[30] which seems to be the opening stage directions for a kind of musical allegory written for another *fête domestique*. (The Chinnerys had an outdoor theatre at Gillwell.) At the bottom of the sheet is Viotti's trademark signature (two treble clefs), that he affixes to any words meant to be accompanied by music, proving his involvement in this production. Viotti's Suite in D major for strings (WVIII:1) was composed for some such theatrical, since the autograph bears the note 'del Teatro Gillwell'. According to Margaret's Journal these comedies were being performed between 1802 and 1806. Music and dancing were a feature of special occasions, and on the twins' tenth birthday in 1801 they were serenaded, as they had been the previous year, by three musicians, probably from the King's Theatre orchestra. Margaret wrote:

> In the morning we were serenaded by a clarinet, bassoon & kettle drum. Fifty three poor children dined with us on the lawn; they assembled at the lodge & were there met by our own little ones, some of our servants, the three musicians &c &c and they were conducted to the house, the music playing. All the time they dined, the music played. In the evening our children, our friends, & most of the servants danced country dances,[31] for an hour before the fire works; and when they were over the dance was renewed. After the children retired we went to a distant room to supper, & the servants with their visitors kept it up till two oclock in the morning.[32]

Viotti probably composed much of his later music at Gillwell. In an 1809 letter to George describing various domestic activities Margaret mentioned that Viotti was composing, but did not elaborate further.[33] Viotti's Violin Concerto No. 28 in A minor was certainly composed at Gillwell. One of the parts of his autograph score for this concerto is entitled 'Carolina Concerto dell'Amico'. If this part is a composing draft rather than a piano reduction, as suggested by White,[34] then putting Caroline's name on it indicates perhaps that she participated in the early

---

[29] The verses of 1807, 1809 and 1810 are to be found in Osborn fd. 11, items 39, 73, 118. The music does not survive.

[30] PHM 94/143/1 – 24/6.

[31] Country dances were popular at home assemblies, as can be seen from later Chinnery letters. One of the best selling items of the important London publishing firm Thompson, was its yearly collection of *Twenty Four Country Dances*.

[32] MC's Journal, [3 September] 1801, p. 141.

[33] MC to GRC, 14 February 1809, Ch.Ch.

[34] *Thematic Catalogue*, p. 36.

trials of the concerto. In 1804, the date of the watermark on the paper, Caroline was only 13, and probably not mature enough to be of use to Viotti in trialling his compositions. But by 1807 Caroline was an accomplished pianist, and it is therefore more likely that the concerto was composed around this time.

Indeed by 1807 Margaret expected Caroline and the other female relatives who were then being educated at Gillwell to help entertain house guests. She stated very clearly her views on this matter in her Journal at the beginning of 1807:

> It is evident therefore, that when so much pain is taken to ornament the mind of a female, and to give her elegant accomplishments, the intent must be that of improving domestic society. I am not here talking of those absurd young persons, and of still more absurd parents who like to exhibit their children like public performers for the amusement of large assemblies! This practice I have ever regarded as a most indecorous folly. But the friends of the family, who occasionally join the domestic circle, *should* partake of its enjoyments whatever they may be, and a young person with every regard to the strictest modesty and the purest delicacy, may assist her mother in the entertainment of her friends.[35]

When the family circle was an intimate one the children participated in the evening music-making at a much younger age, and sometimes helped entertain very close family friends such as William Spencer (affectionately known as Guglielmo), the Grenfells, and their neighbours from Fair Mead Lodge in Epping Forest, the Sothebys,[36] whose children were about the same age as the Chinnery twins.

The Viotti canzonetta 'Vo triste tacito' for soprano and piano, which bears the inscription 'Parole d'un modesto mettre in musica da un timido, il tutto dedicato all'amabile padrona. Gillwell House, 5 Dicembre 1804' ('Words by a modest man, put into music by a shy man, the whole dedicated to the charming padrona'),[37] could have been a collaboration of any of the house guests that were at Gillwell on that weekend.[38] But music *en famille* and concerts for guests were reserved for weekends when William was able to join them. On week nights the principal evening activity was reading aloud. Margaret read Shakespeare, the works of French and Italian poets and dramatists such as Fénelon, Racine, Metastasio, Alfieri, Tasso, and also Greek tragedies. This was a favourite pastime of all the family, particularly of Caroline and Viotti.

The Chinnery concerts at Gillwell House, like the earlier ones at Mortimer Street, drew eminent musicians visiting England and foreign diplomats, as well as British lords and ladies. The weekend musical activities, which featured Viotti and whichever of his colleagues happened to be house guests at the time, took place in comfortable and intimate surroundings with no ceremony, in a house surrounded

---

35 MC's Journal, 16 January [1807], p. 99.

36 William Sotheby (1757–1833), English poet and translator, his wife Mary and their children Hans and Maria.

37 *Thematic Catalogue*, p. 142.

38 MC's Journal, 8 December [1804], p. 77, shows that members of the Grenfell family 'with some others' had been at Gillwell since 5 December.

by a beautiful park and forest, and was attractive to visitors not only on account of the standard of music, but equally for the relaxed yet elegant atmosphere.

The earliest house guest to have kept a record of her visit to Gillwell and of her impressions of the house, the family and the music, was Elisabeth Vigée-Lebrun. The artist became such a close friend of Margaret and Viotti that they would seek her out on each future visit to France, and she even had her own room in Margaret's French country house, purchased when Viotti was appointed director of the Paris Opéra. Among the anecdotes recounted in her *Memoirs* is a description of a two-week visit to Gillwell shortly after her arrival in England in April 1803. She is warm in her praise of the Chinnerys' domestic musical entertainments:

> I began, shortly after my arrival, by spending a fortnight with Mme. Chinnery at Gillwell, where I found the celebrated Viotti. The house was most luxurious, and I was given a charming welcome. On reaching the place I saw that the gate was garlanded with flowery wreaths twined about the pillars. On the staircase, similarly decorated, stood at intervals little marble cupids, holding vases filled with roses. In short, it was a springtime fairy pageant. So soon as I had entered the drawing-room, two little angels, Mme. Chinnery's son and daughter, sang a delicious piece of music to me, composed for me by that good-natured Viotti [see WVII: 2]. I was truly touched by this affectionate greeting; indeed, the fortnight I spent at Gillwell were days of joy and gladness. Mme. Chinnery was a beautiful woman, with much mental subtlety and charm. Her daughter, then fourteen years of age [in fact Caroline was not yet twelve], played the piano astonishingly, so that every evening this young girl, Viotti, and Mme. Chinnery, herself an excellent musician, gave us a delightful concert.[39]

Vigée-Lebrun returned at least three more times to Gillwell, for two weeks in September, a week in November, and a few days in December, bringing with her on these last two occasions the Russian Prince Ivan Bariatinski. It was sometime during these visits that she painted Margaret's portrait (see Figure 2), and made sketches of Viotti for her portrait which would be completed in France in 1805.[40] During the September visit there was music each evening, but the only details in Margaret's Journal were that 'some of the finest compositions of the celebrated Jomelli were executed.'[41] A letter from young George Chinnery to his mother shows that Margaret, Viotti and William also attended a concert at 'Madame le Brun's' in London.[42]

In September 1803, on the eve of her departure for the fashionable health resort of Tunbridge Wells, Vigée-Lebrun wrote to Margaret, also about to set out with her family and Viotti for their yearly autumn vacation in Brighton, for her address in order that she might pay her a visit. Private concerts were again an attraction in the Chinnery drawing room at Brighton, where, Margaret notes, the pianist Mrs Bartolozzi (née Therese Jansen) was a guest on one occasion.[43] The

---

[39] Vigée-Lebrun, *Memoirs*, pp. 192–3.
[40] See above, p. 5.
[41] MC's Journal, 6 September [1803], p. 8.
[42] GRC to MC, *c.*1803, Fisher 2000 – 7/1.
[43] MC's Journal, 16 October [1803], p. 22.

artist's attachment to the Chinnery family and to Viotti is evident from the way she signs off: 'adieu Belle et Bonne, je vous aime de tout mon cœur ainsi tous les votres, et Amico aussi (Farewell beautiful and kind lady, I love you with all my heart, as I do all your family and Amico also). Le Brun'.[44] A letter from Margaret to Viotti thanking him for a bouquet of flowers from Gillwell and sent to her on her birthday in 1804 indicates that Viotti was not in Brighton with the rest of the family on 16 October that year.[45]

Many enthusiastic *amateurs* participated in the Chinnery family concerts. Among them was the newly-wed Scottish couple Lord George and Lady Susan Dunmore,[46] who were also friends of William Spencer. Lady Susan was clearly an accomplished harpist, and wrote from Tunbridge Wells after her 1806 Gillwell visit, 'Tell Amico that the Harp has quite forgot how to play a *Solo* & longs much for the accompaniment to which it has lately been accustomed.'[47] The harp sonata that Viotti dedicated to her (WVI:9) may date from around this time. Miss Sophia Johnstone, the wealthy Chinnery friend who was an intimate of the Prince of Wales and grand hostess to London society was another harp *amateur.*[48] She was admitted by the gossipy diarist Lord Glenbervie, to play and sing well, but he unflatteringly described her person as 'very like a stumpy barrell'.[49] She helped Caroline to prepare for special concerts at Gillwell, writing on one occasion that she was sending her 'the Harp part of Davidde to study for Sunday next.'[50] The illustrious antiquary Richard Payne Knight of Soho Square was always happy to accept a Chinnery invitation: 'Be assured my dear Madam, that this busy crowded Month of May can afford no Engagement more grateful to me than with my friends of Gillwell; whose Musical Attractions are not wanting'.[51]

Then there was the poet William Sotheby, whom the Irish poet and wag Thomas Moore termed 'William Botherby' on account of his flustered, blustering manner. Although they did not pretend to a great knowledge of music themselves, the Sothebys were always ready to bring their children to hear the Chinnerys play. In May 1805 Margaret wrote in her Journal that 'Mr, Mrs and Miss Sotheby' spent the weekend at Gillwell, and Caroline 'endeavoured to entertain them as well as she could on the Harp & Pianoforte.'[52] The jovial poet preferred popular dancing music, and Viotti obliged him on one occasion by providing music for their

---

[44] Elisabeth Vigée-Lebrun to MC, *c.*19 September 1803, Fisher 2000 – 8/1.

[45] MC to GBV, 16 October 1804, Fisher 2000 – 39/1.

[46] Lord Dunmore (1762–1836), was styled Viscount Fincastle until 1809.

[47] Susan Fincastle to MC, 14 September 1806, Fisher 2000 – 5/5.

[48] Sister of George Johnstone (d.*c.*January 1814) and future wife (*c.*1815) of the Count St Antonio (later Duke of Canizaro). The latter was a manager of the King's Theatre in 1821, and he and his wife played an active part in the organization of Lord Burghersh's Royal Academy of Music in 1822.

[49] Douglas, *The Glenbervie Journals*, p. 144.

[50] Sophia Johnstone to CC, *c.*1809, Fisher 2000 – 34/5.

[51] Richard Payne Knight to MC, May [1810], Fisher 2000 – 5/10.

[52] MC's Journal, 18 May [1805], p. 94.

dancing party at Fair Mead Lodge. Thomas Moore, noting Viotti's good-natured forbearance, recorded the event in his *Journal* on 3 September 1818:

> Sotheby, the Poet, (poor Botherby!) once invited the Channings [Chinnerys] & Viotti to his house at Epping Forest, and begged of Viotti (whose little solos are the most touching & romantic things possible) to bring his Violin— The latter good-naturedly promised he would &, on his arrival, Botherby, the barbarian, exclaimed "I am glad you are come— you've brought your fiddle, I hope— now, girls— where are your partners?— stand up— here's Mr. Viotti— what dance will you have?"— Viotti, to the immortal credit of his good-nature, played country-dances for them the whole night.[53]

Perhaps the rendition of popular dance music was not as foreign to Viotti's inclination as Moore believed. After all, before it assumed a respectable place on the concert stage in the eighteenth century the violin was originally the quintessential instrument of dance, and Viotti would have been the first to recognise and indulge in the instrument's capacity to impart joy.

Foreign diplomats, who were invariably of noble lineage and tastes, figured prominently on Margaret's guest lists at Gillwell. The French ambassador to England during the fragile Peace of Amiens, Comte Antoine-François Andréossy, was one of the earliest visitors. Andréossy appears to have first made the acquaintance of William Chinnery through the latter's good offices towards some French *émigrés*. He also shared with William a common love of the fine arts, having purchased in London the valuable collection of drawings that had belonged to the former French finance minister Calonne, Viotti's old Paris acquaintance.[54] Andréossy was invited to Gillwell in 1803, and he too enjoyed the surrounding countryside by day and was entertained, as Madame Vigée-Lebrun had been, with music by night. Andréossy must also have been either a patron of music or a valued *amateur*, as Mozart dedicated a piano sonata (Op. 10) to him.[55] But by March 1803 the Peace was already on the brink of collapse, and in mid-May Andréossy was recalled to France.[56]

Another diplomatic visitor to Gillwell was the Spanish ambassador d'Anduaga, who came with his family in 1804. They too undoubtedly heard the playing of Viotti and Caroline, especially since the younger of their two daughters was about the same age as Caroline. It fell to the elder daughter, Josephine, to write to Margaret Chinnery at the time of their departure from England. In the letter she begged that Mr Viotti would remember his promise to call and see them before their departure, as well as Mr Bianchi, who was at Gillwell when the Anduagas visited.[57] Her father also addressed a letter to Viotti expressing the same sentiments

---

[53] T. Moore, *The Journal of Thomas Moore*, 6 vols, ed. W. Dowden (1983–91), University of Delaware Press, London, vol. 1, pp. 34–5.

[54] Calonne himself had been a house guest of the Chinnerys. See WBC to MC, [March 1812], PHM 94/143/1 – 7/6.

[55] Reviewed by *AMZ*, 26 October 1808, col. 54.

[56] See Andréossy to MC, 15 May 1803, Fisher 2000 – 4/4.

[57] Josephine d'Anduaga to MC, 16 August 1804, Fisher 2000 – 4/6.

of gratitude for the Gillwell hospitality.[58] In December 1804 the cellist Christopher Schram was an overnight guest and probably stayed longer. He was to participate in the trialling of some new string quartets by Viotti in 1812.

The Italian bass Giuseppe Naldi, described by the contemporary opera enthusiast Richard Mount Edgcumbe as an excellent buffo,[59] was probably introduced to Gillwell soon after arriving in England with his family in April 1806. An educated gentleman who had been a barrister in his native city Bologna, Naldi was generous, gregarious and debonair. He was the leading *buffo caricato* at the King's Theatre over the next 12 years. The friendship between the two families went beyond the obligatory appearance in the Gillwell music room, and extended right to his freakish death in Paris in 1820.

On 14 January 1804 the popular Continental contralto Giuseppina Grassini, mistress successively to Napoleon and the Duke of Wellington, made her London debut at King's Theatre. Edgcumbe, who had reservations about the manner by which Grassini reached the pinnacle of her career, noted in his *Musical Reminiscences* that Grassini was not only 'rapturously applauded in public, but she was taken up by the first society, *fêtée*, caressed, and introduced as a regular guest in most of the fashionable assemblies.'[60] One of these fashionable assemblies was Margaret Chinnery's. On the weekend of 5 and 6 February 1804 she was a guest at Gillwell, where she offended her hosts with 'her vulgar and awkward mockery' of English countrywomen's dancing.[61] Nevertheless she was invited back to Gillwell on at least two subsequent occasions.

On one of these occasions Grassini sent word to William Chinnery by the Portuguese ambassador the Chevalier de Sousa Couttinho that she would prefer not to have to sing 'au concert de M[r] Viotti' at Gillwell, as she was fatigued from her previous night's performance. Sousa, who calls Grassini 'la bella Sig[a] Peppina', writes: 'I told her that you would spare her the pain of refusing, by begging your guests in advance to excuse her.'[62] This would have been a severe disappointment to Margaret, who liked to add brilliance to her musical evenings with such famous names. Dragonetti, a mutual friend of Grassini and de Sousa, also wrote to Viotti sometime during this period informing him of the postponement of a musical party that was to have taken place at de Sousa's the following week because Grassini was obliged to sing at the Opera on both Tuesday and Saturday.[63] He may have been referring to Tuesday 7 January 1806, when Grassini performed instead of Mrs

---

58 Anduaga to GBV, [August 1804], NYPL JOB 97-52, item 11. There is a Morillos d'Anduaga listed as a Spanish *amateur* in Havana in the *Annales de la musique pour l'an 1820*, p. 309. This was probably the same diplomat, posted in Cuba in 1819.

59 Edgcumbe, p. 105.

60 *Ibid.*, p. 96.

61 MC's Journal, 7 February 1804, p. 56.

62 'Je luy ai dit que vous lui epargneriés le chagrin de refuser, en priant d'avance les personnes presentes de l'excuser' (Sousa Couttinho to WBC, 23 May [1805 or 1806], Fisher 2000 – 19/9).

63 Dragonetti to GBV, Monday [6 January 1806?], NYPL JOB 97-52, item 64.

Billington in the opera *Gli Orazi ed i Curiazi*, 'on account of the encreased indisposition of Mrs Billington.'[64]

On the eve of her departure from England in November 1806 Grassini sent Margaret Chinnery a letter in which she, like all the other Gillwell guests, expressed her admiration for the talented children, her esteem for the charming hostess, and her appreciation of the idyllic surrounds of Gillwell. She appears to have left England on excellent terms with her hosts, as well as with Viotti, asking Margaret to extend 'to the amiable *Amico* a thousand compliments and beg that he might sometimes remember me.'[65] Margaret was to renew contact with her in 1821 during Viotti's term as director of the Paris Opéra.

In December 1806 the recently arrived celebrated compatriot of Grassini, soprano Angelica Catalani, who would soon eclipse her rival in fame and fortune, was a member of the Chinnery family Christmas party. Catalani's astoundingly powerful and flexible voice was to hold the English music public in thrall for the next seven years. She quickly became the talk of London and the stuff of much newspaper commentary owing to the high fees she commanded. She was accompanied to Gillwell by her husband Paul Valabrègue, whom she had married in Lisbon the previous year. Valabrègue, who subsequently became Catalani's manager, was not a well liked figure on account of his grasping profit-seeking negotiations with theatre managers on his wife's behalf. In one letter to his mother George Chinnery referred to him as Catalani's 'orrido sposo' (horrid spouse).[66]

After Catalani's London debut in the opera *Semiramide* by Portogallo on 13 December 1806, the laudatory newspaper reports, all agog with 'the volume and compass of her voice', her 'neatness and rapidity of execution' and her first-rate acting, were soon succeeded by sarcastic criticism of her elevated fees. She was reported to have demanded £7,000 for her season at King's Theatre, and to have been 'equally moderate […] with respect to private Concerts, requiring but two hundred pounds for her performance each night.'[67] Catalani, whose conduct in private life, was, according to Edgcumbe, irreproachable,[68] was a good friend to the Chinnerys, and was to consent to sing at George's celebratory party in Oxford on the occasion of his winning the Newdigate prize for poetry in 1810, seemingly without charging the Chinnerys the stipulated private concert fee.

Ten days after Catalani's debut at the King's Theatre the Italian tenor Giuseppe Siboni, who had been engaged to sing with Catalani in the 1806–1807 opera season, made his first appearance in London. Shortly after his arrival he too beat a path to Gillwell. The weekend that he spent with the Chinnerys was noted in Margaret's Journal with the remark: 'Caroline accompanied both evenings

---

[64] *Times*, 7 January 1806.

[65] 'a *l'Amico* amabile, mille compliments et priez le qu'il me rappelle quelque fois a son souvenir' (Josephina Grassini to MC, 9 November 1806, Fisher 2000 – 4/7).

[66] GRC to MC, 13 June 1808, Ch.Ch.

[67] *Sun*, 4 February 1807, cited in Smith, *Italian Opera*, p. 84.

[68] Edgcumbe, p. 105.

extremely well.'[69] Siboni had come down to Gillwell with the Viotti/Chinnery friend the Chevalier La Cainea, an amateur singer and theatre impresario. It is clear from a facetious article in the *Gentleman's Magazine* of 1808 that La Cainea was in some kind of managerial position at the King's Theatre. The article recounted a trivial court case in which La Cainea, as defendant, was disputing a singer's claim for higher payment for his services. There were clearly two cliques at the King's Theatre – the gentlemen musicians and the others. Naldi and Siboni, both of the former category, gave what appears to have been blatantly biased evidence in support of La Cainea, who nevertheless lost his case and was ordered to pay the plaintiff (Roselli) the demanded 30 guineas for three nights' singing.[70]

By 1807 Caroline was able to play and sing alongside the best musicians in the country, and her participation in Gillwell concerts increased noticeably: 'Caroline played and accompanied Amico's concerto, and the Chevalier's airs extremely well last night'.[71] On the weekend of 7–8 March the Chinnery home was full of literary house guests (William Spencer, Colonel Henry Francis Greville, Henry Luttrell), and Caroline played for them in a manner which showed Viotti's full influence:

> Caroline played extremely well on the Pianoforte both evenings; on Saturday she played the *Concerto in A* arranged by Mad[me] Montgeroult, and the Adagio was as well as I ever wish to hear it. This great stile of playing an Adagio, I may almost consider as a new and distinct talent she has acquired; in this the merit is all her own. She has made her profit of the good example before her, and has formed her stile upon that of Amico's, which is the most beautiful model she could have found in the world. On Sunday she played a Sonata of Steibelts, just as well.[72]

The only Viotti violin concerto known to have been arranged for piano by Montgéroult is No. 6 in E. But perhaps she also made arrangements of others, which were never printed and are now lost. Many of these private concerts used manuscript music, especially with so many professional musicians present. Viotti composed four concertos in A major, of which only two have an adagio movement (Nos 3 and 9). Both were published in Paris and were therefore likely to have been well known to Hélène de Montgéroult.

A month later Caroline pleased a London drawing room at Lady Anne Hamilton's, a lady-in-waiting to the Princess of Wales. Lady Anne also invited the Chinnery family and Viotti to her South Berkeley Street home on 8 July 1807.[73] Caroline usually consulted with Spencer on the choice of programme and rehearsal arrangements for these musical soirées. For one weekend party at Gillwell she wished to sing the popular English song *Old Robin Gray*. In view of Margaret's

---

[69] MC's Journal, 3 February [1807], p. 102.

[70] *Gentleman's Magazine* (1808), vol. 78, p. 167. La Cainea's name does not appear in Smith's *Italian Opera*.

[71] MC's Journal, 19 January [1807], p. 100.

[72] MC's Journal, 9 March [1807], p. 106.

[73] Lady Anne Hamilton to CC, 6 July 1807, Fisher 2000 – 34/2.

foregoing comments regarding a daughter's duty to aid her mother in domestic entertainments, it was probably from about this time that the note pencilled by Caroline on the third movement of Viotti's piano arrangement of his Concerto No. 24 in B minor dates ('Miss Chinnery begs Mr Walker to take care to make it turn conveniently').[74]

Another Gillwell guest in 1807, and one whom Viotti and the Chinnerys heard in London drawing rooms, was the society singer and pianist Susan Beckford, second daughter of the author William Beckford and future wife of the tenth Duke of Hamilton. J.B Cramer dedicated to her his piano nocturne Op. 32.[75] It was also in 1807 that the 17-year-old harpist Casimir Baecker came to stay at Gillwell. Wishing to promote her adopted son as a virtuoso performer, Madame de Genlis sent him to England in the hope that he would earn enough money from public concerts to ease some of her financial burden, and increase his chances of contracting an advantageous marriage. She relied on Margaret and Viotti to help, and for a period of three or four months his education and music practice were entrusted to their supervision at Gillwell. Viotti was asked to supervise his rehearsals and organize his concerts. Margaret was asked to supply him with tutors, keep him from the dangers of London, and ensure his concerts received favourable press reviews. When Casimir decamped without fulfilling any of his obligations it was left to Viotti to pack up his belongings and arrange for their transport to France, which he did with the help of his friend the harpmaker Sébastien m.[76]

Viotti was later to intervene on Margaret's behalf when Madame de Genlis incorrectly assumed, on Casimir's assertion, that the loss of a precious notebook was due to her carelessness. Madame de Genlis also blamed Sébastien Erard for the loss of some of Casimir's belongings.[77] In *c.*1814 Viotti would write an angry letter to Casimir taxing him with ingratitude and reminding him that he had been welcomed into the Chinnery home Gillwell in 1807 as their own son.[78] In the letter he also made a veiled allusion to a £6,000 loan William Chinnery had earlier made to Erard,[79] probably to help reinvigorate his London piano and harp manufacture in *c.*1807.

---

[74] White, 'Chronology', p. 123. White surmises that Viotti did not have time to complete the orchestration of the arrangement or copy the piano part of the finale, so that Caroline had to play from the full score, and sent it away to be bound with the above request.

[75] Published in Leipzig in 1807 (*AMZ*, 19 May 1807, col. 550).

[76] See Yim, *The Unpublished Correspondence of Mme de Genlis*.

[77] See *Mémoires*, vol. 3, p. 198, and vol. 8, p. 26; and Mme de Genlis to MC, 13 May 1814, Fisher 2000 – 6/35 (Yim, D52).

[78] GBV to Casimir Baecker (copy), [1814], NYPL JOB 97-52, item 65 (Yim, D75).

[79] See above, p. 7.

CHAPTER 11

# Gillwell, London, Oxford, Brighton, 1808–1811

On 14 January 1808 16-year-old George Chinnery departed for Christ Church College, Oxford, where his education would be completed. It was the first time George had left home and his initiation into college life would be hard. William Chinnery being unable to absent himself from the Treasury, the duty of accompanying the frightened young boy to Oxford fell to Viotti and William Spencer.

Viotti was to be like a second father to George during his Oxford years (1808–11). He acted as confidant, adviser, consoler, supporter and loving mentor. He purchased French books for George's private study from London booksellers. He desired to be remembered to George in each of his mother's daily letters, wrote letters of his own, to which George replied in French, and shared in George's trials and triumphs. He even surrendered to George his own writing table. In one memorable letter he advised George, who was struggling to come to terms with the culture of heavy drinking in college, on the art of taking wine convivially without becoming inebriated, describing a technique he himself used frequently when pressed by over-generous hosts to refill his glass. He warned that 'losing one's head and being no longer oneself is, as you know, one of the most humiliating things for a man, even though it may be the fashion in this country.'[1]

Viotti visited Oxford four times during this period: twice in 1808, once in 1809 and once in 1810. During his first visit (15–22 January 1808) he stayed for the first three nights at the home of Spencer's friends the Wall family, then at nearby Wheatfield, the estate of William Spencer's father, Lord Charles Spencer, and home to William Spencer's elder brother Lord John Spencer and his wife Lady Elizabeth. On 18 January he dined with Spencer's uncle and aunt the Duke and Duchess of Marlborough at Blenheim Palace. On his first morning in Oxford Viotti accompanied George to Christ Church cathedral for chapel prayers, which he described as 'an incomprehensible monastic muttering'.[2] Nor was he impressed by the airs of the tutors, saying that everyone in Oxford seemed to be 'infected by a

---

[1] 'de perdre la tête, de n'être plus soi-même, est une des choses, comme tu sçais, les plus humiliantes pour l'homme. Peu importe que ce soit la mode dans ce pays ci' (GBV to GRC, 15 November 1808, Ch.Ch.).

[2] 'un marmotage monastique auquel on ne comprend rien' (GBV to MC, 16 January 1808, NYPL JOB 97-52, item 13).

sultanesque malady'.[3] The second visit (1–10 February 1808) was after a weekend party at the Grenfells' Taplow House, 40 miles from Oxford. The party included the Duke of Cambridge, William, Margaret and Caroline Chinnery and Viotti, William Spencer, the Portuguese ambassador Sousa Couttinho, and the violinist Paolo Spagnoletti (1768–1834), who had arrived in London in 1802. At the end of the weekend William Chinnery returned to London with the Duke of Cambridge, and Margaret, Caroline, Viotti and Spencer proceeded to Oxford.

In October 1808 the Chinnerys and Viotti were again invited to Taplow House, this time to a grand ball in honour of young Charlotte Grenfell's birthday. However because of the manner in which the invitation was issued, Margaret took offence and made her excuses. Viotti of course followed suit, and Mrs Georgina Grenfell's disappointment is made plain in a letter to Viotti in which she writes: 'we will miss you grievously, as you are such a close friend of the Dukes you are absolutely essential, & our Music Alas! will be nothing without you!'[4]

During these visits to Oxford Viotti was to make the acquaintance of several university dons, most of whom were Spencer family friends. Among them was Dr William Howley, a canon of Christ Church College and future Archbishop of Canterbury; Dr Martin Wall, Lichfield Professor of Medicine, with whom he lodged with Spencer on their first arrival in 1808; Dr Marlow, president of St John's College; Italian-speaking music *amateur* Edmund Goodenough, logic and rhetoric lecturer of Christ Church College; and Dr John Cole, rector of Exeter College, who in 1816 would carry back from France Viotti's old baton.[5] During the February 1808 visit Viotti revisited the Wall family, and the doctor enlivened the whole Chinnery party with his 'gaiety, good humour, & delightful conversation' and where 'music was, as usual, *the order of the day*!'[6]

In March 1809 Viotti made a weekend visit to Oxford, travelling again with Spencer, but this time staying at the inn of choice of most Oxford visitors, the Star. The visit had been discussed throughout much of February, and Margaret was sceptical that it would take place at all, writing to George 'perhaps they may set off some day all in a hurry. You know they are both rather odd persons.'[7] What exactly she meant by this is not clear. Clearly both Viotti and Spencer had certain idiosyncracies, but their personalities were quite dissimilar. Spencer was flippant, unreliable and chronically unpunctual, none of which could be said of Viotti. Spencer wanted to be away a fortnight, Viotti only two or three days. 'Amico is put out by Guglielmo's irresolution & uncertainty', Margaret wrote.[8]

When the visit was finally fixed for the weekend of 3–5 March Viotti wrote to say he would bring his violin and entertain George's friends. George planned a party in his rooms on Saturday to which he would invite 'a few men to meet them,

---

[3] 'Il parait que la maladie sultanesque gagne tout le monde ici' (*Ibid.*).
[4] Georgina Grenfell to GBV, [October 1808], Fisher 2000 – 40/2.
[5] See GBV to WBC, 12 February [1816], PHM 94/143/1 – 14/27.
[6] CC to WBC, [8] February 1808, Fisher 2000 – 21/2.
[7] MC to GRC, 20 February 1809, Ch.Ch.
[8] MC to GRC, 24 February 1809, Ch.Ch.

not any of our stiff John Bulls, but pleasant jovial guests.'[9] In the event the party did not take place, owing to the fire at Christ Church on the night of Friday 3 March. Viotti had dined with George in his rooms, returned to the Star, and was about to retire for the night when cries of 'Fire, fire, Christ Church' reached him at the inn. In a state of undress, he rushed to the College ('I raced over almost naked' were his own words),[10] in time to help George move his effects out of his room. George wrote to his mother:

> Scarcely had I entered the Quadrangle, when I saw one whole side of it in an universal blaze. [...] Amico appeared full of affectionate anxiety, & proposed removing as many of my things out of my room as I possibly could. With the assistance of two other men, we carried all the books away, silver spoons &c &c; [...] I then returned to my office of filling buckets, until being quite tired I came & slept for a few hours at the Star.[11]

Viotti's planned visit to Blenheim did not take place either, as the duchess was ill. He therefore spent Saturday visiting the Marlows, the Walls, and Dr Cole, and watched George take a fencing lesson. On Sunday morning Viotti and George breakfasted in college with Goodenough and another Christ Church don, John Conybeare, and Viotti played for them. That evening they dined in the rooms of Pascoe Grenfell's eldest son George, where Viotti gave another informal performance: 'Amico is with us, and has been playing on the violin of a dilettante di musica of this college, who of course came to hear with what unusual sounds his instrument spoke'.[12] Viotti left Oxford on Monday 6 March, and had a comfortable journey on the stage coach, a preferable mode of transport, he claimed, to the more expensive post chaise. Arriving in town at 5 pm, he ate an excellent bowl of soup at Escudier's, the French patissier in Oxford Street, and by 7.15 pm was home at Gillwell.[13]

While in Oxford George attended concerts at the Holywell Music Room and also accepted dinner invitations from local identities, at whose homes he sometimes heard Viotti's music played. On 22 November 1808 he rode over to Wheatfield to dine with Spencer's family, where Louisa Spencer 'play[ed] some of Amico's and of Scarlatti's music; we danced a few reels, and then finished off the evening by playing at cards.'[14] But the music at Wheatfield was not what George had been used to at Gillwell. The following year he wrote that 'Miss Spencer played for a short time, accompanied by the discordant jingle of her father's fiddle.'[15] At Mrs Marlow's party in March 1810 the music was better. A Miss Iffley, who was 'supposed to be an excellent player in these parts', but seemed to George only 'sosoish' compared to Caroline, played Viotti's Concerto in G [as a

---

[9] GRC to MC, 16 February 1809, Ch.Ch.

[10] 'j'y courrûs presque nu' (GBV to MC, 4 March 1809, Ch.Ch.).

[11] GRC to MC, 4 March 1809, Ch.Ch.

[12] GRC to MC, [4 and 5 March 1809], Ch.Ch. MS xlviii a.47, fo 13.

[13] GBV to GRC, 8 March 1809, Ch.Ch.

[14] GRC to MC, 22 November 1808, Ch.Ch.

[15] GRC to MC, 17 May 1809, Ch.Ch.

piano arrangement], which gave George much pleasure. But a duet performed next George thought rather 'massacré'.[16]

William Spencer was employed during these years by the Chinnerys as a classics and prosody tutor to Caroline – undoubtedly to help mitigate his financial difficulties. He therefore lived as a family member at Gillwell for long periods between 1807 and 1811, enjoying the concerts and enlivening the dinners. Margaret's letters to George describing their Sunday evenings painted an idyllic picture in which typical family activites such as card games, needlework and reading were interspersed with musical interludes involving most members of the family. On Sunday 12 March 1809 Margaret wrote from 'my study during Coffee' that the family was waiting for her 'to go into the parlour for music',[17] and on Sunday 7 May of the same year, that after dining and taking their evening walk, they were 'about to hear music, as is our custom on Sunday evenings'.[18]

During these years Viotti's young pupil Nicolas Mori who in 1808 was the same age as Matilda Chinnery – just 11 years old – came to stay at Gillwell every weekend to take his lessons ('Little Mori has just brought down with him your letter of yesterday').[19] At the time of the 1809 Christ Church fire Mori's father rendered an appreciated service to the Chinnerys. With no post leaving Oxford on a Saturday morning, and afraid that Margaret might read frightening accounts of the fire in the newspapers, Viotti had sent a reassuring letter by stage to London addressed to Mori senior, who then took it in person by chaise to Gillwell.

In those days for an aspiring young musician to forge a career it was necessary to be apprenticed to a professional musician to whom he paid a fee and was bound for a term of about six years, during which time a percentage of all his performance earnings were paid to that teacher. Mori was only the second such pupil that Viotti had accepted. (Libon was probably the first.) Mori remained under Viotti's tuition for at least four years (1808–12). He usually travelled down to Gillwell from London with William, who came home from town on Saturday afternoon, and returned on Monday morning.

When he was not asleep over a book in the drawing room, William was either participating in family trios or listening to the playing of Viotti and the children. The children's Aunt Marianne, who lived in the cottage in Gillwell Park, regularly dined with the family on a Sunday. ('Aunt Marianne has dined here, and they are now all in the parlour playing concertos, trios &c.')[20] When the weather was fine Caroline took her harp outside and played, while Margaret, William and Viotti strolled in the garden. ('I walked out a long while this morning with your father and Amico, while Caroline played upon her little Harp seated before the house.')[21]

---

[16] GRC to MC, 23 March 1810, Ch.Ch.
[17] MC to GRC, 12 March 1809, Ch.Ch.
[18] MC to GRC, 7 May 1809, Ch.Ch.
[19] MC to GRC, [20 March 1808], Ch.Ch., MS xlviii a.43, fo 160.
[20] MC to GRC, 1 May 1808, Ch.Ch.
[21] *Ibid.*

On the evening of Sunday 7 May 1808 Margaret wrote to George at half past eight from her study:

> I am just returned from the dining parlour to which we retreated after Coffee, to hear a little music; and I assure you I have been very well entertained. First Matilda played a Sonata, and succeeded to the satisfaction of us all;— then Caroline gave us a beautiful Trio of Amico's, which she played extremely well indeed,— and lastly Mori exhibited his talents to great advantage in a concerto [...] Mori improves rapidly; and Matilda is the only person who at all benefits from your absence, dear George, but she has then a greater portion of my attention to her musical studies.[22]

As a postscript, Margaret added: 'I forgot to say in speaking of the music that your father distinguished himself very much upon the Violoncello to night.'

On the weekend of 5–6 November 1808, the Gillwell family circle was enlarged by Matilda's mother, Mrs John Chinnery and her two young daughters, visiting England from India. In Margaret's letter to George of Sunday 7 November 1808 she depicted the evening scene of the family in the Gillwell drawing room from her writing desk: Mrs J. Chinnery, Marianne, [little] Margaret and Matilda were doing needlework round the table. William on her right was fast asleep, the other two little girls were gone to bed, and Caroline & Amico were in the parlour 'doing something in the musical way together'.[23] They had another small musical party on the weekend of 19–20 November, which included Spencer:

> Mori, who came down on Saturday night, played a concerto also, and very well; but the poor boy is grown strangely awkward and stupid; I believe his father gives him too much salami and macaroni!— Then our concert concluded most divinely by two Duets played by Amico and Mori.[24]

It was the following weekend, when there was a party of poets at Gillwell, that Caroline composed her first romance. She wrote to George at Oxford: 'I courted *Euterpe* lately, who received me graciously enough, and I implored her assistance in the composition of the Romances'.[25] Margaret described the performance of them before Spencer and Samuel Rogers in another letter:

> The evening was rendered delightful by Caroline singing three beautiful things she has composed very lately; they are properly *Lays* in the romance stile, the words in old french by Guglielmo, and set by your sister with admirable truth taste & beauty. Amico and every one feels surprised at her great success,— for really there is nothing of the imperfection of a first attempt in these pieces.[26]

---

22 MC to GRC, 7 May 1808, Ch.Ch.

23 MC to GRC, 7 November 1808, Ch.Ch.

24 MC to GRC, 21 November 1808, Ch.Ch.

25 CC to GRC, in MC to GRC, 26 November 1808, Ch.Ch.

26 MC to GRC, 28 November 1808, Ch.Ch.

On Sunday 18 June 1809 Spencer was again part of the family circle, and for the first time Viotti was absent from the Sunday gathering:

> Caroline & Matilda are playing a Duett, [little] Margaret is looking on; Guglielmo is in an arm chair by a bright wood fire, listening to the music; Papa on the sofa opposite and (wonderful to tell) not asleep. But where is Amico? You will say. He went to dine with the Duke of Cambridge yesterday, slept in town, and went to day with the Duke of Cambridge to dine with the Duke of Cumberland. So that we are quite alone with Guglielmo, for the first time *without Amico*.[27]

Viotti rarely went to town on the weekends. When he did it was usually to visit the Duke of Cambridge, but in the spring season of 1808 he dined in London once with the poet Samuel Rogers, and twice with the collector of antiquities Richard Payne Knight. On the last occasion he spent the morning with the Duke of Cambridge and the evening at Lady Anne Hamilton's.[28]

In May 1809 Margaret wrote that little Mori, now 12 years old, was to make his first appearance on a London stage: 'Mori makes his Debut next monday Evening [22 May] at Mrs Bianchi's concert, in the great rooms Hanover Square!!!' The frequent mention of such youthful musicians in contemporary newspapers shows that their appearance on the performing platform was not uncommon, and that they were by no means considered to be child prodigies. (Julian Baux had performed a Viotti concerto in 1794 at the age of five.) According to Margaret Mori performed creditably:

> Little Mori played extremely well, and was much applauded and admired. He was not in the least frightened or agitated, though the audience was very large; I was delighted to see how profitable an evening it must have been to Mrs Bianchi. As to the music, I will say nothing about it, for music is at a very low ebb in London; perhaps *as times go, it was a good concert*; most certainly it was a very *long* one. I never saw Maestro [Bianchi] look so young and handsome.[29]

Having assisted with musical studies at Gillwell since 1801, the Bianchis had grown close to the Chinnerys and were often included in the Sunday family gatherings. They returned to Gillwell several times in 1809, hence Margaret's interest in Mrs Bianchi's takings on the night of her benefit concert. But Bianchi's wholesome looks on the night of his wife's benefit belied his state of mind. Eighteen months later he was to take his life at his Hammersmith home. Margaret wrote to George that he had been found alone in his bed, and that Madame Bianchi had been performing in the Bath autumn concerts at the time.[30]

Guests continued to come to weekend parties at Gillwell. The most brilliant of all the Gillwell visitors, and one of Viotti's most devoted pupils and Margaret Chinnery's staunchest friends was Adolphus Frederick, Duke of Cambridge. The

---

[27] MC to GRC, 18 June 1809, Ch.Ch.
[28] MC to GRC, 16 June 1808, Ch.Ch.
[29] MC to GRC, 23 May 1809, Ch.Ch.
[30] MC to GRC, 4 December 1810, Ch.Ch.

Duke of Cambridge accepted with alacrity every invitation to play with Viotti at the Chinnerys' concerts, and took equally great pleasure in singing on these occasions. His 15 letters addressed to Margaret Chinnery all contain proof of his eagerness to come to Gillwell: 'I look forward with the greatest pleasure to friday next. Should the hour suit you I will be at Gillwell by twelve O'clock, and I take the liberty of requesting you to desire l'Amico to write me word what Music I am to bring with me'.[31] Possibly the most cultured of George III's sons, and certainly the most principled, Adolphus Frederick was also a lover of the *belles lettres* and enjoyed long *tête-à-tête* conversations with Margaret on literature.

A violin *amateur*, the duke owned a collection of five Stradivari violins that were probably purchased for him by Viotti. Viotti dedicated at least two compositions to him. The Six serenades for two violins, Op. 23 (WIV: 31–36), originally published by Clementi as 'Three duets serenatas for two violins', was probably composed especially for Adolphus Frederick, which would explain the slightly incredulous review given the composition by an 1809 writer. He marvelled at the facile nature of the work, opining that this lightweight ('leichte') composition could in no way be compared with Viotti's longer and better developed duets. Rather, he said, it was made up of a great number of small pieces with a variety of characters, some only two lines long, which typically had a pleasing melody, and were 'as tuneful and as simple as if they had been taken from little airs.'[32] In other words, ideally suited to a student. They were probably composed *c.*1807 or 1808 when the duke's visits to Gillwell were most frequent. (An 1807 reviewer of Viotti's Three duos for two violins, Op. 25, made a similar comment, going so far as to say that these duets could also 'be considered as practice pieces for skilled *amateurs*, or even as student exercises').[33] Viotti also dedicated his Concerto No. 27 in C major to the duke, and there is evidence that in 1812 he also intended to dedicate some quartets to him, although he appears not to have actually done so.[34]

At Gillwell the duke played duets with Viotti, and participated in string quartets or quintets with Viotti, William Chinnery, and any other amateur or professional musicians who happened to be there at the time. He enjoyed singing with Caroline Chinnery, and also accompanied her on the violin when she sang. On the occasion of the duke's 7 January 1808 visit Madame de Genlis's young protégé the harpist Casimir Baecker was also present. Sometimes the duke came to Gillwell exhausted after sitting for long nights in the House of Lords. Once he even dozed off during the music. In a note from Caroline to Spencer discussing the selection of music for the evening's concert at which the duke was to be present,

---

[31] AF to MC, 14 December 1807, Fisher 2000 – 12/3.

[32] 'die durchgängig cantabel und so einfach sind, als wären sie von kleinen Arien genommen' (*AMZ*, 19 April 1809, col. 462).

[33] 'als Uebungsstücke für geschickte Kunstfreunde, oder endlich als Bildungsmittel, in instructiver Hinsicht, betrachten' (*AMZ*, 10 June 1807, col. 598). The three duos may have been part of Viotti's third book of duos, 'Six easy duets for two violins' (WIV: 13–18), published separately as Op. 25.

[34] See below, pp. 167, 175.

she wrote of the necessity of choosing pieces that were not too long or tedious: 'I think 'Caro ogetto' will do for an Aria – it has a little of every thing in it, and *monotony* would make him *snore*, as he did when the Chevalier [La Cainea] sang his *Scena* called *Saul*.'[35]

The episode of the duke's falling asleep occurred during Margaret's weekend party of 28–29 May 1808. Margaret gave George an account of the three days he spent at Gillwell in her letter of 30 May 1808. The duke, she said, arrived at half past 12 on Saturday to breakfast, after which they took a stroll around the grounds. Then they adjourned to the drawing room where 'several trios & duos were played'. During the evening Caroline sang some solfeggios for the duke, who had desired to hear them sung 'in proper Italian style'. The duke expressed his admiration for Caroline's voice and her manner, and 'the evening went off lightly & swiftly between singing & playing'. Margaret did not allude directly to the duke's falling asleep, simply saying that as he had been up all the previous night at the House of Lords, he was tired, and so retired soon after 12. On Sunday they breakfasted at 11, and Viotti's friend the tenor, composer and fashionable singing teacher Luigi Asioli having arrived unexpectedly, the next two hours were devoted to singing. 'The Chevalier [La Cainea] sang the new Scenas of Asioli admirably'.[36]

At two thirty the duke, William Chinnery, William Spencer and another guest went out for a ride on horseback. Dinner was much more animated than the previous day, owing to the addition of Spencer, who had been upstairs ill on the previous evening, and music began at nine. When they tired of singing and playing, the duke waltzed with Miss Johnstone, and they passed an hour doing 'a plain english country dance'. Supper was served, after which several of the guests departed for town after midnight. The party was smaller on the following day, and the duke played with Viotti and William for three hours, both before and after breakfast. He left Gillwell at noon.[37]

Adolphus Frederick came to Gillwell again in October 1808 for another weekend party. Caroline wrote to George that as the duke had a bad cold he at first declined to practise with Viotti, and conversed for a long time with Margaret, wrote some letters, then came downstairs to sing: 'The Duke, Mrs Bianchi the Chevalier & Asioli sang the most delightful *Quartetts*, and Amico joined with *great success* in the Quintetto; now & then M$^{rs}$ Bianchi and the Chevalier sang a Duett; in short we had *really good music*!' Later the duke 'practiced for a couple of hours with Amico and Papa.' Again William Spencer was a member of the party, and was, as usual, 'drole, entertaining, full of wit and pleasantry.'[38] It must have been around this time that Asioli dedicated his four duets to Caroline, as a token of his esteem for her voice, and by way of a compliment to Margaret, who had taught her daughter singing. One of La Cainea's letters to Margaret is endorsed: 'From the

---

[35] CC to WRS, [May 1808], Fisher 2000 – 42/17.
[36] MC to GRC, 30 May 1808, Ch.Ch.
[37] *Ibid.*
[38] CC to GRC, 18 October 1808, Ch.Ch.

Chev. La Cainea on the Dedication of Asioli's Duetts to Caroline'.[39] In 1808 Caroline was singing confidently at Gillwell parties alongside the Duke of Cambridge, Miss Johnstone, the Chevalier La Cainea and Asioli himself.

There are letters proving that Adolphus Frederick made at least ten visits to Gillwell, and several more to Stratford Place, where the Chinnerys and Viotti took a house for the London spring season in 1810. One of the topics touched on in the duke's correspondence with Margaret was the fire at St James's Palace on 20 January 1809. This was reported in a long article in the *Times*,[40] which described the apartments of the palace that were destroyed, including those of the Duke of Cambridge. The reporter remarked that little was saved from the wings that were incinerated. Luckily, the duke wrote to the Chinnerys, he had 'the singular good fortune to save all my things', including his violins: 'Pray tell Amico with my best compliments that I took down my Violins under my arm into my dining room [...] & that I have saved all my Instruments, Music, & even the Music lists[?]. In the same letter he thanked Caroline for 'her kind letter' and assured her that he would be 'delighted to accompany her whenever I have the pleasure of seeing her.'[41]

The Duke of Cambridge's close relationship with Viotti is well documented in the Viotti/Chinnery collection. The are ten letters from Adolphus Frederick to Viotti (eight at the Royal College of Music, one at Fisher Library, and one at the New York Public Library). All are written in passable French, and signed 'Votre très devoué Adolphus Frederick'. In one, Viotti is addressed as 'mon cher Oncle',[42] giving an indication of the closeness that existed between them. Caroline Chinnery used the same appellation for Spencer: 'il mio caro Zio' (my dear uncle).

During the Chinnerys' February–March 1810 stay in London Viotti went frequently to dine or to play with Adolphus Frederick or with his brother the Duke of Cumberland. Margaret wrote to George on one such occasion: 'Amico's dinner [on 7 March] at the Duke of Cumberland's was magnificent beyond description, both in point of *company*, and splendid entertainment.'[43] George remarked to his mother on the Duke of Cambridge's happiness at having Viotti nearby: 'as to the Duke I am sure [...] the satisfaction of having Amico so near at hand must to him be exquisite.'[44] The duke's fondness of Viotti was obvious to all the Chinnery friends, and in arranging parties they usually tried to secure Viotti's presence to please him.

Spencer too became very close to Viotti during these years. Nine of his letters to Viotti survive (1808–12), all written in a bantering tone, and full of witticisms, puns and poems. The intention of some of the letters was to lure Viotti into town with the temptation of female company, lordly dinners and musical entertainment afterwards, such as Spencer himself regularly indulged in. In the first, dated 21

---

[39] La Cainea to MC, 5 November *c.*1808, NYPL JOB 97-52, item 63.
[40] *Times*, 23 January 1809.
[41] AF to MC, 26 January 1809, Fisher 2000 – 12/6.
[42] AF to GBV, 25 July 1811, Fisher 2000 – 38/3.
[43] MC to GRC, 10 March 1810, Ch.Ch.
[44] GRC to MC, 6 March 1810, Ch.Ch.

December 1808, Spencer's ribald teasing on the subject of Viotti's gout indicates the level of intimacy between the two men: 'Besides I do not believe that Madame Gout is the only lady to have become attached to your fine legs! May God forgive you, but I believe you to be a very great sinner! Nevertheless, get better, and let us hope that I shall not find you *in bed*.'[45] The letter is accompanied by an equally irreverent but cleverly constructed poem full of musical allusions, subsequently published in Spencer's *Poems*, also on the subject of Viotti's gout.[46] In the hope of swaying Viotti to come into town for an evening of music at Lady Anne Hamilton's Spencer wrote to Margaret: 'I hope Amico will be well enough to come to town, Lady Anne is in despair, and fears that something has displeased him; the Passione is given up, but the Concerto is eagerly wish'd for, and S[usan] Beckford can not venture upon it unless she tries it over with him tomorrow morning.'[47]

From 1809, when Caroline was old enough to appear in society, she and her mother and Viotti began to visit London more frequently. Viotti's closest acquaintances in London, apart from musicians, were men of letters, art connoisseurs, and aristocratic *amateurs*. Among the latter were Lord Charlemont and his beautiful wife, and above all, in 1808, 1809 and 1810, Lord and Lady Dunmore. In June 1809 after a dinner and concert at the Dunmores' London residence in Berkeley Street, Viotti and Caroline accompanied their hosts to Mrs Cunliffe's. The sole object of the visit, Margaret wrote, was to hear Mrs Cunliffe, 'who was the celebrated Miss Crewe', sing ballads.[48] Mrs Cunliffe's room was brilliantly attended but 'excessively crowded', and they did not get back to Gillwell until 4 am.[49]

Two days later Caroline composed an *adagio* for Lady Dunmore, which was carried to her by Viotti, who was going into town to dine with the Duke of Cambridge. The *adagio* was performed to great acclamation at the next Berkeley Street party (9 June). At this dinner there was 'a small select but brilliant assembly', which included, as well as the Chinnerys and Viotti, Lord Douglas, Lord Webb Seymour, Samuel Rogers, Lord and Lady Charlemont, Lord and Lady Leitrim, the Duchess of Beaufort and her sister Lady Harrowby. After a duet with Lady Susan Caroline played a concerto, and accompanied Amico and the Chevalier La Cainea.[50]

Viotti must have gratified these elegant *amateurs* with copies of songs he composed for some of their parties, as a letter from Lord Charlemont, then on an autumn tour of the country estates of England and Wales, wrote to Caroline: 'Pray

---

[45] 'Au reste Madame La Goutte n'est pas je crois la seule Madame qui ne soit attachée a vos belles jambes! Dieu vous pardonne, mais je vous crois un trés grand Pecheur! Cependant retablissez vous, et espérons que je ne vous trouve pas *allité*' (WRS to GBV, 21 December 1808, PHM 94/143/1 – 29/1).

[46] 'A J.B. Viotti', in W.R. Spencer (1811), *Poems*, Cadell, London, pp. 233–4. In the same work (p. 231) there is another poem addressed to Viotti.

[47] WRS to MC, 15 June 1808, Fisher 2000 – 13/3.

[48] MC to GRC, 4 June 1809, Ch.Ch.

[49] MC to GRC, 5 June 1809, Ch.Ch.

[50] MC to GRC, 11 June 1809, Ch.Ch.

1 G.B. Viotti. Engraving by H. Meyer after G. Trossarelli. Copyright of the Royal College of Music, London.

2 Portrait of Mrs Margaret Chinnery, 1803, by Elisabeth Vigée-Lebrun. Copyright of the Indiana University Art Museum. Photograph by Michael Cavanagh and Kevin Montague.

3 Members of the Chinnery family: Caroline, Walter and Margaret Chinnery. Reproductions after miniatures by Trossarelli from RCM Viotti Papers collection. Copyright of the Royal College of Music, London.

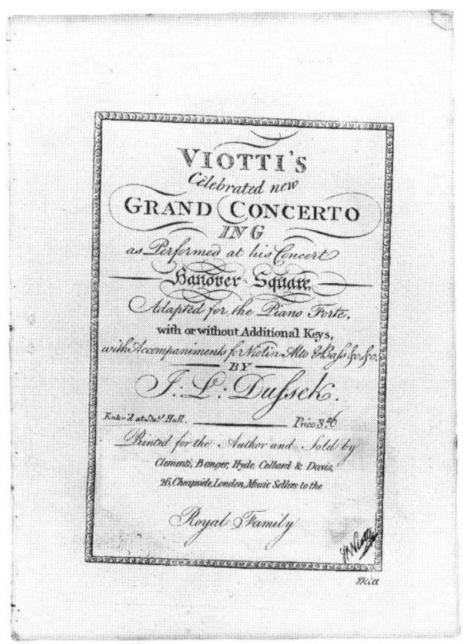


4 Signed title page of Viotti's 'Celebrated new Grand Concerto in G', arranged for pianoforte by J.L. Dussek. Reproduced courtesy of the Powerhouse Museum, Sydney, Australia, E.A. and V.I. Cromc collcction.

5 Title page of Viotti's *Six duos concertants*, Op. 5, showing dedication to William and Margaret Chinnery and engraving of Viotti after a portrait by George Chinnery. Reproduced courtesy of the Music Division, New York Public Library for the Performing Arts, Astor, Lenox and Tilden Foundations.

6 22474 Portrait presumed to be of Giovanni Battista Viotti as a young man, anonymous, late 18$^{th}$C, E.986.1.15. Inscribed on back of painting: 'Viotti di Fontanetto, Vercellese, 1783.' Reproduced courtesy of the Collection Musée de la musique, Paris. Photograph by Jean-Marc Anglès.

7 Black monogrammed seal used by G.B. Viotti on a letter written with Margaret Chinnery to William Chinnery, 6 April 1812. Represents a snake encircled on itself, tail in mouth, a symbol of eternal love or friendship. Bears the inscription 'Donné par l'amitié' (Given in friendship). Reproduced courtesy of the Powerhouse Museum, Sydney, Australia.

8 Gilwell House today, Waltham Abbey, Essex. Photograph by author.

9 Portrait presumed to be of Madame de Montgéroult, by L.-P. Girod de Vienney, France, 19thC. Reproduced courtesy of the Musée des Beaux-Arts de Tours. Photograph by Patrick Boyer.

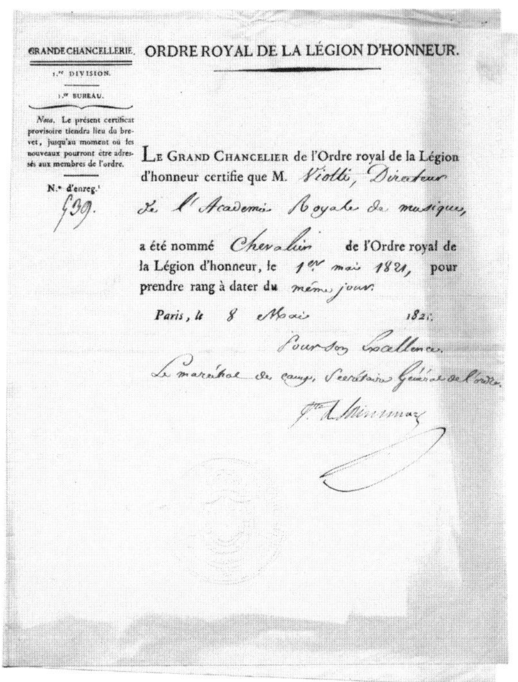

GRANDE CHANCELLERIE.

1.re DIVISION.

1.er BUREAU.

*Nota.* Le présent certificat provisoire tiendra lieu du brevet, jusqu'au moment où les nouveaux pourront être adressés aux membres de l'ordre.

N.o d'enreg.t 939.

ORDRE ROYAL DE LA LÉGION D'HONNEUR.

Le Grand Chancelier de l'Ordre royal de la Légion d'honneur certifie que M. Viotti, Directeur de l'Académie Royale de musique, a été nommé Chevalier de l'Ordre royal de la Légion d'honneur, le 1er mai 1821, pour prendre rang à dater du même jour.

*Paris, le* 8 Mai 1821.

Pour Son Excellence.

Le maréchal de camp, Secrétaire Général de l'ordre.

10 Letter informing Viotti that he has been named Chevalier of the Legion of Honour, 1 May 1821. Reproduced courtesy of the Music Division, New York Public Library for the Performing Arts, Astor, Lenox and Tilden Foundations.

11 Bronze medal representing G.B. Viotti (obverse) and his works (reverse), by Peuvrier, 1824. Copyright of the Royal College of Music, London.

tell him [Viotti] that I am much obliged to him for "Fra Martins", & "Do, Re" & hope to join your Chorus when we meet'. He also asked Caroline for another copy of her 'Troubadour' (one of the lays she had composed in 1808), having misplaced the first one.[51]

Suffering from gallstones in February 1810, Margaret needed to move to London to be closer to her physician, and a house was taken for two months at 24 Half Moon Street. While Margaret convalesced Caroline and Viotti led a gay social life in London, frequenting the drawing rooms of the leading lights of fashion. Spencer, who had spent the previous autumn at Gillwell, moved to Chiswick to stay with his relative the Duke of Devonshire, but called to visit Margaret frequently, and accompanied Caroline and Viotti on their various visits. Viotti sometimes accompanied Spencer to Chiswick while Caroline visited her 'dearly beloved Lady Dunmore'.[52] In one week in March Caroline and Amico dined and played three times at the Dunmores' in Berkeley Street, sometimes 'sans toilette et cérémonie' (with no ceremony), at other times in full dress with the *haut ton* of London. On 23 March Margaret wrote: 'Caroline's playing was amazingly admired, and listened to in perfect silence and with profound attention. Amico too, as usual enchanted his audience, and Lady Susan played better than I ever heard her. The only vocal music was a long air by the Chevalier [La Cainea]. We did not get home till after 2.'[53]

On 26 March Viotti dined with the Chinnerys at Samuel Rogers's elegant mansion at 24 St James's Place overlooking Green Park, together with their usual circle: 'Caroline accompanied the Chev^r and Naldi, and played an Adagio herself'.[54] Viotti also went to a reception with the Chinnerys at the home of the most famous of all London art connoisseurs, Thomas Hope, who inhabited 'a most splendid mansion' on Cavendish Square, which housed a priceless collection of art treasures.[55] When Margaret was well enough she began to participate in the four o'clock round of visits, and in early March received visits from the Chevalier La Cainea, and from Naldi, whom she asked to teach Caroline the *buffo* style of singing.

It was in early February 1810 that Viotti purchased his most famous Stradivarius, the one in his possession at his death. The only mention of its provenance is in a letter from Margaret to George: 'Amico's mind is just now wholly engrossed by the beauties of a new violin he has purchased of Prince Buttera'.[56] The princes of Butera were members of the Sicilian Branciforte family who had had the title conferred in the sixteenth century. How the violin came to London and how Viotti treated with the prince is not known. The intermediary may have been the Chevalier La Cainea, who appears to have been of Sicilian origin,

---

[51] Lord Charlemont to CC, 1 September 1809, Fisher 2000 – 34/6.
[52] MC to GRC, 27 February 1810, Ch.Ch.
[53] MC to GRC, 23 March 1810, Ch.Ch.
[54] MC to GRC, 27 March 1810, Ch.Ch.
[55] *Ibid.*
[56] MC to GRC, 9 February 1810, Ch.Ch.

and may have even been of the same noble family himself. His full name was, according to his marriage licence, Francis Ferdinand Raibari de La Cainea,[57] remarkably similar, given the idiosyncratic English spellings of foreign names, and allowing for the misreading of ambiguous handwriting, to the 'Prince Buttera de Rubari', whose widow married Lord Robert Pembroke in London in 1814.[58] The prince may have been an envoy from the court of the Two Sicilies before Napoleon seized control of the kingdom, remaining in exile in England since that time. Viotti took the instrument with him whenever he played with the Duke of Cambridge or in society, and 'charmed them with his new violin.'[59]

It was around this time that Margaret expected a visit from Catalani, returned to the King's Theatre after a year's absence: 'She sang remarkably well last night at the Opera Amico says, perfectly *in tune*, and was received with the greatest applause. People seem quite delighted at her return.'[60] Undoubtedly at Viotti's instigation Catalani came to sing for the Chinnerys on 16 March 1810 at 24 Half Moon Street, without her unpopular spouse Valabrègue. The elegant Chevalier La Cainea had made clear his opinion of the latter in some *c.*1807 letters to Margaret. Of Catalani herself he wrote: 'She is a good *simple* woman, who, it cannot be denied, possesses a great talent and even more, a great natural gift.'[61] It is clear from his letter that in London society she was considered rather unrefined, and as belonging to an uneducated class of singers who '*should restrict themselves to singing, never speaking or writing*'.[62] This was probably the reason that there were no additional guests, apart from Naldi, on the night she came to dinner. At table were only Margaret, William and Caroline Chinnery, Viotti, Naldi and Catalani:

> Catalani talked a great deal, but she looked tired, for you are to know that she has a new Opera to learn in *five days*, which is to be performed next Tuesday [Guglielmi's *Atalida*]; so that she is hurried to death between learning *her part*, and rehearsing with the others. She very wisely brought her part with her, and instead of singing any other music, sang *that*, which was so much time and trouble saved to her and by which *we* both heard her sing *more* and become acquainted with the forthcoming Opera. Really she surprised me by her wonderful agility,— and quite electrified your sister! Caroline accompanied her, but her astonishment was so great, that it was visible in her countenance; she had forgotten *how* she sings, and scarcely believed such execution possible. Catalani is in full voice,— she has lost something at the top which is compensated by an addition to the lower notes. Upon the whole I think her improved,— she is a much better musician than she was, and seems to have studied her art since I saw her. Lord and Lady Dunmore & Mr [Samuel] Rogers joined us *very late*, when she was tired,— but in order to detain her, and let her rest a little, I asked Naldi to sing his

57 Marriage licence granted by the Vicar-General, 23 August 1792.

58 Burke, p. 1947.

59 MC to GRC, 12 March 1810, Ch.Ch.

60 MC to GRC, 7 March 1810, Ch.Ch.

61 'ella è una buona *semplice* a cui non si può negare un gran talento en ancor più un gran dono della natura' (La Cainea to MC, Thursday, *c.*1808, Fisher 2000 – 4/10).

62 '*ils devroient toujours chanter et jamais parler ou ecrire*' (La Cainea to MC, Wednesday 4, *c.*1807, Fisher 2000 – 4/9).

> *Bastone*, and another buffo air,— after which she repeated some of the new Opera, and then by way of finale Naldi and her sang the Buffo Duet in the Fanatico per la Musica;— I do not know whether you recollect it,— she sings the gammut in it. After this, Catalani took her leave, at about 11 o'clock and Naldi soon after.[63]

In spite of professing tiredness with 'this senseless foolish town' Margaret had Viotti and William take another house for the London season (May–June 1810), this time at Stratford Place. It was here that Caroline made her formal debut into society 'before one of the most brilliant Circles that could be seen anywhere', in William Chinnery's opinion. The guest list of 40 to 50 persons included the Duke of Cambridge; Spencer's relatives the Duchess of Devonshire, Lady Bessborough, and Lady Shaftesbury; Lord Erskine; Lord Crewe; Sir Sidney and Lady Smith; Lord and Lady Granville Leveson-Gower; Lord and Lady Leitrim; the writer George Lamb; the Dunmores and the fashionable brother and sister Mr and Miss Johnstone. Caroline sang and Viotti played.[64]

The spring season in 1810 was a social whirlwind. Margaret wrote of their 'hurry and confusion', 'dressing and visiting', and 'learning and rehearsing' for Caroline's recitals, in which Viotti accompanied her and undoubtedly played compositions of his own.[65] Caroline was now 'quite the fashion!' The Chinnerys and Viotti also received many invitations to balls – at Miss Johnstone's and at Lady Shaftesbury's; to dinners – three at Devonshire House, one at Colonel Greville's, one at Samuel Rogers's; and to after-dinner parties – two at Thomas Hope's Cavendish Square mansion. The company they kept in London became more brilliant as the season progressed, and on 11 June and 24 June they were all invited by the Princess of Wales to Kensington Palace, where Caroline's singing was much admired. On 27 June Margaret gave her last music party for the season, inviting to dinner Spencer and his father Lord Charles, Mr and Mrs St Leger, Mr and Mrs Cunliffe, Lord Valentia, Lord Glenbervie, with 100 others 'mostly of rank and fashion' to come afterwards for music.[66]

The talk of London society at the end of the season was that Catalani had been preferred to Mrs Billington to sing at the next fashionable event on the social calendar, the Installation of the new chancellor of Oxford University. Madame Bianchi would also perform. The Oxford *Encaenia* would be a four-day event (3–6 July), filled with nonstop ceremonies, recitations, balls, private parties, church services and throughout the whole, music. The Chinnerys were to cut prominent figures here too, for George Chinnery had just won the Newdigate Prize for poetry, and was to have the honour of reciting his verses aloud in the Sheldonian Theatre. George would also recite his *encaenia* verses (a tribute to the late chancellor the Duke of Portland), giving him the double glory of appearing twice before the glittering audience in the Theatre. The 1810 Installation would be reported by all the major London newspapers.

---

63 MC to GRC, 16 March 1810, Ch.Ch.
64 WBC to GRC, 28 May 1810, Ch.Ch.
65 MC to GRC, 25 June 1810, Ch.Ch.
66 MC to GRC, 27 June 1810, Ch.Ch.

Accommodation in Oxford during these celebrations was at a premium. Rooms at an inn were taken for Margaret, William, Caroline and their servants. Viotti would sleep at Christ Church in George's sitting room and Spencer in his study. George reminded his mother to bring music, 'Elfrida, Superba Roma or Pandolfetto or any others',[67] for

> many people who have heard of your coming, are crazy to hear dear Caroline; she has already, you know, established some slight reputation here from the short stay she made two years ago. Amico is not forgotten; every body asks whether Monsieur Viotti is to be of the party. As for opportunities of playing, I suppose those will not be wanting, for I trust our *heads of houses* & Canons &c&c will be galant.[68]

The *Morning Chronicle* of 5 July, covering the Oxford events of Tuesday 3 July, was gushing in its praise of George's recitation and of the music. William Chinnery, who had been obliged to return to his office in London, missed his son's performance, but Viotti, who was in the Theatre for the momentous occasion, included a note in Margaret's letter to her husband, saying 'George ['s recitation] went like a charm. Everybody is more than ever enchanted with it.'[69] The same evening George gave a private supper and musical party for about 40 in his college rooms, to which he invited Sir Sidney and Lady Smith and their daughter, many of his Christ Church friends, the Grenfells, some foreign ambassador friends of the Chinnerys, and a few of his Oxford lecturers, including the music-loving Goodenough. The vocalists Catalani and Bianchi were present as private guests, and Caroline wrote to her father the following day that 'Catalani and Bianchi were most kind, and sung as much as George chose.'[70]

Viotti, who had the previous day been distraught at the possibility of being unable to get a piano to George's party, had clearly been successful: 'Can you believe that we cannot find a porter to carry the piano ten yards? If we cannot get one it would be devilish bad luck for poor George. I intend to do my utmost. I shall raise the devil to get my way.'[71] Having been instructed not to forget his 'Buttera', Viotti was himself an important contributor to the entertainment. George's friends, according to Caroline, were impressed: 'Nothing could be more magnificent than the supper, better ordered, better arranged, and better served! Every body was gay animated talkative, and ready to contribute his share to the general amusement –

---

[67] Printed sheet music of favourite overtures, songs, duets, trios and airs from currently performing operas was readily available to *amateurs*, as shown by the numerous newspaper advertisements.

[68] GRC to MC, 24 June 1810, Ch.Ch.

[69] 'George a été comme un charme, tout le monde en est plus enchanté que jamais' (GBV to WBC, in MC to WBC, [5] July 1810, Fisher 2000 – 18/9).

[70] CC to WBC, in MC to WBC, 6 July 1810, Fisher 2000 – 18/10.

[71] 'Croyriez vous qu'on ne peut pas trouver de porteur pour transporter le Piano dix yardes? Si nous ne pouvions pas l'avoir ce seroit par trop diabolique pour le pauvre George. Je m'en vais m'évertuer, je ferai le diable pour en venir à bout' (GBV to WBC, in MC to WBC, [5] July 1810, Fisher 2000 – 18/9).

they all said, that such a College supper had never been seen!!'[72] *Encaenia* week concluded with a ball on Friday 6 July, and the following day the Chinnery party (minus William) rose early to join the throng of carriages going to witness the ascent of Mr Sadler's hot air balloon. An invitation from William Madocks to dine at All Souls' College that evening and the next enabled them to meet two celebrated characters, the statesman and playwright Richard Brinsley Sheridan and the pedagogue Dr Parr. Viotti's talents were again called upon: 'Amico played & Mrs Sheridan sang a little between whiles.'[73]

It was just before Easter 1811 that Caroline caught whooping cough. She was removed to London for the next three months, where Spencer watched devotedly over her, relieved occasionally by Viotti when Spencer left her side to go to the dinners which marked the beginning of the London season. Spencer had tried several times to draw Viotti into town to participate in the spring round of parties, but to no avail. Margaret, who had been ill again with kidney stones, prompting Viotti to remove her notepaper and take over the correspondence duties himself, was later able to write to Caroline that 'Amico is an immense source of comfort, & consolation to me; – he is a *perfect Amico*!'[74] One party that Spencer tried unsuccessfully to arrange for Viotti was at the home of his cousin Lord Bolingbroke, who was anxious to have both Viotti and his pupil Mori at a dinner. After the dinner, Spencer wrote, they would go to the Opera 'where you and I both have duties to fulfill. We shall pay court together to the princess [of Wales], to Lady Charlemont, to your Lady Henrietta [probably Spencer's relative Lady Henrietta Spencer, wife of the Earl of Bessborough] &c&c&c'[75]. Spencer did not want Viotti to object that he could not leave Margaret alone at Gillwell:

> Do not plead as an excuse the solitude of the dear Padrona. George [home from Oxford for Easter] is quite capable of enlivening Gillwell during your short absence— and really you do *owe* some little sacrifices from time to time to this circle of friends who *wish you so much good. All arms are outstretched to you*, but they are not *long enough* to reach you at Gillwell! And anyway it is all good for your *standing*, that is to say your standing with this *little republic of angels* to which you and I have both devoted our hearts and our services of all kinds— do you understand me?[76]

---

[72] CC to WBC, in MC to WBC, 6 July 1810, Fisher 2000 – 18/10.

[73] MC to WBC, Sunday [8 July] 1810, Fisher 2000 – 18/11. See also GBV to WBC, 7 July 1810, NYPL JOB 97-52, item 17.

[74] MC to CC, 19 April 1811, Fisher 2000 – 33/7.

[75] 'ou vous avéz des devoirs a remplir aussi bien que moi, nous ferons notre cour ensemble a la Princesse, a Lady Charlemont, a votre Lady Henriette &c &c &c &c' (WRS to GBV, 6 April 1811, PHM 94/143/1 – 29/2).

[76] 'N'alléz pas m'objecter la solitude de la chère Padrona, George [...] est tres capâble d'animer Gillwell pendant votre courte absence— et réellement vous *devéz* quelques petits sacrifices de tems en tems a cette société qui *vous veut tant de bien. Tous les bras sont ouverts* pour vous, mais ils ne sont pas *assés longs* pour vous atteindre a Gillwell! Et puis tout cela fait du bien a votre *hierarchie* c.a.d. a cette *petite republique d'Anges* a laquelle nous avons, vous et moi, consacré nos ames et nos services en tout genre,— entendéz vous?' (*Ibid.*).

These last words imply a deeper complicity in amorous adventures, but whether they are founded on fact or are mere expressions of male *bravoure*, is difficult to tell. Spencer's philandering is fairly certain, but if Viotti had any relationships outside Gillwell there is no evidence of it in the letters of the CFP collection. Spencer knew Viotti well enough to judge of his reaction, and wrote in mock self-pitying tones: 'I can hear you from here (after several dozen sacre bleu &c &c &c) "because that coxcomb is banished from Gillwell he wants me to be as unhappy as him!"' Nevertheless he concluded optimistically: 'But come anyway, and meanwhile write a line to Mori. Bolingbroke is very impatient to see him.'[77] The next letter announces Bolingbroke's intention of postponing the dinner for Viotti's sake. Spencer apologises for having clean forgotten that it was Holy Week – the reason Viotti must have given as an excuse for not coming into town.[78] His last letter of this period speaks of Lord Bolingbroke's disappointment in not securing Viotti for his dinner, and of Spencer's attendance at a concert that the Italian singer Giacomo Ferrari was giving at the Duchess of Devonshire's.[79]

On 11 May Margaret wrote that Viotti was to receive the French Comte d'Allemand, 'a pleasant intelligent man', who was apparently counting on his help to publish some music of a French *amateur* who had been a participant in one of Madame de Montgéroult's private concerts in Paris in 1802. Margaret's words show not only her diplomatic finesse, but also the power she apparently enjoyed wielding with Viotti, in sitting in judgement of *amateurs*' attempts at composition:

> Who is the french Count you will say? The person who brought the *music* from Mad^me^ de Caumont, the mother of the Mad^lle^ de Caumont who played at Mad^me^ de Montgeroult's the morning we spent with her. This friend of her's is coming tomorrow to hear,— what?— *that the lady's music is too bad for publication*;— *that* is the *english* of it,— we shall dress it up in french as prettily & graciously as we can.[80]

This mention of a morning spent at Madame de Montgéroult's during Viotti's and the Chinnerys' 1802 visit to Paris may help date one of the letters from Viotti to Baillot published by Pincherle. It is a rather formal invitation to Baillot to take part in performing some trios at Madame de Montgéroult's. Baillot's Conservatoire colleague the cellist Charles-Nicolas Baudiot was also invited to assist, since Crosdill was about to leave Paris.[81]

It was not until the end of May that the doctors declared Caroline to be out of danger, and allowed her to return home. However towards the end of April a letter from Viotti at Gillwell addressed to Caroline at Smith's at 3 Duke Street, shows

---

[77] 'Je vous entends d'ici, (aprés quelques douzaines de sacre bleu &c &c &c) "parce que ce coquin est banni de Gillwell il voudroit que je fusse aussi malheureux que lui!" [...] Mais venéz toujours, et en attendant ecrivés une ligne a Mori. Bolingbroke est trés impatient de le voir' (*Ibid.*).

[78] WRS to GBV, [April] 1811, PHM 94/143/1 – 29/3.

[79] WRS to GBV, 16 May 1811, PHM 94/143/1 – 29/4.

[80] MC to CC, 11 May 1811, Ch.Ch.

[81] GBV to Baillot, Wednesday 14 [1802?], cited in Pincherle (1924), Letter 7, p. 109.

that she had recovered sufficiently to play the piano, and that Viotti was planning to come into town to play with her at a domestic concert: 'Yes, my dear, the second [movement?] adagio from the trio will be suitable, or else we shall give him [Smith?] just the two pieces. – George will bring it to you tomorrow and you may do what you like with it.'[82] It would appear from these comments that he intended Caroline to arrange a piano accompaniment to the *adagio* of one of his own trios.

In spite of Margaret's concern about missing the spring season, there was one last social event on the London calendar that the Chinnerys were able to attend. It was the Prince Regent's lavish fête of 19 June 1811 inaugurating the Regency. Caroline was well enough to accompany her parents and Viotti. Indeed they stayed until six in the morning. Margaret, like the rest of London, gushed that 'it was the most beautiful & most princely entertainment that ever was given in any court!'[83] Music was of course *de rigueur*, and Catalani performed the part of Elfrida from Paisiello's popular opera to general acclaim. The occasion was the first of many in 1811 when the prince extended public marks of favour to the Chinnery family.

The fête at Carlton House, falling as it did on the eve of the summer/autumn holiday season, preluded a period of intense social activity for Viotti and all the Chinnery family except George, who was in Oxford reading for his degree examination. In August 1811 the Chinnerys removed to Eastbourne, then proceeded to Tunbridge Wells (where Viotti had already taken a house for them)[84] in September, followed by three weeks in Brighton in October–November, supposedly a 'restorative' vacation for Caroline following her long and debilitating bout of whooping cough. The Chinnerys and Viotti were at Eastbourne before the arrival of the *beau monde* of London and had the place almost to themselves. Their days were filled with walks, tepid sea-bathing, letter-writing, and as soon as Caroline was strong enough, sailing and riding, and excursions to the surrounding places of interest. Their days assumed a quiet, steady rhythm, with few interruptions. By day Caroline read Latin and practised piano, singing and harp-playing with Viotti, and the whole domestic circle enjoyed literary readings in the evenings. Margaret enjoyed the company of her three 'beaux' – William, Viotti and Spencer, and missed them when one or other had to make a visit to London.

The most memorable visit to London was made by Viotti, who on 7 August had his application for British denizenship accepted: 'Amico is going to town tomorrow *pour prêter serment* [to take the oath]', Margaret wrote to George.[85] It was to the Duke of Cambridge that Viotti had appealed to approach his brother the Prince Regent, and denizenship was formally granted on 14 September 1811.[86] Viotti learned of it just before setting out for Eastbourne. One of the most welcome

---

[82] 'Oui Chere, 2[?] Adagio du Trio pourra aller, ou bien nous ne lui donnerons que les deux morceaux.— George vous l'apportera demain et vous ferez comme vous voudrez' (GBV to CC, *c.*23 April 1811, PHM 94/143/1 – 24/5).

[83] MC to GRC, 21 June 1811, Ch.Ch.

[84] GBV to WRS, 6 August 1811, NYPL JOB 97-52, item 26.

[85] MC to GRC, 6 August 1811, Ch.Ch.

[86] PRO HO C97.

letters ever received at Gillwell must surely have been that of the Duke of Cambridge informing Viotti that 'your request has been granted. Knowing the prince's kindly sentiments towards you I am sure that it gave him great pleasure to approve your denizenship, and I am delighted to have been given the charge of presenting to him your application.'[87] In mid-October, stricken with a severe attack of gout, Viotti received his 'Patent', and managed to write letters of acknowledgement to both the prince and the duke.[88]

Spencer also wrote a typically bantering letter, congratulating Viotti on the event. Dated 15 October 1811, it was sent to him at Brighton. Behind Spencer's usual flippancy is a sincere happiness for his friend:

> Long live the red box![89] I have been congratulating myself on having you for a friend for a long time, and now I rejoice to have you as my compatriot.— I say *rejoice*, as a *less emphatic* term than the other, considering that I prefer one *friend* to 20 million compatriots— in spite of John Bull, Jerry Bull and the entire *bovine* family. But my friend, now that you have been received into the bosom of our good mother Great Britain, you must behave yourself. She has a chaste nature, and you must respect her [illegible word] &c&c&c If she offers to suckle you, do not take it into your head to 'prefer the jug to the draught'.[90]

Clearly Viotti accepted Spencer's teasing in good part and cherished his friendship as much as the Chinnerys did. Another congratulatory letter came from George Chinnery's godfather, Sir Charles Flint, who also wrote to Viotti at Brighton: 'nothing could be more flattering or gratifying than the manner in which the Pr. Regent supported your Claim. Without his powerful aid you would once more have fallen a sacrifice to Prejudice and Obstinacy.'[91] After Viotti's ignominious expulsion from England in 1798, British citizenship must have constituted a happy and just compensation. Lady Dunmore also mentions Viotti's 'winning the battle of the *red box*' in her February 1812 letter.[92]

---

[87] 'votre requête a ete accordée. Connaissant les sentiments bienveillants du Prince à votre sujet je suis sur qu'il a donné l'ordre pour votre Denization avec bien du plaisir, et je me rejouis beaucoup d'avoir éte chargé de la communication de lui présenter votre Memoire' (AF to GBV, 25 July 1811, Fisher 2000 – 38/3).

[88] MC to GRC, 14 October 1811, Ch.Ch.

[89] A red leather box used by ministers of state to hold official documents.

[90] 'Vive la boite rouge! il y a longtems que je me felicite de vous avoir pour ami, et maintenant je me réjouis de vous avoir pour compatriote— Je dis *réjouis*, comme phrase *moins energique*, que l'autre, attendu que je prefere un *ami* a vingt millions de compatriotes— Malgré John Bull Jerry Bull et toute la famille *bovine*. Mais mon ami, a present que vous etes recu [sic] dans le sein de notre bonne mere M^me^ La Grande Bretagne, n'allèz pas y faire le polisson, c'est une chaste Nature dont il faut respecter le [bicher?] &c &c &c &c Si elle vous offre à teter, ne vous avisèz pas de "preferer le vase au breuvage"' (WRS to GBV, 15 October 1811, PHM 94/143/1 – 29/5).

[91] Sir Charles Flint to GBV, 24 October 1811, NYPL JOB 97-52, item 27.

[92] 'la bataille que vous avez gagné dans la *boîte rouge*' (Susan Dunmore to GBV, 28 February [1812], PHM 94/143/1 – 28/5).

At the end of August the Chinnerys moved on to Tunbridge Wells. Their travelling party consisted of Margaret, William, Caroline, Spencer, Viotti, the young relatives, little Margaret and Matilda, and various servants. At Tunbridge Wells their tranquillity came to an abrupt end: 'Here is all bustle and visiting', Margaret complained. 'They tell me that when I have received and returned the first visits, I shall be much more to myself.' Two obligatory calls had to be paid straight away to Margaret's Aunt Holland, who had a house not far away, and also to the beautiful Lady Charlemont, who 'has engaged us for the evening to her. So here I am at a late hour come home to settle dresses &c &c, get a little rest and dinner, and then go to work again, for to me (entre nous) all this is *work*. [...] Our Drawing room is full [...] of Vaudreuils,[93] Lady Lambert &c but I am writing in my *bed-chamber*, Caroline is laying down in her's, and Guglielmo & Amico are receiving the company. This is a beautiful place, if there were no people in it and one could enjoy it!'[94]

In Tunbridge Wells the Chinnerys were surrounded by all that was elegant and fashionable in English society. In spite of Caroline's weakened state of health, she was exhibited everywhere as a talented musician. Always paired with Viotti, she was shown off to maximum advantage. At the beginning of September Margaret's Aunt Holland called a large party, for which she procured a harp and a pianoforte especially for Caroline. Margaret reported that her aunt was 'very much pleased with us last night for affording her friends so much entertainment,— Caroline & Amico were as obliging as possible, and literally played all the evening.' At the party 'Lady Dungannon sang a great deal, and Mrs Gordon too, but neither of them knew the least in the world how to sing.'[95] Earlier they had given a dinner for the Comte de Vaudreuil (who was taken ill and had to leave), Lady Mary and Mr Shepherd, Lord Charlemont, the two Misses Berry, and another bluestocking Miss Lydia White. Caroline and Amico had pleased everybody with their playing.[96]

After being forced by fatigue to miss one evening of music at Lady Charlemont's, to which the rest of her family went and at which 'the young Lady Pembroke sang, and Amico played', Caroline resumed her playing and singing the following day, and sent her instruments over to Lady Charlemont's, where 'the most brilliant party assembled', including the Dowager Lady Pembroke, Lord and Lady Pembroke, their daughter Lady Di, and their son Lord Robert, who was a Christ Church contemporary of George, the same who would in 1814 marry the widow of the Sicilian Prince 'Buttera de Rubari'. Margaret found Lord Charlemont 'delightful', but could not say the same of his wife: 'Lady Charlemont does not improve upon acquaintance, but she is [...] *very pretty*.'[97] Spencer and Viotti also found her so.

---

[93] The Comte de Vaudreuil, his second wife and one or both sons.
[94] MC to GRC, 30 August 1811, Ch.Ch.
[95] MC to GRC, 8 September 1811, Ch.Ch.
[96] MC to GRC, 3 September 1811, Ch.Ch.
[97] MC to GRC, 8 September 1811, Ch.Ch.

Included in the Tunbridge set was the Italophile Lord Glenbervie, whose wife was in the Princess of Wales's retinue and whose son had been at Oxford with George. Lord Glenbervie accepted hospitality of the Chinnerys in Tunbridge on 12 September, but repaid them with sneering allusions to William Chinnery's low birth. Later he became a close friend of Margaret and Viotti, who set one of his Italian 'poemettos' to music.[98] Despite his snobbery he was a kind-hearted man, offering to come to the aid of Naldi's widow when the singer was killed suddenly in Paris in 1820.[99] It is to the Chinnery's party of 12 September in Tunbridge that he refers in his seven-page journal entry of 13 September 1811, which is a mixture of gibes and praise for the various Chinnery family members, followed by a lengthy commentary on their friends, including Viotti, Spencer and the Johnstones:

> One of my hostesses (Agnes) [Berry] [...] took me to dine at Mr Chinnery's, where we had an excellent dinner, choice wines, choice spirits, and a considerable portion of beauty, for Lord William Spencer and Viotti were there, and that beautiful *blueish* stocking, Lady Charlemont, besides little Miss Chinnery, who may claim a place among the geniuses as well as with the beauties [...]
>
> Mr and Mrs Chinnery are, in the Society of London, in some respects, the rivals of Mr and Miss Johnstone, whose splendid dinners and walzing balls we partook of at Brighton [...] But the Chinnery parties seem to me more select and more exquisite than those of Hanover Square. [...]
>
> Miss Chinnery is a very pretty, lively, alert girl still under twenty, with good features, black eyes, eyebrows and hair, a clear complexion of natural red and white, a neat person, obliging manners, frank and easy conversation, without being forward or obtrusive, and talents as well as taste, and skill in music in a superior degree. She is also said to write very pretty verses and I believe draws. Viotti has lived in Chinnery's house, I believe, ever since the birth of the daughter— scandal might perhaps insinuate that his residence there is of a little earlier date, but I do not believe that exact chronology would justify this. However, she has been and still continues to be without interruption, the daily and favourite pupil of that first-rate musician for taste, knowledge, and execution, and who adds to such various merits in his profession that of being a very agreeable well-bred and well-informed person in all matters which it becomes a man of the world and of good company to know.
>
> Next to him, as inmate of the House of Chinnery, is William Spencer, nephew to the Duke of Marlborough. [Glenbervie goes on to describe Spencer as 'very profligate and ruined in his fortunes' and 'all high spirits, great good humour, coaxing civility, and irresistible drollery and pleasantry, but never solid, never steady'.][100]

The luminaries listed elsewhere in the same journal entry are the same as those mentioned in Margaret's letter of 13 September 1811.[101] The merry-go-round of dinners, parties, musical suppers and daytime visits and outings continued at a dizzying rhythm. Worn out, Margaret complained bitterly to George: 'I never will

---

[98] Glenbervie to MC, 17 May 1819, Osborn fd. 11, item 1.

[99] Glenbervie to MC, *c.*December 1820, Fisher 2000 – 17/5.

[100] Douglas, *The Glenbervie Journals*, pp. 142–6.

[101] MC to GRC, 13 September 1811, Ch.Ch.

come to Tunbridge again!'[102] Whether Viotti found all the activity as trying as Margaret she does not say, but if he did he successfully hid the fact by being his usual good-natured self, and played with Caroline whenever and wherever it pleased Margaret. Caroline kept up her spirits and managed to please, and was a favourite of lords and ladies alike, making a new friend in the young Marchioness of Lansdowne. The five weeks that the Chinnerys and Viotti spent at Tunbridge were described by Margaret in her first letter from Brighton, their next destination:

> No private individuals certainly ever were received and *courted even* in the way we were by the whole of the society collected at that beautiful place! We seemed to be the soul, the animating spirit of the whole, and they would never leave us a single moment at our disposal;— every day, every hour was filled up, and still they had not days and hours enough they said. Guglielmo says that your sister's success there, was as brilliant and as universal as Susan Beckford's for singing and beauty.[103]

Another excerpt from the same letter shows Viotti's influence on Caroline's music studies. Her piano playing and singing were imbued with so much feeling that those who heard her unfailingly remarked on it, as they did with Viotti. Like Viotti she too was able to move her listeners to tears, and although the account comes from a proud mother, there does seem to be a ring of truth in the detail:

> Her singing was considered as far superior to any other,— people intrigued and plotted to hear her, [...] Last Thursday at Mrs Chaloner's after she had plaid, & sung some little italian things, she sang Old Robin Gray,— and every body was affected to tears,— the ladies all sitting in a row with their pocket handkerchiefs to their eyes, young and old,— made a singular appearance! But it was quite *the fashion* to weep whenever she sung a ballad, and the men did so as well as the women [...] But her greatest success of all was in singing Elfrida last Sunday [...] all agreed that nobody except *Banti* ever sung it at all in that stile.[104]

When the family moved on to Brighton at the beginning of October, it was with a view to obtaining some much needed rest for Caroline, and Margaret intended 'neither to dress or visit'. The previous five weeks in Tunbridge had been fatiguing, 'particularly to Caroline and Amico, who had to perform every night', but, Margaret wrote, 'both [Caroline] and Amico will be admired beyond all others, – indeed Amico's success was as great as Caroline's, – and they will ever be received with delight & *empressement*.'[105] According to Margaret the *haut ton* to be met with at Tunbridge was unequalled anywhere in England: 'As to Tunbridge, there is nothing like it, – and society is now more upon the footing of society at Paris, than any I have ever seen in this country. Amico says the same. The Tierneys[106] are delighted with Amico.'

---

[102] MC to GRC, 15 September 1811, Ch.Ch.
[103] MC to GRC, 4 October 1811, Ch.Ch.
[104] *Ibid.*
[105] MC to GRC, 6 October 1811, Ch.Ch.
[106] George Tierney (1761–1830), respected Whig statesman.

For the first week in Brighton they were alone in their seaside dwelling on the windswept cliffs. The house at 46 West Cliff, chosen for its remoteness, was taken for three weeks, after which Margaret was resolved to return to Gillwell. Margaret enjoyed morning rides in a donkey gig, but Viotti's gout prevented him from accompanying her. Although this was a disappointment, the advantage was that without Viotti Margaret could drive about with a veil covering her face without fear of being recognized. But soon most of the Tunbridge society descended on Brighton, and Margaret and Viotti were obliged to participate in the continuing round of parties or risk being considered aloof. William Chinnery, Spencer and the little girls had left for London, but William returned to Brighton each weekend.

On 29 October the Prince Regent arrived in Brighton, and Viotti, who had just received his denizenship patent, called on him at the Pavilion to thank him. William was also obliged to write his name at the Pavilion 'in order to be sure of not giving offence', since his work at the Treasury frequently brought him into contact with the prince. On 30 October Margaret wrote:

> The Prince regent arrived to a late dinner yesterday,— this morning after breakfast Amico went to pay his respects,— The Prince was not up, but he saw the Duke of Cumberland, who expressed great pleasure at his being here; and told him the Prince would probably see him in the course of the day,— talked to him about the Band, asked him how long it was since he heard it &c&c and desired he would leave his direction with the Porter.[107]

As a result of this visit William was invited to dinner at the Pavilion the same day, and Margaret, Caroline and Viotti in the evening at nine o'clock. Viotti and the Chinnerys had visited the Pavilion previously in 1805, and perhaps also in 1803 and 1804 when they all holidayed at Brighton.[108] Now the prince invited Margaret to play again, but she declined in favour of her daughter: 'Cary sat down and played her own variations, which he said were "quite delicious" and in the stile of Scarlatti. He then took us in to the next room, the band being all ready, and nothing could equal his delight at hearing this *tintamarre* [racket] for three hours.'[109] The Prince Regent's band at Brighton was composed entirely of wind instruments. There is no record of what Viotti thought of the sound, but the prince himself heartily enjoyed it. The latter's Whig friend Thomas Creevey, who was present on another evening when Viotti and the Chinnerys were guests, wrote:

> The Regent sat in the Musick Room almost all the time between Viotti, the famous violin player, and Lady Jane Houston, and he went on for hours beating his thighs the proper time for the band, and singing out aloud, and looking about him for accompaniment from Viotti and Lady Jane. It was a curious sight to see a Regent thus employed, but he seemed in high good humour…[110]

---

[107] MC to GRC, 30 October 1811, Ch.Ch.

[108] MC's Journal, 2 October [1803], p. 14, and 14 November 1804, p. 73; C. Musgrave (1970), *Life in Brighton*, Faber and Faber, London, p. 128.

[109] MC to GRC, 31 October 1811, Ch.Ch.

[110] T. Creevey (1970), *The Creevey Papers*, ed. J. Gore, Folio Society, London, p. 89.

From 30 October Viotti and the Chinnerys were summoned nightly to the Pavilion, where Viotti, according to Margaret, was in high favour with the prince. On 4 and 5 November, when the party at the Pavilion was much smaller, the prince was again 'entirely occupied with his musick' and also, apparently, with Caroline, as he 'offered *her his Band of a morning*, and most graciously assured me that no one shall be present but the Band *and himself* if she will like to try either vocal or instrumental music!'[111] Some members of the prince's band even came to the Chinnerys' house:

> Now at this minute I am writing to you in a corner of our *small drawing room*, where seven or eight wind instruments, & Ferrari at the Pianoforte are trying an air which Caroline is to sing to the Prince tomorrow, and when this is over, (perhaps before it is all over) the Duke of Cumberland is coming to hear Amico & her![112]

Finding them at rehearsal, the duke listened to Caroline, and 'expressed great pleasure at her stile of singing. Amico played three pieces accompanied by Caroline after we had dismissed the Band, – and he was much pleased with these also. He was here about an hour and a half, and thanked me when he took leave'.[113] 'We had proof of the Duke of Cumberland's being highly pleased, for just as we were stepping into the carriage last night to go to the Pavilion, a note was brought to Amico from Col. Bloomfield [the prince's aide-de-camp]'.[114] Addressed to 'Mr Viotti at 46 West Cliff', it reads:

> Lt Col. Bloomfields compliments to M. Viotti & is commanded by the Prince to say that if Miss Chinnery would have the goodness to bring some Musick & M. Viotti his Violin His Royal Highness would be much gratified— Pavila, Nov. 4. [1811].[115]

Margaret's letter to George the following day was bursting with motherly pride:

> I *cannot* give you an idea of the Prince's surprise and delight at your sister's playing!... His *expressions*, his *gestures*, his "tearful eye", every thing was far beyond *any thing* that *any person* has ever said or done before,— he was enchanted with Amico, oh yes quite enchanted,— but to your sister he was... really I cannot find words to tell you all he said and did,— *his attentions,— standing* by her the whole time, handing her to her chair,— telling her "I shall stay by you",— and after the first piece he declared *out loud* that "she was the first player he had ever heard on that instrument and had produced an effect, by a trick peculiar to herself, which he had never thought possible and which he had no idea of". As to *Cramer* added the Prince, "he must hide his face before her"![116]

The prince's penchant for a pretty face was legendary, so perhaps his attentions had more to do with gallantry than with appreciation of her talent.

---

[111] MC to GRC, 2 November 1811, Ch.Ch.
[112] MC to GRC, 4 November 1811, Ch.Ch.
[113] *Ibid.*
[114] MC to GRC, 5 November 1811, Ch.Ch.
[115] Benjamin Bloomfield to GBV, 4 November [1811], PHM 94/143/1 – 28/2.
[116] MC to GRC, 5 November 1811, Ch.Ch.

Margaret may have been well satisfied with the compliment, but Caroline's strength was sapped. The family party, including Viotti, left Brighton on 13 November, spent two nights en route at Thomas Hope's Surrey mansion The Deepdene, one night at Spencer's in Curzon Street, London, and was back at Gillwell by the 18th. This 1811 autumn vacation, during which the Chinnerys were the toast of fashionable society, was to be the last truly happy period in their lives.

CHAPTER 12

# At Charles Street, 1812–1814

If the years 1810 and 1811 were the Chinnerys' *anni mirabili*, the next was definitely an *annus horribilis*. On 16 March 1812 William Chinnery was dismissed from his post as chief clerk at the Treasury. The reason was embezzlement on a massive scale – more than £80,000 over a 12-year period. He did what most debtors then did, and fled to the Continent. The day that William boarded the packet for Gothenburg was 2 April 1812. The following day Caroline died at Spencer's home at 36 Curzon Street in London. A reading of the autopsy report[1] suggests tuberculosis, which she had probably been suffering from for many months, masked by whooping cough, and exacerbated more recently by the frenetic round of parties at Tunbridge and Brighton. Margaret, George, Viotti and Spencer sat with her until the end, and it fell to Viotti to inform William of her imminent death: 'She is still in the greatest danger', he wrote, 'but there is yet a spark of life. Oh! Why cannot I rekindle it with my own life!'[2]

The Chinnerys' *annus horribilis* is well documented in the CFP collection, as is Viotti's unstinting support of William and consolation of Margaret throughout the whole period. Of the 25 miscellaneous letters received by Viotti that exist in the Powerhouse Museum collection, 14 date from 1812 and concern the approaching death of Caroline Chinnery and the scandal attached to William's financial and professional ruin. These letters were all addressed to Viotti at 36 Curzon Street. They came from the Countess Susan Dunmore at Glen Finart in Scotland; from Miss Kingsman, the daughter of Viotti's wine customer; from Sophia Johnstone; from Madame de Vaudreuil, the young and pretty second wife of the Comte de Vaudreuil; from an old French friend A.B. St Leger; from James Perry, editor of the *Morning Chronicle*; from Viotti's business partner Charles Smith; and from Madame Bianchi (now Mrs William Lacy), who was so affected by the Chinnerys' woes that she was 'quite ill with weeping'.[3]

Also dating from this time was a letter to Viotti from the Duke of Cumberland's aide-de-camp C.W. Thornton. It was clearly written in response to an approach Margaret had had Viotti make to the duke regarding George's future career. Thornton wrote:

---

[1] Transcribed in MC to WBC, 6 April 1812, PHM 94/143/1 – 17/2.

[2] 'Elle est toujours dans le plus grand danger mais enfin une etincelle paroit encore. Oh! que ne puis-je la faire reluire avéc ma propre vie!' (GBV to WBC, 2 April 1812, PHM 94/143/1 – 14/4).

[3] 'vraiment malade à force de pleurer' (Jane Lacy to GBV, [March 1812], PHM 94/143/1 – 28/12). The other letters are also at PHM 94/143/1 – 28.

> Previous to receiving your note this day I had communicated your letter, and the enclosure to His Royal Highness The Duke of Cumberland, and I am commanded by His Royal Highness to express his thanks to you for your very kind attention to *him* and also to say every thing kind from him to Mrs Chinnery.[4]

That Viotti was able to act as an intermediary in this way shows his closeness to the royal dukes and indicates the esteem in which he was held by them.

When Margaret had recovered her composure sufficiently to conduct her own correspondence, one of the first people she wrote to was Madame Cherubini. In the letter she described her misfortunes and gratefully acknowledged Viotti's support. Viotti made a copy of the letter, as he made copies of many other letters Margaret was obliged to write at this time, including one to Madame de Genlis (missing). The end of Margaret's letter to Cécile Cherubini reads:

> it is impossible for me to describe all the kindness of Amico!— He is a unique friend and I pray that Heaven may reward his fidelity. He is gentle and kind in the extreme in the way he looks after me, and tries to lessen my woes! […]
> Adieu dear friend,— I have not written to you for a long while because I was told that you were still in Vienna [Cherubini was in Vienna from June 1805–April 1806]. But I never ceased to love you as I loved you in the happy times I spent with you!… I love you and all your family!— excellent Mr Cherubini will also share the pain which overwhelms me…
>
> Forever your affectionate but unhappy friend, M.C.[5]

During these months William's letters to Margaret were full of ruminations and reflections, interspersed with impractical recommendations and suggestions. He remarked several times on Viotti's steadfastness during the crisis, and one of his more perspicacious comments was that Viotti's denizenship put him out of danger of being attacked by a cabal a second time:

> Yes indeed, Amico is incomparable!— He *shames the world* as it goes by his unvaried Conduct towards us at this Moment of pressure! And then what a Blessing it is for us & for him too, that his Patent of Denization which the P. Regent so graciously & generously *ordered to be granted* him, should have put him *out of the reach of the wicked & malevolent*; for had it not been otherwise the Chances would have been heavily against his being secure from their attacks & Indiscretions! But there never was

---

[4] C.W. Thornton to GBV, [1812], PHM 94/143/1 – 28/16.

[5] 'il m'est impossible de vous peindre toute la bonté de l'Amico!— C'est un ami unique, et je prie le Ciel de recompenser sa fidelité; la douceur, et l'extréme bonté avec lesquels il me soigne, et cherche à adoucir mes malheurs! […] Adieu chere Amie,— je ne vous ai point ecrit depuis longtemps, parce qu'on m'assuroit que vous étiez à Vienne. Mais je n'ai jamais cessé de vous aimer comme dans les moments de bonheur que j'ai passé avéc vous!… Je vous aime, et votre famille toute!— l'excellent M$^{r}$ Cherubini partagera aussi la douleur qui m'accable… / À jamais votre aff$^{née}$ mais malheureuse M.C.' (MC to Cécile Cherubini (copy), 1 July 1812, PHM 94/143/1 – 4/7).

a more noble Act done than by H.R.H. in *ordering his Patent* on the Ground of Justice to Amico, as well as personal & royal good will.[6]

The 64 letters from Viotti to William Chinnery (1793–1823) – of which nine date from 1812 – are proof of Viotti's heartfelt attachment to his English protector. Unfortunately only one letter from William's side of the correspondence has been preserved, but Viotti's replies are specific enough to be able to guess at their contents. Viotti's expressions of friendship and support that are to be found in every one of these letters are not empty assurances. He carries his words into deeds and puts the welfare of the Chinnerys above all else in his daily life. He treats with kindness every friend that William sends from Sweden, purchases and dispatches every item that William requests from England, and most importantly, assumes the role of protector and companion to William's wife and family.

One of the more painful tasks that fell to Viotti was to attend the auction of Gillwell Park, ordered by the Government, on 8 April 1813. The house and estate, originally the property of Margaret's father Leonard Tresilian, had been settled on Margaret at the time of her marriage, but had, according to English law, become the property of her husband once she was married. A copy of one of the sale documents is annotated in Viotti's hand with the price each lot fetched, and the name of the purchaser, and was clearly made for Margaret's benefit.[7] At Viotti's request the former Gillwell tutor Herr Trumpf helped Margaret and her family to find accommodation in London after their eviction from Gillwell. In a letter dated 5 August 1812 he writes to Viotti that immediately he received the request he spent the whole morning inspecting properties on their behalf.[8] The house at 10 Charles Street, Manchester Square, which was eventually selected, and where they remained until 1817, was owned by a Mr Treble, whom Margaret found a most difficult landlord. It was small – too small for all the bulky furniture that was retrieved from the auction of the Chinnery effects, and Viotti was constantly complaining of 'this ugly hole, cluttered with furniture'[9] where there was not enough room for his 'Quartett, or a Grand Piano-forte supposing we had one.' The members of the household at Charles Street were Margaret and Viotti, George, Matilda Chinnery and little Margaret Chinnery.

Viotti's 1812 letters to William Chinnery in Gothenburg are mostly concerned with the death of Caroline Chinnery, the choice of a safe haven for William, the actions of the British Government to recover some of William's debt, and the (fruitless) efforts of Margaret to petition the Crown for the right to retain Gillwell House. They also deal with his attempts to seek royal protection in helping both William and George find diplomatic posts. (The Prince Regent was full of empty promises of which nothing came.) In spite of the pressing need to sort out his affairs and find some kind of employment – for Gothenburg had been chosen as a

---

[6] WBC to MC, 16 May 1812, PHM 94/143/1 – 7/12.
[7] Particulars on the sale of Gillwell House and Estate, PHM 94/143/1 – 11/20.
[8] C.L. Trumpf to GBV, 5 August 1812, PHM 94/143/1 – 28/18.
[9] 'ce vilain trou, empifré de meubles'. These are Viotti's words, quoted by Margaret in MC to WBC, 10 October 1813, PHM 94/143/1 – 17/16.

place of refuge as much for its ample commercial opportunities as for its distance from the Napoleonic wars – William seems to have had the leisure to pursue his interest in music.

It is obvious from the letters that he was not short of invitations into Gothenburg society, where he continued to make the acquaintance of musicians, and where he desired to continue his cello playing. From Viotti's letter of 23 June 1812 it may be adduced that William has asked for his cello to be sent to him. Viotti tells William that the export of the cello is causing him headaches. There are imposts to pay and documents to be procured. In the box of provisions, including wigs, pomade, cheese and macaroni that Viotti is preparing to send to William he says he will find some music, but no instrument on which to play it.[10]

William met two musicians in Gothenburg. The first was the German pianist Ludwig Berger, who had been at St Petersburg in 1812 when it was threatened by Napoleon's advancing army, and had fled to England via Gothenburg. The second was Viotti's compatriot, Luigia Gerbini, who, having initially tried to establish a career as a singer, discovered a much stronger talent for the violin, much to the surprise of all who heard her. Her Paris debut at Viotti's Théâtre de Monsieur had drawn the comment: 'She succeeded much better on the violin. She was strongly applauded in a charming concerto by M. Viotti [No. 3 in A major], which she played with a singular precision, and with a dexterity of execution extremely rare in a woman, and which places her on the same level as the best professors.'[11] A reporter reviewing a concert given by Gerbini in Vienna in 1807, went even further, saying that 'her extraordinary bowing power, her strength in passage-work and [mastery of] difficulties almost borders on the unbelievable for a woman.'[12]

Viotti corrects William's misapprehension that Gerbini was a former pupil of his. This belief was apparently widespread, since the *Times* of 13 December 1802, in reviewing Gerbini's performance in *Merope e Polifonte* in London, made the same error, as did Fayolle in his *Dictionnaire*.[13] William appears to have been much struck by her beauty as well as her music, but Viotti is flippantly dismissive:

> Mme Gerbini is a pupil of Pugnani. I heard her for the first time in Paris. I thought that she played very well, that she had a masculine nerve and that she drew a very beautiful sound from an excellent Stradivarius. I do not know if she kept that instrument. Since that time we have seen her in London, and as far as I can recall she did not make an impression on anyone, especially since she came as a singer and only a rather so so one at that... You seem to be quite taken with her appearance! Is it possible that she has

---

[10] GBV to WBC, 23 June 1812, PHM 94/143/1 – 14/7.

[11] 'Elle a bien mieux réussi sur le violon. On l'a fort applaudie dans un charmant concerto de M. Viotti, qu'elle a joué avec une précision singulière, avec une habileté d'exécution fort extraordinaire dans une femme, et qui la place au rang des meilleurs Professeurs' (*Mercure de France*, 27 November 1790).

[12] 'deren ausserordentliche Kraft des Bogens, deren Stärke in Passagen und Schwierigkeiten für ein Frauenzimmer beynahe bis zum Unglaublichen geht' (*AMZ*, 18 March 1807, col. 399).

[13] Choron and Fayolle, *Dictionnaire historique des musiciens*, vol. 1, p. 269.

become tolerable? I have always found her as ugly as sin. She was travelling with her father at that time, now you say that the father has become a brother. Good luck to him, but I have never met him. May God bless my compatriot, and may she have much *success*[?].[14]

In another letter Gerbini's name appears again. William has told Viotti of a private concert at which he played with Gerbini. Viotti, full of regrets for their enforced separation, replies with hearty congratulations on the way William played the cello: 'I must compliment you on the manner in which you played the second cello at Gerbini's concert! Upon my word, the way you made the fourth string vibrate was superb! Dear good Cinnerino, how I would have loved to have heard you!... Oh when shall we be reunited! How cheerfully would I allow myself to be flayed by [your playing]!'[15]

In Viotti's letter of 5 August 1812, he describes a magnificent fête at the Hanover Square home of Sophia Johnstone and her brother at which all of fashionable London was present, including her great friend the Prince Regent. The wealthy Johnstones were indeed as close to the Chinnerys as Lord Glenbervie had portrayed them in his *Journals*, their bond of friendship cemented by a common love of music. Sophia Johnstone, dubbed 'la Signorina' by Viotti, was famous in London for her lavish parties at which the number of musicians rivalled the large contingent to be found at the Chinnerys' home only a couple of years earlier. She too employed singers from the King's Theatre opera company at her assemblies. Margaret, a recluse from society in the first year of her sorrow, was not present on this night, but George and Viotti were.

The high point of the evening, which Viotti described for William in his letter, was the flattering number of enquiries that the prince made of the Chinnery family. Woven through Viotti's highly entertaining narrative, like a recurring melody in a piece of music, is his description of the events taking place in the music room. The prince enters, catches sight of Viotti, bids him good evening most graciously, and passes into the music room, where he sits down on the sofa next to the piano. 'The singing begins. One piece is played, two pieces, then three, during which George

---

[14] 'Mad.[me] Gerbini est éleve de Pugnani, je l'ai entendue à Paris pour la premiere fois, j'ai trouvé qu'elle jouoit trés bien, qu'elle avoit un nerf masculin et tiroit un trés bon son d'un excellent Stradivarius. J'ignore si elle a toujours conservé cet instrument. Nous l'avons revüe à Londres depuis, autant que je m'en rappele elle ne frappa personne, surtout y étant venüe comme chanteuse et chantant alors couci couci... Vous me paroissez assez content de sa personne! Est-ce qu'elle seroit devenüe passable? Je l'ai toujours trouvée laide comme le peché. Elle voyageoit alors avéc son Pere, maintenant vous dites que ce Pere est devenû un Frere; à la bonheur mais je ne l'ai jamais connû. Que le Ciel benisse ma compatriote, et qu'elle puisse gagner beaucoup de *Prix-Daler* [sic]' (GBV to WBC, 14 August 1812, PHM 94/143/1 – 14/9).

[15] 'il faut que je vous complimente sur la maniere dont vous avez éxécuté la seconde Basse au concert de la Gerbini! Parmafois c'étoit superbe, comme vous faisiez ronfler la quatrieme! Cher et bon Cinnerino comme j'aurois voulû vous entendre!... Oh quand serons nous réunis! avéc quelle joie je me laisserois écorcher par vous!' (GBV to WBC, *c.*August 1812, PHM 94/143/1 – 14/10).

and I remained in the first room.'[16] The music is interrupted abruptly by the arrival of a bundle of dispatches from Spain from the Duke of Wellington, whose victories are read aloud to the gathering. During the reading Viotti and George slip into the music room and take up a position close to the prince. 'God Save the King is sung (execrably, incidentally, by Bertinotti, Tramezzani etc), after which the Signorina comes over to me and tells me that the Prince would be very happy to hear me, adding, as you can well imagine, all her usual compliments. I leave my companion, and cross to the small room where I had left my violin.'[17]

Coming back into the music room Viotti is stopped by the prince who, having recognized George, enquires solicitously after Mrs Chinnery, sympathizes with her, remembers Caroline's playing at Brighton the previous autumn, wants to know where William Chinnery is, and remarks on prime minister Perceval's kindness in finding George a situation in the Treasury. 'Meanwhile my turn came round – I took up the violin. The best of princes sat down on a chair near the sofa [...] where Lady Castlereagh and Lady Cholmond[eley] were seated. From there he asked me all sort of questions with the most inexpressible kindness while I tuned the violin with [Francesco] Vaccari and laid out the music [...] I played, and I believe I was fortunate enough to satisfy him. Once my duo was over, he did me the honour of calling me over to ask about you, showing an interest and kindness that brought tears to my eyes.'[18]

Another page of narrative follows, in which the prince also offers sympathy to William, who, Viotti ventures, was a victim of his own confiding nature and his generosity towards others – an opinion with which the prince professes to concur. After holding him in conversation for as long as possible, Viotti finishes by reminding the prince very pointedly of George's talents being wasted in the Treasury and of his suitability to a diplomatic career. Viotti withdraws. 'A duet, *Mia Sorella* was about to commence, so I withdrew. However this charming, magnanimous Prince did not take his eyes off me and kept giving me signs of his appreciation of the music &c.'[19]

---

[16] 'On commence le chant, on éxecute une piece, deux pieces, puis la troisieme pendant lesquelles George et moi nous restions toujours dans cette premiere pièce' (GBV to WBC, 5 August 1812, PHM 94/143/1 – 14/8).

[17] 'On chante God Save the King (détestablement par parenthèse, par Bertinotti Tramezzani &c) aprés quoi la Signorina vient à moi et me dit que Le P. seroit bien aise de m'entendre, ajoutant vous imaginez bien tous les compliments qu'elle sait faire. Je laisse mon compagnon, je traverse le petit cabinet ou étoit mon Violon' (*Ibid.*).

[18] 'Mon tour arrivoit en attendant – je prends le Violon. Le meilleur des Princes s'assoit sûr une chaise prés du Canapé [...] ou étoient assises Lady Castlereagh et Ladi Cholmond^y^. De là il me fait tout plein de questions avéc une bonté inéxprimable pendant que j'accordois avéc Vacari et que je preparois la musique. [...] Je joue, et il m'a parû que j'avois eû le bonheur de le satisfaire. Mon Duo fini, il m'a fait l'honneur de me rappeler à lui, pour s'informer de vous avéc un interet et une bonté qui m'ont fait venir les larmes aux yeux' (*Ibid.*).

[19] 'Un Duo, mia Sorella, alloit commencer, je me retirai. Il ne me perdit cependant pas de vüe cet aimable et magnanime Prince, me faisant des signes sûr la bonté de la Musique

In his letter of 14 August, Viotti comes back to the question of the export of the cello. William must have owned two cellos, one of which was a highly prized Amati, for Viotti says that the Amati has been returned and that he will attempt to send the 'mediocre' cello only, in case of accident. It would appear from a later remark of Viotti, that William subsequently gave the Amati to Crosdill, who promised to bequeath it to William or George on his death.[20] Viotti writes in the same letter that he has sent William some of his music. He is disappointed to learn that part of it was missing on arrival, because Smith had slipped a business letter inside one of the sheets of music – 'in the first violin [part] of the quartets dedicated to Philip C[ipriani].'[21] This last comment identifes the music as the Three quartets for flute (or violin), violin, viola and cello, Op. 22, and proves that they were composed before those dedicated to Viotti's brother André (see below). Philip Cipriani, son of the Italian engraver Giovanni Battista Cipriani, was a senior clerk at the Treasury, and as well as being a colleague of William he was a family friend. William must have asked for different music, as Viotti apologizes for not being able to send his quartets that had been engraved in Paris, as he does not have them in England.[22]

In the same letter is a long description of some new quartets that Viotti has apparently just finished composing, which he intends dedicating to the Duke of Cambridge. These are probably his Three quartets for two violins, viola and cello (WII: 13–15), which are not dedicated to Adolphus Frederick, but to his own brother André Viotti.[23] Because of the smallness of the Charles Street house the four musicians removed themselves to the London home of Lord Dunmore, who had offered it to Viotti while he was at his Scottish seat Glen Finart:

> The other day I tried out the new quartets with Vaccari and the two Schrams.[24] If I were not the author of them I would say that they are really charming, even more than that, but Jean Baptiste's modesty forces him to say nothing. You have no idea how happy these gentlemen were with them. I shall make a copy for Erard — it is a present I wish to make to his nephews.[25] You can imagine how long this copying will take me. When it is completed I shall busy myself selling them here so that they may be engraved and dedicated to the good Duke [Cambridge], who has not yet heard them.— I wanted to have this session behind closed doors, and so that the noise did not disturb the Padrona, we all four went to try out the music at the home of Lord Dunmore, who was in Scotland, and had told me I could use his house whenever I liked.[26]

---

&c' (*Ibid.*).

20 GBV to WBC, 24 February 1814, PHM 94/143/1 – 14/17.

21 'dans le 1[er] Violon des Quatuors dediés à Phillipe C[ipriani]' (GBV to WBC, 14 August 1812, PHM 94/143/1 – 14/9).

22 *Ibid.*

23 See below, p. 175.

24 Cellist Christopher Schram and his brother[?] S. Schram, violinist (see Highfill, vol. 13, p. 232). The viola part was probably taken by Vaccari.

25 One nephew was Pierre Erard (1794–1855), who played the harp in an 1816 Philharmonic concert. He was the son of Sébastien Erard's older brother Jean-Baptiste.

26 'J'ai essayé l'autre jour les Quatuors nouveaux avéc Vacari et les deux Shram. Si je n'en

It is also obvious from these letters that William is still trying to do favours for friends, albeit vicariously. In Gothenburg he has offered the services of Viotti to two of his fellow countrymen, to obtain advantageous terms from Viotti's friend the pianoforte maker John Broadwood. Viotti is ever ready to oblige, but foresees difficulties. The 33 per cent discount that they are seeking is not even given to dealers or professors like himself. The other obstacle is that old Mr Broadwood having just died, Viotti will be obliged to treat with his sons, whom he does not know so well.[27]

During 1812 and 1813 Margaret maintained her reclusive life-style, refusing all invitations, and receiving guests in her own home only in the second half of 1813. After the events of the previous 18 months during which she had seen all her possessions sold at auction, her only consolation was the support of Viotti, who brought with him the consolation of music. Margaret had always been of the opinion that 'music is salutory, both to body and mind',[28] and living with Viotti meant that music was part of her daily life. But it was not until 16 months after her husband's flight and her daughter's death that she was able to admit an outsider into their domestic circle for an evening of music.

Appropriately, their first visitor, Mr Peterson, came from Sweden, sent to them by William. He was an amateur violinist who had shared some musical evenings with William in Gothenburg, and so was warmly received. Catching sight of Caroline's harp in the drawing room, he wished to hear it played. In what must have been a cathartic experience for Margaret, she heard the sounds of her daughter's harp, played by little Margaret, for the first time since Caroline's death. Viotti organized a small family concert:

> Amico made [little] Margaret play a sonata Caroline had taught her,— and he accompanied it. M. Peterson, asked for something else, and heard the variations of the folies d'Espagne. Then Amico proposed playing a Duett with him,— which after some compliments & excuses, was done, and very well done for an Amateur. They played *two* of those dedicated to *us*. I then proposed Amico's letting M. Peterson hear *him alone*,— he complied, and played the famous Minuet of Pugnani, and afterwards a Polacca. To conclude, Matilda played the new concerto just arranged by J. Cramer, accompanied by Amico & M. Peterson.[29]

---

étois pas l'auteur je dirois qu'ils sont réellement charmants, plusque celà meme, mais la modestie de votre Jean Baptiste doit lui imposer silence. Vous n'avez pas d'idée comme ces messieurs en étoient contents. Je vais en faire une copie pour Erard— c'est un présent que je veux faire à ses neveux, et vous sentéz quel temps doit me prendre cette copiade. Quand tout sera pret, je m'occuperai de les vendre ici pour etre gravés et dédiés au bon Duc qui ne les a pas encore entendû.— J'ai voulü avoir cette séance à porte close, et pour que le tapage musical n'affectat pas la Padrona, nous avons été tous quatre faire notre essay chez Lord Dunmore qui étant en Ecosse m'a dit de faire usage de sa maison quand bon me semble' (GBV to WBC, 14 August 1812, PHM 94/143/1 – 14/9).

27 *Ibid.*

28 MC to GRC, 14 March 1810, Ch.Ch.

29 MC to WBC, 18 July 1813, PHM 94/143/1 – 17/11.

The new concerto referred to in the last sentence was Viotti's No. 27 in C major, which is thought to have been composed in 1795, and indeed the wording on the announcement of J.B. Cramer's 1813 piano arrangement, 'Viotti's celebrated concerto in C', indicates that it was already a well-loved piece.[30] Margaret's epithet 'new' therefore seems to refer to the piano arrangement, rather than to the original violin concerto.

Soon after William's arrival in Gothenburg Viotti had written to him saying that he was surprised that Mrs Peterson had not extended the hospitality that was due to him, considering that during her stay in London she had several times attended the Chinnerys' Mortimer Street concerts. It was she who had recommended to Viotti Karl Bärmann, first bassoonist to the king of Prussia. Viotti said he intended to write to her to prod her sense of duty.[31]

Although Margaret refused to go into society in 1812 and 1813, Viotti did, and promoted George Chinnery's cause whenever he could. In 1813 he went reluctantly to a small dinner at Mrs Francis Smyth's, whom he had met with the Chinnerys in Eastbourne in 1811:

> Amico liked his dinner yesterday at Mrs Smyths better than he expected; the party was small and agreeable. Ld & Lady Winchester, Dow[r] Lady Lansdowne, Mr [Payne] Knight & Mr Forbes made up the dinner party,— and at table, during the dinner they talked much of our dear George [...] In the evening a dozen more people came, three of the Royal Dukes, Cumberland, Cambridge & Clarence,— who all enquired after us of Amico.[32]

In 1814 Margaret still hesitated to go into society, but she was happy to entertain in the privacy of her home, and by early 1814 became once more the elegant hostess that she had been before 1812. A letter from the Comte de Vaudreuil, sent from no. 6 Park Lane and dated 7 March 1814, accepts a dinner invitation at Charles Street issued to him, his wife and son Alfred.[33] Other French *émigré* courtiers who were received at Charles Street in 1814, were the philanthropist Baron de Montyon, Colonel Edward Dillon, and M. de Malcor, who, like Vaudreuil, were all attached to Louis XVI's brother the Comte d'Artois (future Charles X), and had accompanied him to England in the early days of the Revolution. From this time on Margaret and Viotti held small select dinners – numbers being limited owing to the size of the dining room – to which Margaret invited more company later in the evening for music.

From Matilda Chinnery's [1814] Journal, undertaken with the purpose of keeping William informed of the minutiae of his family's daily life, it is obvious that family musical evenings continued apace in Charles Street. Margaret's adoring friend Mrs Smyth counted almost as family, and private visits were exchanged

---

30 See White, 'Chronology', p. 123; Milligan, *The Concerto*, pp. 136–7; *Thematic Catalogue*, p. 45.

31 GBV to WBC, 14 August 1812, PHM 94/143/1 – 14/9.

32 MC to WBC, 6 March 1813, PHM 94/143/1 – 17/9.

33 Comte de Vaudreuil to MC, 7 March 1814, Fisher 2000 – 4/11.

almost daily by the two women. Mrs Smyth was also an enthusiastic amateur pianist, as was her daughter Harriet. Matilda's Journal describes an evening of declaiming and music at Mrs Smyth's on 29 March. Margaret had previously given Matilda and little Margaret a lesson 'upon a duet of Dussek's which we prepared to play at Mrs Smyth's':

> After the declaiming, Mrs Smyth begged to have a little Music— & Marg[t] & myself played our duet. Then Harriet [Smyth] played uncommonly well (in Cramer's Stile) some Variations of Beethoven's. She is indeed wonderfully improved. Amico's Concerto finished the whole,— it did not go off as *coulament* [smoothly] & brilliantly as I could have wished! Wine & water was brought after which we came home in the Carriage— first Marg[t] & me,— then Mama & Amico. George staid at home all the Even[g] to read—[34]

The entry of 6 April describes the order of the music after a dinner Margaret gave on Monday 4 April: '[little] Marg[t] & myself played Dussek's Duet, – the Anacreon, – Mrs Smyth played a sonata of Mozart's, & Amico played two little pieces accompanied by me – There was waltzing afterwards.'[35]

Another dinner given by Margaret one week later is described in the same entry:

> The Anacreon opened the concert,— Marg[t]'s March followed, & Mrs Smyth played a sonata of Amico's. After which Miss Smyth began dancing— she danced the Guararcia [guaracha][36] to us with the veil & the Castagnets, and then a Russian Dance composed by [King's Theatre ballet master] Favier on purpose for her. She accomplished them extremely well and afterwards she waltzed with George. Mrs Smyth played the waltzes—'[37]

Catalani's 1814 series of concerts, which opened on 31 March, is also mentioned in the Journal. Having performed at the King's Theatre for the previous four seasons, Catalani now went over to the Theatre Royal, Covent Garden. Matilda thought her fees too high:

> Mad[me] Catalani will have nothing to do with the Opera this year. She is giving concerts (but they are very bad),— The subscription is nine guineas, an exorbitant sum, and the concerts will be twelve in number. A proof that the subscription does not fill is, that there are constant advertisements about them in the Newspaper.[38]

Viotti continued to accept invitations, albeit reluctantly, to perform at private concerts. But in one of his 1814 letters to William, he wrote that he had held out against the persistent overtures of Mr Peterson:

---

[34] MMC's Journal, Wednesday 31 [*recte* 30] March [1814].
[35] *Ibid*, 6 April [1814].
[36] Spanish and Mexican folk dance.
[37] MMC's Journal, 6 April [1814].
[38] *Ibid.*, Thursday 31 [March 1814].

> You remember Mr Peterson, the Viotti of the *amateurs*, the handsome dandy Mr Peterson? You will find enclosed a letter from him telling you how he likes to pass his time. At heart he seems to be a good fellow, and much as I would like to help him out with his fiddling parties, I feel that he only wants to make an exhibition of me, and in truth we are not good enough friends for me to make such a sacrifice for him.[39]

Nevertheless Viotti was on the whole remarkably tolerant of the efforts of amateur violinists, as shown by the large number of private musical soirées ('racleries' as he called them), that he agreed to play at. An invitation to one of the latter was issued by the son of the ex-lord mayor of London William Curtis, and Viotti was agreeably surprised by the standard of music in his home. The old Sir William was an avid Stradivarius collector, and had previously enjoyed Chinnery hospitality at Gillwell.

On 27 January 1814 Viotti wrote to William of his first visit to the Curtis house, which 'was for an *amateurs*' party, where they started the tra la la after dinner with the first bow stroke at 8 o'clock. The old father Sir William was there, and although he is not much of a musician he seemed to play very well.'[40] Viotti found himself invited by Sir William for a repeat performance two weeks later, when George was also included in the dinner invitation. He wrote to William: 'In truth I was well pleased with all those *amateurs*. Each played his part very well and the master of the house put up a very creditable showing on his cello.'[41] Viotti supposes that William will ask why he took it into his head to go and play there. Viotti admits that he had an ulterior motive – to drum up business for his wine commerce!

---

[39] 'Vous rappelez vous de M[r] Peterson, le Viotti des Amateurs, le beau, le miriflore Mr Peterson? Vous trouverez ici joint un billet de lui qui vous dira comment il aime à passer son temps. Dans le fond il me parait bon diable, et je voudrois bien l'aider dans ses parties Racleuses, mais il me semble qu'il voudroit faire de moi une espece d'éxibition, et en verité nous ne sommes pas assez liés pour lui faire un tel sacrifice' (GBV to WBC, *c.*February 1814, PHM 94/143/1 – 14/18).

[40] 'et c'étoit pour une partie d'amateurs, ou éffectivement ils arriverent à la lululu aprés le dinér pour commencer le premier coup d'archet à 8. heures. Le vieux Pere Sir William y étoit, et quoique peu musicien il a parû jouer trés bien' (GBV to WBC, 27 January 1814, PHM 94/143/1 – 14/16).

[41] 'En verité j'ai été trés content de tous ces Amateurs, ils ont fort bien fait chacun leur partie et le maitre de la maison s'en est fort bien tiré sur son Violoncello' (*Ibid.*).

CHAPTER 13

# Paris, 1814

On the Restoration of Louis XVIII to the French throne in 1814 William moved from Gothenburg to Calais. Margaret, Viotti and George went to join him for three months in August, September, October at the nearby town of St Omer, then part of the kingdom of Belgium and Holland. It was their first reunion since William had left England in 1812. William's move to Calais was at the urging of Viotti, who pressed his friend to hasten to take advantage of the commercial opportunities now opening up in France. Calais was strategically an excellent base from which to conduct an import-export business. In the straight-talking tones Viotti so often used with William, especially when the latter was slow to take the initiative, he wrote to goad William into action:

> What the devil are you doing at that outpost from which Mother nature seems to have banished all attractions? As far as I can tell your stay in that place which is inhabited by polar bears can be of no use to you whatsoever, and yet you remain there!… Has the ice frozen your heels to the ground? Why don't you come closer to us? Why don't you come to Holland where we intend to come and embrace you?[1]

Before leaving England Viotti wrote to Pierre Baillot, mooting the possibility of his visiting Paris at some stage during their stay in Holland.[2] Baillot must have previously written to Viotti with an introduction to his pupil Fémy, for Viotti informs him that he sometimes made Fémy play for him – in other words, gave him lessons. In January 1811 some trios by 'Fémi the elder, pupil of M. Baillot at the Conservatoire' were reviewed in the *Allgemeine musikalische Zeitung*. The reviewer could see Viotti's influence in this work, writing that the trios were really accompanied violin solos in the style of Kreutzer and Viotti, even if they were not as good, or as difficult to execute as the latter's.[3] Viotti writes:

> I had the pleasure of making your pupil Fémy play sometimes. He is a very fine boy who is extremely attached to you and with whom I have often had the great satisfaction of talking of you. How dearly would I love to see you and be part of that small circle

---

[1] 'Que diable faites vous à cet Istade ou la mere nature semble avoir bani tous les attraits? Je ne sache pas que votre sejour dans ce lieu habité par les ours puisse en aucune maniere vous etre utile, et pourtant, vous y restez! Est-ce que la glace a gelé les talons de vos souliers? Que ne vous approchez vous pas de nous, que ne venez vous pas en Hollande ou nous comptons aller vous embrasser?' (GBV to WBC, 31 March 1814, PHM 94/143/1 – 14/19).

[2] GBV to Baillot, 12 July 1814, cited in Pincherle (1924), Letter 2, pp. 105–6.

[3] *AMZ*, 2 January 1811, cols 9–10.

> [of musicians] who share my feelings so closely!— Who knows? I leave next week for Holland, and if my affairs permit, it is not unlikely that I shall return to England via Paris… Mrs Chinnery has charged me to give you her very best wishes. She shares my feelings for you, and she has never forgotten your friendliness in *the happy days*. She, her son and I are leaving together to go and rejoin for a couple of months one of the best men on earth— her kind and excellent husband.[4]

Viotti was having the letter carried by their mutual friend the pianist Kalkbrenner, who was now living in England. The letter is signed with feeling: 'Never forget how much I love and esteem you, your sincere friend, J.B. Viotti'.[5]

On 4 August 1814 Viotti wrote to William in Calais announcing his imminent departure from England with Margaret and George. It transpired that Viotti was able to indulge his desire for a reunion with the French musicians who were so dear to him, and he travelled to Paris from St Omer for a week in September (19th – 27th), staying with the Cherubinis at the Conservatoire, as a letter of thanks to Cécile Cherubini shows.[6] Viotti's stay in Paris was recorded by his faithful disciple Baillot, who wrote twice of the visit to Montbeillard:

> This is to inform you, my friend, with as much pleasure as regret, of the arrival of our dear Viotti. He is here for a few days only […] Yesterday, after his arrival, we played some quartets of his, manuscripts, at General Dessolle's house. Tomorrow we shall repeat the performance at Cherubini's house.[7]

> Viotti stayed here for only a week. We played with him four times, and during these sessions he gave us some quintets by Boccherini, his three manuscript quartets, a new concerto in C major and the one in G minor that he arranged as a quartet with some changes. His quartets are filled with song and the happiest of ideas. He has some charming minuets, full of sentiment and grace, and he still has the same elegance and the same passion. You must have seen how we welcomed him at an impromptu

---

4 'J'ai eu le plaisir de faire jouer quelquefois votre élève Remy [*recte* Fémy], c'est un bien bon garçon qui vous est extrêmement attaché et avec qui j'ai eu bien souvent la vive satisfaction de parler de vous. Combien je voudrais vous voir, me retrouver dans ce petit cercle si analogue à mon cœur!— Qui sçait? je pars la semaine prochaine pour la Hollande, et si mes affaires me le permettent ce n'est pas bien sûr que je ne revienne en Angleterre par Paris… M^rs^ Chinnery me charge de vous dire mille choses de sa part, elle partage mes sentiments pour vous, et elle n'a jamais oublié votre amabilité dans *les temps heureux*. Elle, son fils et moi, nous partons ensemble et nous allons rejoindre pour une couple de mois un des meilleurs mortels qui existe— son bon et excellent mari' (GBV to Baillot, 12 July 1814, cited in Pincherle (1924), Letter 2, pp. 105–6).

5 'N'oubliez jamais combien je vous aime et vous estime, votre sincère ami, J.B. Viotti' (*Ibid.*).

6 GBV to Cécile Cherubini, 29 September 1814, cited in Giazotto, p. 269.

7 'Je vous apprends, mon ami, avec autant de plaisir que de regret, l'arrivée de notre cher Viotti. Il est ici pour quelques jours seulement […] Hier, à son débarqué, nous avons fait des quatuors de lui, manuscrits, chez le général Dessolle; nous les referons demain chez Cherubini' (Baillot to Montbeillard, 20 September 1814, cited in François-Sappey, pp. 183–4).

students' concert at the Conservatoire. He departed happy with the welcome we gave him and promised he would return.[8]

The first of the above letters strongly suggests that one from Cherubini to Baillot, transcribed by Pincherle in his 1924 article in the *Revue de Musicologie*, was written around the same time.[9] Both letters appear to be speaking of the same soirée at the *amateur* General Dessolle's house on 19 September 1814.[10] On the eve of his departure for England Viotti wrote a fond farewell letter to Baillot from St Omer, thanking Baillot's brother for some violin strings, for which he insisted on paying, and regretting that his visit was so hurried that he did not have time to visit Baillot at home for 'you know that I like to have a picture in my mind of those I love, and try as I may I am never able to imagine to myself where you play your violin, or where you relax!'[11]

Baillot's bond of friendship with Viotti had been sealed in 1802, when they came to know and love one another, not just as musicians but as men of an extraordinarily similar turn of mind, with a common love of nature, of letters, and with a philosophy that was strongly tinged with Romanticism. Both men railed against fate; both found it hard to be happy. Both were faithful in friendship; both had extremely sensitive natures. Both experienced the inevitable clash of the ideal of the musical art with the reality of the practice of their profession. Baillot had attempted in 1798 to organize a series of concerts with some colleagues. He learned early the dangers of an administrative role. Viotti never did, and was doomed to suffer in each of his stints as a theatre administrator. As musicians, both were fond of chamber music, which to them was like a conversation among friends. The playing of chamber music demanded an implicit understanding among the participants, an exchange of sentiments, of affection even, making it a most intimate declaration of friendship, said Baillot.[12] It must have been a welcome

---

[8] 'Viotti n'est resté que huit jours ici. Nous avons fait quatre fois de la musique avec lui dans lesquelles séances il nous a fait entendre quelques quintetti de Boccherini, ses trois quatuors manuscrits, un nouveau concerto en *ut* majeur et celui en *sol* mineur qu'il a mis en quatuor avec quelques changements. Ses quatuors sont remplis de chants et des idées les plus heureuses. Il a des menuets charmants, pleins de sentiments et de grâce et a toujours la même élégance et le même feu. Vous avez dû voir comment nous l'avions reçu dans un exercice improvisé pour lui au Conservatoire. Il est parti content de l'accueil qu'il a reçu et en nous promettant de revenir' (Baillot to Montbeillard, 9 November 1814, cited in François-Sappey, p. 184).

[9] Pincherle (1924), p. 104. It might be dated *c.*17 September 1814.

[10] Pincherle wrongly assumes that Baillot is speaking of General Degrave, who is not once mentioned in the Viotti/Chinnery letters, and with whom Viotti does not seem to have been in the least acquainted. Lamare spoke of General Dessolle's love of music in his 1803 letter to Baillot written with Rode from Hanover (Rode and Lamare to Baillot, 8 August 1803, PHM E.A. and V.I. Crome collection, A8213).

[11] 'vous savez qu'on aime à suivre avec la pensée ceux qu'on aime, et j'ai beau le tenter, je ne sçais jamais deviner ou vous jouez du violon, ou vous vous reposez!' (GBV to Baillot, 25 October 1814, cited in Pincherle (1924), Letter 3, p. 107).

[12] *Art of the violin*, p. 479.

change for Viotti to be able to play with like-minded musicians, after the many society concerts he had helped animate in London over the past few years.

The three Viotti manuscript quartets mentioned by Baillot in the above letters to Montbeillard were almost certainly those he had composed in London in 1812, which he said he would dedicate to the Duke of Cambridge. The 'new' concerto in C major was his No. 27, which Baillot had not yet heard, it having not been included in the batch of six concertos that Viotti sold to Cherubini's publishing house in 1802. The quartet which he arranged from his Paris-composed Concerto in G minor (No. 19) is the Quartet for two violins, viola and cello in G minor (WIIa: 1). All five works appear to have been sold to Janet et Cotelle (successors in 1812 to the firm of Imbault) at the time of Viotti's 1814 visit to Paris, and were probably published soon after.

The absence of any quartets dedicated to the Duke of Cambridge, and the fact that the only set of three quartets composed by Viotti is dedicated to his brother (Three quartets for two violins, viola and cello, WII: 13–15), seems to indicate that Viotti changed his mind about the dedication. As this was his first meeting with his half-brother André since the latter was a child, he may have thought the dedication an appropriate celebration of the occasion, and switched the promised ducal dedication to his 'new' concerto (No. 27), a more substantial work, and therefore one more befitting a royal dedication. With neither work yet committed to the press, it would have been an easy substitution. Baillot's mention of the Boccherini quintets, which Viotti also frequently performed at private London concerts, as well as one at the fourth 1814 Philharmonic concert, shows the latter's predilection for this composer.

Baillot does not say in his letters to Montbeillard who the other players in the string ensemble sessions were, but Cherubini's letter to Baillot of *c.*17 September 1814 does. In 1814 Baillot had founded a chamber music group, the Quatuor Baillot, with his brother-in-law violinist Charles Guynemer, violist Antoine-Alexandre Tariot and cellist Louis-Pierre Norblin. Three of these were present:

> I am returning the box of strings that you lent Viotti, and take the opportunity to inform you that the musical soirée will definitely take place at the general's [Dessolle] the day after tomorrow in the evening. Let me know if you will take charge of issuing the invitation to your brother, Tariot, Norblin and Baudiot for eight o'clock.[13]

Viotti probably also renewed his friendship with Jean-Louis Duport, who had returned from the Berlin court to take up an appointment at the Conservatoire in 1814. Conservatoire professors whom Viotti had not seen since 1802, for example Kreutzer, Lamare and Hélène de Montgéroult, were probably present at this or other small chamber music sessions, and certainly at 'la belle fête de samedi 24

[13] 'Je vous renvoi la boëte aux cordes que vous aviez prêté à Viotti, et je vous préviens en même tems que la soirée de musique aura décidément lieu chez le général après-demain au soir. Faites-moi savoir si vous vous chargez d'avertir pour huit heures, votre frère, Tario, Norblin et Baudiot' (Cherubini to Baillot, *c.*17 September 1814, cited in Pincherle (1924), p. 104).

[septembre]', which Cherubini organized for his friend.[14] Baillot described this fête in his 1825 *Notice*:

> [Viotti] made another voyage to Paris in 1814, at the time of the Restoration. The Conservatoire only learned of it when he was about to leave. The administrators, who missed no opportunity of keeping the sacred fires burning, arranged an impromptu concert for him in the space of a few hours. However, since quite a large number of artists and *amateurs* were able to be notified in time, the room was full, and Viotti appeared in this family assembly like a father in the midst of his children. The pupils only knew him through his compositions, which, since the inception of the Conservatoire, have been the subject of the annual examinations for the violin prize. The sight of the man who had been their role model filled them with excitement: he was welcomed with an explosion of clamorous transports which proves that if, as a famous lady once said, wit is in France a dignity, then genius will always be a force.[15]

The above shows not only how highly Viotti was esteemed among his confreres for his art, but also how warmly he was regarded as a man. Viotti was now 59 years old, and as Baillot says, a venerated father-figure to the younger Conservatoire pupils. War had kept him out of France for the past 12 years, an absence that had only increased his disciples' reverence. During this time the Conservatoire pupils had been exposed to a whole new expressive dimension of violin playing, thanks to the teaching of Baillot, Kreutzer and Rode.

Margaret's letter of thanks to Cécile Cherubini, written from St Omer, describes just how great an emotional impact the Conservatoire reception had on Viotti, and also shows how close the two families were:

> Dear, very dear Friend!
> Since the return of Amico we have not stopped talking about you and are still far from finished with the topic! Oh how well you welcomed him and looked after him! How warmly did dear M. Cherubini and you and his dear brother cheer our dear Amico's heart. I am enchanted, and filled with the most sincere affection and gratitude! And the high point, the splendid reception of Saturday 24th! That day will forever remain in my heart. It was a magnificent day for our friend, and I do not believe he has ever felt so keenly the sweet sensations of affection, attachment and gratitude. He has very clearly

---

[14] MC to Cécile Cherubini, in GBV to Cécile Cherubini, 29 September 1814, cited in Giazotto, p. 269.

[15] '[Viotti] fit un autre voyage à Paris, en 1814, à l'époque de la restauration. Le Conservatoire n'en fut instruit qu'au moment où il allait repartir. L'administration, qui ne laissait échapper aucune occasion d'entretenir le feu sacré, fit improviser pour lui un concert, en quelques heures; cependant un assez grand nombre d'artistes et d'amateurs ayant pu être avertis à temps, la salle fut pleine, et VIOTTI parut dans cette assemblée de famille, comme un père au milieu de ses enfans. Les Elèves ne le connaissaient que par ses compositions, qui, depuis l'origine du Conservatoire, sont le sujet des concours annuels pour le prix de violon. La vue de l'homme qui avait été leur modèle idéal, les remplit d'enthousiasme: il fut accueilli avec une explosion de sentimens et de transports qui prouve que si, comme l'a dit une femme célèbre, l'esprit est en France une dignité, le génie y sera toujours une puissance' (*Notice*, p. 10).

described his emotion, although he claims that it is inexpressible. Oh how touched you must have been by it, to be sure, and how touching your dear good excellent husband himself must have been! I can picture it all from here, and love you more dearly and tenderly than ever. In short I am thoroughly content for my Amico, delighted with his voyage, and with all that has transpired. It is all engraved on my heart. But delight is as fatiguing as sorrow. He returned very tired, and the energy with which he describes the highlights of his stay with you fatigues him still. In two or three days he will be perfectly recovered. Apart from that, he is in perfect health.[16]

The rest of the letter is taken up with thanks for books, biscuits and a letter written on the same night as the reception. Regretting her happiness of former times, Margaret wishes she were the same person she was 12 years ago when the two women first met. She envies Madame Cherubini her daughter Victorine, who may have been only a little younger than Caroline Chinnery would then have been. Finally she describes Viotti's joy at being reunited with his brother André. Viotti's own letter, which precedes Margaret's on the same sheet, is totally devoted to domestic issues and purchases that the Cherubinis will make for their friends: perfumes, cleaning products, orange water, gloves, stockings, handkerchiefs, grapes, all of which will be sent up to St Omer by coach. In addition Viotti's old pupil Libon, who has been working in Paris since 1800, is to send a bow, Cherubini some violin strings and brother André some chocolate from Turin.

The Cherubinis had been vicariously reunited with the Chinnerys earlier the same year through George, who in May had arrived in Paris in the retinue of Louis XVIII as the latter's bursar, in charge of expenses incurred on the royal journey from England to France. Seconded from the British Treasury to make the historic journey, George had spent only a few days in Paris before being recalled to London. He stayed with the Cherubinis at the 'hôtel des menus plaisirs du Roi, faubourg Poissonniere, n° 23', as a letter addressed to George from the newly reinstated Louis XVIII courtier, the Comte de Vaudreuil, now governor of the

[16] 'Chère! Très chère amie! / Depuis le retour de l'amico nous n'avons pas cessé de parler [de vous] et nous sommes loin encore d'avoit tout dit! Oh comme vous l'avez reçu,— et soigné— comme notre cher M. Cherubini et vous et son cher frère avez fait jouir le cœur de notre cher amico! Tout celà me ravit et me remplit de la plus parfaite affection et reconnaissance! Et le triomphe, la belle Fête de samedi 24 de ce mois! Ce jour là me sera toujours cher, c'était un beau jour pour notre ami, et jamais il n'a éprouvé, je crois, au même point les doux sentiments d'affection, d'attachement, et de reconnaissance, il me peint très bien son émotion tout en affirmant que c'est inexprimable. Oh comme vous en avez été affecté j'en suis sure, et comme ce bon cher ami votre inestimable mari était touchant! Je vois tout cela d'ici, et je vous aime plus tendrement et vivement que jamais. Enfin me voilà satisfaite sur le compte de mon amico, et enchantée de son voyage, et de tout ce qui s'est passé! Tout est gravé dans mon cœur! Mais les jouissances de cœur fatiguent aussi bien que les peines, il est revenu très fatigué, l'energie avec laquelle il me raconte les circonstances intéressantes de son séjour chez vous le fatigue encore,— en deux ou trois jours il sera parfaitement remis,— sa santé est parfaite du reste' (MC to Cécile Cherubini, in GBV to Cécile Cherubini, 29 September 1814, cited in Giazotto, p. 270).

Louvre, shows.[17] George's stay with the Cherubinis is also mentioned in a letter of thanks from Viotti to Cécile Cherubini,[18] and in a letter from Madame de Genlis to Margaret Chinnery saying that she was jealous of the Cherubinis, having wanted George to stay with her.[19]

Viotti's reunion with his young brother André, whom he had not seen since his last visit to Fontanetto in 1793, was an emotional one. A member of the Grenadiers des Gardes de Paris, André had a year earlier been decorated with the Legion of Honour. In a letter from Margaret to William of which the first page, and therefore the date, has been lost, she writes:

> Amico received a letter from his Brother who is you know in the *Grenadiers des Gardes de Paris*,— he has been distinguished, *why* he does not say,— but he was, at the beginning of this month decorated with the Legion of Honour,— in french he says "quand à moi personellement je suis au comble de mes vœux,— sa Majesté [Napoleon] vient de m'accorder pour mes Etrennes, la Decoration de la Legion d'honneur, avec le titre de Chevalier de l'Empire. Son Excellence M. de Lacepede Grand Chancelier m'a honoré et décoré de sa main, en me disant qu'il était charmé de remettre personellement cette marque honorable au frere du celebre____."[20] Amico is very glad to hear he is doing so well,— for in all situations it is right for a young man to do his duty & distinguish himself if he can.

It is clear that the award ceremony took place in January, since André jokes that the decoration was a New Year's gift. As Margaret's letter was to William, who only left England in March 1812, and as it discusses the division into lots of the Gillwell estate preparatory to the sale of the property in April 1813, the date can be narrowed down to January 1813. It is clear from André's last words that 'the famous [violonist Viotti]' was well known to Comte Bernard de Lacépède, who was himself an amateur composer and music writer, having published a work entitled *La Poétique de la musique*.

On the Janet et Cotelle edition of the three quartets that Viotti dedicates to his brother, André is described as 'Chef de Battallion d'Etat-Major et Rapporteur du 2e Conseil de Guerre de Paris'.[21] That André Viotti gained distinction in Napoleon's army doing battle against Britain or her Allies was overlooked by Margaret, who, following her education principles, allowed that it was right and proper for a young man to seek glory in whatever situation he found himself.

---

[17] Comte de Vaudreuil to GRC, 5 April [*recte* May] 1814, Fisher 2000 – 22/11.

[18] GBV to Cécile Cherubini, [May 1814], cited in Giazotto, p. 266. It is clearly the last part of a letter from MC to Cécile Cherubini. The first part has not been transcribed.

[19] Mme de Genlis to MC, 13 May 1814, Fisher 2000 – 6/35 (Yim, D52).

[20] "as for myself, I could not wish for more. His Majesty has just given me a New Year's present— he has decorated me with the Legion of Honour, with the title of Knight of the Empire. His Excellency M. de Lacepede, Grand Chancellor, paid me the honour of decorating me with his own hand, saying that he was delighted to present this mark of honour personally to the brother of the famous___" (MC to WBC, *c.*January 1813, PHM 94/143/1 – 17/4).

[21] See *Thematic Catalogue*, p. 54.

In a letter to William of 1 December 1814 Viotti says he has heard from Cherubini, who will send the music he left behind.[22] This long and entertaining letter is the first that was sent to William after the family's return to England. It gives an account of Margaret's ongoing problem with kidney stones, and contains a hilarious account of the transportation to England of all the food and game birds that William dispatched to them after their departure from France. The following paragraph displays – as do so many of his letters to William – Viotti's playful sense of humour and his determined optimism in the face of any minor domestic crisis:

> Most certainly my dear friend you will not let us die of hunger. Yesterday we received four partridges, five snipe, two teal, and two chickens. Plus— a basket of chestnuts, all tangled up, but excellent. Picture to yourself that they were placed in the stage coach alongside a blue oil pot. Well, apparently they quarelled, and upon my word the chestnuts broke the pot. In order to take his revenge the latter spat his blue dye in their face, so that they arrived all painted blue. Matilda washed them one by one. I cooked eight of them straight away and decided that they had an exquisite taste, so that I can now pronounce your idea to have been excellent.[23]

In the above letter Viotti speaks of sending a reciprocal food parcel to William for diplomat friends in France. In 1814 and on each successive yearly visit to the Continent Margaret and Viotti renewed old friendships and made new ones, especially among the diplomats, whose society Margaret preferred almost above all other. In London they had already met the secretary of the French legation François-Maximilien Gérard, Comte de Rayneval. Rayneval would become under-secretary of state for foreign affairs in the French Ministry of 1820, and he and his wife Alexandrine remained close friends with Viotti and the Chinnerys, and were to be useful to them in facilitating the delivery of cross-Channel mail in diplomatic bags. For the expeditious dispatch of his music, Viotti begs William to efface all other names from his parcel and substitute that of 'M$^{r}$ de Rayneval Premier Secretaire d'Ambassade de France'.[24]

---

[22] GBV to WBC, 1 December 1814, PHM 94/143/1 – 14/23.

[23] 'Trés certainement cher Ami, vous ne nous laisserez pas mourir de faim. Nous avons reçû hier 4. Perdrix, 5 Becassines, 2 Sarcelles, et deux Poulets. Plus— un panier de chataignes bien emberlificotés, mais éxcéllentes. Imaginez vous que l'on les a placés dans le Stage en société avec un pot de couleur bleue à l'huile. Apparemment qu'ils ont querellé, et ma fois les chataignes ont cassé le pot; celui-ci pour se venger leur a craché au visage toute sa matiere bleue, de sorte qu'elles sont arrivées toutes peintes. Matilda les a lavé une à une, moi j'en ai fait cuire huit tout de suite, et j'ai décidé qu'elles avoient un gout éxquis, à cause de quoi je dis que vous avez eû une éxcéllente idée' (*Ibid.*).

[24] *Ibid.*

CHAPTER 14

# The Philharmonic Society, 1813–1814

The establishment of the Philharmonic Society in 1813 heralded Viotti's return to the performing stage after a 15-year absence. He performed at one concert in 1813, one in 1814, and two in 1815, not as a soloist, but as an ensemble player, and the scarcity of his appearances reflects the fact that he was not returning to the career of violinist: his involvement was more important as an administrator than as a musician. Since Viotti was a founding member of the Society, its operations and activities provided a useful distraction for Margaret from her mourning. From the time of its inception she took a personal interest its structure and development, and followed with eager anticipation the reappearance in public of her favourite violinist. As there was at the time no permanent body which performed orchestral or chamber music in London, the Society filled a gap in the performing sphere. It has been claimed that the inspiration for the Society came from Salomon's famous Hanover Square concerts.[1]

Music in London in 1813 was a far cry from the high level it had attained in the last decade of the eighteenth century. In 1809 Margaret had already remarked that it was 'at a very low ebb'.[2] The aim of the Society, according to a preliminary announcement from the original committee of founders, was therefore to 'rekindle in the public mind that taste for excellence in instrumental music which has so long remained in a latent state.'[3] Because the stated object of the Society was to foster instrumental ensemble music, the performance of vocal music without a full orchestral accompaniment was banned, as were solos, duets and concertos, all of which, it was claimed, promoted virtuoso performances over the orchestral whole. To promote 'the best and most approved instrumental music', only 'Full Pieces, Concertantes for not less than three principal instruments, Sestetts, Quintetts and Trios'[4] were allowed. These restrictive rules were soon found to be unworkable, and all of the proscriptions were broken within a few years.

The first meeting to discuss the formation of the Philharmonic Society took place at the home of Henry Dance on 24 January 1813. Brother of the violinist William Dance (1755–1840), who was one of the 30 original members of the Society, Henry Dance was a lawyer, and the Society's first secretary. The first treasurer was William Ayrton, whose strength was writing about music rather than

---

[1] M.B. Foster (1912), *History of the Philharmonic Society of London, 1813–1912*, J. Lane, London, p. 4.

[2] MC to GRC, 23 May 1809, Ch.Ch.

[3] Cited in Foster, *History of the Philharmonic Society*, p. 4.

[4] *Ibid.*

practising it: he was a prominent critic and impresario. Many of the professional musicians who constituted the 30 founding members of the Society had at one time or another graced the Chinnery drawing room: flautist Andrew Ashe, pianists Ludwig Berger and Muzio Clementi, the Cramer bothers Franz and Johann Baptist, and Viotti's Hanover Square concert colleagues Salomon and Janiewicz. Among the Society's associates (again consisting entirely of musicians) was Viotti's pupil Nicolas Mori, who performed in a string quartet in the second performance of the Society on 15 March 1813. Mori was to perform regularly in the Philharmonic concerts, and from 1816 was one of the leaders of its orchestra. At the same time he was leader of the ballet orchestra (1814–17) at the King's Theatre, and in 1822 he would become a professor of violin at the new Royal Academy of Music.

Three other Viotti/Chinnery friends who were associate members of the new Society were Giuseppe Naldi, Paolo Spagnoletti, who had regularly led the King's Theatre orchestra in 1804–1805, and the violinist/violist who had helped trial Viotti's 1812 string quartets, Francesco Vaccari (b.1773). Vaccari and Spagnoletti shared the leadership of the orchestra with Salomon, Franz Cramer and Viotti for the first three years of the Philharmonic's existence. Two of the founders of the Society, Henry Dance and William Ayrton, had additional connections with Viotti. As a lawyer Dance acted for Viotti in his wine partnership with Charles Smith.[5] Ayrton had a selection of literary friends, one of whom was Madame de Staël, who pressed the committee to have tickets to a concert in 1813, and would do so again in 1814 through Viotti. The patron of the Philharmonic Society was the dilettante Prince of Wales, who had lavished attention on Viotti and the Chinnerys at Brighton less than two years earlier.

One of the founding members of the Philharmonic Society and a performer in its concerts was also one of the harshest critics of its proscriptive rules. This was the German pianist Ludwig Berger, whom William Chinnery had met in Gothenburg in 1812 and recommended to Viotti when Berger went on to London. Berger gave his first performance in London on 26 April 1813, when he played a concerto at the Hanover Square Rooms.[6] He composed an overture for the Philharmonic, which was performed on 18 April 1814. Berger was expected to dinner at 10 Charles Street on the evening of 16 July 1813 with William's other Gothenburg friend Mr Peterson, but had disappointed his hosts.[7] Apparently he met Margaret Chinnery on another occasion, for about that time he wrote William a rather jaunty letter – proving that he knew William well enough to jest with him – telling him that he had met his wife, whom he calls 'the epitome of kindness and loveliness'.[8] His criticism of the English public is redolent of Viotti's in his 1794 Bath letters, and like Viotti, he complains of a lack of music appreciation in England: 'Il me parait qu'ici personne *aime* la musique' (It seems to me that

[5] See GBV to Henry Dance (copy), 20 December 1820, PHM 94/143/1 – 28/24.

[6] *Times*, 24 April 1813.

[7] MC to WBC, 18 July 1813, PHM 94/143/1 – 17/11.

[8] 'l'emblême de la bonté et de la douceur' (Ludwig Berger to WBC, *c.*May 1813, PHM 94/143/1 – 15).

nobody here [really] *likes* music). His criticism becomes harsher when he speaks of the Philharmonic Society:

> One of the laws of this Society prohibits the playing of solos, duos and concertos. But concertantes are allowed. So when *Clementi* proposed that I should play a Fantaisie [Choral Fantasy, Op. 80] by Beethoven (a hymn to music), a piece which is in truth not very flattering to the pianoforte, but in which the choir and instrumental solo parts figure the most prominently— Cramer strenuously objected, saying that it was a concerto, and that it was composed specifically to show off the pianoforte, and that he, playing after me, would not be shown to advantage— not to mention the fact that he would be playing three weeks later. Have you ever heard of such absurd behaviour?[9]

In the event Berger performed in a Beethoven quartet for piano and strings at the seventh concert on 14 June 1813, and Cramer in a 'Full Piece for Pianoforte, Wood Wind and Horns' two weeks earlier, indicating that Cramer may have engineered a reversal of the performing order of the two pianists. Judging by the last few words, Berger's criticism was aimed not only at the prohibitive rules of the Society, but also at the professional jealousies which existed among the members of the music fraternity. Cramer was a founding member of the Philharmonic Society, and as one of its most 'assiduous committee men'[10] was duty bound to uphold the rules. However in this instance his objections seem to have been driven by a fear of being upstaged by a rival pianist.

Berger's experience of England was not a happy one according to Viotti, who wrote to William of the pianist's embitterment a month later:

> I gave your message to dear Berger. He is quite convinced that you take a keen interest in him. The poor man has done nothing [no excursions] yet, but he will, I hope. I shall do my utmost to find an opportunity of sending him to the country with some family or other; perhaps I shall succeed. How I wish he might find a reason to come round to liking this country![11]

---

[9] 'Une de[s] lois de cette société defend d'y jouer de[s] Solo et Duo et les Concerto. Mais les Concertantes sont admis. A l'occasion donc que *Clementi* proposoit que je devois y jouer une Fantaisie de Beethoven (la louange de la musique) une piece qui en verité est très peu avantageux au Pianoforte, mais où les chœurs et les Soloparties de l'orchestre font la principale partie— Cramer donc s'opposoit de tout son mieux, disant que c'étoit un Concerto, et qu'il étoit composé exprès pour les delices de Fortepiano, que lui, jouant après ne pourroit plus produire d'effet— sans conter [sic] qu'il devoit jouer 3 semaines plus tard. Avez vous vu jamais conduite plus absurde?' (Ludwig Berger to WBC, *c.*May 1813, PHM 94/143/1 – 15).

[10] C. Ehrlich (1995), *First Philharmonic: A History of the Royal Philharmonic Society*, Clarendon, Oxford, p. 12.

[11] 'J'ai fait votre Commission à ce bon Berger, il est bien persuadé que vous prenez un vif interet à Lui. Pauvre homme, il n'a rien fait jusqu'ici, mais il fera je l'éspere. Je vais tenter l'impossible pour lui procurer l'occasion d'aller à la Campagne avéc quelque famille; qui sçait si je ne réussirai pas. Comme je voudrois qu'il eut enfin quelque raison de se raccomoder avéc ce pays ci!' (GBV to WBC, 19 July 1813, NYPL JOB 97-52, item 30).

It was a landmark for London music when, on 17 May 1813, at the fifth concert of the Philharmonic Society, Viotti returned to the public stage. Although his ensemble performances at the Philharmonic concerts could in no way be compared to his virtuoso performances in the previous decade at the Hanover Square concerts, and although the Philharmonic Society discouraged stardom, Viotti must nevertheless have been an attraction for the concert-goers on this evening. He was both leader of the orchestra and composer of a new string quartet, which he performed with Vaccari, Spagnoletti and the cellist Frederick William Crouch. Although Margaret did not attend, she was sufficiently excited about Viotti's return to the public arena to delay affixing the seal to her letter to William until his return from the concert hall (the Argyll Rooms in Regent Street):

> I have kept my Packet open till now, *10 minutes past midnight*,— and Amico is not yet returned,— I therefore conclude that a great deal has been encored! You must wait till the next Post-day for particulars.
> ½ past 12— Here he is! Nothing can be imagined more brilliant! Amico was caressed, & complimented by almost every individual,— the concert went off to admiration, & it was with difficulty that every one of the pieces was not encored. The Duke sent for Amico between the acts, & said that the Regent fully intended to come, & that if he did, Amico must repeat his Quartett. However he was prevented from coming, which I regret, for as he has *never yet heard these* it would have been a pretty compliment to Amico— All the Boxes were filled and every subscriber there before the *premier coup d'archet*,— the professors are all enchanted,— in short his success was so compleat as *we* could wish![12]

This new quartet by Viotti was probably one of his Three quartets for two violins, viola, and cello (WII: 13–15), that he had trialled the previous year at Lord Dunmore's house. The Duke of Cambridge was naturally keen to hear his admired mentor perform again in public, and a letter to Viotti, which appears to date from the eve of this concert, reveals his eagerness. It is impossible that the duke was referring to any of Viotti's later performances at the Philharmonic, as he had by then left England for Hanover. The fact that William Chinnery is omitted from his salutations shows that the letter postdates 1812:

> My dear Viotti,
> I hasten to acknowledge your note, and tell you that, having forgotten this morning's rehearsal, I sent a messenger to your house to propose a little music, and to have the pleasure of seeing you and finding out how Mrs Chinnery does.
> I will not fail to be at the concert tomorrow in time for the first stroke of the bow.
> Adieu, give my compliments to Mrs Chinnery and George, and be assured of my esteem.
>
> Your very devoted,
> Adolphus Frederick[13]

---

[12] MC to WBC, [17 May 1813], PHM 94/143/1 – 17/55.

[13] 'Mon cher Viotti, / Je m'empresse de Vous accuser le reçu de Votre Billet, et de vous dire qu'ayant oublié la répétition de ce matin j'ai envoyé chès Vous pour Vous proposer une

The Duke of Cambridge was one of the original subscribers to the Philharmonic concerts, as another undated letter addressed to Viotti at 10 Charles Street, Manchester Square, shows. Like Margaret Chinnery, he remarked on the low standard of instrumental music in England at the time:

> I hasten to acknowledge your note and to beg you to put me on the list of subscribers to the Philharmonic Society. It is with pleasure that I shall attend these concerts, and I flatter myself that this Society will succeed in re-establishing the taste for instrumental music, which unfortunately has slipped into decline in this country.[14]

On the top of the letter is a handwritten note, presumably by Heron-Allen, which states: 'Letter in which HRH consents to become a subscriber to the Philharmonic Concerts. Viotti took an active interest in their arrangement, which gives to this letter the date of 1813.' Both the above letters are sent from Cambridge House, and appear to be close in date.

The success of the Philharmonic Society in the year of its inception meant that every one wanted tickets in its second year. In 1814 Viotti was a director of the Society (appointed from among the 30 members to administer the concerts), and was therefore inundated with requests for tickets. Among the rich and famous who came knocking at his door was Madame de Staël, outspoken French writer and critic, irresistible magnet to English high society, and author of the recently published and much talked-about work on Germany *De l'Allemagne*.

Banished from Paris by Napoleon, Madame de Staël had arrived in England in June 1813 accompanied by her son Auguste, her daughter Albertine – who kept a journal of their stay in England – and the 25-year-old ex-hussar husband whom she had secretly wed in May 1811, John Rocca. Lord Glenbervie, as ignorant of the marriage as everyone else in England, identified the latter in his journal as her 'young, handsome, and sickly' secretary-lover 'Mr Raucart or Rocarte'.[15] Soon after Madame de Staël's arrival in England Viotti left a card at her door at Brunet's Hotel, Leicester Square, asking if she remembered him from Paris. He received the following reply, sent to him two hours after his visit in the copperplate hand of her daughter:

---

petite Musique, et pour avoir le plaisir de Vous voir, et de Vous demander des nouvelles de Madame Chinnery. Je ne manquerai pas demain de me rendre au Concert pour entendre le premier coup d'archet. Adieu, faites bien des compliments à Madame Chinnery et à George, et soyez assuré de mon estime. / Votre très dévoué / Adolphus Frederick' (AF to GBV, Sunday [16 May 1813], Viotti Papers, RCM). All the Adolphus Frederick letters in the RCM collection have been translated in van der Straeten (1911).

[14] 'Je m'empresse de Vous accuser le reçu de Votre billet et de Vous prier de me mettre sur la liste des souscripteurs à la Société Philharmonique. C'est avec un plaisir que j'assisterai à ces Concerts, et je me flatte que cette Société réussira à rétablir le goût pour la Musique Instrumentale qui malheureusement est tombée en décadence dans ce pays ci' (AF to GBV, Saturday *c.*March 1813, Viotti Papers, RCM).

[15] Douglas, *The Glenbervie Journals*, p. 220.

> How can Monsieur Viotti possibly suppose that Mme de Staël does not remember his admirable talent. She is extremely desirous of seeing him again, and no one will receive him more warmly than her.
>
> Monday 28 June 1813[16]

Having copied out her words for William, Viotti added the note: 'Is it not very kind of her? Tomorrow I shall pay a vist to the Phœnix, and I hope that her wit will not make me look too much of a fool.'[17] Madame de Staël's formidable reputation for possessing a quick and merciless tongue was a worry to all who met her. Even Margaret Chinnery was alarmed when the grand lady announced her intention of coming to visit.

For the summer of 1813 Margaret and Viotti rented Mr Bell's cottage in rural North Fulham. The same summer Madame de Staël took a house in the pretty country town of Richmond. On the afternoon of Sunday 25 August, just as Margaret, Viotti and George were about to step into the Johnstones' carriage, William Spencer arrived unannounced, accompanied by Madame de Staël, who had herself proposed the visit. In spite of Margaret's trepidation before the meeting, her fine sense of diplomacy and her quick intelligence enabled her both to please Madame de Staël and to guess at her motives. Madame de Staël expressed her profound regret that Margaret and Viotti had not fixed upon Richmond for their summer retreat, and Margaret was alert to her true meaning:

> This [regret] was addressed chiefly to Amico, who seems to be a great favorite, and upon whom she reckoned much I believe for the advantage of her daughter. I took an opportunity of telling her how much the Duke of Cambridge admires Mad$^{lle}$ de Staël, and that he had talked to me a long time about her in a visit he made me a few days ago. *This is true.* I proposed Amico's going to see her at Richmond *with his violin*, telling her that I regretted she had not yet, since her arrival in England, enjoyed the pleasure of hearing him. This was agreeable to her,— and Tuesday next is fixed, for Amico and George to dine & sleep there,— [...] But she also proposed coming *to dine here* in *my hermitage*![18]

Madame de Staël had already met Viotti and George on a number of occasions in the course of her furious round of visits. George's popularity in London society had not wilted under the effects of his father's disgrace, and he accompanied Viotti to numerous dinners, one of which was for Madame de Staël hosted by William Spencer in Curzon Street. Lord Glenbervie was also present, and named all the guests – including 'Viotti with young Chinnery'.[19]

---

[16] 'Comment Monsieur Viotti peut-il supposer que M$^{de}$ de Staël n'ait pas conservé un profond souvenir de son admirable talent. Elle desire extremement le revoir, et personne ne le recevra avec plus d'empressement qu'elle. / Ce Lundi 28 Juin 1813' (Mme de Staël to GBV, 28 June 1813, NYPL JOB 97-52, item 29).

[17] 'N'est-ce pas très aimable? Demain j'irai voir le Phenix, et j'éspere que son esprit ne me rendra pas trop bête' (GBV to WBC, [28 June 1813], PHM 94/143/1 – 14/14).

[18] MC to WBC, 25 August 1813, PHM 94/143/1 – 17/14.

[19] Douglas, *The Glenbervie Journals*, p. 175.

The dinner for Madame de Staël at Margaret Chinnery's Fulham cottage took place on 14 September 1813, slightly bruising Margaret's inclination for seclusion. But there was no gainsaying Madame de Staël. Spencer, one of her intimates during her stay in England, was dragged around with her like a puppy, and Viotti, who was just beginning his social intercourse with her, was soon to find her imperious commands irksome. On 11 September 1813 Margaret wrote that Spencer and Viotti had gone to dine and sleep at Madame de Staël's, returning rather sooner than expected. As for her dinner,

> I must try what can be done in order to receive this great person as well as I can. It is surely a great compliment to me for her & her daughter to come all the way from Richmond and return there late at night. I dare say she does it partly to oblige Amico,—but it is certainly a very great compliment from her.[20]

This dinner must have constituted the breaking of the ice, for hereafter the summonses to Viotti to dine and to play became frenetic. On 3 October Albertine de Staël wrote to Viotti at Fulham, ostensibly to thank him for the complimentary remarks he made about a portrait of her mother, which he may have seen during a visit, but in reality to try to get George to visit her brother who had measles, and to remind Viotti to visit them once they were established in town so that they could hear him play and so that she herself could benefit from some instruction: 'Do not forget your *pupil*. When we are settled in town we shall see you often, shan't we? We do indeed need to hear you to bring a ray of light into this awful fog.'[21] One of the dinners that Viotti and George went to at Madame de Staël's in London may have been in response to an undated invitation, issued apparently on the spur of the moment to Viotti. The note was hand delivered, bore no address, and from its familiar tone, probably dates from 1814:

> If you have nothing better to do, dear Viotti, come and dine with us— we shall give you back the violin which I shall keep as a surety to make you come.
> There will only be family. Will your Chinnery come with you?[22]

Madame de Staël had arrived in England too late for all but the last of the 1813 Philharmonic concerts, and strenuously desired to have tickets to the 1814 season. These were not easy to procure, as the concerts were fully subscribed and transfer of tickets was strictly prohibited. Viotti, who as a director had at his disposal two tickets, furnished her with these – one each for her and her daughter. Matilda Chinnery's Journal, which is largely her own ingenuous rendering of Margaret's

---

[20] MC to WBC, 11 September 1813, PHM 94/143/1 – 17/15.

[21] 'N'oubliez pas votre *pupille*. Quand nous serons établis en ville nous vous verrons souvent n'est-ce pas? Il faut bien vous entendre quelquefois pour éclaircir ce vilain brouillard' (Albertine de Staël to GBV, 3 October [1813], NYPL JOB 97-52, item 32).

[22] 'si vous n'avez rien de mieux à faire caro viotti venez diner avec nous— nous vous rendres le violon que je garde en gage pour vous engager à venir / nous sommes en famille votre chinnery viendra t il avec vous?' (Mme de Staël to GBV, *c.*1814, NYPL JOB 97-52, item 69).

opinions, provides some interesting personal details of the 1814 season, especially at the time of Viotti's own appearance in the fourth concert on 28 March, in which he was once again to perform in one of his own quartets and lead the orchestra.

Even in the midst of all this Philharmonic activity Viotti found time, albeit hurriedly, to attend other concerts. Matilda wrote that while 'Mama, Amico, Margaret and myself' were dining alone on the evening of 23 March 'Amico received a ticket of admission to the Ancients Concert from M. Berkeley Paget. As Amico had asked it of him, Mama persuaded him to dress & go, which he did, though reluctantly. He did not stay long.'[23]

Another interesting piece of information, noted three days before Viotti's concert, was that Margaret Chinnery's pupil Maria [surname unknown], who had until 1806 been raised with the Chinnery children and their relatives, and who had, like them, benefited from music instruction from Viotti, Bianchi and other Gillwell tutors, was also to perform in the Philharmonic concert of 28 March, in a choral work, probably the sextet 'Sacro Pugnal' by Cherubini:

> Maria came here yesterday.— She is to sing in the Chorus on Monday next with Miss Stephens & Mr Braham.— The repetition takes place tomorrow night— Amico is just going to play over some of the pieces down stairs with five people whom he has appointed— This is only a private repetition.[24]

In the month of March Matilda's Journal is full of accounts of the various applications made to Viotti for tickets. On 9 March it was Colonel C. W. Thornton, the Duke of Cumberland's aide-de-camp, who called 'upon a pretext that he wanted to speak to Amico about the Duke of Cumberland's subscription at the Philharmonic'. On 17 March: 'Amico has obtained an admission to the Philharmonic Concerts for the Duke of Devonshire, on the plea that having several times lent Apartments in Burlington House for the repetitions this was due to him'. On 21 March: '[Amico] called upon Miss [Jane] Porter to give her a ticket for the Philharmonic Concert at which he leads himself.' On 24 March: 'Just before dinner, Lady [Elizabeth] Spencer sent her Steward to ask Amico to give a ticket to Miss Chattham for Monday, but Amico told him that his tickets were disposed of – however he promised to do all he could to try and obtain one for her.' On 26 March is noted Madame de Staël's 'selfish' request:

> At 11 o'clock George and him [William Spencer] went together to Mad$^{me}$ de Staël's,— it was a fine assembly & the *Duchess of York* was there.— Only conceive Mad$^{me}$ de Staël's requesting M. Spencer to give up to her his philharmonic ticket for Monday [28 March, the day of Viotti's concert]! This is very selfish of her, for Amico has given her a ticket, and also M. Ayrton's so that her daughter and herself have both got a ticket.— It is therefore evident that she wants to give one to a man, & this man is certainly Mon$^{sr}$ de Rockaur [Rocca] for she has been trying *de toutes les manières* to obtain a ticket for

---

[23] MMC's Journal, 24 March [1814].

[24] *Ibid.*, 25 March [1814]. In 1821 Maria would marry Viotti's and Margaret's great friend the diplomat Baron von Pfeffel in Paris.

him,— but her attempts are without success. We hope M. S. will not give up his ticket to her.[25]

The request that was addressed to Viotti was probably the following half-wheedling, half-imperious one:

> Will you send me, dear Viotti, the address of the subscriber who kindly offered me his ticket. I have lost it and I want to write to him— You have sent me no means for Monday, for I, poor soul, cannot go all alone— You must come to dinner on Sunday— I wanted to persuade Mrs Chinnery and the nieces [Matilda and little Margaret] to give me Sunday evening. Will you obtain it for me? You should call on me one of these mornings and bring me two *very little* tickets for Monday—What about Tuesday?[26]

Another imperious request for tickets was addressed to Viotti, perhaps on a later occasion:

> You are too kind dear Viotti. I dare not risk going in without *tickets*, but between now and Monday fortnight find me two or three— Mr Chinnery will take us if you have only two—[27]

That Madame de Staël's demands on Viotti were becoming a burden to him is hinted at in a letter she addressed to Spencer. Written in her usual hurried scrawl, it implies that a falling out with Viotti has occurred:

> Has the son been found? [Spencer's son William jumped ship from a vessel in Portsmouth harbour in March 1814.] Are you coming to dinner, or at least coming after dinner?—You must make amends for me with Viotti.— I see too little of you. You would never know how to be on affectionate terms in our country—[28]

Viotti's growing impatience with Madame de Staël is also evident in Matilda's entry for the 28 March, the day of his concert:

---

[25] *Ibid.*, 26 March [1814].

[26] 'voulez vous m'envoyer caro viotti l'adresse du souscripteur qui a bien voulu m'adresser son billet. je l'ai perdue et je veux lui écrire— vous ne m'envoyez aucun moyen pour lundi car je ne puis aller toute pauvre[?] seule—il faut que vous diniez chez moi dimanche— je voulois engager Mad. chinnery et les nieces à me donner la soirée de dimanche. voulez vous l'obtenir pour moi? vous devriez passer chez moi un de ces matins et m'apporter deux *tout petits* billets pour lundi— que dites vous du mardi? (Mme de Staël to GBV, Wednesday [March 1814], NYPL JOB 97-52, item 34).

[27] 'vous êtes trop aimable caro viotti, je n'ose pas risquer l'introduction sans *billets* mais de lundi en 15 ayez en trois ou deux— m[r] chinnery nous mennera si vous n'avez que deux' (Mme de Staël to GBV, [March 1814], NYPL JOB 97-52, item 35).

[28] 'le fils est il retrouvé? venez vous diner chez moi, ou venez vous au moins après diner.— il faut que vous me raccomodies avec viotti— je vous vois trop peu. vous n'apprendriés jamais l'intimité de notre pays' (Mme de Staël to WRS, [March 1814], NYPL JOB 79-52, item 31).

> Amico was not of our little dinner party yesterday. For the last week he was engaged to Mad$^{me}$ de Staël's to dinner. He first tried to get off this invitation under the pretext that he must leave her at desert [sic] on account of his repetition at night. But still she would have him & he went. By ten o'clock however he returned home leaving them at Coffee. Fifteen were at table. Madame Catalani, Mr Valabrey, Baron Jacobi, M. Spencer, M. Greville, Lady Mackintosh &c&c. George went to her Evening-party just before Amico came in.[29]

Matilda continues her Journal for that day in the evening, when she describes the domestic accommodations to Viotti's concert. Evidently William Spencer did not give up his ticket to Madame de Staël:

> We dined at ½ past 5 o'clock, that Amico might not eat his dinner in a hurry.— At 7 o'clock he took a cup of coffee, and at a ¼ past 7 o'clock he left us. It has just struck 8 o'clock so I suppose he is *beginning*. George dined with Mr J[ohn] Spencer, and he was to go with them & Mr W. Spencer to the Concert.[30]

Matilda's Journal of the following Wednesday contains an account of the concert of Monday 28$^{th}$, at which Viotti presented a quartet for two violins, viola and cello (undoubtedly another of his 1812 quartets, WII: 13–15), and participated in a quintet by his favourite chamber music composer Boccherini. For the first time Viotti played alongside his pupil Mori:

> Towards 10 o'clock on Monday night just as Mama [Margaret Chinnery] had begun her letter to you we were surprised by Mr Spencer's arrival. The quartetto was over, & had been divinely played,— he would have staid to hear some more of the music had he not been very much *annoyed*,— first by being in a box with five ladies who would chatter about Mr Kean[31] while the quartetto was going on, & secondly by finding himself afterwards by the side of *petty professors*, who instead of admiring the divine music, & Amico's incomparable talents, said that he was weak on the *4$^{th}$ string*, and that the applause given to him was *unmerited*. All this provoked M. Spencer so much that he determined to get away from them;— he then thought of *Mama*, that she was alone, anxious to hear [of] Amico's success, and asked for a Coach & came here.— We made him some tea, & he related to us Amico's Triumph, & his own little adventure!— George dined *tête à tête* with Mr S[pencer] in Curzon St, for Lord Shaftsbury dined at Mr J. S[pencer]'s & Mr S[pencer] did not like it. They were there in time to hear *le premier coup d'archet*. All was over at 11 o'clock & then they returned home & found Mr S[pencer] here.[32]

The professors' criticisms mentioned by Matilda may have been attributable merely to petty jealousy or may have been warranted, given Viotti's long absence from the performing stage. In any case, he was loudly applauded by the public, and

---

[29] MMC's Journal, 28 March [1814].

[30] *Ibid.* William Spencer's brother John was a patron of the Philharmonic Society.

[31] The Shakespearean actor Edmund Kean was then playing in *Richard III* at Drury Lane.

[32] MMC's Journal, Wednesday 31 [*recte* 30] March [1814].

Matilda remarked on the following day that 'Amico excited much more admiration at his concert last Monday than he ever did before.'[33]

The conditions under which the professional musicians laboured to serve the Philharmonic Society were harsh in the first couple of years, as not only were they not remunerated for their labour, but they were obliged to pay a yearly subscription along with all the other members and associates. The duties of the directors were onerous and time-consuming, their committee meetings were riddled with dissention, and their only reward was the gift of two subscription tickets. The day after Viotti's concert, Margaret was obliged to compose a letter in English on his behalf to an unnamed subscriber, whose request for tickets the harried Viotti had clearly forgotten to deal with: 'I have been so hurried and pressed by business since I received your very obliging letter on Saturday, that it has really been wholly out of my power to acknowledge it, and send you a receipt for the cheque you enclosed, before the present moment.'[34]

Subscriptions to the concerts were not promoted. On the contrary, as the Madame de Staël correspondence shows, they were difficult to procure, even for the influential well-to-do. When William Chinnery's friend from Gothenburg Mr Peterson wanted a Philharmonic subscription Viotti said he would try to satisfy him if he could, continuing: 'in any case, as I am this year one of the directors, I am able to give one of my two admission tickets to whoever I like, provided our George does not want it of course.'[35]One close friend who was a subscriber was the Count St Antonio, who lived at Wimbledon. Unable to accept a previous invitation to dine at Charles Street, he invited himself to dinner before the sixth concert on 2 May.[36]

A letter from Clementi to Viotti dated 15 December 1814 shows the manoeuvres that went on outside committee meetings. Having cleared up a couple of unspecified grievances that Viotti had written to him about, Clementi then begged Viotti not to miss the next meeting, at which a new director had to be elected to replace Salomon. Clementi intended to vote for Samuel Webbe and wanted Viotti to second him. Viotti had apparently also written of his desire to resign his directorship for 1815, but Clementi objected:

> As for you yourself (and this is the main reason I take up my pen), remember that I did not accept the directorship before making certain that you were accepting it, as a result of our meeting at Dance's etc. Certainly I am of the view that it would not be worthy in *us* to vacillate now. Think long and hard about it, and I am sure that you will decide in a manner befitting the great man that you are.[37]

---

[33] *Ibid.*, Thursday 31 March [1814].

[34] GBV to unnamed gentleman (copy), 29 March 1814, NYPL *MNY-Viotti.

[35] 'en tout cas, comme je suis cette année un des Directeurs, je pourrai par ci par là lui donner un de mes deux billets d'admition [sic], bien entendû quand notre George n'en voudra pas' (GBV to WBC, *c.*February 1814, PHM 94/143/1 – 14/18).

[36] Count St Antonio to GBV, 27 April 1814, PHM 94/143/1 – 28/19.

[37] 'Quanto a voi stesso, (e questo è il punto principale che mi ha fatto prender la penna in mano) ricordatevi, che io non accettai il Direttoriato prima di assiurarmi se voi

Viotti appears to have retained his directorship in 1815, in spite of his dissatisfaction, expressed in an earlier letter to William:

> Nevertheless I would have very much liked to have got out of this directorship, but no one would consent to my wishes. That is a pity, for it is a lot of trouble for the benefit of no one, as far as I can see. I do hope that next year it will be an *Academy*, otherwise I shall bid adieu to the Philharmonic.[38]

Viotti had already told William of his desire to establish a Royal Academy of Music in his letter dated 19 July 1813. William had asked for details of the structure of the Philharmonic, and in answering his query Viotti wrote of the plans for change, repeating the common refrain of his contemporaries that music was then in decline in England. Even so he was unable to prevent his sense of the ludicrous coming to the fore when he described the undertaking:

> I must tell you that I have collected all the programmes of the Philharmonic concerts and shall send them to you with the first traveller, together with the laws, the rules, the names, etc. But you have surely been informed of our intention of changing all that if we can? Our aim is no less than that of establishing a Royal Academy of Music and of thereby becoming, *all forty of us*, real esquires, esquires by right!— Will it not be fine to be able to call me Amico Esquire? How it will make me puff up! I hope that we shall succeed in spite of the opposition of some stupid Philharmonics, and that we shall have the glory of elevating and giving some credit to a profession which up to now has been in the mire.[39]

The subject of a Royal Academy of Music was also raised by the Duke of Cambridge during a long conversation with Margaret around the same time. Margaret wrote to William on 14 August 1813: 'then he [the duke] asked after

---

accettavate, in consequenza ci siamo radunati da Dance etc. sicchè mi pare non esser degno di *noi* adesso di vacillare. Pensateci bene e riflettateci; e son sicuro che deciderete da grand'uomo come siete' (Muzio Clementi to GBV, 15 December 1814, NYPL JOB 97-52, item 36).

38 'J'aurois cependant bien voulû me dispenser de ce Directoriat, mais on n'a jamais voulû acconsentir [sic] à mes desirs— c'est dommage, car c'est beaucoup de peine pour la satisfaction de je ne sçais qui— J'éspere bien que l'année prochaine, ou ce sera une *Accademie*, ou je dirai adieu aux Philharmoniques' (GBV to WBC, *c.*February 1814, PHM 94/143/1 – 14/18).

39 'je vous dirai que j'ai ramassé avéc soin tous les menûs du Concert Philharmonique et que je vous les enverrai par le premier Voyageur, avéc les Loix les reglements les noms &c&c&c. Mais vous êtes prevenû surement que nous allons changer tout celà si nous le pouvons? Il n'est pas moins question que d'établir une Accademie Royale de Musique et devenir par là *tous les Quarante* de veritables Esquires, des Esquires de droit!… N'est-ce pas que ce sera beau de m'appeler L'Esquire Amico? Comme celà me fera rengorger!… J'espère que nous réussirons malgré l'opposition de quelques bêtes Philharmoniques, et que nous aurons la gloire d'avoir relevé et donné une Consistance à une Profession qui n'a été que dans la Crotte jusqu'ici' (GBV to WBC, 19 July 1813, NYPL JOB 97-52, item 30).

Amico & the Royal Academy of Music, respecting which [...] he observed that with such talents as Viotti's at the head of it, an establishment of that sort must be highly advantageous.'[40] This indicates that the establishment of an Academy of Music was already being mooted in 1813, and that there was talk of making Viotti head of it. Viotti had already had three unhappy or short-lived experiences in theatre management, and was to have another in 1819. Was this yet another move to head a musical institution? If so, it is a pity it was unsuccessful, as administering a school would have been ideally suited to Viotti's talents. Margaret's rejoinder to the duke's remark was that there was as much talent in music in England as in any of the arts, but that it was not '*embodied*', and that a Royal Academy would do just this, 'and then I pointed out to him that as his Royal father [George III] had founded the Academy of Painting, it seemed a natural, and almost necessary consequence that the Prince Regent should found the Academy of Music.'[41]

A 12-page document penned by Margaret Chinnery, entitled 'Observations upon Mr A's Plan'[42] helps explain all this. The document is undated, but judging by the common link to Margaret's conversation with the Duke of Cambridge and Viotti's letters to William, it would appear to have been written in early 1814. The document is a point by point critical analysis of 'Mr A's' [William Ayrton's?] proposals for the establishment of an Academy of Music. William Ayrton, as a non-practising musician with a literary bent, would conceivably have had the time and inclination to put together such a plan. Moreover he was, according to Matilda Chinnery's Journal, a frequent caller on Viotti and Margaret in 1814.

The plan for the new Academy is based on a remodelling of the Philharmonic Society, to which the last section of the document, labelled 'Philharmonic', is devoted. 'The object to be attained', wrote Margaret, is the establishment of a national school [of music]' (p. 3). That this plan was essentially different from the Royal Academy of Music that was ultimately established by Lord Burghersh in 1822, can be seen from the various points discussed. Most importantly, the Academy proposed by Mr A was to be administered, like the Philharmonic, by professional musicians who would be renamed 'Academicians', not by managers drawn from members of the music-loving public. Mr A's plan to fund the new Academy by a public subscription was objected to by Margaret, who hoped to supply the new institution's wants with the present subscriptions of Philharmonic members, and by an increase in the price and number of admission tickets. The success of these proposals was contingent upon the Prince Regent's providing a suitable venue (p. 8).

With regard to the students, Mr A's plan appears to have been that students of all ages would attend daily, whereas Lord Burghersh's Academy was a boarding school for children aged from ten to fifteen, who were given a general education as well as musical instruction. One of Mr A's proposals that was subsequently put into effect by Lord Burghersh was that the students be chosen by ballot. Margaret

---

[40] MC to WBC, 14 August 1813, PHM 94/143/1 – 17/12.

[41] *Ibid.* George IV did become the patron of Lord Burghersh's Academy of Music in 1822.

[42] Draft plan for a Royal Academy of Music, *c.*1814, Fisher 2000 – 16.

proposed that some of the former associates of the Philharmonic Society might become students of the new Academy. Those associates who were too experienced to be placed as students might become honorary members, as would 'all the first rate composers of other countries, Cherubini, Beethoven, Mehul, Paisiello…', and also 'Princes & Noblemen of other countries'. She also wondered (clearly with the Duke of Cambridge in mind) 'whether this compliment should be paid to the brothers of the Prince Regent' (p. 12).

One of the aims of the new Academy was to address the problem of the proscriptive regulations of the Philharmonic Society: 'Surely, it was an error in the plan of the Philharmonic Society to exclude from their concerts the grand Scene et Arie of Jomelli, Piccini, Sachini, Hope, &c&c. The exclusion of Solo instrumental Pieces, is also an error' (p. 9). But while admitting that the reasons for the proscriptions were sound – firstly 'the vanity of the performers', who will always promote their own compositions, and secondly the preference of the public for popular vocal pieces which are not necessarily of a high musical standard – she nevertheless admits that the solution to these problems is difficult to find: 'It seems then that the only protection the Academy can provide for itself by its laws against the encroachment of vanity or bad taste would be by a restriction as to the number of solo performances upon the different instruments' (p. 10).

How does Margaret Chinnery come to be involved in such a plan? Her reputation as both a musician and an educationalist must have been the reason for her opinions being sought. The stamp of her educational principles are evident throughout the document. Her questioning mind, her clear reasoning, her insistence on the definition of terms, her emphasis on the need for strict enforcement of rules governing the students, and her belief in the importance of foreign influences are all in evidence.

Although Margaret's observations begin patriotically, by suggesting that Mr A omit the first paragraph of his introduction 'which gives a french origin to this excellent plan' – the reference appears to be to the Paris Conservatoire – all her other comments testify to her conviction that foreign influences are necessary for the improvement of English taste. For example she criticizes the small percentage of foreigners proposed to be admitted to the Academy as members: 'Does not the english taste in its french state require to be enlightened and improved by the taste & genius of other countries?' (p. 1). The Paris Conservatoire clearly inspired her proposal that 'the Premiums & Prizes […] be presented to the Students *publicly* at the public concerts', which 'will be the beginning of reputation in their Profession and will lead to great results' (p. 5).

The document also stresses the benefits that both students and members will enjoy through their contact with other musicians and a permanent orchestra to work with. On this point Margaret quotes Haydn, proving that he was indeed more than just a casual acquaintance: 'I remember the great Haydn say, that he was more indebted to the circumstance of having the Prince Esterhazy's Band always at his command, for the new & striking effects that were admired in his Symphonies, than to any genius he might possess, as at any hour he could try an experiment in music, & reject or adapt as the result might induce him' (p. 6).

Margaret's remarks on the advantages in 'friendships & connections' that a student of the proposed Academy would enjoy compared to the then prevailing system whereby a pupil studied in solitude, attached to one professor for a fixed term, are enlightening: 'Compare the solitary & melancholy situation of a young professor about to make his Debut in London at the present time; with the enviable advantages I have just been enumerating – and then some idea may be formed of the good that will arise to the Profession from an Institution of this nature' (p. 7). The nineteenth-century musicologist Cazalet also described the position of the English music student before 1822 as melancholy:

> Shut out from all communion with fellow-students, those who shewed an aptitude for music were obliged to bind themselves to some Professor for a term of years, paying a large premium, and sacrificing afterwards, for years, a portion of their hard earnings; and all this but for one branch of their art; harmony, the essential foundation to make a musician, being often entirely neglected.[43]

But Mr A's plan never got off the ground, probably because of a lack of funds. Lord Burghersh's 1822 Academy would not escape the same problem. This plan appears to be the earliest proposal for an Academy of Music in the nineteenth century. It was a great misfortune for Viotti that it was not brought to fruition.

---

[43] W.W. Cazalet (1854), *The History of the Royal Academy of Music*, Bosworth, London, p. 13.

CHAPTER 15

# Between London and the Continent, 1815–1818

In 1815 Viotti performed in the fourth and the sixth concerts (3 April and 1 May) of the Philharmonic Society, both times with his pupil Mori and both times as leader of the orchestra. In the fourth he performed his own Concertante for two violins and cello, and in the sixth a Concertante for two violins, viola and cello. The latter carried a programme note that it was 'arranged from Viotti's Pianoforte Concerto in A minor, by himself'.[1] Since it is not thought that Viotti composed any original piano concertos, the reference is probably to Dussek's arrangement of Viotti's Violin Concerto No. 25, which was dedicated to Mrs Chinnery. Viotti's arrangement of this concerto as a quartet does not appear to have been published.[2] Viotti was still a director of the Society this year, and provided his friend, British Treasury official and commissary-in-chief John Charles Herries, with two tickets to the first concert.[3]

The most important event on the Philharmonic Society's 1815 calendar was a visit from its favourite composer Luigi Cherubini, who was in England from February to June to preside at the performances of his three new works that had been commisssioned by the Society. There is an ambiguous reference to a 'Luigi' in an 1813 Chinnery letter which might indicate that Cherubini made an earlier, unofficial visit to England in the summer of 1813. In a letter to William dated August 1813 Margaret writes of attending a small but splendid dinner at the home of Miss Sophia Johnstone and her brother, and listening to 'Luigi and her [Miss Johnstone] and Amico singing'.[4] This was the dinner at which she and Viotti first made the acquaintance of Miss Johnstone's future husband the Count St Antonio.

In 1815 the Philharmonic Society commissioned three works from Cherubini, a symphony, an overture and a cantata, for which they paid him £200. Cherubini's first appearance was at the third concert (13 March), when he presided at a performance of his popular 'Anacreon' overture. His next was at the fourth (3

---

1 Cited in Foster, *History of the Philharmonic Society*, p. 20.

2 It is not listed in White's *Thematic Catalogue*, and may have been yet another case of a performance from a manuscript, which was subsequently lost.

3 MC to WBC, 9 February 1815, PHM 94/143/1 – 17/19. It was Herries who had seconded George Chinnery from the Treasury to act as bursar to Louis XVIII in April–May 1814 (J.C. Herries to GRC, 22 April 1814, Fisher 2000 – 22/10).

4 MC to WBC, 25 August 1813, PHM 94/143/1 – 17/14. The other possibility is Luigi Asioli. But Margaret generally referred to Cherubini as 'Luigi', whereas she used the surnames of other musician friends.

April), when his new overture and vocal trio 'Et incarnatus est' were given. Viotti shared the stage with his acclaimed friend at the fourth and sixth concerts, and at the sixth Cherubini's new symphony was performed. As a director of the Philharmonic Viotti certainly had a say in fixing the amount Cherubini would be paid for his compositions. But the figure of £50 for a 'Sinfonia' mentioned in Clementi's December 1814 letter to Viotti,[5] probably refers not to Cherubini's symphony, but to that of Ferdinand Ries, commissioned by the Society for the 1815 season, and performed on 15 May. The old Viotti/Chinnery friend Madame Bianchi-Lacy also performed at some of the same concerts as Cherubini, as did the bass Charles T. Smith. (One cannot help but wonder if the latter, who performed 14 times between 1813 and 1816, was the same Smith who was Viotti's partner in the wine business.)

Along with composers Cherubini and Ries there were two French instrumentalists making their first appearance at the Philharmonic concerts in 1815. These were the violinist Charles-Philippe Lafont and the pianist Friedrich Kalkbrenner, both of whom performed their own works. It is highly likely that Viotti was responsible for obtaining their assistance also. Both had studied at the Paris Conservatoire, where they had been prizewinners. Lafont had been trained by Kreutzer and Rode, and was then first violin to the Russian Czar. Kalkbrenner, a close friend of Dussek, had been recommended to Viotti by the latter in 1810, when he made his first visit to England. He had settled in England in 1814 and would make regular appearances at the Philharmonic over the coming years.

During Cherubini's 1815 visit Margaret and Viotti reciprocated the hospitality that Cherubini himself had extended to George and Viotti during their respective sojourns in Paris the previous year. George Chinnery was now in Portugal with the British statesman George Canning, and his absence allowed Cherubini to be comfortably accommodated in the small Charles Street house. (If Cherubini were in England in the summer of 1813 he did not stay with Viotti and Margaret, since there was no room in the tiny Fulham cottage, but he may have been lodged in the home of Mr and Miss Johnstone.) Cherubini accompanied Margaret, Viotti, Matilda and little Margaret twice to Petersham, where they stayed with William Spencer's elder brother John, who was a patron of the Philharmonic Society and other musical societies. The Spencer family home at Wheatfield, where Viotti had stayed in 1808, had burned down in 1813.

Cherubini's first visit to Petersham was in March, one week before his first performance at the Philharmonic concert. His second was on 16 April, when he travelled down from London with Naldi and two diplomats – the Bavarian chargé d'affaires, Baron Christian Hubert von Pfeffel, and Count Francis Jenison-Walworth, William Spencer's brother-in-law. On 8 March Margaret wrote to William that she was grateful for the poultry, cheese and chestnuts he had sent across from France, which she offered as a 'contribution to Mr Spencer's larder, as we came in a large body & have remained here several days.' She continued: 'The girls & Cherubini are gone, – they return a day before us that every thing may be

[5] Muzio Clementi to GBV, 15 December 1814, NYPL JOB 97-52, item 36.

ready for our arrival, & in order that the girls may practise for tomorrow evening.' The following evening Margaret was to receive 'Naldi, Mr [John] Spencer, the Baron [Pfeffel], & the Count [Jenison]' to dinner, with music afterwards.[6]

In May 1815 Cherubini was present at another soirée organized by Margaret at the Charles Street house. With her usual flair and finesse Margaret successfully brought together a convivial selection of musicians, diplomats and close family friends, inviting four guests to dinner and 12 more in the evening. Among the musicians present were the Bavarian Bohrer brothers, violinist Anton (1783–1852) and cellist Maximilian (1785–1867), who had earned great acclaim on their 1810 tour of Europe for their unaccompanied fantasias for violin and cello. Anton Bohrer had been a pupil of Rodolphe Kreutzer, and together with his brother and two Paris musicians he would form the Bohrer quartet. They came to England via Hanover, where in the autumn of 1814 the Duke of Cambridge had heard them. The duke had recommended them to Viotti, writing from Hanover on 15 October 1814:

> I am writing a few words to recommend to you the Bohrer brothers, two young people with much talent who very much desire to meet you. They spent a few days at Hanover, and I derived much pleasure from hearing them play. The one who plays the cello has performed a lot with Romberg and I believe that their duets are in the style of the Romberg brothers.[7]

Margaret reported on the evening in her letter to William of 14 May: 'We had Kalkbrenner, the two Bohrers', & Ramorino to dinner, – in the evening Sir C[harles] & Lady Flint & their sister, – the St Legers, Mary Cipriani,[8] [eminent London physician] M. Lock[le]y & his daughter, – my two neighbours, – Guglielmo, Mr Langersdorff, and Naldi, – these with Cherubini & ourselves made our little room look & *feel* very full.'[9] Ramorino was described by Margaret as a Swiss gentleman. Returning from England to the Continent during the *Cent Jours*, he carried mail for William from Margaret and Viotti. Philipp von Langsdorff, Hessian ambassador to London, was also a close Viotti/Chinnery friend during his years in London.

Margaret goes on to give her opinion of the musicians. Her last remark testifies to the fact that her musical evenings had lost none of their appeal, in spite of her small drawing room and straitened circumstances:

> Kalkbrenner is a very distinguished artist indeed, and far above what I had previously heard of him. One of the Bohrers is extremely clever on the violoncello, and the two

---

6 MC to WBC, 7 March 1815, PHM 94/143/1 – 17/20.

7 'Je Vous addresse quelques mots pour Vous recommander les frères Borer, deux jeunes Gens de beaucoup de mérite qui souhaitent beaucoup de faire Votre connaissance. Ils ont passé quelques jours à Hannovre, et j'ai eu bien du plaisir à les entendre jouer. Celui qui joue le violoncelle a beaucoup joué avec Romberg, et je crois que leurs Duos sont dans le Genre des frères Romberg' (AF to GBV, 15 October 1814, Viotti Papers, RCM).

8 Sister of Philip Cipriani, to whom Viotti dedicated his Three quartets for flute, violin, viola and cello, Op. 22.

9 MC to WBC, 14 May 1815, PHM 94/143/1 – 17/24.

brothers play well together. All this, with Naldi's cheering singing, Amico, & the two girls, made plenty of amusement for them. As usual, they staid it all out, — they were all here by nine oClock, & not gone till half past one![10]

Although there are no more references to Cherubini's 1815 visit in the Chinnery letters, there is no doubt that he remained with them until the end of the Philharmonic concert series on 29 May, returning to Paris one week later.

In July 1815 Margaret and Viotti were again making plans to spend autumn on the Continent. Not yet having heard of Napoleon's defeat at Waterloo they hesitated to venture very far from the coast in case they should be obliged to beat a quick retreat to England. As William was by then established at Calais, Viotti suggested as a meeting place-cum-holiday retreat a choice of the three nearby towns of Lille, Dunkirk or Anvers, from where, in an emergency, William might just as easily hasten across the border to Holland. In the event they spent August in the Netherlands, visiting Ghent, Anvers, Brussels and Lille, then with the threat of Napoleon extinguished, continued on to Paris.

William was ever on the lookout for new commercial opportunities. His good friend John Herries, a former Treasury colleague, looked after his interests on the British side of the Channel and informed Viotti – who passed the intelligence on to William – of any opportunities arising. One very intriguing, but unclear suggestion that was put forward in July 1815 had to do with John Betts the London violin maker, referred to by Viotti in his letter to William as 'Betts the Stradivarius murderer'.[11] This last comment is ambiguous. John Betts and his son Arthur were two of the very few owners of a quartet of Stradivari instruments, which perhaps neither could play very well. On the other hand, in view of the apocryphal[?] story regarding the manner in which John Betts dishonestly ended up the owner of an English nobleman's Stradivarius which had been entrusted to Viotti's care, who had allegedly tried to operate the same trick on the unsuspecting victim, the term 'murderer' may have been used to refer to the manner in which John Betts made the nobleman's instrument 'disappear'.[12] The reference to Betts in the present letter is vague, as is the scheme itself, which seems to have involved selling some popular music in Paris. Like so many of Viotti's and William's schemes it did not come off:

In your last letter you were scratching your head over what it was that our good friend H[erries] proposed that was so advantageous to us! Can't you guess that it concerned what happened at Betts's, that Stradivarius murderer? In the position in which you were, possessing friends of the right sort, such as those whom I know to be friends of

---

[10] *Ibid.*

[11] 'Betz l'estropieur des Stradivarius' (GBV to WBC, 16 July 1815, PHM 94/143/1 – 14/25).

[12] The story of how Viotti took the nobleman's Stradivarius to John Betts to make a copy of, and how Betts himself kept the original, thereby foiling Viotti's same intention, was told by Charles Beare in the *Musical World* of 1837. It is reproduced in *The Strad* (June 1977), vol. 88, pp. 167–73.

yours, and who were formerly the companions of my youth, most certainly there would have been an opportunity of making an immense profit from it. But to make it happen I would have needed to see you, I would have needed to fill the role of Mercury, I would have needed, you would have needed, we would have needed to fly, so to speak, and that was impossible at the time I was told about it. Now unfortunately the secret is out. He is no longer producing these airs and variations that are so astonishing! And the game would not be worth the candle.[13]

Some of Viotti's activities during his autumn 1815 sojourn in Paris (September–end November) may be conjectured from the surviving two or three letters he received while there. The upheaval of the 1814 Restoration of Louis XVIII, followed in quick succession by the *Cent Jours*, then the second Restoration, had a deleterious effect on music in the capital, and the fate of the Conservatoire musicians was left hanging in the balance. By the time Viotti and Margaret arrived in Paris the court had evicted the professors from their lodgings in the rue Faubourg Poissonnière, and closed down the Conservatoire itself (19 September 1815–4 June 1816). There were clearly some of Viotti's friends who remained in the capital, but Baillot had already left for his tour of Belgium and Holland. Presumably Cherubini had no accommodation to offer, since Viotti, Margaret, William and Matilda stayed at the Hôtel de Londres, as a later letter from Viotti to William shows.[14]

A letter to Viotti from his old friend Jean-Louis Duport in answer to his query regarding some misplaced sheets of music may be of this period. It is addressed to Viotti at 'Rue Montabord [Rue du Mont Thabor], Hotel de Londre, A Paris':

My dear friend
It is not I who have your duo in G minor. I put my music in the case of my cello, and so I am sending you the key to the case. Have a look behind the cello. Thank you very much for the pretty music that you let me hear the evening before last.
Your entirely devoted friend ... Duport[15]
Friday morning

---

[13] 'Dans votre derniere lettre vous vous cassez beaucoup la tête à decouvrir ce que le bon Ami H__ a proposé de si avantageux pour nous! Ne devinez vous pas que c'étoit sur ce qui se passoit auprés de Betz l'estropieur des Stradivarius? Dans la position ou vous étiez, possedant des Amis de la bonne éspece, tels que ceux que je vous connois et qui étoient mes compagnons de jeunesse, très certainement, il y auroit eu moyen d'en tirer un parti immense. Mais pour celà il auroit fallu que je vous eusse vû, que j'eusse rempli le role de mercure, que j'eusse, que vous eussiez, que nous eussions volé pour ainsi dire, et celà étoit impossible au moment ou l'on m'en a parlé. Maintenant tout est dit malheureusement, il ne s'éxecute plus de ces aires con variazioni si étonnantes! et le jeu ne vaudroit pas la chandele' (GBV to WBC, 16 July 1815, PHM 94/143/1 – 14/25).

[14] GBV to WBC, 19 February 1816, PHM 94/143/1 – 14/28.

[15] 'Mon cher ami / Ce n'est pas moi qui ai votre duo en Sol mineur. J'ai mis ma musique dans l'Etuit de ma basse, ainsi je vous envoye la clef de l'étui, voyez derriere ma basse. Je vous remercie bien de la jolie musique que vous m'avez fait entendre avant hier soir. / tout a vous ... Duport / ce vendredi matin' (Jean-Louis Duport to GBV, c.1815, PHM 94/143/1 – 28/1).

Taking advantage of Viotti's stay in Paris, the Duke of Cambridge wrote to him with a request to purchase two violin bows, undoubtedly of Tourte manufacture. In the letter, dated Hanover, 6 October 1815, the duke expresses his pleasure that Viotti's friends in Paris have persuaded him to recommence composing and awaits with impatience the new concerto which Viotti has dedicated to him – No. 27 in C major. This was published soon after by Janet et Cotelle,[16] to whom Viotti brought manuscript compositions to be engraved on each successive visit to Paris from 1814. In the meantime, he says, he has been studying Viotti's very beautiful quartets (probably the set of three dedicated to André Viotti, showing that, unless they were brought to him by a friend in the manuscript, they were already printed), and has played one of them with one of the Rombergs, who has just spent a week in Hanover and who thinks it most beautiful.[17]

The third letter of this period was from the French engraver Jissy in England. It concerned a debt he was owed for the engraving of a seal for a M. de Broga, son-in-law of the Bavarian minister in Paris. Jissy says he would like the debt paid in kind – six pairs of silk stockings which he asks Viotti to bring back to England with him.[18]

Meanwhile in London, Pfeffel and Jenison were eagerly awaiting Viotti's and Margaret's return. A three-page letter addressed to Viotti by Jenison expresses his pride that he has earned Viotti's friendship, and his regret that he will soon be posted elsewhere in Europe. He is impatient at the delay in Viotti's arrival, and fills his letter with expressions of tenderness that seem to go deeper than the usual polite niceties:

> How I hate these delays [...] which prolong your absence. Each day, each hour is a new privation for me, a benefit of which you deprive me. Hasten across this channel which for too long has separated us. You will never arrive too early for our liking![19]

Viotti's association with the Philharmonic Society led to many of its musicians performing at private concerts in the Charles Street drawing room. In July 1816 it was the Delihu sisters, or Demoiselles De Lihu, as they were known at the time, popular vocalists who were were to become good friends of Viotti, Margaret, George and Matilda. Apparently of Flemish extraction, the Delihu sisters made their debut at the Philharmonic in 1817 and appeared there again as duettists in 1818, when they 'made quite a sensation by their graceful and sympathetic singing'.[20] Naldi and his daughter were also guests on this occasion. Naldi had been performing at the Philharmonic concerts, along with Viotti's colleague

---

[16] *Thematic Catalogue*, p. 34.

[17] AF to GBV, 6 October 1815, Viotti Papers, RCM.

[18] Jissy to GBV, 20 October 1815, Fisher 2000 – 38/4.

[19] 'Que je hais ces retards [...] qui prolongent votre absence; chaque jour, chaque heure est une nouvelle privation pour moi, un bienfait dont vous me privez. Hâtez vous de franchir ce canal qui nous sépare depuis trop longtems, vous n'arriverez jamais trop tôt au gré de nos vœux!' (Francis Jenison to GBV, 22 November 1815, NYPL JOB 97-52, item 37).

[20] Foster, *History of the Philharmonic Society*, p. 33.

Vaccari, since its inception. Margaret wrote to William of the success of their little concert:

> Amico played some Duetts with Vaccari in his very best stile of finish, tone, & execution! Nothing can be more perfect. The company consisted of Lord & Lady Dunmore, Lady Say & Sele & [her daughter] Miss Twistleton, M. Mrs & Miss Herries, M. St Leger & his daughter, Mrs Cunliffe, Count & Countess St Antonio [formerly Miss Sophia Johnstone], Sir H. Lambert, Baron [Pfeffel], Count [Jenison], the Sardinian minister, M. de Memarin, [Austrian minister] Count Bombelles, Professor Young of Edinburgh &c &c. They were all pleased, and indeed excepting the intolerable heat of the room, every thing else was as well as it could be in this small habitation. I gave them tea, lemonade, cakes & ices.[21]

In December 1815 Pierre Baillot arrived in London, having just completed a successful tour of Belgium and Holland. The following spring he made his debut in the 1816 Philharmonic concerts. Viotti may have been responsible for this invitation also. Baillot already had a reputation as an interpreter of chamber music, having in 1814 established his highly successful chamber music concerts in Paris. He took part in three concerts, playing his own compositions and leading in the sixth and seventh. His old pupil Fémy the elder joined him on stage in all three concerts, and in the sixth a quartet composed by Fémy was performed.

During Baillot's visit Viotti and Margaret Chinnery were both outraged that the popular young French flautist Louis Drouet, who was considered the best wind instrumentalist in France, attempted to capitalize on his reputation by charging Baillot 20 guineas to appear at the latter's benefit concert. Viotti advised Baillot to expose Drouet's greed by stating publicly why he was being dropped from the already printed bills:

> [Mrs Chinnery] and I and her son have all decided that you must not submit to such an outrage, and that you should print on the leaves that are to be distributed at the concert, that you had announced Mr Drouet believing that he would act in accordance with the code that exists among all the professors, that is without interest. But seeing that he absolutely demands 20 guineas for his services, you are obliged to give *something else* in his place, [or] something to that effect.[22]

Now an astute judge of the English character, and able to appreciate the very British sense of fair play, Viotti had come a long way since his damning criticism of the Bath audiences in 1794. He assured his friend that he would have nothing to

---

[21] MC to WBC, 4 July 1816, PHM 94/143/1 – 17/25.

[22] 'Elle [Mrs Chinnery], moi et son fils [George] nous avons tous décidé que vous ne devez point vous soumettre à une telle infamie, et que vous devez mettre sur les cartes que vous distribuerez au concert, que vous aviez annoncé M$^{r}$ Drouet dans la persuasion qu'il agirait dans cette circonstance comme font tous les Professeurs entre eux, sans intérêt; mais que voyant qu'il exige absolument 20 guiné[e]s pour vous rendre ce service, vous vous voyez forcé de donner autre chose à sa place &c &c, [ou] quelque chose de semblable' (GBV to Baillot, 26 May 1816, in Pincherle (1924), Letter 4, p. 107).

fear from disappointed concert-goers: 'Everyone there will take your side, not a single person will blame you. On the contrary, the English are like that, they will share your indignation, and you will [thereby] give a slap in the face to this gentleman, who will have deserved it.'[23]

It was a long while since Viotti had performed in France, and perhaps he was unaware that it was the custom in Paris for musicians to pay for each other's services. A German reviewer of the 1809 Paris winter concerts was just as horrified as Viotti, exclaiming: 'Artists in Paris treat each other like – Jews! They will not play at their best friends' concerts unless they are handsomely paid!'[24] It is difficult to imagine Baillot and his circle doing it, but the practice may have been restricted to the younger generation of musicians (Drouet was only 24). Baillot himself remarked resignedly that he had not expected rich pickings from his English benefit anyway.[25]

An intriguing comment made by Matilda Chinnery in a postscript attached to the bottom of one of Viotti's letters to William in 1816 gives the only clue that Viotti may have had an attachment to any other person but Margaret Chinnery in England. Matilda writes, quite frankly, that 'Amico is quite disconcerted, – he has lost all chance with Miss Keating – reports say she is married to an English Officer at Paris. It is said her mother is dead. I can hardly believe this to be true.'[26] Mentioned in Matilda's Journal as frequent callers at the Charles Street house in 1814, Mrs and Miss Keating are nowhere else mentioned in the Chinnery letters. Perhaps they were the wife and daughter of a George Keating, catholic bookseller and publisher, who had a shop in Piccadilly, and later in Golden Square.

In autumn 1816 Margaret, Matilda and Viotti again travelled to the Continent (August–November), meeting up in Brussels with William and later with George, who had spent August in Paris with his patron George Canning. Margaret's planned visit to Louveciennes to stay with Madame Vigée-Lebrun did not eventuate, and indeed they did not go to France at all this year. The latter wrote Margaret a long letter of regret before their departure, in which she spoke of her fatigue with the world, of the damage done to her property by the Prussian troops, and her relief at the return of the monarchy. At the end of the letter the artist said she was saddened by the length of time that had elapsed since she last had news of Viotti and how much she missed his lively conversation and his playing:

> It has been a very long time since I have had news of Amico. My God, how I wish you could be with me so that I could listen to him speak with so much expression on his face, and the sweet sounds [of the violin] which I so loved hearing. Why do I not hear

---

23 'Tout ce qui sera là prendra votre parti, pas un vous blâmera, au contraire, les Anglais sont comme ça, ils partageront notre indignation, et vous donnerez le soufflet à ce monsieur qu'il aura mérité' (*Ibid.*, p. 108).

24 'in Paris die Künstler einander behandeln, wie— Juden: sie spielen nicht in den Konzerten ihrer besten Freunde, ausser wenn sie tüchtig bezahlt werden!' (*AMZ*, 21 June 1809, col. 606).

25 Baillot to Montbeillard, 12 January 1817, cited in François-Sappey, p. 150.

26 Matilda Chinnery to WBC, in GBV to WBC, 12 February 1816, PHM 94/143/1 – 14/27.

> them any more! They are still in my heart, and I continually say to myself Encore, Encore.[27]

Anxious about a lost crate that had contained one of her portraits of Marie-Antoinette, she asked Viotti to call on Christie in London to find out if the crate had left for France, giving him the name of the dealer in Le Havre to whom it should be addressed. Her final words to Viotti are that as soon as she has finished moving house she will engrave him.[28]

The 1816 visit to Brussels was to be a significant one for Viotti. It was here that he met André Robberechts, a promising pupil of Baillot who had been affected by the closure of the Paris Conservatoire at the time of the Restoration, and who had returned to his native Belgium. Having successfully solicited lessons from Viotti in Brussels in 1816, Robberechts would accompany his master to London and remain in his care for four years. He would remain on affectionate terms with Viotti until the latter's death, and as 'one of the greatest violinists of the classical violin school',[29] he was one of those who passed on the Viotti technique.

Back in England before the end of November 1816, Margaret reported to William in her letter of 24 May 1817 that they had had fewer visitors during the past months.[30] Perhaps Viotti used the period of quiet to compose, as it was in February 1817 that Margaret remarked that Crosdill was delighted with Viotti's new duets.[31] These may have been the Three duets for violin and viola (WIVa: 22–24), arranged from the duets for two violins, 'Hommage à l'amitié' (WIV: 28–30), published by Janet et Cotelle *c.*1817. Margaret attributed the lack of visitors to the inadequacy of their house: 'there is little attraction, – no dinners, no fêtes – a very small dirty house, *now* become extremely shabby.'[32]

But there must have been some musical parties, for the testimony of one contented visitor can be found in a letter to Viotti dated March 1817. This was the Prussian minister Baron Jacobi-Kloest, who was in no way discomforted by the Charles Street house's drawbacks. On the contrary, he praised both the warm hospitality and the fine music which Margaret and Viotti provided, writing to Viotti from Germany, soon after his departure from London:

> Never shall I forget the extreme kindness with which I was treated in your friendly circle. Everything was perfect. The way in which foreigners were received, the rare amiability of the hostess, the delicious music with which we were regaled under your

---

[27] 'En voila bien long ou je n'ai pas entendu parler d'Amico. Mon dieu que vous ét[iez] avec moi aussi je l'entendrais parlé [sic] avec tant de phisionomie et ses doux sons que j'écoutois si bien. pourquoi ne les entendre plus! Ils sont encore dans mon cœur, mais je dis toujours Bis-Bis' (Elisabeth Vigée-Lebrun to MC, 7 July 1816, Fisher 2000 – 8/2).

[28] *Ibid.* It is not known if she did. There is an engraving of Viotti by Frémy after the portrait by Vigée-Lebrun in the RCM.

[29] 'un des plus grands violinistes de l'école classique du violon' (*Almanach musical*, 1861, cited in *MGG*, vol. 11, col. 574).

[30] MC to WBC, 24 May 1817, PHM 94/143/1 – 17/30.

[31] MC to WBC, 20 February 1817, PHM 94/143/1 – 17/28 (torn scrap of a letter only).

[32] MC to WBC, 24 May 1817, PHM 94/143/1 – 17/30.

supervision. In short, throughout my long residence in London I have never known a house where foreigners would have been more gratified than in Mrs Chinnery's [...] Ah! my dear Mr Viotti, what I would not give to hear you *here*. Your divine accompaniment when Miss [Matilda] Chinnery played the piano forte, with all the precision and grace that she was known for, still resonates in my ears.[33]

Jacobi-Kloest's description in the same letter of his own daughter-in-law's playing adds to the overwhelming body of evidence in the Viotti/Chinnery letters that contemporary drawing room *amateurs* played almost exclusively the works of modern composers, snapping up their works as soon as they were published: 'her manner of executing the music of Clementi, Cramer, Dussek, Kalkbrenner, Ries seems to me to be really quite rare. Her expression is perfect. I should like to know if the above *luminaries of the muses of music* have published any new chefs d'œuvre since my departure.'[34] It was usual for these lady pianists to have their sheet music bound into one volume, giving rise to collections such as the one in the Powerhouse Museum, that contains the music of five different composers, including 'Trois sonates pour clavecin ou piano forte avec accompagnement de violon et violoncelle' (Three sonatas for harpsichord or piano forte with violin and cello accompaniment) by Viotti, some easy harp sonatas by Krumpholtz, and piano sonatas by Haydn, Devienne and Boccherini.[35]

But the Charles Street house cramped Margaret's style, and she decided to buy a larger house at 17 Montagu Street, Portman Square, in the parish of St Marylebone, the district frequented by French *émigrés* and wealthy diplomats, who each gave it their own distinctive cachet. By June 1817 she had moved in with Viotti, George and the two girls. Here she clearly intended to entertain on a lavish scale, having in 1816 written to William: 'I might perhaps find a good Swiss servant at Brussels, & bring him home with me. *Here* there is not one who will wear a livery, & a livery servant I must have.'[36]

The Duke of Cambridge alludes to the purchase of the Montagu Street house in his letter to Viotti of 7 July 1817, saying that he intends to call on the family there

---

[33] 'Jamais je n'oublierai les bontés extrêmes dont j'ai été traité dans votre aimable cercle. Tout y étoit parfait. La manière dont les étrangers étoient reçus, l'aimabilité [sic] rare de l'hotesse, la délicieuse musique dont on étoit regalé sous vos auspices— enfin je n'ai pas connu de maison pendant ma longue résidence à Londres, où les etrangers auroient eu lieu d'être plus contents que chés M[me] Chinnery [...] Ah! mon très cher Monsieur Viotti, que ne donnerois-je pour vous entendre ici. Votre divin accompagnement quand M[lle] [Matilda] Chinnery touchoit le piano forte, avec l'exactitude et les graces qui lui étoient propres, raisonne [résonne] encore à mes oreilles' (Jacobi-Kloest to GBV, 24 March 1817, NYPL JOB 97-52, item 38).

[34] 'sa manière d'executer les musiques [sic] de Clementi, Cramer, Dussek, Kalkbrenner, Ries, me paroit reellement peu commune. Son expression est parfaite. Je voudrois savoir si les susdites lumières des muses musicales, ont publié depuis mon départ quelques nouveaux chefs d'œuvre' (*Ibid.*).

[35] Bound velum volume of printed sheet music by various composers, PHM E.A. and V.I. Crome collection, A8213.

[36] MC to WBC, 8 July 1816, PHM 94/143/1 – 17/26.

when he visits England the following year. In the same letter he mentions the purchase of a new violin that Viotti has made for him, undoubtedly another Stradivarius, for which he sends Viotti a bank draft for 50 guineas. He complains that 'La Musique va bien mal' (music fares badly). He has had so little free time that he has been unable to play more than eight or ten times in the last three years. But at least he has managed to sing a little with the Italian vocalist Bolassi.[37]

In June 1817 Margaret and Viotti left again for their annual four months on the Continent, this time accompanied by George. Their destination was Lille, where Matilda's mother Mrs John Chinnery, recently returned from India with her younger children, had taken lodgings. William would meet them there. Margaret and Viotti would later visit Paris, for Viotti looked forward to his yearly reunions with his brother. The normally eloquent Baillot is silent on Viotti's 1817 visit to Paris, but it may be imagined that Viotti renewed contact with at least some of his colleagues, especially Madame de Montgéroult, with whom plans may have been laid for her visit to England the following year. In Lille Margaret seems to have held some musical parties, as shown by a letter from Viotti, written from the rue Royale, where they were staying, to his friend [Louis?] Vogel. Viotti apologised for having to postpone a large private concert to which Vogel had invited several colleagues. This was clearly the same Monsieur Vogel whom Louis Spohr would visit in Lille in February 1820, calling him 'the best violinist in town [...] and director of the dilettante-concerts'.[38]

In 1817 William was still residing at Calais, but he was soon to move to Le Havre in search of new trading opportunities. In Calais he appears to have led a quiet existence acting as an agent for Viotti's and Smith's wine importing firm, with a certain Jacques Le Veux as his assistant. William's inactivity in Calais frustrated Viotti, who condemned his lack of initiative. Writing of a recent conversation with their friend Herries regarding William's future, Viotti reported: 'I told him how irritating it was that we could not find you some occupation! Something to keep you busy, even if it is not lucrative! For, I told him, the mind becomes just as rusty as the body if it is not exercised!'[39]

In her large house in Portman Square Margaret could now move right back up to the very top echelon of London society and circulate with comfort. The feeling of shame that had held her in check for the first few years after William's disgrace had all but evaporated, and although she complained privately of some 'slights and

---

[37] AF to GBV, 7 July 1817, Viotti Papers, RCM. Bolassi was a member of the King's Theatre opera company, 1810–14, and later ran a music school in Paris.

[38] Spohr's *Autobiography*, vol. 2, p. 70; see also GBV to Vogel, 17 October 1817, cited in Giazotto, p. 272. It is unclear if this is the same 'much-travelled' Vogel who in c.July 1811 gave a successful flute concert in Warsaw (AMZ, 3 July 1811, col. 458). Goodkind (p. 740) names a Louis Vogel as a Stradivarius owner. *New Grove 2*'s entry for Louis Vogel, flautist and violinist, is inconclusive.

[39] 'Je lui dis combien il étoit facheux que nous ne puissions vous trouver quelque occupation! Quelque chose enfin quand même ce ne seroit pas lucratif, pour vous tenir en éxércice! Car, lui disai-je, l'esprit se rouille tout aussi bien que le corps si on ne le remue pas!' (GBV to WBC, 7 March 1816, PHM 94/143/1 – 14/30).

buffetings', she did not hold back from appearing in public again. With a more spacious house, Margaret's social connections expanded. And with the obliging Viotti by her side it was impossible to stand in the shadows for long. The English nobility did not care what had taken place six years previously, and the aristocratic foreigners did not know. For Margaret and Viotti the year 1818 was to be the busiest since Caroline's death.

On 25 May 1818 Margaret held a large glittering party, to which the most select of London society were lured by the multiple attractions of fine music, a fine home and fine company to rub shoulders with. The following day Margaret wrote to William, 'Our party last night went off as well as possible dear Chinnery! – a very good assortment of company came, notwithstanding *all* there was, going on in the town. Our rooms looked well, the music was good, refreshments plentiful.'[40] As Glenbervie had once said, the art of good entertaining consisted in knowing who wanted to be with whom.[41] Margaret possessed this skill. She named 78 of her carefully chosen guests. Among them were many titled diplomats. Not included in the list were the 'ten professional persons' (musicians) and themselves, bringing the number to nearly 100. Considering that her party clashed with a very popular Delihu concert, this represented a resounding triumph. An astute judge of character, Margaret assessed the excuses of those who declined her invitation:

> The Saltouns went to the De Lihus,— their concert of course kept away some of my company,— for I had invited above an hundred— Lady Ousley was detained with dinner company at home, Sir Gore said,— but I suspect that she is very fine & very absurd,— I have seen her three times, & like her less each time. The people began coming in about ten,— & continued coming & going all the evening,— some went away & came back again. About two they were all gone but the professors. We began with a Symphony of Haydn's,— then a vocal Quintett from Rossini's Barbiere di Seviglia,— then Amico & Robberecht played. Then a vocal Duett by Miss [Caroline] Naldi & [Spanish tenor Manuel] Garcia. After this the Bohrer's played (which they never shall do again here). Then a Duett by Naldi & Garcia,— after that a Duett by Lady Flint & Miss Naldi which terminated the whole [...] Amico went on Tuesday, the night following mine, to Lady Grey's.[42]

Anton and Maximilian Bohrer were on the point of leaving for the court of Berlin, where Anton was appointed concertmeister to Friedrich Wilhelm III, and Maximilian first chamber violoncellist. They appear to have encountered a problem with the British authorities over the export of their instruments, the same obstacle that Viotti had come up against in his attempt to export William's cello in 1812. George Chinnery, who was then still employed in the British Treasury, which was responsible for the Department of Customs and Excise, was able to assist. The intermediary who approached him was the Viotti/Chinnery friend the Comte de Caraman, a member of the French legation in London. He wrote to

---

[40] MC to WBC, 26 May 1818, PHM 94/143/1 – 17/33.

[41] Douglas, *The Glenbervie Journals*, p. 144.

[42] Wife of 2$^{nd}$ Earl Grey, Whig statesman. MC to WBC, 26 May 1818, PHM 94/143/1 – 17/33.

George thanking him for his 'obligeance' in the matter of the Bohrer brothers' violins, adding that he would hasten to let them know of 'this decision which gets them out of a serious predicament.'[43] The Delihu sisters, having performed in the Philharmonic concerts of 1817 and 1818, remained in London until mid-November, then left for Ireland, George informed his mother, who was by then in Paris with Viotti, Matilda and William.[44] The popular sisters returned for the 1819 Philharmonic season.

With an acute awareness of social rank through keeping company with aristocracy and royalty, and an exquisite taste in music through associating with Europe's best musicians, Margaret was critical of any music and company that did not measure up to her high standards. In the same letter to William she wrote in withering tones of an evening of music at Mrs Curtis's (Sir William Curtis's daughter-in-law):

> We all went to Mrs Curtis's last night— there was music in *their* way,— instrumental quartets & symphonies, with english Glees. I did not know a creature there, excepting Sir Gore & Lady Ousley,— in number there might be forty persons, or thereabouts. A fine house, an agreeable good-natured mistress, a worthy master, a parcel of fine children, plenty of fresh delightful flowers, and awkward unfamiliar servants, who seemed to belong to the last century. The general effect to me was *ponderous*. I shall stay at home for the rest of the week to refresh myself![45]

The subtle snobbery that pervades those words may be likened to Glenbervie's regarding the Chinnerys themselves seven years earlier. But as Glenbervie himself eventually became a dear friend of Viotti and one of Margaret's most admiring correspondents, it is clear that private thoughts were not allowed to impinge on public enjoyments. Still in the same letter to William Margaret mentions yet another 'grand Dinner' that she will give to 'the foreigners', the following Saturday, and another she had given to Lord Limerick previously. Now comfortably established on the top rung of society, Margaret was impatient with anything but the best: 'I took Mad de Mongeroult [who had arrived in London in *c.*June 1818] to Lady Flints [in Birdcage Walk] last night, – There was an enormous crowd, & *who* composed it I cannot tell you, – very second-rate company I believe. Music so-so.'[46]

Another grand dinner that Margaret did not elaborate on was described by one of her guests, Lord Glenbervie:

---

[43] 'cette decision qui les tire d'un grand embarras' (Georges de Caraman to GRC, 15 May 1818, Fisher 2000 – 22/35).

[44] GRC to MC, 9 October 1818, Fisher 2000 – 7/6.

[45] MC to WBC, 26 May 1818, PHM 94/143/1 – 17/33.

[46] MC to WBC, 11 June 1818, PHM 94/143/1 – 17/34. Lady Flint was also a patron of music, and held regular concerts in her home. Viotti and his colleagues had in the past been called upon to perform in them, and on one occasion Janiewicz had been obliged, on account of the incessant buzz of conversation and rattling of tea cups, to remind the audience of its manners (N. Bentley (ed.) (1977), *Selections from the Reminiscences of Captain Gronow*, The Folio Society, London, pp. 90–91).

> In the evening [3 July 1818] I went to a select concert at Mrs Chinnery's, where the *amico*, as she calls him, played on his violin, with and without accompaniment, to the great admiration of the connoisseurs. [He goes on to list the diplomats and others present.] Fiotti [sic] talked to me of Madame d'Esmangart, whom he had known last winter at Paris at his brother's, who he told me is a colonel and Attorney General at Paris, a strange union of situations, but I found he meant that he has the same sort of office and duties with our Judge *Advocate*.[47]

In May 1818 the Duke of Cambridge was back in London for the English celebration of his marriage to Princess Augusta Wilhelmina, daughter of the Landgrave of Hesse-Cassell. He was eager to see Viotti again and make music. On 26 May Margaret wrote: 'The Duke and Dutchess of Cambridge arrived on Tuesday 26th to dinner; Amico and George wrote their names at Cambridge House this morning.'[48] And on 11 June: 'Tomorrow there is a probability of his [Viotti's] having a Quintetto at Cambridge House.'[49] A few days before, the duke had introduced his bride to London society at a ball at Almack's to which George was invited, but not introduced to the duchess personally. Margaret desired that Viotti would remind the duke to make the introduction, which he did at the party at Cambridge House on the 12th.

Margaret wrote to William: 'Amico dined again with the Duke of Cambridge, – he went in the morning by appointment to play Duetts, & the Duke desired he would dine there, saying "I have only one place, so that I cannot ask George to dinner, but tell him to come at 10 oClock." Amico dined with the Duke and Dutchess of Glocester [sic], Princess Sophia of Glocester, the Landgrave of Hesse, and their ladies & suites making up a full table.'[50] George added a postscript to his mother's earlier letter for his father, saying 'Amico dines again at Cambridge H° to-day & I am asked to join the party which is to take place in the Evg. Had I been a foreigner I suppose I should have been a guest.'[51]

Later the same month the Duke of Cambridge paid Margaret the promised visit, and having announced his intention of calling on her the following Sunday evening, Margaret felt obliged to arrange a party. She tried unsuccessfully to have Crosdill, who, despite Viotti's dire predictions of 1814 when he complained of Crosdill's neglect of the family,[52] had regularly called to enquire after William, but did manage to secure at short notice Schram and the Naldis, who agreed to come before their performance at the King's Theatre: 'We have therefore got Schramm, – & the Naldis will come for an hour before they go to their evening's engagement. Madme de Mongeroult will play also. For company I have secured Lady & Miss Dashwood, & Lady Augusta Leith, & – about a dozen men chiefly from the

---

47 Douglas, *The Diaries of Sylvester Douglas*, vol. 2, p. 319.

48 MC to WBC, 26 May 1818, PHM 94/143/1 – 17/33.

49 MC to WBC, 11 June 1818, PHM 94/143/1 – 17/34.

50 MC to WBC, 15 June 1818, PHM 94/143/1 – 17/35.

51 MC to WBC, 11 June 1818, PHM 94/143/1 – 17/34.

52 GBV to WBC, 24 February 1814, PHM 94/143/1 – 14/17.

Diplomatic corps.'[53] On Monday morning she gave William an account of the evening:

> It is all over, and barring the heat, *well over* I think! [...] the Duke of Cambridge came in at half past nine Oclock. He was very amiable, spoke to every body, desired the ladies to sit down & while this was going on the venerable Landgrave of Hesse Cassel entered, and without any ceremony, entered into conversation with me, & sat down on the Sofa by me— I then desired they would sing a Quintetto, of Rossini's— this went off well & tea having been handed round, the Duke took the second violin part in a Quintetto of Boccherini's— I never heard him play better,— but the heat was so overpowering, that he declined playing any more. As the singers were obliged to leave us at 10 oClock in order to attend a prior engagement I proposed before they went away a Duett between Caroline Naldi & Garcia, which went off well also. Ices were then handed round. But the Duke began to grow fidgetty,— he is desperately in love with his wife, and it was the greatest sacrifice he could possibly make to me, to stay so long from her. He waited however to hear Amico and Robberecht play a Duett, & then vanished [...] I forgot to say that Madame de Mongeroult played a Solo,— but alas!— her execution & her taste are much fallen off![54]

Another tenor who assisted on this night was the Frenchman Pierre Begrez, who had made his London debut at the King's Theatre in 1816 and also sang with Naldi in that season's Philharmonic concerts.

A long letter written by Hélène de Montgéroult from Paris shows that she had remained in London until February 1819. She thanks Margaret for making various domestic purchases for her, and regrets the Montagu Street concerts: 'I miss the musical evening of 15 February, and all those that will have followed it. I felt so comfortable in that beloved drawing room listening to and admiring dear Amico!'[55] Since her return she has given some private concerts of her own: 'for my part, my dear Madam, I have held two musical assemblies, on Saturday 24 February and the other on the 25th of this month. My excellent p[iano] made an impression.'[56] The piano was one that she had bought from Broadwood while in London: 'Broadwood treated me very well, except for the fact that he forgot to send me a protective cover for this fine instrument, a [illegible word], a key and an assortment of strings, but that can be remedied.'[57]

In Margaret's letter of 22 June 1818 her mood has changed. For the first and only time in the whole correspondence she complains about Viotti: 'It is not

---

[53] MC to WBC, 27 June 1818, PHM 94/143/1 – 17/37.

[54] *Ibid.*

[55] 'j'ai regretté cette soirée musicale du 15 février, et toutes celles qui l'auront suivie; je me trouvois si bien dans ce salon aimé écoutant, admirant ce bon amico!' (Hélène de Montgéroult to MC, 30 March 1819, Fisher 2000 – 4/18).

[56] 'quand à moi, ma chere dame j'ai eu deux réunions musicales. Samedi le 24 février l'autre le 25 de ce mois; mon excelent p[iano] a fait son effet' (*Ibid.*).

[57] 'broadwood m'a fort bien traitée si ce n'est qu'il a oublié de m'envoyer une housse pour ce bel instrument, une [disporue?], une clef, et un assortiment de cordes; mais cela peut se réparer' (*Ibid.*).

always an easy thing to bear with Amico's temper, at all times, – I have always regretted that among the many fine qualities he possesses there should be an *over-bearingness* that at times renders both his actions & expressions harsh.' What upsets her most is Viotti's turning his back on music: 'For a long time past Amico hates music, – he never composes, – would never touch a violin if he could avoid it, – his delight is in reading novels!'[58]

A March 1816 letter from Viotti to William gives an early clue to his bad mood. William Spencer's brother, John Spencer, one of Charles Smith's and Viotti's biggest wine customers, has defaulted on his debt to the shop:

> If it were up to me, dear friend, I would not be writing to you, because I am in a bad humour! Why? Because everything is going to the devil in this world, and life is one long headache, and we shall probably lose everything that that unlucky John Spencer owes to the shop![59]

John Spencer has amassed such enormous debts that he has been stripped of his Government office as Receiver General, and the Government has issued him with an 'Extent' thereby freezing his assets and preventing his creditors from being paid, complains Viotti. He goes on: 'You can imagine the pretty kettle of fish at Duke Street, and what a foul temper Charles & Co are in! Anyway, that is how it is, and all we can do is regret having had anything to do with these petticoated dandies.'[60] John Spencer's financial difficulties were also noted in a letter from Margaret, in which she wrote that 'J.S.' had 'terribly misled poor Guglielmo in his affairs', obliging his brother to pay more than £400 in sureties, a sum that William Spencer could not afford.[61] It was John Spencer's debt, then, that precipitated the dissolution of Viotti's and Smith's business.

Not wanting to dwell on this unpleasant subject, Viotti passes on quickly to describe for William the surprise party for Naldi's Saint's Day. While Madame Naldi made preparations at home for receiving guests, and transformed the drawing room into a theatre for the *fête domestique*, Viotti, Margaret, George and Matilda and their closest diplomatic friends Pfeffel and Jenison kept him in ignorance of the arrangements by making him believe that after dining at Margaret's, he was to go to a performance of the popular London puppets, the *fantoccini*, at the Strand.[62] Viotti described the surprise party for William:

---

[58] MC to WBC, 22 June 1818, PHM 94/143/1 – 17/36.

[59] 'Si je m'en croyois, cher Ami, je ne vous écrirois pas, à cause que je suis de mauvaise humeur! Pourquoi? parce que tout va à la diable dans ce monde, qu'on n'y peut vivre qu'au milieu des tracasseries, et que probablement nous perdrons presque tout ce que ce malheureux John Spencer doit à la boutique!' (GBV to WBC, 21 March [1816], PHM 94/143/1 – 14/31).

[60] 'Imaginez la belle besogne que Duke Street a fait et quelle humeur de chien possede Charles & Co! Enfin celà est comme ça et il ne nous reste qu'à regreter d'avoir jamais eu à faire à ces paniers parés' (*Ibid.*).

[61] MC to WBC, 4 July 1816, PHM 94/143/1 – 17/25.

[62] The *fantoccini* began as a simple Punch and Judy show, but gradually became more ambitious, presenting Shakespearean plays and opera of a high standard.

Last night we had a charming fête at Naldi's. It was his Saint's Day, and in order to surprise him his wife begged me to invite him to dinner at the Padrona's and to bring him home about nine in the evening. I carried out *to the letter* what she asked, and at the appointed time M[essrs] de Pfeffel, Jenison, Matilda, George and I simply took him home, making him believe that we were taking him to see the Fantoccini at the Strand. He walked right into the trap, and it was only when he arrived at his own front door, which he saw was all lit up, and [noticed] all the activity, that he realised it was a trick, but the trick was played to touch his heart. We found the drawing room turned into a theatre, about a hundred guests waiting for the play to begin, and an orchestra composed of Vaccari, Spagnoletti, Sor, and Crouch. They began with a charming short French comedy in which his wife and daughter took the principal roles, and finished with a short Italian opera, words and music having been written especially for the occasion. Bouquets of flowers were presented to the accompaniment of music, and tears of emotion came to many eyes, particularly those of the happy Papa.— We waltzed for a little while afterwards, and ate an elephant— made of biscuit of course. Then we went to bed.[63]

Two years later, in Paris on his yearly autumn visit, Viotti would himself be the object of a public display of affection at a fête staged in his honour. The fête was arranged by Baillot and other Conservatoire professors and their pupils. It is possible that Margaret, being anxious for Viotti's state of mind after the collapse of his wine business and his resultant distaste for music, might have proposed it as a way of bringing Viotti back to his art. She certainly played an important part in the preparations and in the precautions necessary for keeping Viotti in ignorance, since it took place at their own dwelling. As was apparent from the account of Naldi's party, such surprises relied heavily on the co-operation of those closest to the recipient. Baillot gave two accounts of the fête, one private and one public. The first was in a letter to Montbeillard dated 6 November 1818:

[63] 'Nous avons eû hier au soir une fête charmante chez Naldi. C'étoit le jour de sa fête, et Madame sa femme, pour lui faire une surprise, m'a prié de l'inviter à diner chez la Padrona et de le lui ramener vers les 9. heures du soir. J'éxecutai à pontino ce qu'elle desiroit, et à l'heure convenüe, M[ssrs] de Pfeffel Jenison Matilda George et moi nous le conduisimes tout simplement chez lui, lui faisant croire que nous le menions voir les Fantoccini dans le Strand. Il donna completement dans le paneau, et ce n'est qu'en arrivant à sa porte qu'il vit tout éclairé, beaucoup de remû menage qu'il s'apperçût de l'attrappe, mais l'attrappe étoit faite pour toucher son cœur. Nous y trouvames le sallon changé en Theatre; une centaine de personnes attendre que la piece commençat, et un orchestre composé de Vacari, Spagnoletti, Sor et Croutch [sic]. On commença par une petite comedie françoise charmante ou sa femme et sa fille jouoient les roles principeaux, et on finit par un petit opera italien, paroles et musique fait éxprés pour l'occasion, ou les bouquets ont été présentés harmonieusement et ou les larmes d'attendrissement sont venües offusquer les yeux de beaucoup de personnes, particulierement ceux de l'heureux Papa.— On valsa un petit peu aprés, on mangea un Elephant— bien entendû en biscuit, et on alla se coucher' (GBV to WBC, 21 March [1816], PHM 94/143/1 – 14/31). At the end of the letter is a note from Naldi.

I saw M. de Louvois at a morning assembly at Viotti's, whom I had the pleasure of hearing at two of these assemblies and at a small fête that we gave him on Sunday 25 October, two days before his departure. A young poet wrote a cantata in his honour, which the good-hearted Habeneck set to music, with solos and choruses. I slipped in eight lines on which he based a charming chorus as a finale to the cantata. We went to Viotti's lodgings after we came out of the king's mass. He had not been forewarned. We had assembled an orchestra and all our pupils. This surprise caused him so much emotion that he could neither walk nor speak when he came in, and he was choked by tears. The ritornellos were made up of a dozen *motifs* from his concertos, quartets, etc, and you can imagine how closely I shared in the emotion of the one who was listening to them, as I played. Once he had recovered from the first shock, the cantata was given a second time, then our dear Viotti, seeing himself surrounded by his children and his friends, agreed to take up his violin and play for us a superb concerto in E minor, from the manuscript. How could he not have played it with divine passion? His soul was vibrating in unison with ours. [...] Finally we presented dear Viotti with the words of the cantata, written by a *real* poet [A.P. de Montférier], and those written by yours truly, which I placed below his portrait. Here they are. I send them to you with no ceremony, believing them not good enough for him, but worthy of indulgence for the sentiment that dictated them:

His sounds exert their dominion over all hearts,
He surpassed his teacher and had no rivals.
Under his brilliant bow there is a living god
And his happy genius crowns his works.
Moving from the serious to the sweet, from the pleasing to the severe,
Without ceasing to be great, he knows how to express everything.
Within his touching harmonies his soul is complete,
And his sweetest triumph is to be beloved.[64]

---

[64] 'J'ai vu M. de Louvois à une réunion du matin chez Viotti que j'ai eu le plaisir d'entendre à deux de ces réunions et à une petite fête que nous lui avons donnée le dimanche 25 octobre, l'avant-veille de son départ. Un jeune poète a fait en son honneur une cantate que le brave Habeneck a mise en musique avec des récits et des chœurs. J'y ai glissé huit vers sur lesquels il a fait un chœur charmant qui a terminé la cantate. Nous sommes allés chez Viotti en sortant de la messe du roi. Il n'était prévenu de rien. Nous avions rassemblé un orchestre et tous nos élèves. Cette surprise lui a causé tant d'émotion qu'il ne pouvait en entrant ni marcher ni parler et que les larmes le suffoquaient. Les ritourelles étaient composées d'une douzaine de motifs de ses concertos, quatuors, etc et vous devez penser combien, en les jouant, je partageais l'émotion de celui qui les écoutait. Remis du premier saissisement, la cantate a été dite une seconde fois, puis notre cher Viotti, se voyant au milieu de ses enfants et de ses amis, ne s'est point refusé à prendre le violon et nous a joué un superbe concerto manuscrit en mi mineur. Comment ne l'aurait-il pas dit avec un feu tout à fait divin? Son âme répondant à la nôtre était toute en vibration [...] Enfin nous avons remis au bon Viotti les vers de la cantate faits par un véritable poète, et ceux de votre serviteur, que j'avais écrits au bas de son portrait. Les voici. Je vous les envoie sans façon, les trouvant non pas assez bien pour lui, mais dignes d'indulgence en faveur du sentiment qui les a dictés: Ses chants sur tous les cœurs exercent leur empire / Il surpassa son maître et n'eut pont de rivaux / Sous son archet brillant, c'est un Dieu qui respire / Et son génie heureux couronne ses travaux. / Passant du grave au doux, du plaisant au sévère / Sans cesser d'être grand, il sait tout exprimer / Dans ses accords touchants son âme est toute entière / Et son plus doux triomphe est de se faire aimer' (Baillot to Montbeillard, 6

There is no clearer proof of Baillot's love and admiration for Viotti than in the above verses. What the modest Baillot omitted to mention in his letter was that it was he who performed the solos.[65] Baillot understood Viotti's yearning to be among true artists again, and restricted the number of guests to 30, not including the musicians. Alive to the emotions provoked in both the musicians and the one being honoured, he wrote in his public eulogy on Viotti's death:

> This little fête took place amidst the liveliest of emotions. One circumstance in particular rendered it still more moving. After the cantata was sung before the guest of honour, he was begged to play. His emotions were boiling over, yet he did not demur. It must be remarked that apart from a few friends, no one had heard him play a concerto for more than thirty years. He performed his No. 29 in E minor [Letter I], with his usual verve. Alas! it was his swansong. We were listening to him for the last time. But this farewell was an introduction for most of the audience. Imagine, if it be possible, how such a conjunction of circumstances must have added grandeur to the artist's talent, and pathos to the effect of the piece. We had brought several of our pupils. One of them, at the first sound of Viotti's instrument, was so moved that he burst into tears. Soon he was sobbing so loudly that we were obliged to place ourselves in front of him to hide him from the view of the player who held our souls captive, like Poussin's shepherd, who hides the dying Eurydice from the eyes of Orpheus, so as not to miss the sounds of the divine poet.[66]

Viotti's own letter of farewell to Baillot, even though written four days before the above fête, was full of similar emotion and affection. Addressed to Baillot at no. 6, rue Buffault, Faubourg Montmartre, Viotti wrote:

> It is very sad, dear kind Baillot, to say adieu!... However I must, and being unable to say the word in person, allow my writing of it as a substitution. I shall never forget all your tender affection, and your generous acknowledgement of my talent. In order to be so liberal it is necessary to possess all the talent that you do. How dearly would I have

---

November 1818, cited in François-Sappey, p.184). The verse translation is from White's *Thematic Catalogue*, p. xx.

65 Michaud, vol. 43, p. 589. It is highly probable that Miel was present on the occasion.

66 'Cette petite fête se passa au milieu des plus vives émotions. Une circonstance particulière la rendit encore plus touchante. Après la scène lyrique chantée devant celui qui en était l'objet, on le pria de jouer; son attendrissement était porté au dernier degré; toutefois il se rendit aux instances. Il faut remarquer qu'à l'exception de quelques amis, personne ne l'avait entendu dans le concerto depuis plus de trente ans. Il exécuta son 29e en mi mineur [Lettre I], avec sa verve accoutumée. Hélas! ce fut le chant de cygne; nous l'entendîmes pour la dernière fois; mais cet adieu était un début pour la plupart des auditeurs. Qu'on imagine, s'il est possible, ce qu'un tel concours de circonstances devait ajouter de grandeur au talent de l'artiste, et de pathétique à l'effet du morceau. Nous avions amené plusieurs de nos élèves. L'un d'eux, au premier son tiré de l'instrument par VIOTTI, fut tellement ému, qu'il se mit à fondre en larmes; bientôt il sanglotta si haut, que nous fûmes obligés de nous placer devant lui pour le dérober aux regards de celui qui captivait notre âme tout entière; comme ce berger de Poussin, qui cache aux yeux d'Orphée Eurydice défaillante, pour ne rien perdre des accens du chantre divin' (*Notice*, p. 11).

> liked to see more of you!... But is a heart ever satisfied in a Paris or a London?... Adieu, I embrace you tenderly and beg that you never forget
> Your affectionate friend, J.B. Viotti
> The ladies [Margaret and Matilda] send all their best wishes.—[67]

Viotti's 1818 visit to Paris did not go unnoticed by the French press. In the *Annales de la musique pour l'an 1819*, which contains a directory of Parisian musicians, as well as miscellaneous musical news, there is a revealing paragraph that highlights Viotti's interest in innovative teaching methods:

> NOVEMBER [1818]
> The celebrated Viotti did not want to leave Paris without ascertaining the happy results that have been achieved in France of applying the monitorial system to the teaching of music.[68] He has recently visited the school run by [prizewinning Conservatoire piano graduate] Mlle Renaud d'Allen, rue Charlot, n° 14, which for some time has been drawing large numbers of students to the Marais. Having closely observed the classroom exercises, charming to both eye and ear, he saw for himself that the success of such an establishment was due to the excellence of the method employed, and not to some transient fashionable fad for frivolous novelties that all too often appeal to idle minds. It is regrettable, he said, that such simple and ingenious methods were not applied earlier in the development of a charming art, the study of which has, in times gone by, wasted so many young people's time and caused them to turn away from music.[69]

---

[67] 'C'est bien triste, cher et bon Baillot, de dire adieu!... Il le faut cependant, et ne pouvant prononcer ce mot là en personne, permettez que l'écriture y supplée— Je n'oublierai jamais toute votre tendre affection, et votre genereuse bonté pour mon talent. Il faut avoir tout celui que vous avez pour etre si liberal. Combien j'aurois voulu vous voir d'avantage!... Mais peut-on satisfaire entierement le cœur dans un Paris ou un Londre?... Adieu, je vous embrasse avéc tendresse et vous prie de ne jamais oublier / Votre Aff[né] Ami, J.B. Viotti / Les Dames me chargent de vous dire mille choses de leur part' (GBV to Baillot, 21 October 1818, NYPL *MNY-Viotti).

[68] This system originated in England and was popular in France during the Restoration. It involved training the brightest pupils in the class to become monitors to instruct their fellow students in small groups. Its application to music teaching is described in the *Annales de la musique pour l'an 1819*, pp. 283–5.

[69] 'NOVEMBRE / Le célèbre Viotti n'a point voulu quitter Paris sans connaître les résultats heureux que l'on obtient aujourd'hui en France de l'application de l'enseignement mutuel à la musique. Il a visité dernièrement l'école tenue par mademoiselle Renaud d'Allen, rue Charlot, n°. 14, qui attire, depuis quelque tems un grand concours au Marais. Après avoir observé dans le plus grand détail les exercices de cette classe faite pour charmer également l'œil et l'oreille, il s'est convaincu par lui-même que les succès d'un pareil établissement sont dus à l'excellence de la méthode qu'on y a adopté, et non à cet engouement éphémaire que la mode inspire trop souvent à l'oisiveté pour des nouveautés futiles. On doit regretter, disait-il, que des procédés si ingénieux et si simples n'aient pas été plus tôt appliqués aux progrès d'un art charmant, dont l'étude coûtait jadis tant de dégoûts et de perte de tems à la jeunesse' (*Ibid.*, pp. 306–7).

Back in London Margaret recommenced her bi-weekly letters to William (there are none from Viotti to William during this period), and seven letters dated January 1819 give the names of those they saw in Paris in 1818. They were mainly diplomats, politicians, and old friends of Viotti, with some new acquaintances. Among them were the Comte de Rayneval, the statesman Elie Decazes, the Marquis de Grimaldi, the judge M. de Bourguignon, General Dessolle (now a marquis), and André Viotti's friends Messrs de Mortier, de Lausac and Cunietti. Viotti, Margaret and Matilda would also undoubtedly have attended the weekly *soirées musicales* held by Baillot and the Bohrer brothers in their respective homes in the rue Buffault and the rue d'Artois, if these had begun before their departure. And it was probably during this 1818 visit that Viotti sold Janet et Cotelle his Three divertimenti for violoncello with accompaniment for piano, Nos 1, 2 and 3, which, along with his identical set for violin, were dedicated to Jean-Louis Duport, perhaps with foreknowledge of his friend's approaching death. They were published in Paris in 1819, the year Duport died.[70]

Margaret seems to have given fewer parties in London in 1819, but when she did her guests were as usual members of foreign diplomatic corps. For her party of 8 January 1819, she invited the Neapolitan, the French, the Swedish, the Bavarian and the Saxon ambassadors and their wives. As she said in her letter to William of 10 January, all her entertaining was very expensive and her motive for keeping it up was solely to further William and George's interests.[71] As usual there was music, although not many professors. Margaret reported that Lady Flint 'sang her own compositions' accompanied by the French tenor Pierre Begrez, and Matilda played the piano accompanied by Robberechts.[72]

Another description of a private concert, at which 'Amico played beautifully', seems to date from the Philharmonic season of 1819. Margaret writes that Viotti 'was accompanied by his pupil, [Charles] Guinemer, Col. West,[73] and [Richard] Ashley', and that he was 'quite delightful, & in high good humour all the evening.'[74] Guynemer would play at the Philharmonic concerts of 25 February, 11 March, 29 April and 27 May 1822. The other pupils whom Viotti inherited from Baillot, Fémy and Robberechts, also played at the Philharmonic concerts, Fémy in 1814, 1816 and 1818, and Robberechts in 1819, when he performed a Viotti concertante for two violins with Mori. Fémy also played with Mori. Violist Richard Ashley performed in Philharmonic concerts in 1818 and 1819.

Yet another party Margaret gave during the London season of 1819 for about 30 persons included ten diplomats, among them the Baron Armand de Séguier, the French consul general who was to render an important service to Margaret in 1827 at the time of one of her Paris court cases. This party, Margaret wrote in an undated

[70] Both sets of divertimenti were listed in the *Annales de la musique pour l'an 1820*, under the heading 'Répertoire de la musique vocale et instrumentale publié en 1819', p. 161.

[71] MC to WBC, 10 January 1819, PHM 94/143/1 – 17/41.

[72] MC to WBC, 8 January 1819, PHM 94/143/1 – 17/40.

[73] Probably the younger brother of John Richard West, 4th Earl Delawarr.

[74] MC to WBC, c.April 1819, PHM 94/143/1 – 17/57 (incomplete).

letter to William, was also 'rich in poets': Samuel Rogers, Thomas 'Anacreon' Moore, Henry Luttrell and William Spencer. 'The music', Margaret wrote, 'which was to be instrumental by agreement, was very fine, – some Quintetts of Bocherini's, – a Duett between Amico & Robberecht, – a Trio by Amico.'[75] This tiny undated scrap of a longer letter has been separated from its beginning, but can be precisely dated from an entry in Thomas Moore's *Journal* concerning the same party. His entry for Tuesday, 8 June 1819 reads: 'we went in the evening to Mrs Chinnery's, where I heard Viotti, Ashley &c play a beautiful Quintett of Boccherini's, full of sweet melody. The Demoiselles Liker [Lihu] sung too.'[76]

One potentially useful French diplomat friend in London, the Baron Edouard Decazes, was the cousin of Elie Decazes, statesman and favourite of Louis XVIII, who had risen to power in the French Government at the end of 1818, following the resignation of the Duc de Richelieu and the entire French cabinet. On the first day of 1819 Margaret wrote to William with news of the demise of the extreme right wing royalist element of the French government. The Ultras, she proclaimed, 'are all beaten, & the Cousin of a man who sat with me for an hour & a half yesterday, is now the most powerful minister in Europe! – I must write directly to compliment young E[douard] de Calze'.[77] As Margaret had said before, she was always on the lookout for connections who might further her family's and Viotti's interests. With her unerring nose for scenting out men at the pinnacle of power, she unashamedly cultivated those who were likely to be best able to do so.

To her connections with the new French Government Margaret was able to add an old friend of Viotti: 'M. Dessolles is an old friend of Amico's you know, – so that upon the whole I do not think we shall have lost ground at head quarters.'[78] Two weeks later she wrote: 'The Marquis de Dessoles has written a *very kind* answer to Amico's complimentary letter to him, – *very very* kind!'[79] The Marquis Dessolle, that same music *amateur* who was a friend to the Conservatoire professors, who frequently received them in his home, and who, during his command of a division of the French reserve army in Hanover in 1803, had invited Lamare to lodge and make music with him in Osnabruck,[80] having gone over to the Bourbons in 1814, was now minister for foreign affairs, and nominally president of the new 1819 Government.

Margaret's reference to their knowing the key players at 'head quarters' in France had some bearing on what was to become Viotti's next career move. With his wine business insolvent, Viotti needed a new direction to his life. Knowing influential men in the new French Government, he was able to ask for favours. He decided to apply for the directorship of the Paris Opéra.

---

[75] MC to WBC, [8 June 1819], PHM 94/143/1 – 17/56 (incomplete).

[76] Moore, *Journal*, vol. 1, p. 185.

[77] MC to WBC, 1 January 1819, PHM 94/143/1 – 17/38.

[78] MC to WBC, 4 January 1819, PHM 94/143/1 – 17/39.

[79] MC to WBC, 19 January 1819, PHM 94/143/1 – 17/43.

[80] Rode and Lamare to Baillot, 8 August 1803, PHM E.A. and V.I. Crome collection, A8213.

CHAPTER 16

# Paris, 1819–1820

On 1 January 1820 a five-page report on Viotti's appointment to the position of director of the Paris Opéra was published in the influential German music journal the *Allgemeine musikalsiche Zeitung*. It begins:

> From Paris, beginning of December 1819.
> The most important event of the past month in the world of good music has incontestably been the appointment of Mr Viotti as director of the *Grand Opéra*. There has been so much controversy surrounding it, and detractors have made such contradictory comments and have at times spread so many false rumours in the press, that I believe that I can render the readers of this music journal no better service than to give the following report on the matter, gleaned from authentic sources.[1]

The controversy surrounding the appointment of a new director for the Paris Opera centred on whether this person should be from inside or outside the French opera world, and the above article was strongly in favour of the latter. In the view of the writer the reason Viotti was appointed to this post was that the French authorities correctly decided to eschew the appointment of a candidate from within the ranks of the stage composers, among whom were Cherubini, Spontini, Berton and Plantade. By virtue of their profession, the writer maintains, these men would not have been unbiased in their selection of operas. Viotti, on the other hand, can lay claim to the post for several reasons. Although he has lived mostly in England, he has retained both professional and personal ties with France, firstly through his compositions, which continue to be published in Paris, and secondly through his brother, who is is a decorated French army colonel and a judge advocate in the highest military court. The writer also applauds Viotti's alleged intention of seeking new composers and singers from abroad, especially from Germany. The last two pages of the report are devoted to the conflict between Viotti and Spontini, with a strong bias in favour of Viotti, over the completion of Spontini's opera

---

[1] 'Aus Paris, zu Anfange Dezember 1819. Das wichtigste Ereigniss in der hiesigen musikalischen Welt des vorigen Monats ist unstreitig die Anstellung des Hrn. Viotti als Direktor der grossen Oper gewesen. Es ist darüber so verschiedenartig geurteilt worden und beeinträchtige Personen haben bey dieser Gelegenheit so widersprechende und mitunter auch falsche Gerüchte im Publikum verbreitet, dass ich glaube, den Lesern der musikalischen Zeitung keinen unangenehmen Dienst zu erweisen, wenn ich ihnen über den in Frage stehenden Gegenstand folgende, aus authentischen Quellen geschöpfte Nachrichten gebe' (*AMZ*, 1 January 1820, col. 3).

*Olympie*, which was due to be premiered on 15 December, but which was not ready until the 22nd.[2]

The conflict surrounding Viotti's appointment to the directorship of the Paris Opéra continued into the beginning of the twentieth century, with a highly critical article by French musicologist Lionel de La Laurencie entitled 'Les Débuts de Viotti comme directeur de l'Opéra en 1819' (The beginnings of Viotti's directorship of the Opéra in 1819).[3] It paints a very unflattering portrait of Viotti as a grasping entrepreneur, an authoritarian director and a disloyal friend. The Chinnery correspondence during this period of Viotti's life gives a more complete picture of Viotti's motives and aspirations. Although the letters that Viotti writes to the Chinnerys during his tenure of the directorship do not discuss in detail his functions at the Opéra owing to his reluctance to burden his friends with his professional problems, those written after this two-year period do throw some light on the matter.

Through a reading of the Chinnery letters both of the above articles on Viotti's appointment as director of the Paris Opéra can be shown to be faulty: the German writer in his assertion that Viotti did not seek the appointment, and La Laurencie in his assessment of Viotti's character. There is no doubt that Viotti did seek the position. The reason was the failure of his wine business in 1818. Margaret had earlier injected a sum of £2,600[4] into the business, and the desire to repay this debt was his top priority, and clearly the principal reason for his turning his sights towards the Paris post. He also needed a regular income to be able to contribute to household expenses, which he shared with Margaret. Having decided upon this course of action, he set about achieving his goal with his characteristic determination and energy.

The person to whom Viotti made his application was the minister of the Maison du Roi, the Comte de Pradel, who was known to George Chinnery[5] and undoubtedly also to Viotti, from his yearly visits to Paris. A letter that the Comte de Pradel sent to Viotti on 2 November 1819 acknowledges receipt of Viotti's own letter in which he offered himself as a candidate to take the place of Louis-Luc Loiseau de Persuis,[6] who had held the post from 1817 to 1819, and who was due to retire at the end of the year. It was public knowledge that Persuis's health had been deteriorating since the beginning of the previous summer, but it is probable that Viotti had begun to lay the groundwork for his application long before that date. Pradel approved Viotti's appointment, and on 13 November wrote of his decision to the Baron de La Ferté, superintendant of the king's *Menus-Plaisirs*.[7]

---

[2] *AMZ*, 1 January 1820, cols 3–12.

[3] La Laurencie (1924), pp. 110–22.

[4] See MC to WBC, 5 February 1821, PHM 94/143/1 – 17/51.

[5] See Comte de Pradel to GRC, 6 November 1816, Fisher 2000 – 22/24.

[6] Cited in La Laurencie (1924), pp. 113–14.

[7] *Ibid.*, p. 115. This term referred to all royal entertainments (including music), which had been administered since 1547 by a special ministry. The *QMMR* (1824, vol. 6, no. 24, p. 528), took umbrage at the fact that music was lumped in the same category as the royal hunt, writing that it was 'offensive [...] to the professors of [this] liberal art, who consider

Viotti was officially appointed 'directeur de la scène et du personnel des artistes' (stage and artistic director) of the Opéra, or more correctly the Académie royale de musique,[8] on 30 October 1819, to take up his duties on 1 January 1820. This was a provisional appointment to enable Persuis to introduce Viotti gradually to his duties. As it transpired, Persuis died on 21 December, and Viotti took over from that date. The appointment gave him an annual salary of 12,000 francs and an accommodation allowance of 3,000.[9] Luigi Cherubini had indeed been a contender for the same position and there is evidence that Viotti, in a letter to Cherubini denying knowledge of how he came to be appointed to the position, was less than honest with his friend. Viotti was clearly embarrassed at his triumph over the offended Cherubini, writing 'I cannot help feeling extremely troubled at having been the rival of a friend whom I love, of a friend whose genius I have always respected and admired, and of someone whom I shall always love, whatever may be the changes which may operate in his heart',[10] and did his best to make amends by dedicating a 'Duet' for solo violin to him (WV:23). The autograph manuscript is headed: 'Duetto a un Violino Solo composto da G.B. Viotti, per il suo amico Cherubini' and finishes: 'This production has merit only in the fact that it pays homage to a friend of 37 years, who will accept it in the spirit in which it is offered.' It is dated Paris, 15 March 1821.[11]

In an era when position depended on patronage it is understandable that Viotti, when hard-pressed, made use of his old Parisian friends, as well as of the extensive network of contacts that Margaret had so carefully established over the previous few years with French politicians and diplomats. The one consolation for Cherubini was that as superintendant of the royal chapel, he was in a better financial position than Viotti, and by 1822 would have the additional emolument from his directorship of the Paris Conservatoire.

In speaking of Viotti's entrepreneurial endeavours, La Laurencie criticizes him for his ill-will, his acerbic pen, and his general bad humour. It is true that Viotti was intolerant of fools, could be tenacious and obdurate in confrontations, was single-mindedly determined in all his initiatives, and was short-tempered when under duress. But to single out Viotti's 'caractère agressif et autoritaire'[12] while ignoring his praiseworthy qualities is not to do him justice. His sense of humour

---

that the delights of music have a title to be ranked above the boisterous animal gratifications of the chase.'

[8] The two terms are used here synonymously.

[9] La Laurencie (1924), p. 113.

[10] 'je ne puis m'empêcher d'éprouver une peine extrême d'avoir été le concurrent d'un ami que j'aime, d'un ami dont j'ai toujours respecté et apprécié le génie et d'un être que je ne cesserai d'aimer, tels que soyent les changements qui peuvent s'opérer dans son cœur' (GBV to Cherubini, 5 November 1819, cited in Pougin, p. 92).

[11] 'Cette production n'a de merite que dans l'hommage que j'en fais a un Ami de 37 ans, qui l'acceptera d'aussi bon cœur que je la lui offre.' The manuscript was advertised for sale (price US $2,000) by music dealer Oscar Shapiro of Washington in his 1979 catalogue no. 14 entitled 'The Violin Family'.

[12] La Laurencie (1924), p. 118.

was sparkling, and his good nature and obligingness were remarked upon by many different witnesses, including his fellow musicians. His most outstanding quality – the very one that La Laurencie implies he lacks – is evident in nearly every one of his letters in the CFP collection. It was his absolute loyalty and unstinting generosity towards his friends.

The role of theatre impresario inevitably involved stress. It was not a situation for a weakening 64-year-old. As Viotti himself confided to a friend, the appointment, 'although an honour, upsets my 27-year tranquillity within the bosom of the best family in all of England.'[13] Since 1817 the Académie royale de musique had comprised two opera companies at two different theatres: the Italian comic opera, usually referred to by contemporaries as the Théâtre-Italien, in the rue Favart, and the *grand opéra*, usually referred to as the French opera, in the rue de Richelieu, where *opera seria* was performed. The strict hierarchical nature of the administration of the Opéra during the Restoration meant that 'its director was hardly more than a puppet cleverly manipulated by the minister or the sovereign himself'.[14]

As Viotti had been warned in 1789, 'c'est une bien grande machine que l'Opéra' (the Opéra is a huge machine).[15] In 1831 there would be more than 80 musicians, 70 members of the chorus, 80 walk-ons, about 100 dancers, and 60-odd stage-hands.[16] There do not appear to have been many fewer in 1819. It was not an easy task to balance finances – the *grand opéra* was the most expensive to run of all the Paris theatre companies – fulfil the wishes of the king's minister, appease difficult prima donnas and at the same time please the public. It was rare to find, either in England or in France, a successful and popular theatre impresario, and none seems to have found the task easy or escaped criticism. It was as a result of Madame Catalani's incompetent three-year directorship of the Théâtre-Italien that this theatre had passed to the control of the Académie royale de musique in 1817.

When Viotti applied for the directorship of the Opéra, Margaret had little reason to remain in England, and decided to make France her principal abode. As early as January 1819 there were signs that Margaret and Viotti were intending to establish a home in France, which leads to the assumption that Viotti had begun negotiations with the king's minister, or with some other highly placed member of the Government, during his 1818 sojourn in Paris or shortly after. In her letter to William of 21 January 1819 Margaret wrote that she had asked her diplomat friend Langsdorff, who was leaving on the morrow for France, to retrieve from Le Veux at Calais all her effects that had been sent from Dover, and deliver them to Madame de Rayneval in Paris.[17]

---

[13] 'tout en m'honorant, bouleverse ma tranquillité de 27. ans au sein de la meilleure famille de toute l'Angleterre' (GBV to [Jacques Le Veux], 8 January 1820, NYPL *MNY-Viotti).

[14] 'son directeur n'est guère qu'une marionnette savamment manipulée par le ministre ou le souverain lui-même' (P. Barbier (1987), *La Vie quotidienne à l'Opéra au temps de Rossini et de Balzac, Paris 1800–1850*, Hachette, Paris, p. 53).

[15] 'Mémoire au roi', Paris, 1789, cited in La Laurencie (1924), p. 111.

[16] Barbier, *La Vie quotidienne à l'Opéra*, p. 50.

[17] MC to WBC, 21 January 1819, PHM 94/143/1 – 17/44.

The other indication that Viotti and Margaret intended to settle in France was Margaret's purchase of a property at Châtillon, then a tiny village six miles south of Paris in the fertile horticultural area of Montrouge. The date of purchase of this elegant domain with a chapel and substantial orchards is unclear, but a letter from Margaret to William reveals that in April 1819, a month before their departure for France, she had set aside a sum of money for the purchase of a property – originally intended to be at Louveciennes, near the home of her friend Madame Vigée-Lebrun.[18]

A letter from Viotti's brother André to the 'incomparable amica' (Margaret Chinnery) dated June 1819 shows that he and another friend, M. de Lausac, had been given the task of finding a suitable country house for Margaret and Viotti:

> Mr Lausac followed your instructions and has located a charming house which would fulfil all your desires, and even more. It is situated in one of the most beautiful regions on the outskirts of Paris. It is situated in the promised land, or to put it better, in a terrestial paradise on the banks of the European Jordan, at *Chennevières*[?], in a word, in the land of the rudd [freshwater fish].
> Now all that remains, according to the last [letter] of my dear brother, is to find a temporary pied-à-terre so that you can breathe the pure air of beautiful, seductive France.[19]

At the end of the letter André mentions a cherished portrait that is 'enveloppé d'un mystère impénetrable' (shrouded in deep mystery) and a bust which is rumoured to be a chef-d'œuvre. Both clearly apply to Viotti. But he gives no further particulars. The bust is mentioned again by Viotti in 1822 and by George in 1821: 'Nothing could possibly gratify me more than to hear that the long expected bust of Amico both as a likeness & a work of art pleases you in all respects, for upon such a point you were not easily to be satisfied.'[20] George wishes to know the sculptor's name. Miel wrote of a bust of Viotti executed in Paris by the sculptor Jean-Jacques Flatters,[21] who also made a bust of Haydn. In 1885 a plaster bust of Viotti measuring two feet seven inches high and one foot ten inches wide was in the possession of Algernon Greene,[22] but its whereabouts today is not known.

The property mentioned in the above letter was not the one that Margaret ended up purchasing at Châtillon, since Châtillon is not situated on a river. But the Châtillon property does appear to have been purchased in 1819, judging by Viotti's

---

[18] MC to WBC, 19 April 1819, PHM 94/143/1 – 17/47.

[19] 'M.[r] Lausac a agi en conséquence, et il a pointé une maison charmante qui remplirait tous vos vœux même au dela, elle est située dans une des plus belles Régions de la Banlieue de Paris, elle se trouve dans la terre promise, ou pour mieux dire dans le paradis terrestre, aux bords du jourdain européen, a *chennevieres*[?] enfin, dans le pays des Rosses. Reste maintenant, conformement à la dernière de mon cher frère, trouver un pied à terre provisoire pour y respirer l'air pur de la Belle et séduisante france' (André Viotti to MC, 27 June 1819, NYPL JOB 97-52, item 41).

[20] GRC to MC, 21 March 1821, Fisher 2000 – 7/10, and see below, pp. 252–3.

[21] Michaud, vol. 43, p. 589n.

[22] Algernon Greene to Edward Heron-Allen, March 1885, Viotti Papers, RCM.

remark in his 1819 letter to Cherubini that he had been called from Châtillon to take up his appointment at the Opéra.[23] A temporary residence in Paris was found at 38 rue Basse-du-Rempart, and then, after Margaret's return to England for the winter, at 46 rue Neuve-des-Mathurins. It appears that Viotti may have lodged with friends, as the first was the address of a violinist of the Théâtre-Italien (Godefroy), and the second perhaps that of his old friend Maret.[24]

The village of Châtillon was situated on a rise with magnificent sweeping views over the villages of Bagneux, Montrouge, the city of Paris and the river Seine. George Chinnery, who had just completed a grand tour of the Continent with his patron George Canning, described it in his travel journal:

> Just returned from Chatillon sous Bagneux distant about two leagues from Paris, where my mother has purchased a country residence, & where I joined her on Saturday as soon as M[r] C[anning] had settled himself in the Hotel de Bristol. At Chatillon Blucher had his head quarters in the year 1814, and the home which now belongs to us was formerly the property of the Comtesse du Tessé Grande Ecuyere de la Reine in the time of Louis XVI. The view which it commands of Paris is most extensive, & as a habitation it is as delightful a Villa as can anywhere be seen.[25]

In the nineteenth century the Montrouge region was famous for its orchards. The Châtillon property had fruit trees, grape vines and copious crops that were sent to market for extra income. For Viotti and the Chinnerys Châtillon was a second Gillwell, and Viotti and Margaret's French friends referred to her as the 'chatelaine of Châtillon'. Madame Vigée-Lebrun had her own room there.

Margaret was well supplied with servants at Châtillon, and carried on her entertaining, receiving a cosmopolitan mix of diplomats, French statesmen, musicians and personal friends and family for dinners and music just as she had done at Gillwell. It was now Viotti who commuted each weekend from Paris, as William had commuted to Gillwell from London, and Margaret went periodically to Paris, just as she had gone to London in the old days to hear an opera or attend a play. William's visits, on the other hand, were now restricted to a short summer/autumn vacation and to assisting with those periods of great upheaval, the bi-annual moves. Idyllic though it was in spring, summer and autumn, their little château was practically uninhabitable in winter owing to heating and water problems, and Margaret spent the winters in London.

One of Margaret's English friends who attended the Paris Opéra in September 1819, before Viotti took over the reins, was Lady Dashwood King. The latter wrote

---

[23] GBV to Luigi Cherubini, 5 November 1819, cited in Pougin, p. 92.

[24] The first address was on a letter from Lady Dashwood King to MC, 24 September 1819, Fisher 2000 – 5/28. The street no longer exists. It was absorbed by the boulevard de Bonne-Nouvelle. The 1819 address given for Viotti in the *Annales de la musique pour l'an 1820* (p. 314), 'passage du Cendrier, 38', is the same one. The entrance was probably in the old covered *passage* near where it joined the boulevard. The second address was on two letters: GBV to [Le Veux], 8 January 1820, NYPL *MNY-Viotti, and GRC to GBV, 1 September 1820, PHM 94/143/1 – 28/23. For the owner of the last property, see p. 252.

[25] GRC's Travel Journal, vol. 3, pp. 166–7.

to Margaret on her return to London, giving her an account of a performance in which Madame Fodor had been poorly received by the French audience. Joséphine Fodor-Mainvielle had starred with Naldi in the first London performance of Rossini's *Barbiere di Siviglia*, and had sung at the Philharmonic concerts of 1816 and 1817, also with Naldi. At her debut in London in 1816, her voice was described by the *Morning Post* as 'rich, harmonious, and, without possessing extraordinary power, of a considerable compass. Her taste is chaste, her execution correct, easy and elegant, and her science evidently profound.'[26] 'Chaste' was also the epithet given to her singing style by Lady Dashwood King. Regretting that Madame Fodor was no longer in England where she was appreciated, she commented to Margaret: 'She sings too chaste to please the french. Never shall I forget the screams of the three first female Singers at the french Opera [...] squalling away in the most disgusting manner – I would have liked to go to the opera with Mr Viotti one night to see the effect it would have produced upon him.'[27] The Paris correspondents for the *Allgemeine musikalische Zeitung* had been complaining for years of the screeching of the French singers, one saying that each tried to sing more loudly than the other, another begging for mercy for the ears of the audience.[28] Viotti was unable to procure better singers owing to budget constraints.[29]

Viotti needed to re-employ Joséphine Fodor in 1820, or face the prospect of having only one principal female singer, Madame Ronzi-De Begnis, who was notoriously prone to indisposition, both real and imagined. After the piteous humiliation that Madame Fodor had endured in 1819, he must have used all his considerable skills as a negotiator to keep her. Lady Dashwood King tells Margaret that after her performance, when she went to shake hands with her, 'she seemed ready to cry'.[30] Nevertheless Viotti was able to capitalize on his friendship with the singer to negotiate a contract with her for 25,000 francs for the following year, plus a guaranteed 15,000 francs from benefits. Madame Fodor was apparently happy with the contract, and Viotti remained on good terms with the Fodor-Mainvielle couple, as shown by the fact that in October 1820 Mainvielle carried a personal letter from Viotti to William Chinnery in Le Havre.[31]

Another Chinnery friend who arrived in Paris in September 1819 was the melomaniac poet Thomas Moore who, like William Chinnery, had fled to France to escape his creditors. Having first met Viotti at Gillwell, and having been struck by his good nature, Moore wrote again of his pleasure in meeting Viotti, when he noted in his journal on 23 April 1820: 'Viotti, too, was there, whom I always like to meet.'[32] Moore's song 'Love thee dearest' was based on the second movement

[26] Cited in *New Grove 1*, vol. 6, p. 682.
[27] Lady Dashwood King to MC, 24 September 1819, Fisher 2000 – 5/28.
[28] *AMZ*, 21 June 1809, col. 605, and 4 March 1818, col. 184.
[29] GBV to La Ferté, 26 November 1819, cited in La Laurencie (1924), p. 115.
[30] Lady Dashwood King to MC, 24 September 1819, Fisher 2000 – 5/28.
[31] GBV to WBC, 19 October 1820, PHM 94/143/1 – 14/35.
[32] Moore, *Journal*, vol. 1, p. 313.

of Viotti's Concerto No. 5.[33] According to Moore's *Journal*, he went to the opera five times in ten days after his arrival in France.

When Viotti took over the directorship of the Opéra, rehearsals for Spontini's new opera *Olympie* were already in progress, but were not running to schedule. Various illnesses and other impediments caused many of the female members of the cast (Mme Albert, Mlle Grassari, Mlle Armand and Mlle Paulin) to offer excuses as to why they were unable to perform, putting Viotti in an untenable position and the opera out of production for a total of two months. One had a sore throat and asked for more time to learn her part, another had just been bled and was too weak to rehearse, the third refused to perform in more than the first act, and the fourth blamed constant visits to the copyist for her omission to learn her part in time.[34] It was no wonder that Viotti complained of them, and that his friend the Comtesse de Boigne, in writing to Margaret Chinnery of a visit Viotti had paid her mother in December 1821, said that he seemed happy to have escaped the whims and caprices of 'ces demoiselles de l'Opéra.'[35] Viotti himself said that he was 'wearied, beset and disgusted by the annoyances inflicted on him by these ladies.'[36]

The acrimonious exchange of letters between the director and the composer over the completion of Spontini's *Olympie* marked the beginning of what was to be a continuous stream of problems that lasted throughout Viotti's tenure of the post. If the correspondence cited by La Laurencie proves that Viotti possessed an aggressive and dictatorial nature, as La Laurencie claims it does, then it must also prove Spontini's equally belligerent and obstinate character. Even La Laurencie admits that Spontini was 'violent et autoritaire', and that he generated enormous copying costs, yet still seems to lay the blame for the argument with Viotti.[37] Copying costs of musical scores were borne by the Opéra administration and could cause an enormous budget blow-out if the score was reworked too often. The perfecting of the score of Spontini's opera *La Vestale*, for example, lasted a year and cost 10,000 francs in copyists' fees. Moreover Viotti appears to have had the opera-goers on his side in the argument with Spontini. The latter had been working on *Olympie* for four full years, and the public, tired of the constant procrastinating, was more than happy to see Viotti take a firm hand in the matter.[38]

The problems recognized today as being inherent in Spontini's *Olympie* tally with Thomas Moore's opinion of the opera, which he saw in rehearsal on 18 December 1819, four days before its premiere. In his journal of that date he writes: 'Went to seek for Viotti in order to get permission to attend the Rehearsal of Spontini's new Opera Olympie this evening – met him & he promised to admit Lord G., myself & Fitzgerald […] the rehearsal very singular – the stage lighted

[33] See *Thematic Catalogue*, p. 146.

[34] Barbier, *La Vie quotidienne à l'Opéra*, p. 71.

[35] Comtesse de Boigne to MC, 13 December 1821, Fisher 2000 – 4/23. The letter is signed with her trademark signature 'Osmond de Boigne'.

[36] 'las, obsédé et dégoûté des tracasseries que j'éprouve de la part de ces dames' (A. Soubies, *Théâtre-Italien de 1801 à 1913*, p. 17, cited in La Laurencie (1924), p. 121).

[37] La Laurencie (1924), pp. 117–18.

[38] *AMZ*, 1 January 1820, cols 9–10.

up, all the scenery in form & the actors in their every-day clothes – the music [was] too full of notes & overloaded harmonies, & the way it was squalled & mewled out by Mades Branchia [sic] & Albert detestable.'[39] With this last criticism Moore echoes the opinion of his compatriot Lady Dashwood King, although when he heard the finished opera performed on 23 December 1819 he made no mention of the quality of the singing, restricting his comments to the stronger points of the production, and writing, 'nothing can be more poetically imagined than the scenery & ballet of this Opera.'[40]

Margaret and Matilda returned to London at the end of November 1819. Alone in his empty apartments Viotti was disconsolate. He wrote to William, now back in Le Havre having accompanied the ladies to Calais, 'My God, what a feeling of abandonment, what a desert all this is! But we shall not speak of it, however, for once I get started on the subject there will be no stopping me.'[41] George Chinnery's travel journal shows that he too was in Paris with his patron George Canning for a very brief period (15–19 November) in 1819, but the time he could spend with Viotti and his family would have been disappointingly brief. However he did bring with him some violin strings from Naples, much to Viotti's delight. With the simultaneous departure of Margaret, William, George and Matilda, Viotti found himself totally alone for the first time in 27 years. His anxieties were compounded by the knowledge that a variety of problems awaited Margaret in London, the most pressing of which would be her attempt, through her lawyer, to recover the money she had lent to Viotti's wine business.

The winding-up of Viotti's affairs with his former business partner Charles Smith called him back to London in early 1820, and he departed France on 15 January,[42] arriving in London a couple of weeks before the death of George III. A copy of a letter from Viotti to his lawyer and power of attorney Henry Dance, whose chambers were at 33 Lincoln's Inn Fields, explains that the partnership was dissolved in the winter of 1819, that Smith was to repay the capital that Viotti had contributed to the firm in three instalments, and that a promissory note for the sum of £500 was to be payable on demand.[43]

Margaret wrote to William on 1 February 1820 that 'Amico […] is gone to have his first conversation with C.S. this morning, upon the arrangement of their affairs. By their articles of association it is stipulated that payment is to be made at the periods of *six*, *twelve* & eighteen months, – so as to be compleated by that period.' In the same letter she complained that the time restraints of such a short stay made arranging parties difficult: 'However we have now fixed a dinner for next Saturday, & another for the Wednesday following. I shall also try to give two

---

[39] Moore, *Journal*, vol 1, p. 268.

[40] *Ibid.*, p. 270.

[41] 'Mon Dieu quel abandon, quel desert que tout ceci! Ne disons rien cependant, si une fois j'attaque ce chapitre, je n'en finirai plus' (GBV to WBC, 21 November 1819, PHM 94/143/1 – 14/34).

[42] See GBV to [Jacques Le Veux], 8 January 1820, NYPL *MNY-Viotti.

[43] GBV to Henry Dance (copy), 20 December 1820, PHM 94/143/1 – 28/24.

or three music parties; but really time flies so fast when a period is fixed, that one can hardly do any thing.'[44]

During his two-month stay in London Viotti attended the first Philharmonic concert of the season on 6 March 1820. The gifted, supremely confident German violinist Louis Spohr had just arrived in London at the invitation of the Society, and his demands for the programming and conducting of his concerts succeeded in bending the Society's rules and altering the future course of the Philharmonic Society. He wrote in his *Autobiography* of the pieces he performed:

> I therefore at the first Philharmonic concert, came forward with my cantabile scena, and in the second part with a solo quartet in E major, and met with great and general applause [...] As a violinist [it afforded me an especial gratification] that old *Viotti*, who had always been my pattern, and was to have been my instructor in my youth, was among the auditory and spoke to me in great praise of my play.[45]

Viotti had only been away for four weeks when the assassination of the Duc de Berry occurred outside the Paris Opéra (rue de Richelieu) on 13 February 1820. The nephew of Louis XVIII had accompanied his pregnant wife to her carriage during the performance, and was stabbed by Louis-Pierre Louvel on re-entering the opera house, dying of his wounds in the antichamber at dawn. A contemporary account of the events of that night at the Opéra shows that André Viotti represented his brother in the latter's absence: 'The brother of M. Wiotti [sic] administrator, [who was] away on personal business in England, paced the floor between the antichamber and the office doors.'[46]

As the Duc de Berry was an heir to the throne of France, his assassination had serious ramifications for the French Government, and created immense upheaval for the administration of the Opéra. The building was immediately condemned, its occupants turned out, and all theatres in Paris were closed for a period of ten days' mourning. There would be a two-month delay before another opera could be staged. The *grand opéra* was moved to the much smaller Salle Favart for 16 months until a new opera theatre could be built. This unforeseeable catastrophe compounded Viotti's problems. It can only be imagined that Viotti rushed back to Paris as soon as he was able – which was not until one month after the event – and that his absence on the occasion placed him in a severely embarrassing position vis-à-vis the king's minister.

The date of Viotti's return to Paris is given in his letter to Baillot, which is dated 16 March 1821 [*recte* 1820?]. The letter is addressed to 'rue Buffot N° 6', an apartment which Baillot left on 1 April 1820. Viotti writes: 'Here I am back again.

---

[44] MC to WBC, 1 February 1820, PHM 94/143/1 – 17/48.

[45] Spohr's *Autobiography*, vol. 2, p. 77. This programme does not correspond to the published one (see Foster, *The Philharmonic Society*, p. 44).

[46] 'Le frère de M. Wiotti, administrateur et absent pour ses propres affaires en Angleterre, s'est promené de long en large depuis l'antichambre jusqu'à la porte de l'administration' (*Récit historique des événements qui se sont passés dans l'administration de l'Opéra la nuit du 13 février 1820*, Paris, 1820, cited in Pougin, p. 95).

I arrived yesterday, [filled] with a great desire to embrace you; all the greater since I was perforce deprived of seeing you last autumn and winter.'[47] The date of the letter could not have been 1821, since Viotti did not leave Paris in early 1821, as shown by his correspondence with Margaret. Moreover he was not deprived of Baillot's company in the winter of 1820–21, as this was the time of Spohr's visit to Paris, when there were convivial meetings with other violinists. It was in the autumn and winter of 1819–20, when Viotti was undergoing his tumultuous introduction to the directorship of the Opéra, that he would have felt most isolated. Yearning to see his friend again, Viotti asks Baillot to call at the Opéra the following afternoon.

By April 1820 Margaret too had returned to France, and soon after was established at Châtillon. A letter dated July [1820] to Viotti from the Comte de St Sauveur, who owned a property nearby, and who kept Margaret supplied with coaches, horses and footmen, seems to contain an offer to provide a carriage,[48] an essential appurtenance to enable Margaret to attend the opera and other entertainments in the capital. One of the performers whom Margaret particularly wished to hear was Caroline Naldi, who made her controversial Paris debut at the Théâtre-Italien in Mozart's *Cosi fan tutte* in September 1820.[49] Young Caroline Naldi had sung frequently with her father at Margaret Chinnery's musical parties, and it may have been on account of Viotti's friendship with her father, rather than for her talent, that he had employed her.

Although the nineteenth-century musicologist Félix Clément counts Caroline Naldi among the 'brilliant constellation of singers'[50] who performed at the Théâtre-Italien in the post-Restoration years, the anonymous author of an advice-giving pamphlet published at the beginning of 1821 entitled *Disinterested observations on the administration of the Royal Italian Theatre, addressed to M. Viotti*[51] was scathing in his criticism: 'Mademoiselle Naldi, who has allegedly just been engaged [...] for 18,000 fr, has not sufficient voice to fill the tiny space of the Théâtre-Italien; her intonation is not sure; her pronunciation is quite English, and her acting ability nil.'[52] Margaret, who noted the review of the performance in the

---

[47] 'me voici de retour depuis hier avec une envie éxtreme de vous embrasser; d'autant plus grande que j'ai été forcément privé de vous voir l'Automne et l'hiver dernier' (GBV to Baillot, 16 March 1821 [*recte* 1820?], NYPL *MNY-Viotti). For Baillot's different addresses, see François-Sappey, p. 149.

[48] St Sauveur to GBV, 3 July [1820], NYPL JOB 97-52, item 43. See also GRC to MC, 20 May 1824, PHM 94/143/1 – 12/23.

[49] MC to WBC, 24 September 1820, PHM 94/143/1 – 17/49.

[50] 'brillante pléiade de cantatrices', *Histoire de la musique depuis les temps anciens jusqu'à nos jours* (1885), Hachette, Paris, p. 486.

[51] *Observations désintéressées sur l'administration du Théâtre Royal Italien, adressées à M. Viotti*, Boucher, Paris, 6 February 1821, transcribed in Giazotto, pp. 276–85.

[52] 'Mademoiselle Naldi qui vient, dit-on, d'être engagée [...] pour 18.000 fr., n'a point assez de voix pour remplir la très petite enceinte du Théâtre-Italien; ses intonations ne sont pas sûres; sa prononciation est tout anglaise, et son jeu nul' (*Ibid.*, p. 282).

French newspaper the *Drapeau blanc* of 21 September 1820, objected to the choice of opera, writing to William:

> Caroline Naldi's debut was very successful, in spite of their having fixed upon the most disagreeable opera I ever heard in my life,— the *poem detestable*, all the characters odious, and the music heavy. In the first act she was completely overcome by fear,— her voice was without power, and would not obey her efforts,— I trembled, thought she would be judged unfairly,— and certainly the audience seemed disappointed during the Entr'acte. However in the second act, from having had ice put round the outside of her throat, and having swallowed a great deal of iced water, the extreme hoarseness subsided sufficiently to enable her to sing her air *most beautifully*; then the plaudits began, and were loud & universal. They saw she was mistress of her profession, which she really is,— they thought her pretty, graceful in her actions, natural, a good actress; in short they were delighted with her […] She was over-fatigued by constant rehearsals, & has not been able to sing again,— but on Tuesday she will make her second appearance in that frightful opera, which I should like to see committed to the flames.[53]

But the anonymous author of the *Observations* laid the blame for the failure of this opera squarely on the shoulders of Caroline Naldi. '*Cosi fan tutte* failed because of Mlle Naldi's weak voice', he wrote categorically.[54] Another music critic, however, attributed Caroline Naldi's weak beginning to nerves, and like Margaret, thought her performance improved in the second act: 'The debutante is young and pretty. We thought her voice was a little weak, but this young lady was overwrought […] Mademoiselle Naldi sang very well in the second act.'[55]

Another witness to Caroline Naldi's debut in France was the novelist Jane Porter, who wrote to George asking him to thank Viotti for the generous packet of tickets he had sent her.[56] Miss Porter also wrote twice to Viotti in September on the eve of her departure to England, jestingly addressing him as 'faithless Amico' for failing to come to her house for an appointed morning visit. Apparently insensitive to Viotti's time constraints, she had wanted to introduce to him her diplomat brother who wished to be admitted to Mrs Chinnery's 'admired society'. She also wanted him to deliver a letter to Naldi.[57]

Another who made demands on Viotti's limited time was the *amateur* Comte de Lamorlière, who, having already published a violin piece that had been favourably received in private music societies, sent Viotti one of his concertos to be appraised. Viotti having done so, and having made some favourable comments, this persistent (and canny) count wanted permission to quote Viotti's comments 'en facsimile' on the published music, saying that knowing how occupied Viotti

---

[53] MC to WBC, 24 September 1820, PHM 94/143/1 – 17/49.

[54] '*Cosi fan tutte* est tombé par la faiblesse de la voix de Mlle Naldi' (*Observations*, cited in Giazotto, p. 277).

[55] 'La débutante est jeune, jolie; sa voix nous a paru un peu faible, mais cette jeune personne était fort émue [...]. Mademoiselle Naldi a fort bien chanté, au second acte' (*Journal de Paris*, 21 September 1820).

[56] Jane Porter to GRC, [September 1820], Fisher 2000 – 22/65.

[57] Jane Porter to GBV, [19 September, 1820], NYPL JOB 97-52, item 45.

was he would not demand a reply, but would simply take Viotti's silence as assent.[58] The letter was addressed to Viotti at the Hôtel des Iles Britanniques (5 rue de la Paix), which Viotti and the Chinnerys used as a poste restante address. It appears that Lamorlière was a devoted admirer of Viotti, for he composed an elegiac piece entitled *Les Adieux de Viotti* for two violins and basso *ad libitum*,[59] presumably at the end of 1821 when Viotti left the Opéra, although it could have been on the occasion of any one of Viotti's departures from Paris for England.

From Venice on 1 September George Chinnery had written to Viotti at 46 rue Neuve-des-Mathurins, confirming his arrival in Paris with George Canning on 1 October, and asking Viotti to take rooms for his travelling party at the same hotel on the Place Vendôme where they had stayed the previous year.[60] On George's arrival Viotti wrote to him, delighted that he was able to prolong his stay in Paris.[61] In fact George remained for six weeks, as Canning, having been an intimate friend of the former Princess of Wales, was reluctant to return to England while her trial (the trial of Queen Caroline, prosecuted by her husband George IV) was going on. George accompanied Canning on a continuous round of visits, dinners, and theatre-going during the week, but spent each weekend at Châtillon, returning to the Cannings' hotel in Paris on Monday morning to resume his secretarial duties.

In the first week of their stay George and the Canning party went several times to the opera. On 3 October they saw the popular dancer and mime Mademoiselle Bigottini in the ballet *Clari*.[62] This was one of the six new works (all short operas or ballets), that Viotti had succeeded in staging at the Salle Favart in the face of severe space restrictions. On 5 October they attended the Italian opera to hear Rossini's enormously popular *Barbiere*, 'the most perfect performance of the kind ever got up both in regard to the composition of the music, the perfection of the orchestra & the excellence of the vocal performers'.[63] On 9 October George accompanied his mother to a performance of Mozart's *Don Giovanni*, another successful production. He heard it again the following evening with Canning.

In his journal entry of 3 October George described the celebrations for the birth of the Duc de Bordeaux, son of the lately assassinated Duc de Berry. His birth assured the succession of the Bourbon line. A public holiday was declared, there was distribution of bread, meat and wine in the Champs Elysées, as there would be for the young prince's baptism seven months later, and banquets and games took place in every part of the capital:

> In the Evening at 8 O'clock splendid fireworks were let off from the Pont Royal, not equal though I think to our weekly display at Vauxhall, & to conclude the fête couplets appropriate to the occasion were sung at all the theatres: the theatre to which we went

[58] Lamorlière to GBV, 27 November 1820, NYPL JOB 97-52, item 48. See also *Annales de la musique pour l'an 1820*, p. 8.
[59] See Pougin, p. 162, and *Annales de la musique pour l'an 1820*, p. 190.
[60] GRC to GBV, 1 September 1820, PHM 94/143/1 – 28/23.
[61] GBV to GRC, 30 September 1820, NYPL JOB 97-52, item 46.
[62] GRC's Travel Journal, vol. 3, p. 167.
[63] *Ibid.*, p. 169.

> was the Italian Opera, beyond all comparison the best now in Europe, & the piece performed was the Agnese by Paer; the principal characters by Pellegrini, Garcia, & Mad. Fodor.[64]

The custom of composing celebratory couplets to be sung on special occasions had not changed over the last century. Since Madame de Genlis's childhood the tradition had continued, practised by the Chinnerys at special family celebrations, and upheld at private and public occasions right into the nineteenth century. George's comment on the excellence of the Théâtre-Italien concurs with the testimony of the large number of contemporaries who described this theatre as the hub of fashionable Paris. It was the rendez-vous of society's elite, and was especially popular with the foreigners.

On the morning of 8 October Canning and his family paid a visit to Margaret, George, Matilda and Viotti at Châtillon. Also present were André Viotti, Monsieur de Ladébat, Louis-Pierre Norblin, principal cellist of the Opéra orchestra, and retired French statesman, Comte Louis-Nicolas Lemercier. Margaret offered fruit, wine and biscuits, and did her best to encourage conversation:

> Soon afterwards George asked Mr Canning if he should present Amico to him, & when this was done, they both talked together a little, always on the opposite side of the room— Amico begged leave to present his brother, & Mr C entered into conversation with André and made many enquiries of him with regard to the military courts of justice here. At length I proposed a walk in the garden,— they liked both house and garden very much, but M.C. was particularly pleased with the terrace on top of the house.[65]

George's journal entry of the 9 October reads simply: 'M$^{r}$ and M$^{rs}$ C. came in the course of the morn$^{g}$ yesterday to pay my mother a visit, & we had afterwards a party to dinner & music in the Evening.'[66] Margaret was a little taken aback by Canning's reserve, as was Viotti each time he met Canning thereafter, but George put it down to shyness, saying that he usually succeeded in breaking it down by means of frank and open conversation: 'Whenever I see M.C. after a certain interval of time I am struck like Amico with his air embarrassé and his manière boutonnée [buttoned-up manner], but like Amico again I try to get the better of his diffidence by excessive frankness on my part.'[67] On Wednesday 8 November George entered the brief note in his journal: 'My mother & Amico dined with the Cannings – in the Ev$^{g}$ we went to the Opera.'[68] On the same evening in London, 8 November 1820, a Miss Greene (apparently the same who inherited the Chinnery/Viotti papers), played Olivia in a Covent Garden performance of Shakespeare's *Twelfth Night*, arranged for the first time as an opera by Henry

---

[64] *Ibid.*, p. 168.

[65] MC to WBC, 9 October1820, PHM 94/143/1 – 17/50.

[66] GRC's Travel Journal, vol. 3, p. 169.

[67] GRC to MC, 13 March 1821, Fisher 2000 – 7/9.

[68] GRC's Travel Journal, vol. 3, p. 180.

Rowley Bishop. Miss Greene was highly praised for her singing by William Parke.[69]

Viotti's problems with the Opéra administration increased as time went on. The conditions under which he toiled in the aftermath of the assassination of the Duc de Berry were particularly frustrating. This, combined with the constant juggling of his private and public life, surely contributed to his declining health. In November 1820, immediately after Margaret, Matilda and George had departed for England, Viotti scrawled a desperately unhappy note to William, who, having spent the autumn with his wife and Viotti, had now returned to Le Havre: 'How upset I am dear friend, that you have left me! How lonely I am! I can well say that my life is a continuing renewal of ceaseless troubles.'[70]

---

[69] *MM*, vol. 2, pp. 155–6. See also Henry Rowley Bishop to Mary Greene, 3 August and 19 August 1843 (Fisher 2000 – 49/11 and 49/12).

[70] 'Comme je suis faché cher Ami, que vous m'ayez quitté! Comme je suis seul! Je puis bien dire que je passe ma vie dans des peines qui se renouvellent tous les jours' (GBV to WBC, 25 November 1820, PHM 94/143/1 – 14/36).

CHAPTER 17

# Paris, 1821

At the end of 1820 and beginning of 1821 Viotti experienced a succession of personal losses. First it was the death, which Viotti may well have witnessed, on 14 December 1820 of one of his dearest friends, Giuseppe Naldi, killed at the home of another close friend, Manuel Garcia in Paris, when a newly-invented pressure cooker exploded in his face. By the end of 1820 it was also becoming clear that Smith would be unable to fulfil the terms of his promissory note, as a letter from Viotti to his lawyer Henry Dance shows.[1] Margaret spent the three winter months in meetings and discussions with Dance in London in a vain bid to recover some of her own debt. In February 1821 she also endured the painful departure of Matilda, who was to be married in India. Matilda had lived with Margaret and Viotti as a daughter for the past 20 years, and her departure left a vast gap in their lives.

Unable to be at Margaret's side in her legal struggles, Viotti felt both helpless and guilty. To Margaret he tried to appear resolute, but to William he gave way to his true feelings. Alternately resigned to and rebellious against his fate, he wrote that there was no other option than to suffer the blows courageously, resigning oneself to the will of He who directs all. But he was unable to hide his despair over Margaret's misfortunes: 'Oh, the thought of this rends my heart! – I only pray to God that I may live long enough to repair the harm done by that infamous Charles S[mith], and then I shall die happy.'[2] Finally, afraid of alarming his friend, he made a supreme effort to reassure William also, ending his letter: 'I took up my pen in a moment of bad humour, of weakness – but that is not my usual state. Calm yourself, my friend. Generally speaking I am more heroic than I appear to be just at this moment.'[3]

When the date of Margaret's return to France drew near he wrote in great relief: 'But [now] you are leaving the land where you had so much suffering; you are coming back to me. I feel myself being reborn. Oh you will see if I shall not be able to lessen your sorrows and lighten your troubles!'[4] He refrained from

---

[1] GBV to Henry Dance (copy), 20 December 1820, PHM 94/143/1 – 28/24.

[2] 'Oh cette idée me dechire l'ame!— Je ne demande à Dieu que la grace de vivre assez pour réparer le mal de l'infame Charles S__ et puis je fermerai les yeux content' (GBV to WBC, 28 January 1821, NYPL JOB 97-52, item 49).

[3] 'J'ai pris la plume dans un moment de mauvaises dispositions, de faiblesse— mais ce n'est point mon état habituel, tranquillisez vous mon ami, je suis plus Heros en general que je ne le parois dans ce moment ci' (GBV to WBC, 28 January 1821, NYPL JOB 97-52, item 49).

[4] 'Mais vous quittez cette terre ou vous avez tant souffert; vous arrivez auprès de moi, je me sens renaitre. Oh vous verrez si je ne saurai adoucir vos chagrins, alleger vos peines!'

mentioning his own troubles. Public criticism of his administration of the Opéra was growing, and it was only a month since he had received the ten pages of advice from the anonymous author of the *Observations*. Although the latter wished Viotti well, he must nevertheless have added to Viotti's sense of frustration with his long pages of hints and suggestions on repertoire, artists, and fees.

Describing himself with romantic mystique as an *amateur* who always sat in the right hand balcony, this well-meaning dilettante proceeded to dissect the administration of the Théâtre-Italien over the past year in minute detail. He warned that although the Italian opera may be in vogue at the present time, it would not always be so if Viotti did not provide a vigilant and enlightened administration. He noted the role of the Théâtre-Italien in catering to the needs of a large foreign audience who did not appreciate the more learned Conservatoire music, saying that it had 'become the customary topic of conversation in the best company'.[5] Foremost on his list of criticisms were the French singers, whom he thought would be better replaced by properly trained Italian ones. He decried the fact that the Théâtre-Italien was being used as a finishing school for the young and inexperienced pupils of the rue Bergère (the Conservatoire). While sympathetic to the woes of Viotti in regard to the *grand opéra*, he too complained of the 'discordant, tremulous or thundering voices' of the male singers, and the screeching of the females.[6]

Concomitantly, the celebrated German violinist Louis Spohr, who had just made his mark in London, was penning his extremely critical letters from Paris for the *Allgemeine musikalische Zeitung*. Having arrived in Paris at the beginning of December 1820 for two months, he submitted four letters to the German journal dated 15 December 1820–30 January 1821, which he reproduced in his *Autobiography*.[7] In tones that are breathtakingly egotistic, he found fault with every aspect of music in Paris, coming to the curt conclusion that 'the French are not a musical nation'.[8] Like the author of the *Observations* he criticized the voices of the singers, disliked the presentation of older operas that were outmoded, and deplored the dreadful disfigurement of Mozart's masterpiece the *Magic Flute* in its reworking as the *Mystères d'Isis*. Although he did make some allowances for the *grand opéra*'s cramped performing conditions, there was not much that met with his approval in either of the opera companies. He praised Kreutzer's music to *Clari*, but the Parisian ballet in general, he opined, 'may sometimes afford agreeable amusement, until one becomes wearied with the monotony of the mimic movements, and of the yet greater sameness of the dances.'[9]

---

(GBV to MC, 3 March 1821, NYPL JOB 97-52, item 52).

5 'devenu un des sujets de conversation et d'intérêt le plus habituel de la meilleure compagnie' (*Observations*, p. 276).

6 'les voix discordantes, chevrotantes ou tonnantes' (*Observations*, p. 279).

7 Vol. 2, pp. 107–132.

8 Spohr's *Autobiography*, vol. 2, p. 115.

9 *Ibid.*, p. 111.

Many of Spohr's pronouncements were justified. Without exception all foreign visitors to Paris agreed that the French Opéra singers screeched. An anonymous English music critic writing for the contemporary *Quarterly Musical Magazine and Review* noted that the first thing that struck a foreign visitor to the opera was 'the screaming (*criallerie*) of the singers and the noise of the orchestra.'[10] In this last point he was in agreement with Spohr, who also found the Opéra orchestra loud and lacking in cohesion, in spite of the fact that it was composed of very fine individual players. Among them were the two Kreutzers, Baillot's pupils Habeneck and Guérin, and many other Conservatoire graduates.

While in Paris Spohr took part in private concerts, playing before professional musicians, dilettanti and connoisseurs, as well as giving one public concert. He met with many of the Conservatoire professors, including Cherubini, both Kreutzer brothers, Baillot and Baudiot, and it is likely that he found Viotti at more than one of their assemblies. With Margaret in England during the winter months, Viotti undoubtedly took advantage of any free moments to seek out his old violinist friends. Spohr mentions one musical party that was given at Rodolphe Kreutzer's:

> At *Kreutzer*'s, in particular, almost all the first composers and violinists of Paris were present. I gave several of my quartets and quintets, and on the second day my nonet. The composers present expressed themselves to me in very laudatory terms upon the composition, and the violinists upon my play. Of the latter, *Viotti*, both the *Kreutzers*, *Baillot*, *Lafont*, *Habeneck*, *Fontaine*, *Guerin*, and several others whose names are not so well known in Germany, were present.[11]

This musical party is also mentioned by Baillot in a letter to Montbeillard: 'I had the pleasure of hearing [Spohr] at Kreutzer's, and our dear Viotti was present.'[12] Spohr would have had to negotiate with Viotti when, to lessen the financial risk of giving a public concert, which he described as a Herculean task, he hit upon the idea of sharing costs and receipts with the Opéra. His proposal was that the first half of the programme should consist of his own concert, the second of a ballet. This arrangement was satisfactory except for the delay in obtaining permission from the minister,[13] yet another frustation for Viotti, who undoubtedly would have liked to help a fellow violinist, but had no power to act independently of his superiors.

The observations made by Spohr in 1820 show that nothing had changed in the Paris concert scene since Viotti had performed there 38 years ago: the newspaper critics were still as venal, musicians still played pieces calculated to surprise, rather than to exhibit any knowledge of music, audiences still accorded equal acclamation to serious and trivial music, and in the theatres *claqueurs* were paid by the singers

---

[10] 'Sketch of the State of Music in Paris', *QMMR* (1820), vol. 2, no. 8, p. 507.

[11] Spohr's *Autobiography*, vol. 2, p. 113. Kreutzer then lived at no. 17 rue de Provence.

[12] 'J'ai eu le plaisir de l'entendre [Spohr] chez Kreutzer où était venu notre cher Viotti' (Baillot to Montbeillard, 4 January 1821, cited in François-Sappey, p. 185).

[13] Spohr's *Autobiography*, vol. 2, pp. 120–21.

to burst into applause at appropriate moments.[14] Expressing a sentiment that must have been remarkably similar to Viotti's own in 1783, Spohr confessed that when a listener applauded his composition he could not feel gratified, 'since immediately afterwards he bestows the same admiration upon the most trifling things. One blushes to be praised by such connoisseurs.'[15]

Meanwhile Viotti did his best to improve the Théâtre-Italien. The suggestion of the anonymous author of the *Observations* to employ Italian singers appears to have been heeded. On 8 February 1821, just two days after receiving the advice, Viotti apparently wrote to the composer Ferdinand Herold, who was chorus master at the Théâtre-Italien, charging him with a secret mission to Italy to recruit new singers.[16] It was during his stay in Naples that Herold met Rossini, who, according to a letter from Herold to his mother, expressed a burning desire to come to Paris to direct his operas.[17] As a result of Herold's visit Rossini himself wrote to Viotti offering him an adaptation of his oratorio *Mosè*.[18] Rossini had in fact been hoping to direct one of his operas in Paris since two years previously, when, in May 1819, he had been approached by the diplomat Jean-Alexis Artaud de Montor to write music to a libretto by the composer and poet Marc-Antoine Désaugiers. The letter detailing these secret negotiations was addressed to fellow diplomat François-Maximilien de Rayneval, close friend of Viotti and the Chinnerys.[19]

It seems more than a coincidence that this letter from Artaud should have been addressed to Rayneval, whom Viotti had known since 1814 in London, whose company Viotti and Margaret had constantly kept in Paris in 1818, and to whose wife Margaret had sent all her belongings in January 1819, in anticipation of permanent settlement in France. And even more of a coincidence that the letter should have ended up in the hands of Viotti, who endorsed it 'Lettre de Rome à M$^r$ de Rayneval au sujet de Rossini'. It seems therefore fairly certain that the overtures to Rossini had been initiated by Viotti himself, proving that he had been or anticipated being promised the directorship of the Opéra as early as May 1819. In the letter Artaud does not reveal who charged him with the mission, but the fact that he gave Rossini detailed notes about the different voice types of the Paris singers, and that Rossini promised to have his score ready by the following winter, when he hoped to come to Paris to direct the opera, is all information that would have been of great interest to Viotti. As the Viotti/Chinnery correspondence shows, Viotti was in the habit of giving such missions to his diplomat friends. For example in October 1820 he asked the Sardinian envoy Charles de Pralorme, then on his

---

[14] See also *QMMR* (1820), vol. 2, no. 8, p. 509.

[15] Spohr's *Autobiography*, vol. 2, p. 114.

[16] Privately owned letter cited in Pougin, p. 100.

[17] Ferdinand Herold to Mme Herold, 10 April 1821, cited in Pougin, p. 101.

[18] Rossini to GBV, [1821], cited in Pougin, pp. 101–2.

[19] Artaud de Montor to Rayneval, 29 May 1819, NYPL JOB 97-52, item 40. See F. Barulich (2000), 'Il Segreto: The Viotti/Chinnery Correspondence in New York', *Fontes Artis Musicae*, vol. 47, pp. 311–13.

honeymoon in Turin, to enquire about some undisclosed regulation governing the administration of La Scala opera theatre.[20]

The new theatre that was to house the *grand opéra* was finally finished in August 1821. It was in the rue Le Peletier only a few hundred yards from the original site. Viotti wrote in exasperated tones to William on 6 July 1821, that he expected to receive keys to the new venue towards the end of the month: 'The theatre is making good progress, and I think that the keys will be handed over on the 25th of this month. So much the better, for this cursed toil is causing us enormous difficulties.'[21] The inauguration took place on 16 August with a grand spectacle, including a performance of *Vive Henri IV*, with variations for orchestra by Ferdinand Paer, music director of the Théâtre-Italien.

The modern composers such as Mozart, Rossini and Paer were clearly the favourites of Paris audiences. Viotti too seemed to prefer their works, and did his best to present as many as he could under the circumstances. A letter from Paer to Viotti, which dates from some time during Viotti's directorship of the Opéra or shortly after, shows that he was also a personal friend, one of those musicians who came to Châtillon to make music with Viotti. The letter is a reply to a dinner invitation from Margaret Chinnery, in which he begs that his lateness will be excused, as he has to keep his usual appointment to play with the musical Duc de Duras on Sunday afternoon from one o'clock to quarter to five.[22]

A few months before the opening of the new opera theatre Viotti received an anonymous piece of rollicking rhyme laced with sharp-edged wit, which was intended to be set to a popular tune, and which was penned by a Viotti satiriser with a sense of humour:

| | |
|---|---|
| Air la Bonne aventure o gué | To the tune of A fine adventure, olay. |
| 1er Couplait<br>Nous sommes bien convaincus<br>que l'opera tombe<br>et que ce sont des intrus<br>qui creusent sa tombe<br>mes en sortant de favard [Favart]<br>ils seront mis a l'écart<br>la Bonne aventure o gué &c | 1st verse<br>We are quite convinced<br>that the opera will fail<br>and that it is intruders<br>who are digging its grave.<br>But on leaving Favart<br>they will be cast aside.<br>A fine adventure, olay. |
| 2eme<br>Viotti pour directeur<br>… belles espérances<br>Courtin administrateur<br>ah pauvres finances | 2nd<br>Viotti as director<br>… high hopes.<br>Courtin as administrator<br>oh poor finances. |

[20] Pralorme to GBV, 18 October 1820, NYPL JOB, 97-52, item 47.

[21] 'La salle avance à grands pas, je pense que le 25 de ce mois on remettra les clefs. Tant mieux car cette maudite besogne nous donne terriblement d'embarras' (GBV to WBC, 6 July 1821, PHM 94/143/1 – 14/38).

[22] Paer to GBV, [n.d.], NYPL JOB 97-52, item 70.

| | |
|---|---|
| un Grandsire deteste<br>méprisable et méprisé<br>la Bonne aventure o gué &c | Hated Grandsire,<br>despicable and despised.<br>A fine adventure, olay. |
| 3eme<br>l'un ne parle pas français<br>et juge les pieces<br>l'autre ne parle jamais<br>et prend les espèces<br>le Secrétaire a son tour<br>fait ici comme a Cherbourg<br>la Bonne aventure o gué &c | 3rd<br>One does not speak French<br>and assesses the librettos.<br>The other does not speak at all<br>and takes the cash.<br>As for the Secretary,<br>he acts as if he were in Cherbourg.[23]<br>A fine adventure, olay. |
| 4eme<br>quand enfin on ouvrira<br>la Salle nouvelle<br>et qu'on demenagera<br>la triste sequelle<br>Comme on se réjouira<br>Comme chacun chantera<br>La Bonne aventure o gué &c | 4th<br>When at last<br>the new room is opened<br>and they rehouse<br>the sad company of players<br>How we shall rejoice<br>How everyone will sing<br>A fine adventure, olay[24] |

This parody of the misfortunes of the Opéra and of the incompetence of its administrators was addressed to Viotti, but included as objects of the author's scorn Courtin, who was in charge of stage sets, and Grandsire, the general secretary who was responsible for finances. The first two lines of the third verse clearly refer to Viotti, as it was the director who presided over the committee that selected the operas to be performed. It was the libretto that was considered in the first instance, the music being only a secondary consideration, hence the attack on Viotti's French. The Opéra's practice of giving more weight to the poem than to the music may have been driven in part by the newspaper critics, who, Spohr complained, devoted whole columns to the poem, while dismissing the music with a few words only.[25]

The above rhyme was addressed to Viotti at the 'hotel choiseul, rue Grange Batelliere, paris'. The Hôtel Choiseul, formerly the grand residence of the Duc de Choiseul, contained apartments provided by the State for opera administrators. An advertisement for the sale of the contents of this mansion, including furniture, furnishings, mirrors, and candelabras, appearing in the *Journal de Paris* of 5 December 1807, shows that the apartments had long since been stripped of their former glory. In writing to the superintendant of the king's *Menus-Plaisirs* in January 1821 to request furniture for these now empty apartments, Viotti

---

[23] Apparently a reference to the time of Louis XIV, when extravagant extensions to the château of Cherbourg were immediately demolished on completion.

[24] Anon. poem addressed to GBV, *c.*19 March 18[21], PHM 94/143/1 – 28/20.

[25] Spohr's *Autobiography*, vol. 2, p. 115.

complains, 'Everyone who comes to live in the administration [apartments] has furniture. Only I, who have returned after a 29-year absence, have none. Nor have I the means to purchase any!'[26] A letter from George to his mother shows that Viotti did not move into these apartments until June 1821. George writes: 'My father writes me word that Amico is removed to the Hotel de Choiseuil [sic]. Have you seen his apartments & are they thoroughly comfortable?'[27]

Viotti's letters to the Baron de La Ferté in the spring of 1821 testify to his frantic preparations for the traditional annual Holy Week concerts organized by the Opéra. This year they were a particular source of tension, for they were conducted amidst simultaneous rehearsals for the forthcoming *pièce de circonstance*, the specially commissioned opera written to celebrate the baptism of the royal heir to the throne, the Duc de Bordeaux (see below). In his letter of 8 April Viotti admits to having, in a moment of impetuosity, made the rash offer to pay out of his own pocket the members of the Bohrer Quartet (Anton and Maximilien Bohrer, violinist Théophile Tilmant and violist Chrétien Urhan). It may be surmised from the apologetic tone of this letter that the sum that Viotti had originally promised his friends had exceeded the Opéra budget and been refused.[28] There is evidence in a letter from Muzio Clementi to his Leipzig publisher Härtel that Viotti had also invited his old friend to preside over the performance of a new symphony at the same concerts.[29]

Yet another distraction for Viotti around this time came from the French diplomat Georges de Caraman – now posted in Bavaria – asking for Viotti's protection of the nine-year-old pianist son of a Bavarian friend, who wanted her son to take lessons at the Paris Conservatoire. This was probably a request that Viotti dreaded: according to the cynical *AMZ* Paris correspondent G.L.P. Sievers, it was 'raining' child wonders in Paris during these years.[30] The letter is addressed to 'Monsieur Viotti, Directeur du Conservatoire royal de Musique, Rue Taitbout N° 9 à Paris',[31] where Viotti had apparently moved after quitting 46 rue Neuve-des-Mathurins, sometime after September 1820.

There was a close affiliation between the Conservatoire (since 1816 the Ecole royale de musique) and the Opéra (Académie royale de musique). In 1818 Pradel had created the Ecole primaire de chant, whose classes were specifically designed to train future members of the Opéra company. Viotti, along with Paer, Boieldieu, Cherubini, Le Sueur and Berton, were members of the jury responsible for examining the pupils of the Ecole primaire. But they soon came to the conclusion

---

26 'Tout ce qui va habiter l'administration a des meubles, moi seul revenu après 29 ans d'absence je n'en ai point et n'ai pas le moyen de m'en procurer!' (GBV to La Ferté, 27 January 1821, Viotti Papers, RCM).

27 GRC to MC, 20 June 1821, Fisher 2000 – 7/24.

28 See Giazotto, pp. 273–4, esp. GBV to La Ferté, 8 April 1821, cited in Giazotto, p. 274.

29 Clementi to Härtel, 2 April 1821, cited in M. Unger (1971), *Muzio Clementis Leben*, Da Capo, New York, p. 222.

30 *AMZ*, 30 September 1818, col. 692.

31 Georges de Caraman to GBV, 2 March [1821], Fisher 2000 – 38/5. The *Annales de la musique pour l'an 1820* (p. 92) lists this as Charles Lafont's address.

that such a school was costly and of little value, and advised its closure at the end of 1820, with a new post for its director Alexandre Choron to be created at the Ecole royale de musique.[32] An 1821 letter from Viotti to Choron concerning the audition of a pupil indicates that the recommendation was implemented.[33] Two more of Viotti's 1821 letters were written from the Ecole royale de musique, one being marked 'Conservatoire à l'examen des Eleves' (from the Conservatoire during the pupils' examination), the other simply 'Conserv. de Musique'.[34] Clearly Viotti and his contemporaries preferred the old name.

Another letter of the same period came from Lord Dunmore, who wrote to George expressing the hope that 'my old Friend Viotti enjoys appearing again on the broad Theatre of Life. It rarely happens that a person in full possession of those powers which command public applause can completely withdraw from such avenues[?] without casting a long look behind.' Half suspecting the truth, he added that he hoped Viotti had not been 'dragged there against his will.'[35]

An advertisement in the *Times* of 19 March 1821 shows that some of the members of the Paris Opéra performed in Rossini's opera *La Gazza ladra* in the 1821 London season. The 'free list' mentioned at the end of the advertisement refers to the practice, common in both London and Paris, of members of the upper classes applying to their friends in theatre management for free tickets to performances, as George did to William Ayrton, now musical director of King's Theatre, for this very performance.[36] It was a practice which was largely responsible for the many failures in theatre management, and was not entirely eradicated at the Opéra until the reign of Louis-Philippe in 1830. Viotti received many such requests from acquaintances, some of which he was happy to grant (Thomas Moore's and Jane Porter's), others not (a request from an unknown applicant, to whom he made the discouraging reply that 'apart from the fact that the police take a dim view of this private indulgence, the ticket office is presently closed').[37]

Seventeen letters from George Chinnery in London to his mother at Châtillon (March–July 1821) are a rich source of information on the London stage in the 1821 spring season. In George's letter of 21 March 1821 he writes that certain singers and dancers from the Opéra were 'on loan' to the King's Theatre, and that they would return to Paris at Viotti's bidding:

> Mad[lle] Noblé [French ballet dancer] is very much admired for face figure à-plomb & general style of dancing, but she is thought to move rather heavily, & certainly her feet

---

[32] Lassabathie, *Histoire du Conservatoire impérial de musique*, p. 53.

[33] GBV to Choron, 14 July 1821, Viotti Papers, RCM.

[34] GBV to WBC, 29 June 1821, PHM 94/143/1 – 14/37, and GBV to an unidentified gentleman, 30 October 1821, cited in Giazotto, p. 275.

[35] Lord Dunmore to GRC, 28 March 1821, Fisher 2000 – 22/70.

[36] GRC to MC, 21 March 1821, Fisher 2000 – 7/10.

[37] 'outre que la police se met de mauvaise humeur contre cette condescendance privée, le caissier n'est pas chez lui dans ce moment ci' (GBV to unknown gentleman, 30 October 1821, cited in Giazotto, p. 275).

do not twinkle like those of Melanie. The public will however be very unwilling to part with her whenever Amico sends his summons over.[38]

Another letter from George, written at the beginning of May 1821, informed his mother that he had written to Amico to give him an account of the Parisian singers and dancers whom he had sent over to London. He reported that they were all liked except Madame Albert, and that 'Amico had better send for her back'.[39] Poor Madame Albert, George wrote to Viotti, was disadvantaged by her physical appearance: she was fat, her arms were too short, and her face was expressionless. Moreover her voice was too weak to fill the theatre.[40] In yet another letter George regretted being too late to go to the opera to give Viotti a report on the singers he sent across, but to 'tell Amico also that people are not by any means unanimous in favour of Ronzi, but that De Begni seems to be more generally liked.'[41]

One of the concerts George made a point of attending during the spring season of 1821 was Caroline Naldi's benefit at the Argyll Rooms, under the 'express' patronage of the new king, George IV, on 19 March, three months after her father's death: 'Caroline Naldi looked an interesting figure in her deep mourning, & a plume of black feathers in her hair, [and] with no other ornament, was very becoming.' The programme of the concert, published in the *Morning Chronicle* of 17 March 1821, names Mori as orchestral leader, and Sir George Smart as conductor. Mori also played a violin concerto, but the advertisement does not name the composer. It is George Chinnery who informs us that Viotti was the composer, but that Mori, lacking his master's 'grandioso' manner, was unable to do the (unidentified) work justice. George also reveals that he found the Beethoven symphony 'execrable', but liked the Finale to the first act of Rossini's *Tancredi*.[42]

During Viotti's tenure of the directorship of the Paris Opéra George was able to be of service to him in London in a variety of ways. He delivered mail for him, made purchases of small personal items, was prepared to help visiting French dignitaries from the Opéra find accommodation, and acted as Viotti's legal signatory to copies of his music, then being published by Clementi and Co. During the early period Viotti was in constant touch with his musician friends in London, including Naldi. In a postscript to one of George's letters to his mother he says: 'Tell Amico that I have forwarded his note to Clementi by the 2 penny post and shall leave the other for the Naldis at their home [8 Mount Street] myself presently.'[43]

The note to Clementi concerned the publication of what appears to be Dussek's piano transcription of Viotti's Violin Concerto No. 23 in G major. Another letter from George proves that in Viotti's absence it was he who was the

---

38 GRC to MC, 21 March 1821, Fisher 2000 – 7/10.

39 GRC to MC, 9 May 1821, Fisher 2000 – 7/13.

40 GRC to GBV, 8 May 1821, NYPL JOB 97-52, item 55.

41 GRC to MC, 21 May 1821, Fisher 2000 – 7/17. The bass Giuseppe de Begnis was married to the soprano Giuseppina Ronzi. He also sang in some 1821 Philharmonic concerts.

42 GRC to MC, 21 March 1821, Fisher 2000 – 7/10.

43 GRC to MC, 23 March 1820, PHM 94/143/1 – 12/1.

signatory to each copy of the concerto that was printed, enabling Viotti to obtain royalties on it: 'Cher Amico – Je viens de signer et d'expédier chez Collard cent exemplaires de l'immortel Concerto in G.' (I have just signed and sent to Collard a hundred copies of the immortal Concerto in G.)[44] A *c*.1802 Clementi and Co. edition of Dussek's piano arrangement of this concerto in the Powerhouse Museum bears Viotti's signature on the title page (see Figure 4). The continuing brisk sales of this 'immortal' concerto in 1821 show that it was still very popular with the *amateurs*.

George continued to act in this capacity on behalf of Viotti until the beginning of 1824, when he left London for Spain to take up his post as commissioner of claims. As late as 19 September 1823 he wrote to Margaret to ask her to reassure Viotti that he was still more than happy to carry out this task for him: 'What could possess Collard to fancy that I was not in the way to sign more Titles of the Concerto in G?' He asked his mother to tell Amico that he went immediately to Cheapside, got a packet of 100 title pages, and signed them the same evening, so that by now they would be ready for sale.[45] When Viotti died, and Margaret moved to France, there was no one to whom she could turn to perform this task. George, then in Spain, wrote:

> You were of course much too agitated & oppressed with grief in London to make any application to Clementi Collard & C° before you came away; but you should bear the point in mind, &, if necessary, send them a certified copy of the will. Having no friend whom you can conveniently ask to sign Title Sheets of the Concerto in G you had better perhaps accept a given sum for the Copyright.[46]

At the beginning of May 1821 a specially commissioned work was performed by the *grand opéra* as part of the celebrations which took place for the baptism of the late Duc de Berry's seven-month-old son, the Duc de Bordeaux. It was the one-act opera in three tableaux, *Blanche de Provence*, on which Viotti's colleagues Berton, Boieldieu, Cherubini, Paer and Kreutzer, who was now leader of the Opéra orchestra, collaborated. The celebrations for this event, which was much publicized both in Paris and London, continued over three days, 1, 2 and 3 May. Thomas Moore, who was still in Paris, witnessed the festivities, writing in his journal on 3 May 1821 that he 'Dined [...] at the Café Français, and went to the French Opera in the evening – saw a new allegorical opera got up in honour of the occasion called "Blanche de Provence" – the music (by Cherubini, Paer and two others) very pretty & the dancing delightful.'[47]

The full programme of the three-day fête was published in the *Times* of 4 May 1821. On the first day the royal infant would be baptised in Notre Dame, on the second there would be a grand ball at the Hôtel de Ville, and on the third there would be public balls. Illuminations, fireworks, and distributions of wine and

---

[44] GRC to MC, 21 March 1821, Fisher 2000 – 7/10.
[45] GRC to MC, 19 September 1823, Fisher 2000 – 7/29.
[46] GRC to MC, 20 May 1824, PHM 94/143/1 – 12/23.
[47] Moore, *Journal*, vol. 2, p. 448.

victuals would take place on all three days. The production that was, as George wrote, the object of Viotti's 'labours *extraordinary*', was performed at the small Théâtre-Italien, probably under extremely trying conditions. The London newspapers reported that the event was a success.[48] *Blanche de Provence* was the last French opera given in the Salle Favart.

On 1 May 1821 Viotti was decorated Chevalier of the Legion of Honour by Louis XVIII. Coming right at the time of his hardest labours for the baptism of the Duc de Bordeaux, it was probably awarded as a gesture of royal gratitude. Viotti's copies of the two documents that deal with his admission to the order, one of which is the letter of notification (see Figure 10), are in the New York Public Library Viotti/Chinnery collection.[49] In George's letter of congratulations of 8 May he remarked that his joy was crowned by the thought that Cherubini, who had been admitted to the same order in 1814, could no longer boast of being more distinguished than 'mon Amico'.[50] One month later George mentioned that 'Amico gained public eulogium in Paris at a ceremony',[51] probably the formal presentation of the award. Another congratulatory letter in very idiosyncratic French seems to be from Viotti's old friend, later to become his intractable debtor, Lourenço da Lima, the former Portuguese ambassador to London.[52] An engraving by H. Meyer from a portrait of Viotti by Trossarelli bears the inscription 'Knight of the Legion of Honour' (see Figure 1), and a lithograph by Antoine Maurin, reproduced at the front of White's *Thematic Catalogue*, shows him wearing the cross. Miel believed that the former bore the greatest likeness to Viotti of all his portraits.[53]

Viotti's admission to the order of the Legion of Honour seems to have been also commemorated by the *Société académique des enfants d'Apollon*, of which he was a member, by a cantata composed for the occasion by his friend Habeneck. It was performed in the presence of Viotti at a meeting of the *Société* in the Conservatoire's concert room on 31 May 1821, with solo parts sung by Chenard and Garcia.[54]

At the end of George's letter dated 21 May 1821 is a cryptic message for Viotti: 'Tell Amico that Collins the Chandelier man has not sent me the measures according to promise.'[55] Two weeks later he writes that Amico will by now have received his letter enclosing 'one of the identical tubes of the Haymarket Gas Chandelier'.[56] The lighting in the old Paris opera theatre had been very poor, and clearly Viotti intended to remedy the situation in the new theatre by installing a

---

48 GRC to MC, 4 May 1821, Fisher 2000 – 7/12.

49 NYPL JOB 97-52, items 53 and 54. The official copy of the record of Viotti's admission to the order was destroyed by fire in Paris in 1871 (La Laurencie (1924), p. 122).

50 GRC to GBV, 8 May 1821, NYPL JOB 97-52, item 55.

51 GRC to MC, 11 June 1821, Fisher 2000 – 7/22.

52 [Lourenço da Lima?] to GBV, *c.*May 1821, PHM 94/143/1 – 28/22.

53 Michaud, vol. 43, p. 589n.

54 M. Decourcelle, *La Société académique des enfants d'Apollon*, p. 56, cited in Pougin, p. 162.

55 GRC to MC, 21 May 1821, Fisher 2000 – 7/17.

56 GRC to MC, 1 June 1821, Fisher 2000 – 7/20.

replica of the King's Theatre gas chandelier. The King's Theatre was the best illuminated theatre in Europe at the time. In 1803 the *Allgemeine musikalische Zeitung* had made a point of commenting on this fact,[57] and in George's travel journals of 1819 and 1820 he repeatedly complains of dark theatres on the Continent – especially La Scala at Milan. In George's next letter he replies to Viotti's question regarding payment to Collins, who has provided the French administrators with a set of specifications and a sketch of the chandelier:

> I see no necessity for communicating further with Collins the Chandelier Manufacturer unless he should of his own accord make a demand for what trouble he has had. If Mons$^{r}$ Delaferté should as a point of honour wish to remunerate the man, it will at any time be easy to ask him to set a value on his services. The only object for which M. Delaferté appears to me specifically indebted to Collins, is a certain finished drawing of the Haymarket chandelier.[58]

It was almost certainly La Ferté's plan to acquire a replica of the King's Theatre chandelier that brought him to London at the end of June 1821. George even offered to help him find accommodation: 'I will have pleasure in seeing M. De la Ferté here & will immediately put myself on the look out for an apartment for him.'[59] In the event George's offer of assistance was not needed, as Viotti sent word that La Ferté would stay at Deshayes's apartment, which George would have 'inspected', he said, if Amico had sent him an address.[60] A few days later George reported that André Deshayes had 'lately arrived from Paris' and had been to visit him. It had been agreed that Deshayes would make all the arrangements concerning La Ferté's stay.[61]

A riot which took place in the Salle Favart in 1821 probably came as the final straw for Viotti's sorely-tested patience. It was described in the *Memoirs* of Hector Berlioz – rather sheepishly, since it was he and his young friends who, albeit unintentionally, caused it. The disturbance occurred during a performance of the ballet *Nina*, and had its origins in the then common practice of featuring a favourite member of the Opéra orchestra in a solo performance. On this night the advertised artist was Baillot, but for some reason the promised solo piece was cancelled, causing an uproar in the parterre. The players fled as angry members of the audience spilled into the orchestra and began to damage and destroy instruments.[62]

By the end of 1821 Viotti was near breaking point. Indeed it was remarkable that he could juggle as many conflicting occupations as he had done up till then. In the second half of the year he had helped William with his Le Havre commerce, writing of exports of brandy, madeira and green tea. His old complaint of gout had

---

[57] *AMZ*, 6 April 1803, col. 475.

[58] GRC to MC, 11 June 1821, Fisher 2000 – 7/22.

[59] GRC to MC, 20 June 1821, Fisher 2000 – 7/24.

[60] GRC to MC, 29 June 1821, Fisher 2000 – 7/25.

[61] GRC to MC, 3 July 1821, Fisher 2000 – 7/26.

[62] Berlioz, H. (1870), *The Memoirs of Hector Berlioz*, ed. and trans. D. Cairns, Alfred A. Knopf, New York, 2002, p. 58.

resurfaced. Margaret's health was frail – although he continued to give William reassuring reports – and his attempts to recover his debt from Charles Smith had failed, depriving him of the means to repay his debt to Margaret. After her consultation with Henry Dance at the beginning of the year Margaret informed William that in the lawyer's opinion 'nothing can be done in Amico's unfortunate case. He says that if Amico refuses to release Charles Smith from his promissory note, the great creditors will agree to make a bankrupt of C.S. and exclude Amico from the benefit of the bankruptcy, retaining his liability to all unpaid debts.'[63]

Before Margaret returned to England at the end of October 1821 Viotti had been forced to resign his directorship of the *grand opéra*. With the help of his 'Patron' he was able to retain the directorship of the Théâtre-Italien, but owing to the uncertain state of French Government affairs at the time, an agreement on the pension he was to receive was not concluded. It may be fairly safely assumed that this 'Patron' was the minister of the Maison du Roi, Jacques Alexander Bernard Law, Marquis de Lauriston, who had been appointed on 1 November 1820 following the Ultras' rise to power after the assassination of the Duc de Berry.[64]

Three letters from Viotti to Margaret written at the end of 1821 shed light on his relations with the minister, and also underscore Viotti's undying attachment to his long-time companion. On 1 November 1821, the date of his official resignation as director of the *grand opéra*, he wrote:

> We are coming to the moment when my fate will be decided. I saw the minister yesterday; I see him often and always find him kindly disposed and friendly, swearing that I shall be content, liberated and tranquil [...] My affair will be decided once and for all in under a few days, and I certainly hope that I shall soon be in a position to send you some good news.[65]

Viotti's 'affair', which was definitely not decided in the following days, appears to have been a promise of a pension of 6,000 francs a year,[66] representing half of his salary for the management of both theatres. Viotti said that he did not envisage that he would be allowed to keep his apartments in the Hôtel Choiseul. He clearly thought it of no consequence, since he and Margaret intended finding an apartment in Paris once the London house in Montagu Street was sold:

> I foresee that I shall not be able to keep the apartment. It is only natural that those coming into this galley should at least have lodgings. But what does it matter? I have never liked it except lately, when it was embellished by [the presence of] a cherished friend. So after all we shall have the opportunity of carrying out our plan of finding a

---

[63] MC to WBC, 5 February 1821, PHM 94/143/1 – 17/51.

[64] On Lauriston see the *Memoirs of the Comtesse de Boigne*, vol. 3, pp. 96–8.

[65] 'Nous touchons au moment ou mon sort sera décidé, j'ai vû le ministre hier, je le vois beaucoup et toujours je le trouve bon et aimable me jurant que je serai content, libre et tranquille [...] Mon affaire va être entierement decidé sous peu de jours, et j'éspere bien que bientot je serai à même de vous envoyer de bonnes nouvelles' (GBV to MC, 1 November 1821, Fisher 2000 – 2/2).

[66] See GBV to WBC, 7 May 1822, PHM 94/143/1 – 14/42.

small apartment just for us, where we shall be entirely our own masters, free of any histrionics.[67]

It was clear that Viotti was looking forward to some calmer years ahead. The forthcoming four-month separation from Margaret, who was as usual to spend the winter in London without him, would be a torture. The letters of these months reveal the toll that the past two years have taken on his health, his nerves and his morale. Above all they highlight his love for his companion of 20 years:

> Alas for four months, the darkest of the year, I must suffer you to be alone!... It will be the last time, I promise you. We shall live and die together hardly leaving one another's side. Every day I am more certain of it [...] Perhaps at the most I shall make a few voyages to Italy... Who knows if we shall not be able to make them together!!![68]

He ended the letter 'Oh please God let this be last time that I must bid you adieu from such a distance',[69] and signed it 'Votre tendre Amico'. Sadly, Viotti's hopes for a last visit to his native land were not realised, but his prediction that he and Margaret would be parted only by death proved accurate.

One week later he wrote again, frantic at having not yet heard from her, and unwilling to believe that the mail packets from England had been delayed for such a long period of time: 'It is unbelievable! You have been gone for a fortnight, my dear good Amica, and you must have been in London for more than nine days, and [still] not a word from Montagu Street!!! It seems impossible that a contrary wind can last for so long, and I do not know what to think. Oh my God preserve me from bad news.'[70] Praying for a letter to quell his anxiety, he this time signs himself 'Votre Amico à tout jamais' (Your Amico forever).

During Margaret's absence Viotti watched over the running of the Châtillon estate. He went each weekend to check on the servant caretakers, supervising the fruit picking and the dispatch of the produce to market. Playing down his health

---

[67] 'Je prévois que je ne pourrai garder l'appartement, il est bien naturel que ceux qui viennent dans cette galere ayent au moins de quoi loger. Mais qu'est-ce que celà fait. Je ne l'ai jamais aimé que dernierement qu'il a été embelli par une tendre Amie; ainsi après tout nous aurions l'occasion de mettre notre plan à éxecution, nous chercherons un petit appartement qui nous servira à nous seuls et ou nous serons entirement maitres sans mélange d'Histrions' (GBV to MC, 1 November 1821, Fisher 2000 – 2/2).

[68] 'Helas pour quatre mois, les plus noirs de l'année, il faut vous savoir seule! ... Ce sera bien pour la dernière fois je vous en répons, nous viverons et nous mourrons ensemble sans presque nous quitter; tous les jours j'en acquiers de plus en plus la certitude [...] Que je n'aurai à faire tout au plus que quelques voyages en Italie... Qui sçait que nous ne puissions pas faire cette petite éxcursion ensemble!!!' (*Ibid.*).

[69] 'oh fasse le Ciel que ce soit la derniere époque ou je doive vous dire adieu de si loin'.

[70] 'C'est incroyable! Voilà quinze jours que vous êtes partie ma bonne chere Amica, en voilà plus de neuf que vous devez etre à Londre, et pas un mot encore de Montagu Street!!! Il me parroit impossible que le vent contraire dure si longtemps et je ne sçais que penser. Oh Mondieu préservez moi de mauvaises nouvelles' (GBV to MC, 8 November 1821, Fisher 2000 – 2/3).

problems, he assured Margaret that he now had plenty of time to do this. He also claimed that he was optimistic regarding the granting of his pension:

> Do not fear that I am harming my cause by making these little excursions— Progress is being made, and we are drawing close to a conclusion— Yesterday evening at half past eight I was coming down the stairs of the Opera on my way home, when Mr Sorconnes, who has replaced Mr de La Boulaye as general secretary, stopped me. On behalf of the minister he reiterated yet again most kindly, graciously, and with great concern, that I should set my mind at rest, not be impatient, and that they were not wasting a minute in formulating their plan, that all would be finalised, and that I should be perfectly happy.[71]

The Vicomte de Sorconnes, the new secretary to the minister of the Maison du Roi, had almost certainly been a guest at Châtillon. After Viotti's death in 1824 George was to write to his mother: 'Among your Parisian acquaintances the name of Sorconnes naturally occurs to me; & I am sorry to hear that he should have ceased to be Sec[re] général du Min[re] de la Maison du Roi, – unless indeed he has got a better situation.'[72] Viotti's fate was still not decided on 12 December 1821.

Margaret was not reassured by the letter, wanting to know where Viotti was living, and venting her indignation that he had been stripped of one post before being firmly established in another. François Habeneck, who had been a regular visitor to Châtillon, was appointed the new director of the *grand opéra*, and had in turn made his old master Baillot first violin of the orchestra.[73] Margaret wondered how Habeneck was conducting himself, as well as all the others 'who were so recently your subjects'. She worried that they had also taken from him 'les Bouffes' (the Italian opera), saying that if Viotti had charge of no theatre at all she would cease attending the opera and bury herself at Châtillon summer and winter.[74]

But a little later Margaret was glad to learn that Viotti finally had found time for some composing:

> I rejoice at the thought that you are pursuing music again— Heaven be praised!— That will do you an *immense amount of good*, to your health, your peace of mind, your inclinations, and finally, will be of enormous *benefit* to the world at large!— Happy is the man of genius who possesses so many things without going out of himself![75]

---

[71] 'Ne craignez pas que je fasse du tort à mes affaires par ces petites éxcursions— Tout marche, et nous touchons à la conclusion— Hier au soir à 8. heures et demies je descendois l'escalier de l'opera pour me retirer. M[r] de Sorconnes secretaire General à la place de M[r] de la Boulaye m'arreta pour me repeter encore de la part du Ministre, et avec une douceur, un interet et une grace infini, qu'il me prioit d'être parfaitement tranquille, de ne point m'impatienter, qu'on ne perdoit pas une minute dans l'organisation de leur plan, que tout celà alloit etre terminé, et que je serois parfaitement content' (*Ibid.*).

[72] GRC to MC, 20 May 1824, PHM 94/143/1 – 12/23.

[73] This and other administrative changes announced in *Journal de Paris*, 2 and 3 November 1821.

[74] MC to GBV, 13 November 1821, NYPL JOB 97-52, item 57.

[75] 'Je me rejouis de la pensée que vous vous occupez de la musique avec un peu de suite,— le ciel soit loué!— Celà vous fera *mille biens*, a la santé, a la paix de l'ame, a vos gouts, et

Viotti appears not yet to have received this last letter of hope, as the following is a reply to Margaret's earlier anxieties:

> Your last letter again caused me pain.— How quick you are to torment yourself. This time it is I who have been the cause of your tender anxiety.— From all those [letters] that you have probably now received you will see that there is not the slightest reason to be afraid on my account— Whatever the administrative changes may be, if indeed there are any, my Patron is in a separate camp, and has nothing to do with party arrangements. So on that front we are safe. Let us suppose that even of his own volition or by accident he leaves his post. Mr Séguier is right, he will not leave it before settling my affair, especially since it is already so near conclusion. Besides, the thing is too well known, as he so rightly says, too just, to be thrown off course now.[76]

If Viotti was anxious about the outcome of his 'affair' he certainly hid the fact from Margaret, whom he tried to protect at all times from any upsetting news. But he did admit that the waiting frustrated him: 'It is detestable for someone like me, who likes a decision, even if it brings misfortune upon me.'[77] In private he must have been anxious, as it was in November 1821 that he wrote an appealing letter to his debtor, the former Portuguese diplomat Lourenço da Lima, begging him 'to fulfil a sacred duty to an unfortunate friend!'[78] In this letter he admitted what he had not admitted to Margaret – that he was truly in great need.

In her letter of 29 November Margaret had complained that she did not have a spare moment in which to play the piano that she had recently installed. Viotti advises her to borrow some music from Hüllmandel, Kalkbrenner or Madame de Montgéroult, who must have then been in England. His reply confirms that he had been composing at Châtillon:

> My Amica, how I regret that you did not take my trifling little manuscript writings for violin and piano! Do you wish me to send them to you? I am not doing anything at all

---

ensuite *un bien*, tres grand, au monde entier!— Heureux l'homme de génie qui possede tant de choses, sans sortir de lui meme!' (MC to GBV, 29 November 1821, NYPL JOB 97-52, item 58).

[76] 'Votre dernière lettre m'a encore fait de la peine.— Comme vous êtes prompte à vous tourmenter, c'est moi cette fois ci qui cause votre tendre inquietude.— Par toutes celles que sans doute vous avez reçues maintenant vous verrez qu'il n'y a pas la moindre raison de vous mettre en peine pour mon sort— Que tel changement de ministere, si tant est qu'il en aye, mon Patron fait bande à part, n'a rien à faire aux arrangements de partis— Ainsi de ce coté là nous sommes en sureté. Supposons même que par son bon plaisir, ou accident, il quitte sa place; M[r] Seguier a raison, il ne la quittera pas sans terminer mon affaire d'autant plus qu'elle avance fort vers la conclusion— D'ailleurs la chose est trop connûe, comme il dit fort bien, trop juste pour que des entraves s'y mettent' (GBV to MC, 12 December 1821, Fisher 2000 – 2/4).

[77] 'C'est détéstable, pour moi qui aime la décision, même pour les malheurs qui doivent m'arriver' (*Ibid.*).

[78] 'de remplir un devoir sacré vis-à-vis d'un ami malheureux!' (GBV to Lourenço da Lima (copy), 11 November 1821, PHM 94/143/1 – 28/25).

with them. They are just as they were when I brought them from Chatillon. I have not touched them.[79]

These writings may have been Viotti's *Andante et rondo pour le piano forte et le violon* (published by Simrock, 1823), which were arranged from his newly revised Violin Concerto No. 19, published by Janet et Cotelle in 1819.[80] Viotti may also have then been preparing his Violin Concerto No. 28 for publication. Clearly composed when Caroline Chinnery was still alive, it was published by Janet et Cotelle as 'Lettre H', with a dedication to the Marquis de Lauriston, around this time.[81] The dedication was surely made either in gratitude for the pension his patron managed to procure for him, or in anticipation of it. In the end Viotti did not send the above-mentioned compositions, writing blackly on 23 December:

> I shall not send you my musical scribblings. I shall keep them for us to amuse ourselves with here, or else I shall bring them to you, if, as I hope, Heaven permits that I go and fetch you. My life is very hard, at a loose end and isolated as I am! I say isolated, for I count as nothing all [those] whom I see, or might see. You, … you dear Amica, George and Chin, you are all I have in this world. Separated from you, I am without support. I have not a soul to whom I would pour out my heart. Judge what a penance my life is![82]

One of the last letters to reach Viotti in 1821 was from his friend the Duke of Cambridge in Gotha, recommending the young violinist Peterson, son of a Hamburg musician, and pupil of Hanover's foremost violinist Thielmuller. He also asked Viotti for some more bows from Tourte *le jeune*, saying that the ones Viotti himself used suited him perfectly. At the end of such a troubled year it is doubtful that Viotti would have been comforted by even Adolphus Frederick's warm assurances of esteem, attachment and devotion.[83]

---

[79] 'Comme je regrette mon Amica que vous n'ayez pas emporté avec vous mes petites bettises manuscrites pour violon et Piano! Voulez vous que je vous les envoye? Je n'en fais rien du tout, elles sont là comme je les ai apportées de Chatillon sans les avoir jamais touchées' (GBV to MC, 12 December 1821, Fisher 2000 – 2/4).

[80] *Annales de la musique pour l'an 1820*, p. 157; *Thematic Catalogue*, p. 126.

[81] *Thematic Catalogue*, p. 36.

[82] 'Je ne vous enverrai pas mes gribouillages musicaux, je les garderai pour nous en amuser ici, ou je vous les apporterai si le Ciel décide, comme je l'espere, que j'aille vous chercher— ma vie est bien dure libre et isolé comme je suis! Je dis isolé car je compte pour rien tout ce que je vois ou pourrois voir. Vous, … vous chere Amica, George et Chin, voilà tout ce que j'ai a ce monde. Separé de vous, je reste sans appuis, je n'ai pas une ame à qui mon cœur voudroit dire un mot d'epenchement. Jugez dans quelle penitence de vie je suis!' (GBV to MC, 23 December 1821, PHM 94/143/1 – 2/27).

[83] AF to GBV, 7 December 1821, NYPL JOB 97-52, item 59.

CHAPTER 18

# Viotti's final years, 1822–1824

February 1822 saw Viotti back in England with Margaret, still without his promised pension. A letter from Robberechts dated 11 February 1822 shows that Viotti's last pupil was then living in Paris, where he found time to give six lessons a day, work on his concertos, and perform at private concerts, as well as at Baillot's *soirées musicales*. He was clearly popular with the *amateurs*, and was gaining in confidence with all the playing. Robberechts moved in the same circles as Viotti and Margaret, and acted as a go-between in Viotti's communications with his friends in Paris. He passed on messages from the Englishwoman Mrs Popkins, whose parties Margaret and Viotti attended regularly during these years, and from Madame de Lausac, Madame Vigée-Lebrun, and Madame de St Sauveur, as well as from Lauriston's old friend M. de Cailleux, now Director of Museums. The latter had twice written to Viotti, undoubtedly in regard to the long-awaited pension.[1]

At a *grande soirée* arranged by Madame de La Briche and attended by the *amateur* Duc de Duras, Robberechts's piece was called for twice. The hostess claimed to know positively that Viotti had received his pension. Another *soirée* was given by Madame de La Bouillerie, wife of the future minister of the Maison du Roi. Robberechts also reported on the subscription got up for the sale of a collection of Boccherini quintets, segments of which had been released at monthly intervals over the previous four years. Viotti appears to have had a hand in the organization of the subscription, as it was to him that the publisher Janet's inquiries were directed. The last release was imminent and Janet wished to know how he would send the subscribers their copies and how he would be paid. Robberechts's fondness for his 'cher Maître' is evident in his closing words, 'I embrace you with the warmest affection and will keep you in my heart all my life'.[2]

In April a letter was addressed to Viotti from the Vicomte de Sorconnes, which had probably not reached him by the time Viotti wrote to William in May, saying that he intended to continue to harrass the minister until he obtained his pension: 'As for me, do not think that I am going to leave the minister in peace. Let us begin by ending all the bureaucratic dithering regarding the pension of 6,000 francs.

[1] André Robberechts to GBV, 11 February 1822, NYPL JOB 97-52, item 60.

[2] 'Je vous embrasse avec la plus vive affection et vous porterai dans mon cœur toute ma vie' (*Ibid.*). See advertisement for the *Collection des quintetti de Boccherini pour deux violons, alto et deux violoncelles* (Janet et Cotelle, Paris, 1818–22), in the *Annales de la musique pour l'an 1819* (pp. 182–3).

After that I shall bring forth all the batteries of demand that are in my power.'[3] The letter from Sorconnes was in response to one from Viotti dated 9 April. He begged Viotti not to be anxious, promised to speak to the minister again, and hoped he would soon be in a position to inform Viotti of His Excellency's intentions.[4]

Viotti was now in such straitened circumstances that he was obliged to ask William for some financial help for Margaret. He also revealed that he owed William's business partner in Le Havre, Joseph Cary, 2,500 francs – a fact that he wanted kept secret from Margaret to spare her anxiety. His intention was to repay this debt with the proceeds from the sale of his Feydeau Theatre box, which he had retained since the period of his involvement with the Theatre. But his ownership of the box had been contested, causing him additional worry: 'Whether it be a little or a lot, I shall certainly get something from the box. I have won my lawsuit, but a devil of a cad has, without any right, contested it, and it will take some time to extract it and be rid of these obstacles raised by people without faith, law or honour.'[5] His postscript shows a delicate feeling of protection towards Margaret, whose health was then weak: 'I assume that you will reply directly to the Padrona regarding the money. If you happen to write a few lines for me do not mention my affairs. We know what they are, and any details would be superfluous.'[6]

The time spent waiting for Margaret's recuperation from her long illness before they could both return to France for the summer was all the more painful for Viotti, as he was impatient to pursue his affairs. En route to France they spent a restful few days in the country at Sittingbourne. Viotti had always loved the beauty and tranquillity of the country, and wrote in a lyrical vein reminiscent of his earlier missives from Bath: 'The weather is superb, the air is fragrant with the most delicious perfumes, the beans are in flower, the clover is perfect, and roses are intertwined in the hedges.'[7] Margaret added a note for George at the end in which she expressed her gratitude for Viotti's kind attentions: 'God bless you dearest George – nothing can be good without you, as Amico says, but he is all kindness

---

3 'Quant à moi, ne croyez pas que je veuille laisser tranquille le ministre. Commençons par laisser terminer toutes les ceremonies des bureaux concernant la pension de 6 000F.— Aprés je drésserai toutes les batt[e]ries réclamantes qui sont en mon pouvoir' (GBV to WBC, 7 May 1822, PHM 94/143/1 – 14/42).

4 Sorconnes to GBV, 20 April 1822, NYPL JOB 97-52, item 62.

5 'Peu ou beaucoup, il est certain que je tirerai quelque chose de la Loge. J'ai gagné mon procés, mais un demon un canaille a mis sans en avoir le droit opposition, et il faut du temps pour la faire oter, et se delivrer des embar[r]as suscités par des gens sans foix [sic] ni loi ni honneur' (GBV to WBC, 7 May 1822, PHM 94/143/1 – 14/42).

6 'J'imagine que vous repondrez directement à la Padrona au sujet de l'argent,— si par hasard vous m'écrivez quelques mots ne faites pas mention de mes affaires— nous les savons, des détails seroient inutiles' (*Ibid.*).

7 'Le temps est superbe, l'air est embomé par les plus délicieuses éxalésons possibles, les fêves en fleurs, le Tréfeuil [trèfle] dans sa perfection, les roses en guirlandes dans les hayes' (GBV to GRC, 2 June 1822, PHM 94/143/1 – 25/4).

and attention to my wants and wishes, and is never tired of doing everything he can to make me comfortable.'[8]

By the end of June 1822 Margaret and Viotti were back in France, and judging by the lack of correspondence with William over the next four or five months, spent all or most of that time with him at Châtillon. On 16 August 1822 comes the first indication that Viotti's 'affair' has been settled. In a letter addressed to Cailleux Viotti writes:

> If my affair is *truly* resolved and concluded, not only are you the first, but the *only* person to inform me of it, for I have had no word from anyone on this interesting subject. Moreover I am grateful for your heartfelt solicitude in wanting to set my mind at rest. You can probably guess how very sensible I am to it, and I would be even more so, if it be possible, if you had, as you promised, come yourself to inform us of it. Patience, I shall come and see you in Paris straight away and we shall arrange a date for you to pay us a visit. The poor patient [Margaret] is improving and is hopeful of seeing you again soon. Her husband also desires so much to know you. If by any chance you know where I must present myself in order to receive [the pension], please let me know.[9]

Cailleux was clearly another intimate of the Châtillon circle, judging from the familiar way that Viotti speaks of Margaret Chinnery as 'the poor patient'. But he did not meet William Chinnery until the end of 1823, when it appears that William, without stopping to consider the consequences of his action, informed him that Viotti was in London. The hoped-for pension of 6,000 francs had not eventuated. Instead, Viotti had been awarded a yearly stipend of 3,000 to continue as director of the Théâtre-Italien, albeit apparently part-time, given that the salary was now halved. Clearly it was expected that Viotti would reside in Paris. In writing to William, Viotti can only guess at what he said to Cailleux, but the tone of the letter is one of ill-concealed exasperation with William's gaffe:

> I was dying to know, my dear Chin, what action you took with Cailleux. And you ask me if I would approve of it! Today you have informed us what it was, and so I hasten to reply. I disapprove of it so strongly, my friend, that I am seriously considering leaving London to come to Paris to undo the harm that might result from it, that is of losing 3,000F in income, which is indispensable to me. I do not at all like the sound of what M. de Sorconnes is saying, that is, that *I can live in London instead of Paris*. I flattered myself that I was regarded as still being of use to them. If they think otherwise, then

---

[8] MC to GRC in GBV to GRC, 2 June 1822, PHM 94/143/1 – 25/4.

[9] 'Si mon affaire est *vraiment* décidée et terminée, non seulement vous êtes le premier à me l'apprendre, mais *l'unique* car je n'ai reçu un mot de personne sur cet interessant sujet. Au reste je reconnois bien la sollicitude de votre cœur à consoler le mien. Vous devinez sans doute combien j'y suis sensible; je le serois encore plus s'il est possible, si, comme vous me l'aviez promis, vous étiez venu nous l'apprendre vous même. Patience, j'irai vous voir incessamment à Paris, et nous arrangerons le jour que nous devrons vous posseder ici. La pauvre patiente va mieux et elle est tout éspoir de vous revoir bientôt, son mari aussi desire tant vous connaître! Si par hasard vous savez ou je puis me présenter pour toucher, faites le moi savoir' (GBV to Cailleux, 16 August 1822, Viotti Papers, RCM).

> adieu to the 3,000 that I receive from the administration, for this amount represents a salary not a pension. What a shame! I had arranged everything so well before my departure!!! Now dear Chin, you can no doubt feel the full extent of the inappropriateness and even danger of your action. Anyway, all that can be done now is to try to remedy the situation, and that is what I shall try to do [...]
> P.S. I must beg that you do not utter a word of this to anyone again. I know Cailleux better than you, and I shall think about whether or not I can put things back the way they were by letter...[10]

The matter is not mentioned again in the Chinnery letters. There is a possibility that if Viotti's salary was cut off, he may have initiated proceedings to have it reinstated, and that this may have been the subject of one of the lawsuits that Margaret Chinnery inherited after Viotti's death.

The winter of 1822–23 was the first that Margaret did not spend in England. She and Viotti remained in Paris in an apartment in the rue d'Artois, although a December 1822 letter from Viotti, then temporarily living alone at Châtillon, shows that Margaret and William were at that time staying at [46] rue Neuve-des-Mathurins, and that Viotti would shortly be joining them there. This address, where Viotti appeared to have lived for most of 1820, was an *hôtel* that had in 1783 belonged to the Marquis de Louvois, who was exiled by Louis XVI for his dissolute lifestyle.[11] It now belonged to a duke (Hugues-Bernard Maret, Duc de Bassano?),[12] judging by Viotti's closing words, 'Que le Bon Dieu soit avéc vous et avéc sa Grace' (May God be with you and with his Grace). Most of the letter is taken up with a discussion about parcels of food and household items (two irons, saucepans, hat stand, two corkscrews, scissors, three serviette rings, cheeses, potatoes, onions, coffee), that Viotti is preparing to send into town by a servant, along with what appears to be his sculpted bust: 'I hope that the famous head will

---

[10] 'Je me tuois, mon cher Chin, à deviner quelle étoit la demarche que vous avez fait auprés de Cailheux, et dont vous me demandiez si je l'approuverois! Aujourd'hui vous nous l'apprenez, et je me hâte d'y répondre. Je l'approuve si peu, mon Ami, que je pense serieusement à quitter Londre pour me rendre à Paris, et remedier au mal qu'il en pourroit résulter, celui de perdre 3 000fr de rente, qui me sont indispensables. Je n'aime pas du tout les dires de M^r de Sorconnes, que *je peux vivre à Londre au lieu de Paris*— Je me flattois qu'on me regardoit comme pouvant leur etre utile encore, s'ils pensent autrement, adieu les 3 000. que je reçois de l'administration, car cette somme est en appointement et non en pension. Quel domage! J'avois si bien arrangé le tout avant mon départ!!! Maintenant cher Chin, vous sentez sans doute toute l'inconvenance et le danger même de votre demarche— Enfin reste à y remedier maintenant, et c'est ce que je tacherai de faire [...] / P.S. Il faut que je vous prie de ne plus en dire un mot de plus à qui que ce soit— Je connois Cailheux mieux que vous, et je vais réfléchir si par lettre je ne pourrai pas redonner la même face à cette malheureuse affaire...' (GBV to WBC, 14 November 1823, PHM 94/143/1 – 14/63).

[11] Hillairet, *Dictionnaire historique des rues de Paris*, vol. 2, p. 111.

[12] See below, pp. 262–3.

arrive safe and sound with its face wrapped in fresh cotton wool.– I hope you will admire my packaging.'[13]

But Viotti's cheerfulness may have been a little forced, as he was still recovering from an unspecified illness: 'I am feeling better, much better. But although I am able to get about in the garden, the granaries and the yards, I do not think I should leave this place so quickly.'[14] Perhaps Viotti was feeling worse than he revealed, as it was only a few days later that he penned his will. Tormented by his failure to repay Margaret's loan, he wrote: 'Not only do I die without fortune, but in addition I die with a debt that tears my heart out [...] This cursed debt is the bane of my life and I shall not rest in the grave if I am not fortunate enough to be able to discharge it.'[15] Viotti left everything he possessed to Margaret, with the exception of a small debt to his brother André, which he asked her to repay. His morale was at rock bottom. He did not want any money set aside for a burial: 'a sod of earth is enough for a miserable creature like me.'[16] Viotti appointed William Chinnery and their friend Gustave Gasslar, of 17 boulevard de la Poissonnière, executors of his will.

Another anxiety that preyed increasingly on Viotti's mind as he felt his health failing was his inability to make contact with Madame de Genlis to inform her of the facts surrounding Casimir Baecker's abrupt departure from England in February 1808, when he and Margaret had been appointed the youth's de facto guardians, and given charge of his London concerts, which never eventuated. He also wanted to explain the loss of some of Casimir's personal effects. Margaret herself eventually succeeded in reaching Madame de Genlis a year after Viotti's death by means of a letter which was hand-delivered by William. In it she described Viotti's fruitless attempts to have the truth acknowledged:

> A few months before his death M. Viotti wrote you a detailed letter to clarify once again the truth about M. Casimir's effects, to tell you that he had taken full charge of them, and to describe the steps he had taken. This letter was written in France. He felt his health weakening, and told me in this very same room from which I am now writing to you, "I shall send this explanation to Madame de Genlis, written and signed by me, so that she is fully informed of the truth; and I shall keep a copy, for I do not want all the trouble that that young man [Casimir Baecker] has caused me to rebound on you or on my friend Mr Chinnery, in the event that I am no longer here to declare the truth." I

---

[13] 'J'espere que la fameuse Tete arrivera saine et sauve avec son visage enveloppé de coton nouveau.— Vous admirez j'espere mon embalage' (GBV to WBC, 7 December 1822, PHM 94/143/1 – 14/44).

[14] 'je me porte mieux, beaucoup mieux. Mais quoiqu'en état déjà de courir par le jardin, dans les grainiers et les cours, je ne crois pas que je doive quitter ces lieux si vite' (*Ibid.*).

[15] 'Non seulement je meurs sans fortune mais de plus je meurs avec une dette qui me déchire l'Ame [...] Cette dette sacrée fait le malheur de ma vie et troublera le repos de mes ombres, si je suis assez infortuné pour ne pouvoir l'acquitter' (Viotti's will, 13 December 1822, Viotti Papers, RCM).

[16] 'un peu de terre suffira pour un miserable comme moi' (*Ibid.*).

believe that a copy of that letter is with other papers at his [Viotti's] lawyer's in London. The original was transmitted to you (I believe) by post.[17]

Thirteen of the twenty 1823 letters from Viotti to William were written during this winter in Paris. They speak mainly of William's business affairs, Viotti's debt to Joseph Cary, and Margaret's investments in the French funds which Gustave Gasslar managed when she and Viotti were in England.[18] All the letters mention financial worries of some sort.

Viotti spent the beginning of 1823 in Paris in frantic buying and selling at the Bourse on behalf of Margaret with money that William sent from Le Havre. 'I am all ruffled by the knocks I received at that infernal Bourse', he complained on 22 January.[19] The risky business of bond trading was both physically and mentally wearing, and by the end of January the impending war between France and Spain was causing additional anxieties, both to merchants and to the general public. Margaret wrote to William: 'People are all in suspense here too, – many of the english are hurrying home, – but no creature seems to know any thing *really* or *clearly* about the matter.'[20]

Fearing that his business would be adversely affected, William was thrown into turmoil by the prospect of war, and Viotti found himself obliged to comfort him. He wrote philosophically: 'No one in Paris is displaying as much anxiety as you. I am not saying what must or may happen, one would have to be more than a magician to predict that, but while waiting for fate to take its course we are remaining calm and we do not predict anything very black. Calm your own mind too my dear friend. Your judgement will be more sound.'[21] In his letter of 31 March Viotti again chastised William for his pessimism: 'Your business is going well, judging by your letters, the wind is by the stern, the dear Padrona's health is

---

[17] 'Quelques mois avant de mourir Mons^r^ Viotti vous a écrit avec détail, pour vous déclarer, encore une fois, l'exacte vérité sur tout ce qui regardoit les affaires de Mon^r^ Casimir pour vous dire qu'il s'en étoit chargé entierement, et les démarches qu'il avoit faites. Cette lettre étoit écrite en France,— il sentoit que sa santé s'affoiblissoit, et il me dit dans ce meme cabinet d'ou je vous écris à présent "j'enverrai ce détail à Madame de Genlis, écrit de ma main et signé, afin qu'elle soit bien pleinement instruite de la vérité; et j'en garderai copie; car je ne veux pas que tous les ennuis que ce jeune homme m'a causé, retombent sur vous, ou sur mon ami M^r^ Chinnery, dans le cas ou je ne serois plus là pour affirmer la verité." Je crois que la copie de cette lettre est, avec d'autres papiers, chez son Avoué à Londres; l'original vous a été transmise (je crois) par la poste' (MC to Mme de Genlis, 1 July 1825 (copy), Fisher 2000 – 6/36; Yim, D53).

[18] See Gustave Gasslar to GBV, NYPL JOB 97-52, item 61.

[19] 'Je suis tout froissez [sic] par les hurtons [heurts] qu'on m'a donné à cette infernale bourse' (GBV to WBC, 22 January 1823, PHM 94/143/1 – 14/45).

[20] MC to WBC, in GBV to WBC, 30 January 1823, PHM 94/143/1 – 14/46.

[21] 'Personne dans Paris ne témoigne l'inquiétude qui parroit [sic] vous obseder. Je ne dis pas ce qui doit, ou peut arriver, il faudroit etre plus que sorcier pour celà, mais en attendant les évolutions du sort, nous nous tenons tranquilles et nous ne prévoyons rien de trés noir. Tranquillisez votre ésprit aussi mon bon Ami, votre jugement sera plus parfait' (GBV to WBC, 13 February 1823, PHM 94/143/1 – 14/51).

improved, thank Heaven, so why so many jeremiads, so much melancholy? Come, come my dear Chin, lift your spirits.'[22]

In 1822, unburdened of his Opéra concerns, Viotti had had time to return to composing. In February 1823 he sent what he said were two new concertos to Joseph Cary, perhaps copies of those mentioned in his will ('you will find among my music two manuscript concertos').[23] It is most improbable that two Viotti concertos would have remained unpublished, even after his death. Therefore it seems likely that the concertos in question were his last two, Nos 28 and 29, both published by Janet et Cotelle around this date. Originally composed, apparently, much earlier (before 1811), they might possibly have been revised *c.*1822.[24] Viotti himself could have sold the concertos to Janet et Cotelle after sending copies to Cary. Viotti's debt of 2,500 francs to Cary is mentioned in three of his letters to William – those of 7 May 1822, 25 February 1823, and 5 March 1823, but exactly when this loan was made is not stated. In his letter of 25 February 1823 Viotti says:

> I am writing a couple of words to Cary by this mail, just to tell him that I shall be sending him two new concertos, and to talk about my debt. But in replying to this letter do not mention any of that. You know that Amica is supposed to know nothing about it. Not even the poor concertos.[25]

The fact that the two reasons for writing were mentioned in the same breath might imply a connection. Was Viotti sending Cary his concertos as an appeasing gesture, as he was unable to repay his debt? In that case the loan must have been quite recent. It has been claimed that a 'John' Cary gave Viotti a loan to prop up his wine business in 1810.[26] And Viotti did dedicate his Three duets for violins, 'Hommage à l'amitié', to a Mr Cary *c.*1803.[27] This is puzzling – unless 'Mr Cary' was a different person altogether – given that neither William nor, apparently, Viotti even knew Joseph Cary before the middle of 1818, when William moved to Le Havre to enter into partnership with him, a fact that is established by Margaret's

---

[22] 'Le commerce de votre Maison va bien à ce qu'il paroit par vos lettres, le vent se soutient en poupe, la santé de la chere Padrona va mieux grace au Ciel, ainsi à quoi bon tant de jérémiades, tant de tristesse? Allons, allons mon cher Chin— reveillez votre Spirit' (GBV to WBC, 31 March 1823, PHM 94/143/1 – 14/57).

[23] 'On trouvera parmi ma musique deux concertos manuscrits' (Viotti's will, 13 December 1822, Viotti Papers, RCM).

[24] See White's comments ('Chronology', p. 124) about the likelihood of later dates for the slow movements of both these concertos. However his conjecture that the andante of Concerto No. 29 in E minor might have been composed in 1818 for the occasion of Viotti's swansong performance before his Conservatoire colleagues in Paris is impossible, as this was a surprise party, at which Viotti performed impromptu.

[25] 'J'écris deux mots à Cary par ce courier, rien que pour lui annoncer que je lui enverrai deux concertos nouveaux, et lui parler de ma dête. Mais en répondant à celle ci ne parlez de rien de tout celà. Vous savez que l'Amica n'en doit rien savoir. Pas meme des pauvres concertos' (GBV to WBC, 25 February 1823, PHM 94/143/1 – 14/53).

[26] Giazotto, p. 155.

[27] *Thematic Catalogue*, p. 95.

note in Viotti's letter to William of 2 October 1823, when it was discovered that Cary had been taking money from the firm.[28]

On 22 April 1823 George wrote to his mother of a new composition of Viotti, which had been sent to him in manuscript form via the Swedish ambassador in London: '[Baron de] Stierneld has sent me the two packets of music & the £6.3 [undoubtedly reimbursement for purchases made for him by either Margaret or Viotti]. I enclose his note. Amico's titre is indeed as S. says a titre de gloire for me, of which I feel unworthy. Thank him a thousand times for this token of affection, & for having immortalised me.' And as a postscript: 'Pray send me Amico's instructions as to what I am to do with the music. Is it for Collard?'[29] There is no mention of the title of the piece of music in question, but it is clear that Viotti has dedicated it to George. George's next letter confirms this: 'The *Presentation* Copy of Amico's new publication, since I am to consider it as such, shall be bound & deposited in my library. Pray tell him so with renewed and additional thanks. The other copy I *think* of giving to Cha$^{s}$ Staniforth.'[30]

The music dedicated to George Chinnery was Viotti's Violin Concerto No. 29 in E minor (Letter I). It is positively identified by Baillot in his *Notice* as the one that Viotti performed before his Conservatoire friends in 1818. Viotti must have instructed George not to send the concerto to Collard, as he intended it to be published by Janet et Cotelle. In the latter's edition the concerto is dedicated to Mr and Mrs Chinnery, a mistake which is typical of the confusion surrounding the names of the different members of the Chinnery family, a confusion that continued until fairly recently. The bound 'presentation copy', presumably inscribed with a dedication to George, has not yet been found, but there is a good chance that it has survived, since it would have been among the family papers that were bequeathed to Miss Mary Greene at Margaret Chinnery's death, and which subsequently came onto the market at various Sotheby auctions in the 1960s.

Viotti and Margaret moved back to Châtillon in spring, but by the summer of 1823 Viotti must have felt a marked deterioration in his health, and with his spirits in need of lifting, he addressed a moving plea to his old soulmate Baillot to come and play with him. The tone of the letter is reminiscent of another one to Baillot expressing the same desire, written, perhaps, at the end of 1822,[31] but here Viotti's fatigue, discouragement, and need for consolation are even more apparent:

---

[28] MC to WBC in GBV to WBC, 2 October 1823, PHM 94/143/1 – 14/61. Not much is known about Joseph Cary. It is certain that he played the violin (see GBV to WBC, 21 November 1819, PHM 94/143/1 – 14/34, in which Viotti says he will share some violin strings with Cary). As well, Goodkind (p. 740) names Cary as an owner of a Stradivarius.

[29] GRC to MC, 22 April 1823, PHM 94/143/1 – 12/13.

[30] GRC to MC, 6 May [1823], PHM 94/143/1 – 12/16. Charles Staniforth was the son of a prominent London banker, and close family friend.

[31] GBV to Baillot, [n.d.], in Pincherle (1924), Letter 6, pp. 108–9. It seems to be written from Paris, not Châtillon, and Margaret is apparently with him.

My dear good Baillot
I feel a very great need to play a duet with you, and an even greater need to embrace you. Would you be able to sacrifice one of your Sundays to us, and come and dine with us *this coming Sunday*? That would be charming, and good Mrs Chinnery, who, thank Heaven, is beginning to feel better, would be enchanted to see you again at last, and to hear again your interesting instrument [probably Baillot's 1737 Stradivarius]. Reply immediately with a word, I beg you. Send it to the Hotel des Iles Britanniques, no. 5 rue de la Paix, where I shall go and retrieve it on Thursday morning.

Remember me to your dear family, and believe me to be always

Your affectionate Amico
JB Viotti[32]

In August William's letters were full of self-pitying laments about having been forced into the merchant's life against his will. By October the reason became clear. Joseph Cary, on his own admission, had been taking money from the firm for his own use, bringing the business to the point of bankruptcy. For the second time in his life, William's reputation was under threat, but this time the tables were turned, and William was the victim of another's misdeeds.

Viotti gives the amount of capital that William brought to the firm Cary & Co as 100,000 'livres' (francs?), a sum that had been lent him by George and Viotti himself when William had been without a sou.[33] If this statement is true, the debt seems to have been generously forgotten by Viotti, and it is not once mentioned in the enumeration of his losses. Once more Viotti chastises William for his complaining, and this time he is more severe: 'Madame is reading a letter from you that rends her heart. Is it possible that you persist in reiterating statements that have been made a thousand times before, and which I have already blamed you for? In the name of God, pause for reflection, and look to her situation!!! P.S. I took hold of your letter and threw it in the fire. You can pick a bone with your Amico if you are unhappy about it.'[34]

It seems incredible that Viotti had the energy to look after still more friends' concerns in 1823, yet this was indeed the case. General Edme-Etienne

---

[32] 'Mon cher bon Baillot, / Je sens un besoin très grand de faire un Duo avéc vous, et un plus grand besoin encore de vous embrasser. Seriez vous capable de nous sacrifier un de vos Dimanches? et venir ce *Dimanche prochain* diner avéc nous? Celà seroit charmant, et la bonne Mad[me] de Chinnery [sic], qui commence grace au Ciel à se sentir mieux, seroit enchantée de vous revoir enfin, et d'entendre encore votre interessant instrument. Repondez moi de suite un petit mot je vous prie, adressez le à l'hôtel des Iles Britanniques rüe de la Paix n.° 5 ou j'irai le chercher jeudi matin. / Rappelez moi au souvenir de votre aimable cercle et croyez moi toujours / Votre aff[né] Amico / JB Viotti' (GBV to Baillot, 29 July 1823, in Schwarz, 'Beethoven and the French Violin School', p. 444).

[33] GBV to WBC, 27 October 1823, PHM 94/143/1 – 14/62.

[34] 'Mad[me] lit une lettre de vous qui lui arrache l'ame, est-il possible, que vous vouliez revenir sans cesse sur des éxpressions répétées mille fois, et sur les quelles je vous ai déja tant blamé? Au nom de Dieu reflechissez mieux, et occupez vous un peu plus de la situation!!! P.S. Je me suis emparé de votre lettre et je l'ai jetée au feu. Prenez vous en à votre Amico si vous en etes mécontent' (*Ibid.*).

Desfourneaux, a decorated French hero who 25 years previously had been governor of the French colony Guadeloupe, had probably been introduced to Viotti by his brother André, and both the general and his son (who was at a military college in England), became close to Viotti and the Chinnerys. Desfourneaux was seeking compensation from the British Government for an incident that had occurred in Guadeloupe in 1794.[35] Viotti had asked George, who in 1823 was working in the Foreign Office, to ask his patron, British foreign secretary George Canning, to intervene.

On 18 April 1823 George wrote to Margaret with instructions for Viotti regarding Desfourneaux: 'Amico must explain to the General [...] that M. de Marcellus [French ambassador in London] has not neglected his affair, – far from it – but that *publick* business of the deepest interest on which he has had occasion to see M.C.[anning] has necessarily put individual cases rather out of sight for the present.' He went on to ask Viotti to 'discourage all thoughts of the General's coming to Eng$^{d.}$', as it would not assist his cause: 'Amico should also say to the Gen$^{l}$ that if I do not write to him myself it is because I really have no spare moments, – & that considering Amico as an "autre moi-même" I request him to be my substitute.' But George thought that Canning could do little for the general, as the matter came under the jurisdiction of the Treasury, not the Foreign Office.[36]

Then there was Viotti's preoccupation with Lima's debt of £930, which, in the present circumstances, became more pressing. But Lima was an inveterate gambler. He had paid Viotti one instalment of the debt in 1821, but nothing since his return to Portugal. George took up the matter on behalf of Viotti, writing at least three letters to Portugal between 1823 and 1824, the last to the former Portuguese ambassador in London and Chinnery friend, the Marquis de Palmella, now a minister in the Portuguese Government.[37] Palmella had been the intermediary through whom the first instalment had been paid.

Before leaving for London in November 1823 Viotti sat for a portrait by the French artist Peuvrier. After his death it was cast into a series of bronze medallions, one of which is in the Royal College of Music, London (see Figure 11). It depicts a profile of Viotti above a small violin, with the surrounding inscription: 'J.B. VIOTTI NE A FONTANETTO EN 1758 [sic] MORT EN 1824'. On the reverse is a representation of a sun, with a central inscription, 'NEC PLUS ULTRA', from which radiate the names of the different genres of Viotti's compositions: 'CONCERTOS QUATUORS NOCTURNES METHODE SONATES TRIOS DUOS SYMPHONIES'. Two months after Viotti's death George wrote to his mother from Spain:

> I read in one of the Paris journals (with reference to a series of medallic portraits) "Le meme artiste, Peuvrier, s'occupe du portrait de Viotti, composé d'après nature avant son départ pour Londres. Il paroitra incessament chez l'auteur Rue Mazarine No. 26; et

[35] See MC to WBC, 25 February 1819, PHM 94/143/1 – 17/45.

[36] GRC to MC, 18 April 1823, PHM 94/143/1 – 12/12.

[37] GRC to Palmella (copy), 11 March 1824, PHM 94/143/1 – 25/6.

> chez l'Eveque graveur, Palais Royal No. 121, passage Seraphin." Doubtless my Father will be anxious to secure you a good impression before the die is worn.[38]

The 'METHODE' mentioned on the bronze medallion refers to Viotti's violin treatise, which was only a fragment, and which Viotti had probably tried unsuccessfully to find time to write in between his frenetic visits to the Bourse. He had spoken of it to Baillot, perhaps at the Sunday chamber music party at Châtillon of 3 August 1823.[39] In his *Notice* Baillot wrote:

> In the last meeting we had with him, in 1823, he spoke of an elementary work he had commenced. [...] A violin treatise written by VIOTTI, with his unerring judgement, and with the delicate and profound sensibility that was his hallmark, rich in examples of his own compositions, must be of the greatest interest. Such a work would be welcomed with both respect and enthusiasm by all friends of the musical art. Let us hope that the executors of his last will and testament will yield to our wishes, and publish soon this precious work.[40]

Baillot seems to have had little idea of the strain Viotti was under at the time. To write such a treatise Viotti would have needed health and leisure, neither of which was granted him in 1823. The fragment that he had begun, which does not show any signs of developing into the excellent method that Baillot himself authored in 1835, was left in his will to Margaret, whom Baillot knew well, and who was clearly the target of the above plea. Margaret did make the fragment available for publication by passing it on to Baillot's pupil François Habeneck, who published a facsimile of it inside his own *Méthode*.[41]

Viotti's continuing anxiety over Margaret's indifferent health, over the Chinnerys' deteriorating affairs, and the burden of the supportive role he was expected to assume for William as well as for Margaret, capped by his own financial worries, finally took its toll. In November 1823 he wrote to William from London, where he and Margaret had returned for the winter, informing him that Margaret's health was holding out, but that his own was not: 'Unfortunately I am not as well as I should like. Not gout, but a cough, a cold, some damned thing is

---

[38] "The same artist, Peuvrier, is working on a portrait of Viotti, drawn from life before his departure for London. It will be available shortly from the artist's, Rue Magazine No. 26; and from L'Eveque the engraver, Palais Royal, No. 121, passage Seraphin." (GRC to MC, 20 May 1824, PHM 94/143/1 – 12/23).

[39] This would have been the date of the Sunday mentioned in GBV to Baillot, 29 July 1823, cited in Schwarz, 'Beethoven and the French Violin School', p. 444.

[40] 'Dans le dernier entretien que nous eûmes avec lui, en 1823, il nous parla d'un ouvrage élémentaire qu'il avait commencé: [...] Un traité didactique sur le violon, écrit par VIOTTI, avec cet esprit juste, ce sentiment délicat et profond qui le caractérisait, et riche d'exemples composés par lui, doit être du plus grand intérêt; un tel ouvrage serait accueilli par tous les amis de l'art musical avec autant de respect que d'empressement. Espérons que les dépositaires de ses dernières volontés céderont à nos vœux, et qu'ils feront bientôt paraître ce précieux travail' (*Notice*, pp. 12–13).

[41] *Méthode théorique et pratique de violon*, Canaux, Paris, *c.*1840.

making me as lethargic as an old hack.'[42] Viotti's correspondence with William ceases at this point, and the next undated letter from Margaret announces his approaching death:

> You will have understood that I have little hope of saving Amico— in fact he breathes, and that is all! But he says he is perfectly comfortable, has no pain any where, sleeps a great deal, indeed almost always, but his strength diminishes daily, & his countenance is dreadful to behold! [...] I am collecting all the fortitude I can muster for this [...] great trial, and I feel that I shall go through it if God continues the support & inward strength now granted to me. I dare not complain, or bewail, or think of any past days or things that would soften me,— *we must say but little about it*, for it will not bear dwelling upon. Your reflections upon the evils of our lives *would kill me*, were I to do more than hurry through them, as one would walk upon hot cinders![43]

Not yet having sold her Montagu Street house, Margaret had vacated it to allow it to be let while she and Viotti were in France, and had rented lodgings at 5 Upper Berkeley Street, which is where Viotti died. The news of his death comes in a letter dated 4 March 1824 and shows just how important Viotti was to Margaret as a companion and sharer of her fortunes, and as a buffer to William's pessimism. The letter also depicts a man sadly tormented in his death throes. One cause for his torment was the lack of reply to the letter he had written to Madame de Genlis in 1823 defending Margaret's honour, noted in Margaret's indignant 1825 letter to Madame de Genlis: 'When he [Viotti] was on his death-bed in London he remarked to me more than once, Madame, that you had never answered his letter!'[44] Margaret wrote to William the day after Viotti's death:

> My dearest Chinnery
> For your sake, and for George's I am exerting myself to the utmost to bear up against this afflicting dispensation of Providence: Amico died yesterday morning at 7 oClock,— I wish I could say he had died easily or comfortably, but quite the reverse of that was the case. However it is all over now,— the deep impression the horrid sounds have left, can only wear off by degrees, and by my endeavours & prayers to Heaven.
> Remember that I have now no *companion* nor *present comfort* but yourself,— Therefore if you give way to grief, all will soon be over with us both! Keep up your courage for my sake and for George's. I have long been aware that the sad event was inevitable,— or at least very probable.[45]

Viotti died aged 69 on 3 March. His death was announced in the 1824 *Gentleman's Magazine* (vol. 94, pp. 284, 380), and in the *Morning Chronicle* of 8

---

[42] 'Moi, malheureusement je ne suis pas aussi bien que je le voudrois, point de goute, mais une toux, un rhume, un diable que sais-je, qui me rend si peu agissant qu'une vieille rosse' (GBV to WBC, 17 November 1823, PHM 94/143/1 – 14/64).

[43] MC to WBC, *c.*March 1824, PHM 94/143/1 – 17/53.

[44] 'Lorsqu'il étoit sur son lit de mort à Londres, il m'a observé plus d'une fois, Madame, que vous ne lui aviez jamais répondu!' (MC to Mme de Genlis (copy), 1 July 1825, Fisher 2000 – 6/36; Yim, D53).

[45] MC to WBC, 4 March 1824, PHM 94/143/1 – 17/54.

March 1824, where the notice was equally brief: 'It is with very sincere regret that we announce the death of Mr Viotti, the celebrated performer on the violin. He died in London on the 3rd instant, after a short illness, in the 69th year of his age. Mr Viotti was a native of Piedmont.'

There was also Fayolle's eulogy in the *Harmonicon* of April 1824, but surprisingly, no death notice in either the *Allgemeine musikalische Zeitung* or its British emulator the *Quarterly Musical Magazine and Review*. The *AMZ* however did mention it in the context of a report on the annual general meeting of the *Société académique des enfants d'Apollon* of 27 May 1824, during which the speaker welcomed new members, among whom was young Liszt, and regretted the passing of some old ones, among whom were Viotti and Salieri.[46]

Viotti's funeral service, conducted by Reverend R.H. Chapman, was held on 11 March 1824 in the church of St Marylebone in the parish where he died.[47] The church register states that he was buried in vault no. 6 under Paddington Street,[48] now Paddington Street Gardens. It is sad to reflect that Viotti, who hated the confinement of big cities, and who loved nothing better than to roam purposelessly in the countryside, losing himself in the contemplation of nature, should have been laid to an uncertain repose in one of London's most overcrowded cemeteries. By the end of the nineteenth century the ever-expanding population of the city caused the graves to mount to eight deep, before many of the bones were removed to an ossuary. As grim proof of the inadequacy of the site, the tiny rectangle that constitutes the gardens today sits well above street level, one preserved sarcophagus displayed as a reminder of the site's original function.

Baillot, having made a pilgrimage to the St Marylebone cemetery sometime in 1824, included an account of the visit in his beautiful testimony to Viotti, written on the anniversary of his death. It finishes on a note of real regret:

> We have especially heeded our heart's dictates and have religiously scattered some flowers on the tomb of VIOTTI, of this head of a school, on whom heaven had lavished its favours, whose talent always followed the noble impulses of his soul, who combined grace and sublimity, sweetness and strength, unity and variety, the natural and the elegant, and who unconsciously displayed the goodness of his heart in all that he did, an excellent human being as well as an admirable artist, whom we have always honoured and whom we miss like a father![49]

---

[46] *AMZ*, 19 August 1824, col. 554.

[47] 'Mort et enterrement de J.-B. Viotti', *Revue de musicologie* (1924), vol. 5, pp. 131–2.

[48] Directions for Burials, St Marylebone parish records, London Metropolitan Archives.

[49] 'Nous avons surtout écouté la voix de notre cœur, et nous avons jetté religieusement quelques fleurs sur la tombe de VIOTTI; de ce chef d'école, à qui le ciel avait prodigué ses faveurs, dont le talent suivit toujours les nobles impulsions de son âme, qui joignit la grâce à la sublimité, la douceur à la force, l'unité à la variété, le naturel à l'élégance, et qui manifesta, sans y songer, la bonté de son cœur dans tout ce qu'il fit; homme excellent autant qu'artiste admirable, que nous avons constamment honoré et que nous regrettons comme un père!' (*Notice*, p. 13).

CHAPTER 19

# After Viotti's death

After Viotti's death Margaret sold her Montagu Street home and moved back to Châtillon on 25 May 1824, having spent the intervening weeks in mourning at Orpington with her sister Mrs Elizabeth Marsh. She remained at Châtillon for the summer of 1824 and the winter of 1824–25. George was in Spain at the time of Viotti's death, and the subject takes up much space in his 53 letters to his mother of this time. Margaret's side of this correspondence has been lost, and with it much information concerning the aftermath of Viotti's death. But there nevertheless remains enough detail in George's replies to understand some of the circumstances.

Margaret received many condolences on the death of Viotti. One which particularly touched her heart was was from Hugues-Bernard Maret, now the Duc de Bassano, who had been one of the objects of Viotti's concern during his anxiety-filled voyage on the Continent 30 years earlier, and who had probably renewed contact with Viotti and the Chinnerys in 1820 on his return to France after a five-year exile. He wrote to Margaret:

> It seems impossible to be condemned to never again see a friend of 34 years [...] After weeping for this friend who was so lovable, so kind, so true, and so dear, all my sad thoughts turned to you. Your sorrow is a subject of very painful concern to my wife and me. We who share [your sorrow] have a need to know how you are supporting it. Is your health able to withstand these assaults? Madame de Chinnery [sic], will you return soon to France? When shall we be able to attempt to console you by grieving with you? My son will ask all these questions of our dear George. How earnestly shall we interrogate him on his return![1]

The letter was signed, sincerely and respectfully, 'Le Duc de Bassano'. After his imprisonment at the hands of the Austrians (1793–95), Maret had returned to France a hero, and at the time of the 18 brumaire coup d'état, was plucked by Napoleon from semi-retirement and projected into prominence. He was appointed to successively higher and higher offices, was made a count in 1807, a duke in

[1] 'Il me sembloit impossible d'etre condamné à ne plus revoir un ami de 34 ans [...] Après avoir pleuré cet ami si aimable, si bon, si vrai, si cher, toutes mes tristes pensées se sont tournées vers vous. Votre douleur est pour ma femme et pour moi le sujet d'une préoccupation bien pénible. Nous qui partageons, nous avons besoin de savoir comment vous la supportez. Votre santé résiste-t-elle à ces atteintes? Reviendrez vous Madam de Chinnery? bientôt en france? Quand pouvons nous tenter de vous consoler en nous affligeant avec vous? Mon fils aura toutes ces questions à [poser à] notre cher Georges. Avec quel empressement nous l'interrogerons à son retour!' (Duc de Bassano to MC, 30 March 1824, Fisher 2000 – 4/25).

1809, and minister of foreign affairs, 1811–13. His only rivals for Napoleon's favour were Fouché and Talleyrand, and he displaced the latter when Talleyrand fell from grace in 1807. At the Restoration Maret came under attack from all sides, and retreated to the country. During the *Cent Jours* he rallied again to Napoleon's side, accompanying him to Waterloo. From 1815 he had been living in exile in Switzerland, imprisoned in Austria, given his freedom in Italy, finally returning to France in 1820. The familiar tone of the above letter lends weight to the likelihood that it was indeed the Duc de Bassano who had given Viotti and Margaret intermittent shelter in Paris over the previous few years.

It is ironic that one of Napoleon's most loyal supporters should have been on such close terms with a patriotic English family who hated Napoleon with an implacable British hatred. But such was the strength of Viotti's friendships that they were able to cross political borders. The duke, who did not know of George's posting to Spain, enclosed a letter for him, to be delivered in person by his eldest son, named, appropriately, Napoleon. He asked George to receive his son with the same friendliness that he had felt for George himself since George was a child (a reference to the 1802 meetings in Paris). By the duke's own words we learn that he first met Viotti in 1790.[2]

Among the mourners who visited Margaret after Viotti's death were his friends Cailleux and the Comte de St Sauveur. The latter made contact with George in Madrid in May 1824 when he came to Spain as an officer of the Garde du Corps in the French army of occupation. George wrote to his mother: 'The Cte de St Sauveur knew the full extent of grief which you had suffered on the occasion of poor Amico's death; for he had received, he said, a long letter from you at the time on that heart rending subject.'[3] Of Cailleux he wrote: 'Cailleux's first visit [after Viotti's death] must in truth have been a painful one, – & so will my first meeting with him be, at any distance of time: there are certain fountains of grief, as I have often heard you say, which never can be dried up.'[4] In the same letter George mentions another name connected with the Paris Opéra, Baron de La Ferté, who had suffered a 'reverse of fortune' as a result of having been 'engaged in some manufacturing speculation' which had failed. Margaret also received a visit from Rode, who dined at Châtillon in May 1825, to the surprise of George, who thought he had settled for life in Berlin.[5]

While in Madrid George paid a nostalgic visit to Viotti's old friend Francesco Vaccari, who, having lost his court position as first violinist to King Ferdinand of Spain, now found himself in unhappy circumstances. Having sent the violinist an engraved portrait of Viotti, George was invited to a private concert at Vaccari's home:

---

[2] Duc de Bassano to GRC, 30 March 1824, Fisher 2000 – 4/25.

[3] GRC to MC, 20 May 1824, PHM 94/143/1 – 12/23.

[4] GRC to MC, 15 July 1824, PHM 94/143/1 – 12/30.

[5] GRC to MC, 28 May 1825, PHM 94/143/1 – 12/63.

> I [...] had brought with me three or four impressions of Amico's Print, & I sent one two days ago, framed, with a corresponding letter *in Spanish*, to poor Vaccari, who is very low in health & spirits, so much so that his dejection nearly amounts to an alienation of intellect. His undeserved expulsion from the King's service through the intrigues of rivals who are unfit even to rosin his bow, has been the cause of it: but my present & letter gave Mad. V. (who is just the same as when you knew her) sincere pleasure, & she immediately invited me to a private concert at their house given yesterday morning, where for the first time since I have been in Madrid I heard something like music. Vaccari himself though distressingly grave & silent plays as well as ever, & Mad. Vaccari's brother, [Francesco] Bruneti, is a prodigy on the Violoncello, quite equal to Duport & Crosdill & very superior to Lin[d]ley. A *female* pupil of Vaccari's executed one of Amico's concerto's [sic] on the violin, & this was almost too much for me, those sounds not having vibrated on my ear since they last came from the "parent-lyre"— Amico's print occupies the most distinguished place in Vaccari's drawing room, & though the poor man's finances are probably slender his habitation is excellent, being the rez de chaussee of the hotel of the Duque de Tamame's.[6]

Margaret was the sole beneficiary of Viotti's small estate, as his will attests. Among the items Viotti bequeathed to Margaret was the famous 1712 Stradivarius which George referred to in his letters as the 'Buttera', after the Sicilian prince from whom Viotti purchased it. 'Buttera' may have been a nomenclature known only to Viotti's contemporaries, or perhaps one used privately by Viotti and the Chinnerys. The violin was well known among Viotti's string-instrument colleagues. It was 'of the maker's largest and boldest form, extremely handsome in appearance, the tone being remarkable for luscious maturity of quality and sympathetic responsiveness to the lightest possible touch of bow and finger.'[7]

Another Stradivarius known to have been owned by Viotti was the 1709 one used by Marie Hall (1884–1956), a pupil of the Czech violinist Pisek Sevcik who had studied at the Prague Conservatoire under Anton Bennewitz, himself a pupil of Friedrich Pixis, thereby aptly giving Marie Hall direct lineage, in terms of violin playing principles, to Viotti. The Sotheby auction catalogue of 7 November 1968 shows that this violin was purchased by Jack Morrison for £22,000.

Soon after Viotti's death Margaret received a request to buy the 1712 'Buttera' from G. Duport, son of Viotti's good friend the cellist Jean-Louis Duport. G. Duport, also a cellist, wished to preserve the violin in company with the Stradivari cello that had belonged to his father. Addressed to Madame Chinnery, 17 Montagu Street, Portman Square, London, he wrote from Paris 11 days after Viotti's death:

> Madame,
> The irreparable loss that the arts have suffered in the person of Monsieur Viotti has dismayed all those who have the honour of praticising them, and even more especially, those who had the honour of knowing him.

---

[6] GRC to MC, 4 July 1825, PM 94/143/1 – 12/69.

[7] W.H., A.F. and A.E. Hill (1963), *Antonio Stradivari: His Life and Work (1644–1737)*, Dover Publications, New York, p. 153.

It is with deep sadness and with no other title than that of being one of his great admirers and as the son of his oldest and best friend, that I dare address you, Madame, with the object of having a very precious souvenir of this great man. I should like, if it is at all possible, to purchase his violin. M. Robberechts thinks that it is at your disposal. I would be very obliged to you, Madame, if you would let me know if you would consent to let me have it, and at what price?

It would give me great pleasure to reunite his instrument with my father's cello, and preserve both precious instruments together.

I dare to hope that you will be so kind as to reply.

Please accept, Madame, the assurance of my respect and utter devotion.

Your sombre servant

G. Duport

Violoncello professor

Rue Veuve S[t] Médéric 12° n° 3[8]

This application must have been refused, as the 1712 violin, according to Herbert Goodkind's *Violin Iconography*, was sold in 1824 by the French auction house Hôtel Bouilleron for £152. The month was August, according to a letter from George to his mother, in which he wrote: 'Poor dear Amico's best violin appears from your statement to have sold tolerably well'.[9] It was subsequently sold in 1853 for £240 by Puttick and Simpson (now Phillips), and again in 1860 for £220 by the Hôtel Bouilleron.

Among the owners that Goodkind lists for the 1712 violin is the name Hill (London violin dealers William E. Hill & Sons). A letter from 'William E. Hill & Sons, 140 New Bond Street, London W' to Edward Heron-Allen, dated 26 March 1901, written after they had learned of the latter's acquisition of the recently discovered Viotti papers, states that they had 'acquired one of the finest Stradivarius violins that exists' and attached to it was a statement that it was in the possession of Viotti at his death. The letter also seeks information regarding prices that violins fetched in Viotti's day, to be used 'for our book on Stradivari',[10] which would be published in 1902.

---

[8] 'Madame, / L'irréparable Perte que les Arts ont fait dans la Personne de Monsieur Viotti a consterné tous ceux qui se font honneur de les professer, et plus particulierement encore ceux qui avaient le Bonheur de le connaître. / C'est avec une profonde affliction et sans autre titre que celui d'un de ses grands admirateurs et comme fils de son plus ancien et meilleur Ami que j'ose m'adresser à vous, Madame, pour avoir de ce grand homme, un souvenir bien precieux; c'est [que] je desirerais[?], si toutefois la chose est possible acheter son Violon. M[r] Roberechts pense qu'il est à votre disposition. Je vous serais obligé, Madame, de me faire savoir si vous consentiriez à me le céder, et à quel Prix? / Il me serait bien agréable de réunir son Instrument à la Basse de mon Père pour les conserver précieusement. / J'ose espérer une réponse de vos Bontés. / Agréez, Madame, l'Assurance de mon respect et de mon entier devouement. / Votre sombre Serviteur / G. Duport / Professeur de Violoncelle / Rue Veuve S[t] Médéric 12° n° 3' (G. Duport to MC, 14 March 1824, Fisher 2000 – 4/24).

[9] GRC to MC, 23 August 1824, PHM 94/143/1 – 12/36; Goodkind, p. 29.

[10] William Hill to Edward Heron-Allen, 26 March 1901, Viotti Papers, RCM.

The other item that Margaret needed to sell to realise some ready cash was the grand piano at Châtillon. George wrote to her on 26 October 1824 that he was 'quite miserable' at the thought that Margaret had now 'ceased to benefit by contribution from my Father & poor Amico', and that although the sale of Viotti's property would cover 'his part of the deficit' in the present year, they would have to make provision for the coming one.[11] The piano, one of Broadwood's best, should fetch a good price, George thought. George's advice to his mother on making use of Viotti's name to sell the piano, even though he had not been its owner, was astute, and the venues he suggested for its advertisement were likely to have attracted the desired buyers:

> I have a hint to give you with regard to the Pianoforte, if you like it. People will certainly not take the trouble of going out to Chatillon on a venture for that purpose, & it is not easy to find a safe person to whom you could entrust it at Paris;— but why not cause it to be known at Galignani's, and at Imbaut's (if I spell the name right, meaning a great publisher of music & some of poor Amico's compositions) or at several of the great Magazins de Musique & Lutiers; describing the Pianoforte as having been imported direct from England by the late celebrated J.B.V. & allowed to be one of the finest instruments which had ever come out of M. Broadwood's atelier, & finished in all respects proportionably to the excellence of it's tone. Might not Cailleux be very useful in mentioning it, & ought not the professors who so often came to make up a trio or quartett, to bestir themselves, if applied to by Cailleux or some other person, to find a purchaser. And why not Mad. De Vaudreuil & Mad. De Boigne among their friends?[12]

The Galignanis had an English bookshop and circulating library in Paris, and published *Galignani's Messenger*, a daily newspaper circulating among English residents all over Europe. Their headquarters served as a club where the English and other visitors to Paris met, and as such was an ideal location to attract prospective English buyers. Viotti's old friend and colleague Imbault had sold his publishing business to Janet et Cotelle in 1812, and the shop, which must have retained the name of Imbault, was located in the precincts of the Théâtre-Italien, where recent memories of Viotti still lingered.

Margaret's friends the Comtesse de Vaudreuil and the Comtesse de Boigne had both lived in London, and had both known Viotti well. Madame de Boigne was the daughter of the Marquis d'Osmond, Louis XVIII's ambassador to London, 1815–18, who himself was a *habitué* of 17 Montagu Street in 1818, and whose wife was farewelled by Margaret in early 1819 before the couple returned to France.[13] Madame de Boigne owned a small manor in the village of Châtenay near Sceaux, in the vicinity of Châtillon. She had a fine singing voice and probably sang at some of Margaret's and Viotti's Châtillon parties. The Vaudreuils had attended Viotti/Chinnery concerts in England and France from 1809 to 1817, the year of the Comte's death.

---

[11] GRC to MC, 26 October 1824, PHM 94/143/1 – 12/43.

[12] GRC to MC, 6 August 1824, PHM 94/143/1 – 12/33.

[13] MC to WBC, 25 February 1819, PHM 94/143/1 – 17/45.

Part of Viotti's legacy to Margaret were three lawsuits, which George mentions in his letter of 27 June 1824: 'I thought poor Amico had only left one law suit, but you talk of three. If there is to be a priority of decision I hope it may be in favour of the Feydeau one.'[14] Viotti had been unable to realise any money in his lifetime from the sale of his Feydeau Theatre box, still being contested in the French courts. A letter from George to his mother dated 20 October 1824 indicates that Margaret had won the case, but had not yet concluded a successful sale: 'Though so ancient a date, I fear that you will not even now be able to tell me that poor Amico's contested box-property is made over to you, and that from the prospect held out, the present year may almost close before you actually touch the possible 3,000 francs.'[15]

At the beginning of 1825 there was news of a successful sale of the box, yielding twice the expected sum. William Chinnery's proposal to keep the box for their own use had clearly been overruled by Margaret:

> The greater part of your letter is devoted to the subject of the Feydeau box. Many many thanks for putting me so completely in possession of the merits of the case & especially for the gratifying result with which you wind up the whole disquisition. Situated as we are the possession of the 6 000fr. is preferable to any ulterior benefits,— & besides when my father, in the preceding letter, argued the advantages of the opposite course, there was no prospect held out of the sale producing such a sum. It really is a capital result and I am willing to hope, since it is part of the same property, that what you are entitled to on the score of the other 8.$^{m}$ may not fall short of the additional 2 000: you have, alas, an abundance of losses to set off against this little gain.[16]

The other expected sum of money which George says is to come from 'part of the same property' must have been a share of some other entitlement from the Feydeau Theatre that was Viotti's due.

The year 1825 brought two crushing blows for Margaret. The first was the publication of the first three volumes of Madame de Genlis's controversial *Mémoires*, which rocked Paris and were the talk of society for many months. The *Mémoires* were a medley of jumbled reminiscences, recommendations, recriminations and opinions, in which her friends, all named, were alternately praised and savaged. The first volume contained a very warm tribute to Viotti:

> The following year I admired the playing of the famous Pugnani, one of whose claims to glory consists in his having been the master of Viotti, an artist born to serve forever as a model to all those who devote themselves to the arts, through his prodigious talent, his cultured mind, his morals, his pure and noble conduct at all times, and the qualities of his heart.[17]

---

[14] GRC to MC, 27 June 1824, PHM 94/143/1 – 12/27.

[15] GRC to MC, 20 October 1824, PHM 94/143/1 – 12/42.

[16] GRC to MC, 20 January 1825, PM 94/143/1 – 12/50.

[17] 'L'année d'ensuite, j'entendis avec admiration le fameux Pugnani, dont l'un des grands titres de gloire est d'avoir été le maître de Viotti, artiste fait pour servir à jamais de modèle à ceux qui se consacrent aux arts, par son prodigieux talent, la culture de son esprit, ses

But in the third volume Madame de Genlis accused Margaret of losing her precious notebook, a manuscript containing her reflections on the death of her daughter, which Casimir Baecker had brought to England in 1807.[18] The spread of such a rumour was precisely what Viotti had tried to avert by his 1823 letter to the famous author, which she never answered, and which was the cause of much of his distress on his death-bed. George wrote indignantly from Spain:

> The Memoirs in question, the first two volumes at least, have found their way to the Spanish libraries, & the misrepresentation is therefore generally circulated [...] What you add of the difficulty of getting letters to reach Mad. de G. proves that Casimir is as mischievously artful as ever, & that his pretended retirement to a troisieme Etage apparently en grande dévotion (which poor Amico once told me of) is mere hypocrisy. The tribute to Amico in the Memoirs is unquestionably gratifying to us; but it is more than neutralized by the other paragraph.[19]

The second far more severe shock for Margaret was George's own sudden death from an unknown illness in Madrid, just three months later. The letter from George Canning describing to Margaret the circumstances of his death survives in the Royal College of Music Viotti collection.[20] It was presumably then that William rejoined his wife in Paris, where they resided at 88 rue du Faubourg-St-Martin, living as a couple for the first time since 1812. William himself died in 1827, leaving Margaret embittered and sickened of life. To make matters worse Margaret's reputation was attacked in a lawsuit, the subject of which is not known. This was apparently additional to the three lawsuits mentioned earlier by George.

It may be conjectured that the attack on Margaret's reputation arose from her 24-year cohabitation with Viotti. The attack is spoken of in a letter from the French consul general in London, Baron Armand de Séguier, clearly written in response to one from Margaret seeking a testimony to her good character. Margaret was about to appear before Séguier's brother, president of the Royal Court in Paris. The baron, who had been a guest at Margaret's and Viotti's musical parties at Montagu Street, supplied the testimony, adding: 'Her adversary is using the most odious means against her and is seeking to slander her. While she was living in England Mme Chinnery had no need to give proof of the high esteem in which she was held in London, and which I was witness to.'[21] There is no further reference to this court case in the Chinnery papers.

Margaret died at her home, 78 avenue des Champs-Elysées, on 5 November 1840, attended by Miss Mary Whitaker Greene, who inherited the entire CFP

---

mœurs, sa conduite noble et pure dans tous les temps, et les qualités de son cœur' (*Mémoires*, vol. 1 p. 144).

[18] *Mémoires*, vol. 3, p. 198; Yim, *The Unpublished Correspondence of Mme de Genlis.*

[19] GRC to MC, 4 July 1825, PHM 94/143/1 – 12/69.

[20] George Canning to MC, 31 October 1825, RCM.

[21] 'Sa partie adverse emploie contre elle les moyens les plus odieux et cherche a la calomnier— dans l'existence qu'elle avoit en angleterre, Mme Chinnery vivoit sans avoir besoin à faire attester la consideration dont elle jouissoit a Londres et dont j'ai été temoin' (Baron Armand de Séguier to MC, 30 May 1827, Fisher 2000 – 4/28).

collection, including the Viotti papers. Three years later Miss Greene received two letters from London from the composer Sir Henry Rowley Bishop, written on behalf of Prince Albert, seeking Madame Cherubini's address in Paris.[22] These are the last letters in the Chinnery collection.

* * *

It might be wondered what course Viotti's life would have taken had he not met the Chinnerys. Would he have resumed a lifelong performing career in London if he had not succumbed to the temptation of a lucrative career as a merchant? Would he have returned to Paris to pursue a musical career there? The indications are that he would not. Viotti's temperament was not suited to the drudgery of a musician's life, especially that of a musician at Napoleon's court, where, according to Baillot, artists were treated worse than servants. Viotti was proud. He was a man of action, who disliked indecision and procrastination. He had a strong entrepreneurial drive, and might have succeeded very well in his entrepreneurial endeavours if, like many of his colleagues, he had chosen a music publishing business instead of one in which he was so completely at the mercy of his debtors. Viotti had early acquired a taste for aristocratic and moneyed society, and through commerce he meant to, and did, initially, with the Chinnerys' help, acquire the necessary wealth to enable him to continue this lifestyle.

But therein lay the essential contradiction with his art. Entrepreneurial activities did not leave him the leisure to pursue what he loved best, although his overriding love of music meant that he did not cease composing. Did his cohabitation with the Chinnerys have a stultifying effect on his creativity? Daily life in the bosom of a family was not, as Viotti himself said, compatible with the career of musician, and may not have been ideal for composing either, but it did offer the advantages of a comfortable and regular life. However Viotti's most important works, his violin concertos, were written when he had an orchestra at his disposal – in Paris the fine orchestras belonging to wealthy aristocrats or private societies, and in London the King's Theatre orchestra. After those times his output consisted essentially of chamber music, much of which seems to have been written specifically for his pupils or for dilettante co-performers in private concerts.

It must be emphasised that although Viotti's decision to throw his lot in with the Chinnerys' made the practice of his musical art very difficult, the decision to take this course was entirely his own. In assessing Viotti's ignominious fall from hailed artistic genius to failed entrepreneur White writes that 'the factors that brought Viotti's career to a sad close are not alone the result of his own poor judgement in leaving the fields in which his superb talent lay', and that the reason for his demise was essentially that he had had the misfortune to be born into the wrong era – 'too late to settle into the subservient position of a court musician but too early to enjoy the fortune and prestige of the next generation of violin

[22] Dated 3 and 19 August 1843, Fisher 2000 – 49/11, 49/12.

virtuosos.'[23] Perhaps the true reason lay within Viotti himself. It was more than anything else his temperament that caused him to follow the path he did. Just as his pride and impetuosity prevented him from becoming a subservient court musician, so his intolerance of ill-educated public audiences would have prevented him from pursuing the career of a violin virtuoso, even if such opportunites had been available in his time. But in the final analysis it was Viotti's loyalty and devotion in friendship that determined his fate. Fidelity was his strongest character trait, and in the end it triumphed even over music.

---

[23] White, *From Vivaldi to Viotti*, p. 332.

# Appendix

**Letter from Pugnani to Viotti, 16 October 1793**

*NYPL JOB 97-52, item 1*
*Address*: A Monsieur / Monsieur Viotti / Celebre Proffeseur de Musique / A Gant / dans la flandre Autrichienne

Turin, 16 October 1793

My dear Viotti, you have come to life at last and sent me news of yourself. It has been two years since I heard from you. I would have given a pound of my blood to have seen you here, but since the thing is impossible, I shall confine myself to expecting you next year, or else I shall come and see you if my affairs permit. For more than a year my head has been incapable of thinking of music. Those French dogs have caused us such anxiety. You know that we ceded Savoy to them, and Nice. We thought that at any moment they would cross the Alps. But the right time for them has passed, and for the moment (even though they would like to) they are no longer able to threaten us. But the sums that we are obliged to lay out to maintain large armies make us uneasy.

We are holding out this year but if things continue this way I do not know what we shall do. We also had to send troops to Toulon to support the English. In short we hope that the outlook will change, for soon there will be 35,000 men in garrison there (including English, Spanish, Neapolitans and Piedmontese). We hope they will prevail. Princes and kings are in the army and that has given courage to our troops who have displayed incredible valour.

Now to you, my dear friend. I learned with great pleasure that you had covered yourself in glory in London. You will do the same again this year, and my joy will know no bounds. I played one of your latest concertos in E major. It pleased me very much, the style is new, and [it] is well written. I wrote a letter to you in London four or five months ago, which you will undoubtedly find on your return at the post office.

Now to my private affairs. I will tell you that having putting aside a little money, and owing to the king having increased my salary, I thought I would be able to live out my days in comfort. But this unfortunate war has spoiled everything. Firstly the king is keeping back a quarter of all salaries, and as well as that, he is deducting an eighth and a quarter on life annuities, and on all other ordinary annuities. As you can imagine that makes a hole in my purse.

What have I been doing? A certain Salomon passed through here and told me with assurance of the power he wielded in London in matters musical. I extended to him every kindness in my power, and he offered me his services. I accepted them, and an opportunity presented itself. I therefore wrote to him to beg him to do what I am about to describe to you. I should tell you that I took the novel Werther[1] (which you certainly know) and set it to music. I made a melodrama out of it. I wanted to have it printed with some new symphonies, and some concerto or other. I wrote to tell him that I would associate him in the venture if he would take the trouble to sell this music, and correct it after it was printed. Which I did. That gentleman did not even reply to my letter. Having ascertained that he did receive it, I wrote to Borghi.[2] You are well aware that he owes me this service out of gratitude. I pressed him with the same proposition. Do you know what he replied (politely, but I understood the gist of his letter)? He said that my music was no longer in vogue in London, and that Haydn alone had a reputation, along with other new composers, and that he would not take charge of it. That, my dear friend, was the worthy reply that I had from him. If it were possible to get through France I would have set off immediately to show them my music and my talent, and to see who was right or wrong. But for the moment there is nothing to do but vent one's rage in silence. I assure you that that really hurt me. If you could do me this service you would oblige me greatly. I should also tell you that Werther has also been transcribed and reduced for harpsichord. Without giving yourself too much trouble, see what you can do, and write immediately and tell me what I must do. Between ourselves, you would be doing me a very great favour.

Do not forget to send me your address when you arrive in London, otherwise you know that letters do not arrive at their destination. My family is well, and we would have prepared a bed and *some good sauce* for you, but that will have to be for next year.

Adieu. Love me, do not forget me, and know that no one in the world loves you more than your friend Pugnani.

---

Turin ce 16 8[bre] 1793

Mon cher Viotti, vous vous reveillés a la fin, et vous m'avéz donné de vos nouvelles, qu'il y avoit plus de deux années que je n'en avoi recu [sic]. j'auréz donné une livre de mon sang pour vous voire ici, mais puisque la chose est impossible, je me bornerai a vous attendre l'année prochaine, ou que j'yrai vous voire si les affaires s'arrangent. il y a plus d'une année que je n'ai plus la tête pour penser a la musique. ces chiens de francais nous [ont] fort inquiété. vous savez que nous leurs avons abbandonée la Savoje, et Nice. nous avons cru qu'a tous moments il auroient passée les Alpes. mais le bon moment pour eux c'est passée et pour à present (malgré leur volonté) il n'est plus possible qu'il nous inquietent. mais les depenses que l'on est obligé de faire pour entretenir des grandes armées nous mettent mal a notre aise.

Patience encore pour cette année mais si les choses continuent je ne sai pas comme nous ferons. il a encore fallu envoier des troupes a Toulon pour soutenir les Anglois. enfin nous esperons que les choses changent de face, car dans peu il y aura a Toulon 35m. hommes de garnison (entre Anglois Espagnols, Napolitains, [et] Piemontois) et qu'il[s]

---

[1] Goethe's novel *Die Leiden des jungen Werthers.*

[2] Luigi Borghi, former pupil of Pugnani and assistant manager of O'Reilly's opera company at the Pantheon in 1791.

passeront outre— les Princes, et le Roj sont a l'armée. celà a donnée du courage a nos troupes qui ont donnée des preuves d'une valeur incroiable.

Venons a vous mon cher, j'ai appris avec bien du plaisir que vous vous etes couvert de gloire a Londre. vous continueréz de mesme cet année, et celà me comblera de joie. j'ai jouée un de vos derniers concerto[s] en mi naturel. il m'a beaucoup plu, il est heureux pour le stil, [et] bien ecrit. je vous ai ecrit a londre il y a quatre, ou cinq mois, que vous trouveréz (la lettre), indubitablement a votre arrivée a la poste.

Venons a present a mes affaires particulieres. je vous dirai qu'après avoir mis a côté un peu d'argent, et le Roj ayant augmenté ma paye je croioi de pouvoir vivre avec toutes les comodités de la vie le reste de mes jours mais cette malheureuse guerre a tout desconcertée. Primo le Roj retient le quart sur toutes les payes outre celà le 8ème et le quatème sur les rentes viageres, et sur les autres rentes ordinaires. celà (comme vous sentéz bien) fait un voïde dans ma bourse. qu'ai-je fait. il est passée ici un certain Salomon qui m'a assurée sur le pouvoir qu'il avoit a londre sur la partie musicale. je lui ai fait toutes les politesses que j'ai pu, il me a offert ces [ses] services. je les ai acceptée a [et] l'occasion s'est presentée. je lui ai donc écrit pour le prier de ce que je vais vous ecrire. il faut que vous sachiéz que j'ai pris le Roman de Werther, que vous conaisséz assurement) je l'ai mis en musique. j'en ai fait un Mellodrame. je voulai le faire imprimer avec des sinfonies nouvelles, et quelque concerto. je lui ai ecrit que je l'associerai s'il vouloit se donner la peine de vendre cette musique, et de la coriger quand elle seréz imprimée. che farci. ce Monr ne m'a pas meme repondu. ajant scu qu'il avoit recu ma lettre je me suis adressée à Borghi, vous savéz s'il devoit par reconnoissance s'emploier a me rendre ce service. je l'ai prié instament lui faissant les memes propositions. Savéz vous ce qu'il m'a repondu avec politesse mais que j'ai très bien compris le sens de sa lettre: que ma musique n'etoit plus goutée a londre. que le seul Hayden avoit de la reputation et d'autres auteurs nouveaux et qu'il ne s'en chargeréz pas. Voilà mon cher la digne recompense que j'ai recu. Si l'on avéz pu passer par la france je serai parti sur le champ pour leur faire voire par ma musique, et mon talent s'ils avoient tort, ou raison. mais dans ce moment, il faut enrager, et se taire. je vous assure que cela m'a bien fait de la peine. si vous pouvéz me rendre ce service vous m'obligeriéz beaucoup. je dois encor vous dire que Werther est aussi mis et reduit pour le clavecin. sans gêne vojéz ce que vous pouvéz faire, et ecrivéz moi tout de suite ce que je dois faire. entre nous vous me rendriéz un très grand service. n'oubliéz pas de m'envoier votre adresse quand vous seréz a londre sans quoi vous savéz que les lettres ne parviennent pas a son adresse.

Ma famille se porte bien et nous vous aurions preparée un lit et *de bonne sausse*. mais celà sera pour l'année prochaine. adieu aiméz moi, ne m'oubliéz pas et croiéz que personne au monde ne vous aime plus que votre ami Pugnani.

# Bibliography

## Primary sources

Australia, Sydney, Powerhouse Museum:
The Chinnery Family Papers, 1789–1837, PHM 94/143/1.
Printed music in E.A. and V.I. Crome collection:
Viotti's 'Grand Concerto in G', arranged for pianoforte by J.L. Dussek from Violin Concerto no. 23, published by Clementi, Banger and Hyde, PN 561, watermark 1802, 88/1167-51.
Viotti's Violin Concerto no. 3, published by Sieber, *c.*1782, 95/190/1 – 1:8.
Viotti's Violin Concerto no. 5, published by Sieber, *c.*1782, 95/190/2 – 1:8.
Bound collection of sheet music by various composers, A8213.
Autograph letters in E.A. and V.I. Crome collection, A8213:
R. Kreutzer / N. Isouard to Citizen Bonnet, 21 ventôse [12 March 1801].
P. Rode / J.-M. Hurel de Lamare to P. Baillot, 8 August 1803.
P. Baillot to Baron de Schonen, 15 September 1831.
N. Mori to M. Ollivier, 11 September 1837, among others.
Australia, University of Sydney, Fisher Library, The Chinnery Family Papers, *c.*1795–1843, 2000 – 1-49.
France, Archives nationales, Département de Paris:
Will of Margaret Tresilian Chinnery, proven Paris, 12 December 1840, -ET/LX/761.
Deed of succession of Margaret Tresilian Chinnery, 4 May 1841, D. $Q^7$ 3465.
U.K., British Library, The Travel Journals of George Robert Chinnery, 1819–20, 3 vols, Add MS 64093, Add MS 64094, Add MS 64095 (Microfilm copies in Fisher Library).
U.K., Lambeth Palace Library, Vicar-General marriage licences.
U.K., London Metropolitan Archives, St Marylebone parish records.
U.K., Oxford, Christ Church College Library, Chinnery correspondence, 1808–11, 14 vols, MS xlviii a.42a–a.55 (Microfilm copies in Fisher Library).
U.K., PRO, Lists of Grants by Letters Patent, 1801–73.
U.K., Royal College of Music Library, Viotti Papers, 1798–1905, MS 4118.
U.K., Surrey Record Office, 1881 Surrey census index.
U.S.A., New York Public Library for the Performing Arts (Music Division):
Viotti/Chinnery correspondence, 1793–1822, JOB 97-52, 72 items.
Viotti correspondence, 1814–23, *MNY-Viotti, 6 items.
U.S.A., Yale University, Beinecke Rare Book Library, Osborn Collection, MS Osborn fd. 11, Chinnery poetry, 148 items (Microfilm copies in Fisher Library).

## Secondary sources

'Account of the Encaenia at Oxford', *Gentleman's Magazine* (1810), vol. 80, pt 2, pp. 69–73.
'A J.B. Viotti', in W.R. Spencer (1811), *Poems*, Cadell, London, pp. 233–4.

Bachaumont, L. Petit de (1783), *Mémoires secrets pour servir à l'histoire de la république des lettres en France depuis 1762 jusqu'à nos jours*, 21 vols, vol. 20, John Adamson, London [Paris?].

Bachmann, A. (1925), *An Encyclopedia of the Violin*, reprinted Da Capo, New York, 1966.

Baillie, L. (1981–87), *The Catalogue of Printed Music in the British Library to 1980*, 62 vols, British Library, London.

Baillot, P. (1835), *The Art of the Violin*, ed. and trans. L. Goldberg, Northwestern University Press, Evanston, Ill., 1991.

__ (1825), *Notice sur J.-B. Viotti*, Hocquet, Paris.

Balteau, J., Barroux, M., Prévost, M. (1933–), *Dictionnaire de biographie française*, 18 vols to date, Letouzey et Ané, Paris.

Barbier, P. (1987), *La Vie quotidienne à l'Opéra au temps de Rossini et de Balzac, Paris 1800–1850*, Hachette, Paris.

Basso, A. (ed.) (1985), *Dizionario Enciclopedico Universale della Musica e dei Musicisti*, 12 vols, Editrice Torinese, Turin.

Barulich, F. (2000), 'Il Segreto: The Viotti/Chinnery Correspondence in New York', *Fontes Artis Musicae*, vol. 47, pp. 310–42.

Bénézit, E. (1976), *Dictionnaire des peintres, sculpteurs, dessinateurs et graveurs*, 10 vols, Librairie Gründ, Paris.

Bentley, N. (ed.) (1977), *Selections from the Reminiscences of Captain Gronow*, The Folio Society, London.

Benton, R. (1976), 'J.-J. Imbault (1753–1832), violoniste et éditeur de musique à Paris', *Revue de musicologie*, vol. 62, pp. 86–103.

Berlioz, H. (1870), *The Memoirs of Hector Berlioz*, ed. and trans. D. Cairns, Alfred A. Knopf, New York, 2002.

Blom, E. (ed.) (1954), *Grove's Dictionary of Music and Musicians*, 5th edn, 9 vols, Macmillan, London.

Blume, F. (ed.) (1949–86), *Die Musik in Geschichte und Gegenwart*, 17 vols, Bärenreiter, Kassel.

Boigne, A. de (1907–13), *Memoirs of the Comtesse de Boigne*, 4 vols, ed. C. Nicoullaud, Heinemann, London.

Boyce, M.F. (1973), *The French School of Violin Playing in the Sphere of Viotti: Technique and Style*, Ph.D. diss., University of North Carolina, Chapel Hill.

Boyden, D. D. (1965), *The History of Violin Playing*, OUP, London.

Brewer, J. (1997), *The Pleasures of the Imagination: English Culture in the Eighteenth Century*, HarperCollins, London.

Broglie, G. de (1985), *Madame de Genlis*, Perrin, Paris.

Brown, C. (1988), 'Bowing Styles, Vibrato and Portamento in Nineteenth-Century Violin Playing', *Journal of the Royal Musical Association*, vol. 113, pt 1, pp. 97–128.

Burke, B. (ed.) (1938), *Burke's Genealogical and Heraldic History of the Peerage Baronetage and Knightage*, 96th edn, Shaw, London.

Campbell, M. (1980), *The Great Violinists*, Granada, Frogmore, St Albans, Herts.

Carroll, C.M. (1976), 'A Beneficient Poseur: Charles Ernest, Baron de Bagge', *Recherches sur la musique classique*, vol. 16, pp. 24–36.

Cazalet, W.W. (1854), *The History of the Royal Academy of Music*, Bosworth, London.

Chastel, A. (1976), 'Etude sur la vie musicale à Paris à travers la presse pendant le règne de Louis XVI', *Recherches sur la musique française classique*, vol. 16, pp. 37–70.

Choron, A.-E. and Fayolle, F.-J. (1811), *Dictionnaire historique des musiciens: Artistes et Amateurs, morts ou vivants*, 2 vols, reprinted Georg Olms, Hildesheim, 1971.

Clément, F. (1885), *Histoire de la musique depuis les temps anciens jusqu'à nos jours*, Hachette, Paris.

Colles, H.C. (ed.) (1927/1940), *Grove's Dictionary of Music and Musicians*, 3rd and 4th edns, 5 vols, Macmillan, London.

Corder, F. (1922), *A History of the Royal Academy of Music from 1822 to 1922*, Corder, London.

Creevey, T. (1970), *The Creevey Papers*, ed. J. Gore, Folio Society, London.

Delalain, P. (1900), *L'Imprimerie et la librairie à Paris de 1789 à 1813*, reprinted Gregg, Farnborough, 1972.

Deutsch, O.E. (1955), *Handel: A Documentary Biography*, Black, London.

Douglas, S. (1928), *The Diaries of Sylvester Douglas (Lord Glenbervie)*, 2 vols, ed. F. Bickley, Constable, London.

__ (1910), *The Glenbervie Journals*, ed. W. Sichel, Constable, London.

Dulaure, J.-A. (1838), *Histoire physique, civile et morale des environs de Paris*, revised J.-L. Belin, 2nd edn, 6 vols, vol. 6, Furne, Paris.

Edgcumbe, R. M. (1827), *Musical Reminiscences of an Old Amateur Chiefly Respecting the Italian Opera for Fifty Years from 1773 to 1823*, 2nd edn, W. Clarke, London.

Ehrlich, C. (1995), *First Philharmonic: A History of the Royal Philharmonic Society*, Clarendon, Oxford.

__ (1985), *The Music Profession in England since the Eighteenth Century: A Social History*, Clarendon, Oxford.

Ernouf, A.A. (1884), *Maret, duc de Bassano*, 2nd edn, Perrin, Paris.

Escudier, M. and Escudier, L. (1856), *Vie et aventures des cantatrices célèbres précédées des musiciens de l'Empire et suivies de la vie anecdotique de Paganini*, Dentu, Paris.

Eymar, A.-M. d' (1799–1800), *Anecdotes sur Viotti*, Luc Sestié, Geneva.

Fayolle, F. (1824), 'Memoir of Giovanni Battista Viotti', *The Harmonicon*, no. 16, April, pp. 55–7.

Fétis, F.-J. (1834–44), *Biographie universelle des musiciens et bibliographie générale de la musique*, 8 vols, Leroux/Méline, Brussels.

Foster, J. (ed.) (1968), *Alumni Oxonienses: The Members of the University of Oxford, 1715–1886*, 2 vols in 1, Kraus Reprint, Nendeln/Liechtenstein.

Foster, M.B. (1912), *History of the Philharmonic Society of London, 1813–1912*, J. Lane, London.

François-Sappey, B. (1978), 'Pierre-Marie-François de Sales Baillot (1771–1842) par lui-même', *Recherches sur la musique française classique*, vol. 18, pp. 127–211.

Fuller Maitland, J.A. (ed.) (1904–10), *Grove's Dictionary of Music and Musicians*, 2nd edn, 5 vols, Macmillan, New York.

Gardeton, C. (ed.) (1819–20), *Annales de la musique ou Almanach musical pour l'an 1819 et 1820*, Minkoff Reprint, Geneva, 1978.

Gautier, Eugène (1873), *Un Musicien en vacances*, Leduc, Paris.

Genlis, S.-F. de (1782), *Adèle et Théodore, ou Lettres sur l'éducation*, 3 vols, Libraires associés, Paris.

__ (1825), *Mémoires inédits de madame la comtesse de Genlis, sur le dix-huitième siècle et la Révolution française depuis 1756 jusqu'à nos jours*, 8 vols, Ladvocat, Paris.

__ (1811), *Nouvelle Méthode pour apprendre à jouer de la harpe*, Minkoff Reprint, Geneva, 1974.

'On geometrical proportions [in music]', *QMMR* (1820), vol. 2, no. 8, pp. 434–47.

Giazotto, R. (1956), *Giovan Battista Viotti*, Edizioni Curci, Milan.

Golby, D. (1999), 'Violin Pedagogy in England during the First Half of the Nineteenth Century, or *The Incompleat Tutor for the Violin*', in B. Zon (ed.), *Nineteenth-Century British Music Studies (I)*, Ashgate, Aldershot, Hamp., pp. 88–104.

Goodden, A. (1997), *The Sweetness of Life: A Biography of Elisabeth Louise Vigée Le Brun*, André Deutsch, London.

Goodkind, H. (1972), *Violin Iconography of Antonio Stradivari, 1644–1737*, Larchmont, New York.

Grove, G. (1878–90), *A Dictionary of Music and Musicians*, 1st edn, 4 vols, London.

Harvey, B. (1995), *The Violin Family and its Makers in the British Isles: An Illustrated History and Directory*, Clarendon, Oxford.

Heartz, D. (1984), 'Portrait of a Court Musician: Gaetano Pugnani of Turin', *Imago Musicae*, vol. 1, pp. 103–19.

Highfill, Philip H., Burnim, K.A. and Langhans, E.A. (1973–93), *A Biographical Dictionary of Actors, Actresses, Musicians, Dancers, Managers and other Stage Personnel in London 1660–1800*, 16 vols, Southern Illinois University Press, Carbondale, Ill.

Hill, W.H., Hill, A.F. and Hill, A.E. (1963), *Antonio Stradivari: His Life and Work, 1644–1737*, Dover Publications, New York.

Hillairet, J. (1997), *Dictionnaire historique des rues de Paris*, 10th edn, 2 vols, Editions de Minuit, Paris.

Hogarth, G. (1848), *Musical History, Biography and Criticism*, reprinted Da Capo, New York, 1969.

*The Honours Register of the University of Oxford: A Record of University Honours and Distinctions completed to the end of Trinity Term 1883*, Clarendon, Oxford, 1883.

Horwood, R. (1813), *The A to Z of Regency London*, ed. P. Laxton and J. Wisdom, Harry Margary, Lympne Castle, Kent, 1985.

'Impromptus', *The Musical Standard*, 2 June 1888, p. 343.

James, K.E. (1987), *Concert Life in Eighteenth Century Bath*, unpub. Ph.D. diss., University of London.

__ (1990), 'Venanzio Rauzzini and the Search for Musical Perfection', *Bath History*, vol. 3, pp. 90–113.

Kassler, M. (1979), 'The Chinnery/Viotti Papers in Sydney', *Musicology Australia: Journal of the Musicological Society of Australia*, vol. 5, pp. 237–41.

Kelly, M. (1826), *Reminiscences*, ed. R. Fiske, OUP, London, 1975.

Kennedy, M. (ed.) (1994), *The Oxford Dictionary of Music*, 2nd edn, OUP, Oxford.

King, N. (1971), 'Le Séjour de Madame de Staël en Angleterre', in S. Balayé (ed.), *Les Carnets de voyage de Madame de Staël: Contribution à la genèse de ses œuvres*, Librairie Droz, Genève, pp. 354–406.

La Laurencie, L. (1924), 'Les Débuts de Viotti comme directeur de l'Opéra', *Revue de musicologie*, vol. 5, pp. 110–22.

__ (1971), *L'Ecole française de violon de Lully à Viotti*, 3 vols, vol. 2, Minkoff Reprints, Geneva.

Landon, H.C. Robbins (1976), *Haydn in England 1791–1795*, Thames and Hudson, London.

Larousse, P. (ed.) (1866–76), *Le Grand Dictionnaire universel du XIXe siècle*, 15 vols, Larousse, Paris.

Lassabathie, T. (1860), *Histoire du Conservatoire impérial de musique et de déclamation*, Michel Lévy Frères, Paris.

Lesure, F. (1984), 'Deux contrats d'édition de Viotti (1796–1802)', in R. Elvers (ed.), *Festschrift Albi Rosenthal*, Schneider, Tutzing, pp. 221–6.

Lewis, T. (ed.) (1865), *Extracts of the Journals and Correspondences of Miss Berry, 1783–1852*, 3 vols, Longmans, London.

Lister, W. (2002), 'New Light on the Early Career of G.B. Viotti', *ML*, vol. 83, no. 2, pp. 419–25.

__ (2003), '"Suonatore del Principe": New Light on Viotti's Turin years', *Early Music*, vol. 31, no. 2, pp. 233–45.

__ (2001), 'Wilhelm Cramer and the Opera Concert Orchestra: "Damnatio Memoriae"', *ML*, vol. 82, no. 1, p. 78.

Lyons, D. (1805), *The Environs of London*, 6 vols, Caddell and Davies, London.

McVeigh, S. (1999), 'The Benefit Concert in Nineteenth-Century London: From 'tax on the nobility' to 'monstrous nuisance', in B. Zon (ed.), *Nineteenth-Century British Music Studies (I)*, Ashgate, Aldershot, Hamp., pp. 242–66.

__ (1994), 'Brahams's Favourite Concerto', *The Strad*, vol. 105, April, pp. 343–7.

__ (1993), *Concert Life in London from Mozart to Haydn*, CUP, Cambridge.

__ (1989), *The Violinist in London's Concert Life 1750–1784: Felice Giardini and his Contemporaries*, Garland, New York and London.

'Memoir of Viotti', *QMMR* (1820), vol. 2, no. 5, pp. 52–5.

Miall, B. (1913), *Pierre Garat, Singer and Exquisite: His Life and his World, 1762–1823*, Unwin, London.

Michaud, J.-F. (ed.) (1843–65), *Biographie universelle ancienne et moderne*, 45 vols, reprinted Akademische Druck und Verlagsanstalt, Graz, 1966–70.

Milligan, T.B. (1983), *The Concerto and London's Musical Culture in the Late Eighteenth Century*, UMI Research Press, Ann Arbor, Mich.

Monnais, E. (1844), *Esquisses de la vie d'artiste*, Jules Labitte, Paris.

Moore, T. (1983–91), *The Journal of Thomas Moore*, 6 vols, ed. W. Dowden, University of Delaware Press, London.

Morellet, A. (1822), *Mémoires inédits de l'abbé Morellet sur le dix-huitième siècle et sur la Révolution*, 2nd edn, 2 vols, Slatkine Reprints, Geneva, 1967.

Morris, W.M. (1904), *British Violin Makers*, Chatto and Windus, London.

'Mort et Enterrement de J.-B. Viotti', *Revue de Musicologie* (1924), vol. 5, pp. 131–2.

Musgrave, C. (1970), *Life in Brighton*, Faber and Faber, London.

Norway, A.H. (1895), *History of the Post-Office packet service between the years 1793–1815*, Macmillan, London and New York.

'Origin and History of the *Concert Spirituel*', *The Harmonicon* (1824), no. 16, April, p. 57.

Palmer, F. (1997), *Domenico Dragonetti in England (1794–1846): The Career of a Double Bass Virtuoso*, Clarendon, Oxford.

Parke, W.T. (1830), *Musical Memoirs*, 2 vols, reprinted Da Capo, New York, 1970.

Petty, F.C. (1980), *Italian Opera in London 1760–1800*, UMI Research Press, Ann Arbor, Mich.

Pincherle, M. (1927), *Feuillets d'histoire du violon*, Paris, pp. 172–81.

__ (1924), 'Quelques Lettres de Viotti à Baillot', *Revue de musicologie*, vol. 5, pp. 103–9.

__ (1964), *The World of the Virtuoso*, trans. L.H. Brockway, Victor Gollancz, London.

Pohl, C.F. (1867), *Mozart und Haydn in London*, reprinted Da Capo, New York, 1970.

Pougin, A. (1888), *Viotti et l'école moderne de violon*, Maison Schott, Paris.

Quoy-Bodin, J.-L. (1984), 'L'Orchestre de la Société Olympique en 1786', *Revue de musicologie*, vol. 70, pp. 95–105.

Raina, R. (1994), 'Nuovi documenti biografici su Giovan Battista Viotti', *Nuova Rivista Musicale Italiana*, vol. 28, pp. 251–6.

'Rode, Baillot, and Kreutzer's Method of Instruction for the Violin', *QMMR* (1824), vol. 6, no. 24, pp. 527–31.

Rogers, P. (1998), *Gilwell Park: A Brief History and Guided Tour*, The Scout Association, London.

Rufer, A. (1941), *Novate: Eine Episode aus dem Revolutionsjahr 1793*, Büchergilde Gutenberg, Zurich.

Sadie, S., ed. (1980), *The New Grove Dictionary of Music and Musicians*, 20 vols, Macmillan, London.

__ (2001), *The New Grove Dictionary of Music and Musicians*, 2nd edn, 29 vols, Macmillan, London.

Saint-George, H. (1896), *The Bow, its History, Manufacture and Use*, The Strad Library, London.

Sainty, J.C. (1972), *Office-Holders in Modern Britain (I): Treasury Officials 1660–1870*, Macmillan, London.

Sales catalogues of various English and U.S. music manuscript dealers, 1973–85, PHM E.A. and V.I. Crome collection.

Schiffer, L. (1914), *Johann Ladislaus Dussek: Seine Sonaten und seine Konzerte*, reprinted Da Capo, New York, 1972.

Schnapper, E. (ed.) (1957), *British Union-Catalogue*, Butterworths, London.

Schueneman, B. (1995), 'Search for the Minor Composer: The Case of Giovanni Battista Viotti', *Music Reference Services Quarterly*, vol. 4, no. 2, pp. 29–42.

Schwarz, B. (1958), 'Beethoven and the French Violin School', *MQ*, vol. 44, no. 4, pp. 431–49.

__ (1987), *French Instrumental Music between the Revolutions (1789–1830)*, Da Capo, New York.

__ (1983), *Great Masters of the Violin*, Robert Hale, London.

__ (1972), 'Problems of Chronology in the Works of G.B. Viotti', *International Musicology Society Congress Reports*, vol. 11, pp. 644–7.

Scorgie, M.E. and Wilkinson, D.J. (1997), 'William Bassett Chinnery: 1787–1812. Australia's Premier Accountant and Embezzler', unpub. paper presented at the Conference of the Accounting Association of Australia and New Zealand (AAANZ), Hobart, Australia (extract in *Conference of the AAANZ*, Melbourne, July 1997, p. 115).

Scott, M.M. (1951), 'The Opera Concerts of 1795', *Music Review*, vol. 12, pp. 24–8.

'Sketch of the State of Music in Paris', *QMMR* (1820), vol. 2, no. 8, pp. 507–18.

Smart, G. (1907), *Leaves from the Journals of Sir George Smart*, ed. H.B. Cox and C.L.E. Cox, Longman, Green and Co., London.

Smith, W.C. (1955), *The Italian Opera and Contemporary Ballet in London, 1789–1820*, Headley Bros, London.

Soboul, A. (1989), *Dictionnaire historique de la Révolution française*, PUF, Paris.

Sotheby and Co., *Catalogue of Valuable Printed Books, Autograph Letters and Historical Documents*, 1961–64, 1967–68.

Spencer, W. R. (1811), *Poems*, Cadell, London.

__ (1835), *Poems*, 2nd edn, Cochrane, London.

Spohr, L. (1865), *Autobiography*, 2 vols, trans. from the German, Longman Green, London.

Stephen, L. (ed.) (1888–1900), *Dictionary of National Biography*, 63 vols, Smith, Elder and Co., London.

Stolberg-Wernigerode, O. (ed.) (1952–96), *Neue deutsche Biographie*, 18 vols, Duncker und Humblot, Berlin.

Stowell, R. (1985), *Violin Technique and Performance Practice in the late Eighteenth and early Nineteenth Centuries*, CUP, Cambridge.

__ Review of White's *From Vivaldi to Viotti* in *ML* (1993), vol. 74, pp. 294–5.

Straeten, E. van der (1933), *The History of the Violin*, 2 vols, reprinted Da Capo, New York, 1968.

__ (1914), *The History of the Violoncello*, reprinted W. Reeves, London, 1971.

__ (1902), 'J.B. Viotti, wie er sich selbst geschildert', *Die Musik*, vol. 1, nos 18 and 19, cols 1635–43 and 1736–44.

__ (1911), 'Viottiana', *The Connoisseur*, November, pp. 152–60.

Stubbings, K. (1982), 'Gilwell Park', *Essex Journal*, vol. 17, no. 2, pp. 10–18.

Tulard, F., Fayard, J.-F., Fierro, A. (1987), *Histoire et dictionnaire de la Révolution française, 1789–1799*, Laffont, Paris.

Tyson, A. (1963), *The Authentic English Editions of Beethoven*, Faber and Faber, London.

__ (1967), *Thematic Catalogue of the Works of Muzio Clementi*, Hans Schneider, Tutzing.
Unger, M. (1971), *Muzio Clementis Leben*, Da Capo, New York.
Vallas, L. (1971), *Un Siècle de musique et de théâtre à Lyon (1688–1789)*, Minkoff Reprints, Geneva.
Vannes, R. (1975), *Dictionnaire universel des luthiers*, 3rd edn, Les Amis de la Musique, Brussels.
Vigée-Lebrun, E. (1903), *Memoirs of Madame Vigée Lebrun*, trans. L. Strachey, Doubleday, New York.
__ (1835–37), *Souvenirs*, 2 vols, ed. C. Hermann, Edition des Femmes, Paris, 1984.
'Viotti, Old Betts, and the Straduarius', *The Strad* (1977), vol. 88, June, pp. 167–73.
Welply, W.H. (1927), 'George Chinnery, 1774–1852, With Some Account of his Family and Genealogy', *Notes and Queries*, vol. 152, pp. 21–4, 39–43, 58–61, 75–8.
White, C. (1969), 'Did Viotti Write any Original Piano Concertos?', *Journal of the American Musicological Society*, vol. 22, pp. 275–84.
__ (1992), *From Vivaldi to Viotti: A History of the Early Classical Violin Concerto*, Gordon and Breach, Philadelphia.
__ (1985), *Giovanni Battista Viotti: A Thematic Catalogue of his Works*, Pendragon Press, New York.
__ (1973), 'Towards a More Accurate Chronology of Viotti's Violin Concertos', *Fontes Artis Musicae*, vol. 20, pp. 111–24.
Yim, D. (2000), *The Chinnery Family Papers, 1793–1843*, 2 vols, unpub. Ph.D. diss., University of Sydney.
__ (2001), 'Madame de Genlis's *Adèle et Théodore*: Its Influence on an English Family's Education', *AJFS*, vol. 38, no. 1, pp. 141–57.
__ (ed.) (2003), *The Unpublished Correspondence of Mme de Genlis and Margaret Chinnery and related documents in the Chinnery Family Papers*, *SVEC*, vol. 2.

## Newspapers and periodicals

*Allgemeine musikalische Zeitung*, 1798–1825
*Almanach musical* (1782–83), vols 7–8, Minkoff Reprints, Geneva, 1972.
*Bath Chronicle*, 1793–98
*Bath Herald and Register*, 1793–95
*Bath Journal*, 1793–95
*Calendrier musical universel, suite de l'Almanach musical* (1788–89), vols 9–10, Minkoff Reprints, Geneva, 1972.
*Diary, or Woodfall's Register*, 1792–93
*Gentleman's Magazine*, 1808–14, 1824
*Journal de Paris*, 1782, 1807, 1819–21, 1824
*London Gazette*, 1818–21
*Mercure de France*, 1782–83, 1787, 1790, 1804–1807
*Le Moniteur*, 1820
*Morning Chronicle and London Advertiser*, 1782
*Morning Chronicle*, 1791–1801, 1805, 1810, 1818, 1824
*Morning Herald*, 1781, 1793–99, 1818
*Morning Post and Daily Advertiser*, 1789
*Morning Post*, 1794, 1811
*Oracle*, 1793–98, 1800
*Public Register, or the Freeman's Journal*, 1796–98
*Quarterly Musical Magazine and Review*, 1820–24

*The Sun*, 1794–95, 1824
*The Times*, 1792–1806, 1809, 1812–14, 1818, 1821, 1824

# Index

Giovanni Battista Viotti is abbreviated to V, Margaret Chinnery to MC, William Bassett Chinnery to WBC, George Robert Chinnery to GRC, William Robert Spencer to WRS, and Adolphus Frederick, Duke of Cambridge to AF.